COLOUR MATTERS

Essays on the Experiences, Education, and Pursuits of Black Youth

Based on research conducted in Black communities, along with over thirty years of teaching experience, *Colour Matters* presents a collection of essays that engages educators, youth workers, and policymakers to think about the ways in which race shapes the education, aspirations, and achievements of Black Canadians. Informed by the current sociopolitical Canadian landscape, *Colour Matters* covers topics relating to the lives of Black youth, with particular, though not exclusive, attention to young Black men in the Greater Toronto Area.

The essays reflect the issues and concerns of the past thirty years, and question what has changed and what has remained the same. Each essay is accompanied by an insightful response from a scholar engaging with topics such as immigration, schooling, athletics, mentorship, and police surveillance. With the perspectives of scholars from the United Kingdom, the United States, and Canada, *Colour Matters* provides provocative narratives of Black experiences that alert us to what more might be said, or said differently, about the social, cultural, educational, political, and occupational worlds of Black youth in Canada. This book probes the ongoing need to understand, in nuanced and complex ways, the marginalization and racialization of Black youth in a time of growing demands for a societal response to anti-Black racism.

Colour Matters

Essays on the Experiences, Education, and Pursuits of Black Youth

CARL E. JAMES

UNIVERSITY OF TORONTO PRESS
Toronto Buffalo London

© University of Toronto Press 2021
Toronto Buffalo London
utorontopress.com
Printed in the U.S.A.

ISBN 978-1-4875-0867-8 (cloth)   ISBN 978-1-4875-3879-8 (EPUB)
ISBN 978-1-4875-2631-3 (paper)   ISBN 978-1-4875-3878-1 (PDF)

Library and Archives Canada Cataloguing in Publication

Title: Colour matters : essays on the experiences, education, and pursuits of
   Black youth / Carl E. James.
Names: James, Carl E., author.
Description: Includes index.
Identifiers: Canadiana (print) 20200410644 | Canadiana (ebook) 20200410776 |
   ISBN 9781487508678 (hardcover) | ISBN 9781487526313 (softcover) |
   ISBN 9781487538798 (EPUB) | ISBN 9781487538781 (PDF)
Subjects: CSH: Black Canadians – Ontario – Toronto. |
   CSH: Black Canadians – Ontario – Toronto – Social conditions. |
   CSH: Black Canadians – Education – Ontario – Toronto. |
   CSH: Black Canadians – Ontario – Toronto – Social life and customs. |
   LCSH: Toronto (Ont.) – Race relations. | LCSH: Toronto (Ont.) – Ethnic relations.
Classification: LCC FC3097.9.B6 J36 2021 | DDC 305.8960713/541 – dc23

Funding for this publication came from the SSHRC Major Collaborative Research Initiative (MCRI) program and the Jean Augustine Chair in Education, Community & Diaspora, Faculty of Education, York University.

University of Toronto Press acknowledges the financial assistance to its publishing program of the Canada Council for the Arts and the Ontario Arts Council, an agency of the Government of Ontario.

Canada Council for the Arts / Conseil des Arts du Canada

ONTARIO ARTS COUNCIL
CONSEIL DES ARTS DE L'ONTARIO
an Ontario government agency
un organisme du gouvernement de l'Ontario

Funded by the Government of Canada / Financé par le gouvernement du Canada

Contents

Foreword: The Long Game vii
D. ALISSA TROTZ

Introduction: Exploring the Social and Educational Experiences of Black Canadian Youth over Time xv

1 Historical and Social Context of the Schooling and Education of African Canadians 3

  Response: Complicating Gender and Racial Identities within the Study of Educational History 43
  FUNKÉ ALADEJEBI

2 Generational Differences in Black Students' Education Pursuits and Performance 47

  Response: It's the Same with Black British Caribbean Pupils 72
  SHIRLEY ANNE TATE

3 "To Make a Better Future": Narrative of a 1.5 Generation Caribbean Canadian 76

  Response: Using Gender to Think Through Migration, Love, and Student Success 107
  AMOABA GOODEN

4 Students "at Risk": Stereotypes and the Schooling of Black Boys 112

  Response: Black Lives Matter in the USA and Canada 141
  JOYCE E. KING

5 More than Brains, Education, and Hard Work: The Aspirations and Career Trajectories of Two Young Black Men   150

Response: What Folks Don't Get: Race and Class Matter   169
ANNETTE M. HENRY

6 Class, Race, and Schooling in the Performance of Black Male Athleticism   174

Response: Basketball's Black Creative Labour and the Mitigation of Anti-Black Schooling   191
MARK V. CAMPBELL

7 Troubling Role Models: Seeing Racialization in the Discourse Relating to "Corrective Agents" for Black Males   197

Response: Black Role Models and Mentorship under Racial Capitalism   216
SAM TECLE

8 "Up to No Good": Black on the Streets and Encountering Police   221

Response: It Could Have Been Written Today: A Montrealer's Reflection   246
ADELLE BLACKETT

9 "Colour Matters": Suburban Life as Social Mobility and Its High Cost for Black Youth   251

Response: "What Floats in the Air Is Chance": Respectability Politics and the Search for Upward Mobility in Canada   278
ANDREA A. DAVIS

10 Towards Equity in Education for Black Students in the Greater Toronto Area   283

Response: "I Will Treat All My Students with Respect": The Limits of Good Intentions   309
LEANNE TAYLOR

Epilogue   315
MICHELE A. JOHNSON

Acknowledgments   327

Contributors   331

Index   335

Foreword: The Long Game

D. ALISSA TROTZ

For Maud Fuller, Jamaican-Canadian educator (1933–2013)

We could start with this story: A parent, herself a Black teacher, runs into her son's French teacher, who is white. She tells him that her son has transferred to one of the technical high schools. He congratulates her, assuring her that she has made the right decision since – he tells her confidently – her beloved child will be good with his hands.

Or we could begin by introducing a Black university student, also a parent, who leaves her seminar discussion almost every week as she keeps getting calls from her child's school about his disruptive behaviour. At one point, her son is physically restrained by a teacher. Efforts to challenge this – including contacting the school superintendent – continue all year. Unsatisfied with the responses she has received, she eventually transfers her son to another school, making her commute to his school and her university significantly longer. No changes are made at her son's former school.

Another student-parent learns that her son has been moved to a special education classroom without consultation. The special ed class is taught by the school's only Black teacher, and most of the students in that class look like her child.

The children in the above two stories are both five years old.

Or we could simply begin by reflecting on what it means to be a parent of Black children in North America, what it means to watch them grow into an understanding of themselves as part Caribbean – as affirmation to be sure, but also as the expression of a tentative relation to a place where they were born and raised and schooled.

School (noun). A space where Black parents are acutely aware that our children spend most of their waking weekdays. Where big pieces of them are (de)formed. A space of damage. Where we are yet to understand the spiritual and psychic costs, even as we know that racism and mental health are inextricably linked (see Sinai Health System, Human Rights & Health Equity Office, 2017; Taylor & Richards, 2019).

School (verb). To put a person in their place.

Add up the experiences. Multiply the slights that are not slight at all. Divide and subtract. Take away the sense of a self that is valuable. This is not an abstraction.

* * *

In this thoughtful collection, Carl James walks us through the difficult calculus of young Black lives. The essays gathered here were published over the course of two decades and represent research with young people in Ontario conducted over an even longer period – across NDP, Liberal, and Conservative governments. Taken together, these essays give rise to a temporal dissonance that is, to say the least, disconcerting: on one hand, the awful immediacy of the issues foregrounded in these pages; on the other, the long horizon of anti-Black racism. This dissonance is underlined in the chapters that track the subduing of Black aspiration in longitudinal surveys with young people. The essays are punctuated by responses from other Black educators, with titles that underline congruence across time and Black diasporic space ("It Could Have Been Written Today: A Montrealer's Reflection"; "It's the Same with Black British Caribbean Pupils"; "Black Lives Matter in the USA and Canada"). The final essay, on consultation sessions with members of Black communities in the Greater Toronto Area in 2016, seems to reprise decades-old issues covered in earlier chapters. And the urgency of the times we inhabit – let us be clear, this is a state of emergency – is most starkly conveyed in the evidence James offers us, from Toronto District School Board figures, that when it comes to suspension, expulsion, and dropout rates, the figures are higher for succeeding generations of Black children (chapter 2). What these data tell us, to put it bluntly, is that the longer Black folk are here, the worse it becomes.

In meticulous detail, and drawing on primary and secondary research, James lays out the materialization of anti-Black racism. This is the storying of how the Canadian school system produces the Black child as a problem, as academically inferior and unteachable. It does this via a series of systemic practices: stereotypes (like the trope of the Black male as immigrant, fatherless, athlete, troublemaker, underachiever); streaming; surveillance (in her response to chapter 8, Adelle Blackett describes this as "perpetual policing," which moves from street to school and back again); suspicion; suspensions; and "safe schools" acts that, in operating to evict, render schools anything but safe for Black children. The absence of representation in the official curriculum, barely disrupted by compartmentalized multicultural pedagogies like the annual celebration of Black History Month, provides an early lesson to all children on whose lives count and which communities are valuable. The damage is deepened via what has been described as the "hidden" curriculum of misconceptions and culturally biased attitudes that shape teachers' interactions with and expectations of their Black students (see Aladejebi's response to chapter 1) – surely a misnomer, since nothing is hidden when we take into account what a child hears, sees, senses, and feels.

In these pages, we also see how anti-Black racism is deftly reconfigured when challenged, as in the example James offers of how, when faced with the official recording of suspension rates, several schools simply shifted to other forms of exclusion that flew under the radar, and that even included attempts to "encourage" Black parents to voluntarily relocate their children. He shows how neoliberal logic obscures enduring structures of anti-Black racism, returning us to cultural deficit models that valorize and place responsibility on the individual (the Black mentor, the Black role model, the all-you-need-to-do-is-put-your-head-down-and-work Black student), while putting the blame for so-called Black underachievement on Black communities and on Black families in particular. And he lists an avalanche of official reports, royal commissions, consultations, strategies, legislation, working groups – each succeeding intervention a rehearsal of what we already know. While calling for a response, the reports themselves become the sum total of the response, instantiating erasure through acknowledgment. Coming with promises but no resources, the recommendations constitute the action meant to subdue and reassure, the action that turns out to be no action at all (Ahmed, 2012).

In tracking the operation of white supremacy in the Canadian school system, it is important for us to simultaneously attend to aggregation (showing how anti-Black racism universally produces the Black student as inferior and unbelonging) and disaggregation (properly attending to differences among Black students through an intersectional approach). In her response to chapter 1, Funké Aladejebi offers crucial insights into what this might look like across gender, geography, and itineraries of Blackness that speak to the specificity of Canadian-, Caribbean-, and continental-African-born youth. Drawing primarily on and making space for the experiences and voices of Black male youth living in the Greater Toronto Area, the book does an excellent job of laying out the deeply restrictive and pathologized notions of masculinized heteronormativity with which they must contend, raising other crucial questions of the consequences of such tropes for cis and trans girls and gender-nonconforming youth (Maynard, 2017).

Some of the response essays further develop this point, noting that an emphasis in the literature on Black male youth can sometimes run the risk of eliding the varied production of Black femininities. In this text, James recognizes the importance of explicating the specific ways in which Black girls, as students, experience and navigate the Canadian school system (see introduction and chapter 9). These are urgent considerations, requiring us to attend to how Black children are differently disciplined by the gender and sexual politics of respectability and social mobility. What corresponding stereotypes attach themselves to Black female-presenting bodies? How does the trope of the absentee father as explanation for Black "underperformance" also require denigrating Black mothers and pathologizing households where the only adults are women?

Another area that calls for more detailed consideration is that of the deeply gendered circuits of social reproduction that offer support and care for Black children in and out of school. Again, some of the responses offer a glimpse into these support networks, such as the "othermothering" practices of Black women teachers as identified by Funké Aladejebi (response, chapter 1). With this in mind, we might reread Carl James's interview with Mark, a 1.5 generation (that is, immigrated to Canada between the ages of eight and twelve) Caribbean Canadian, for the clues it supplies about the affective and material support of his mother. Centring Mark's mother's migratory journey from Trinidad and Tobago yields a different kind of narrative, one that foregrounds transnational familial relationships that are central to the reproduction of Caribbean diasporic space and belie truncated and nation-bound notions of the single-parent household (chapter 3 and response by Amoaba Gooden). Such an approach might also compel us to revisit and renarrate the story of the mobilization of Black communities that is presented to us in chapter 1, exploring instead why and how women were often at the forefront of this organization that centred Black children's needs. It offers an alternate entry point into thinking across spaces and communities, and listening for the lessons that emerge about the unwaged, caring, invisible, and deeply gendered labour that is the foundation of the frontlines of struggle.

As is poignantly captured in these pages, education has long been held up for Black communities as a space for redressing inequities, a route to social mobility, intergenerational stability, and security. It unfolds here in multiple ways: in the dreams of families who migrate from the Caribbean in the hope of ensuring what they imagine to be better futures; in the savings of those who scraped together enough to move to the suburbs – many escaping the deepening racial and class inequalities produced by the displacement of gentrification – to give their children a better start. And repeatedly we see how aspirations are thwarted, how the meritocratic promise of individual effort is short-circuited by the structural persistence of anti-Black racism, and how suburban respectability comes at a price paid by Black students.

The cruel irony is that when "success" comes, despite all these roadblocks, and as exception rather than rule, it is held up in some quarters as singularity detached from collectivity, and as evidence that we inhabit a postracial world where brains and hard work are all it takes. When in fact – and this is "the heart of the matter," as James Baldwin observed – the young Black people whose lives are the point of departure in this collection are interpellated by a system designed to fail them, a system that requires them not "to aspire to excellence ... [but] to make peace with mediocrity" (Baldwin, 1963/1992, p. 4).

We would do well to recall Ruth Wilson Gilmore's (2007) incisive definition of racism as "the state-sanctioned or extralegal production and exploitation of group-differentiated vulnerability to premature death" (p. 247). In other words, this is not an aberration. Education as liberation thus comes up against the school as a key site for the social reproduction of inequality. This is a tension that James recognizes (see, in particular, chapter 4). And it therefore requires that we attempt to be as clear as possible about the questions we pose and the terrain we are fighting upon. I write this as a Black educator at the University of Toronto, an institution that trains large numbers of the teachers who populate our schools and is continually ranked as one of the top academic institutions in the world. At the very same time, it is a space from which, as Carl James points out in this volume, only 51 per cent of Black students who entered from the Toronto District School Board between 2004 and 2016 graduated (chapter 2). What – and who – must be disappeared for the celebratory narrative to hold? What does this moment, and "facts" like these, demand from us? As Sylvia Wynter (1992) said to her colleagues in the face of the 1992 Los Angeles riots and the disclosure that the police used NHI – No Humans Involved – as a code to refer to young Black men they apprehended and whose rights they routinely violated, "What are we, as grammarians of our present epistemological order, to do?"

In her response to chapter 4, drawing on Toni Morrison and Sylvia Wynter, Joyce E. King underlines the importance of reframing how we tell these stories, to "disconnect the implicit language of dominance ... from a vocabulary that Wynter theorizes ineluctably affirms the supposed inferiority of conceptual Blackness in alter ego relation to conceptual whiteness." King makes a compelling argument for the use of "action verbs instead of descriptive adjectives and nouns" (e.g., absented fathers, absented histories, impeded achievers, resource-starved, impoverishment). Such language can *consistently* direct a method and mode of analysis that uncompromisingly names the settler colonial context of Canada and the culturally lethal practices stitched into the seams of this country's educational system that fall with particular weight on Indigenous and Black communities.

Taking the frame of racial capitalism and the Black radical tradition as a point of departure enables us to see education as part of what James notes is "a capitalist system which [produces] large populations of unemployed, working-class, poor, and racialized youth" (chapter 5). It teaches us that confronting anti-Black racism is not a piecemeal endeavour, and that the seductive politics of inclusion and accommodation are highly selective, legitimizing ongoing systematic dispossession and exploitation while deepening class and other divides within the Black community. And this framework also cautions us against occasional slippages, such as when James refers to studies that quantify the cost of students' not completing high school, inadvertently deploying neoliberal logic to make a case for supporting Black student success as the "cheaper" option (chapter 10).

James opens this book with a historical overview of the educational experiences of Black youth, a discussion that gestures to the important work of initiatives and organizations. While he recognizes that it is not the largesse of successive governments but the insistent interventions of Black folk that has produced some changes (like the introduction of the Africentric Alternative School), this book does not specify the kind of sustained work this entails. The task of dismantling structures that deny Black people's humanity also requires the careful gathering-up of archives of contestation and reading them in relation to the household, the neighbourhood, the school, the school board, the city, the province, the country, and beyond. This is not just an exercise in rendering Black resistance visible – although that is surely important, particularly when it comes to the deeply gendered caring work. It also holds the promise of better understanding the conditions of possibility; of exploring the processes through which demands for change can get dissolved via incrementalism or the institutional politics of incorporation and reform (see, for instance, the thoughtful response to chapter 7 by Sam Tecle in which he reckons with the necessity, peril, and promise of the "Black mentor"); of thinking about the spaces for coalition-building; and of being clear-eyed about short-term demands while always keeping an eye on the long game, however far off the horizon and however much others might dismiss it as wishful thinking. The responses that follow each chapter foreground the transnational dimensions of the Black diaspora; in our examination of how students come to understand themselves as Black in school, it is imperative that we carefully map the connections across these experiences and movements across space and time.

In the opening chapter, Carl James gestures to the transnational dimensions of anti-Black racism and names Black British struggles in the 1970s and 1980s. One of the references he mentions is a 1971 pamphlet by Bernard Coard titled "How the West Indian Child Is Made Educationally Sub-Normal in the British School System." The pamphlet was published by New Beacon, one of the first Caribbean and African diasporic publishing houses in the UK and part of a sturdy infrastructure of Black organizing that was deeply diasporic in terms of both the migratory trajectories of the parents, students, and community activists involved and the international relations that informed collective practices in specific places (Walcott, 1997). The British school system was part of a colonial apparatus that also structured the curriculum in Coard's Grenada. Eight years after that pamphlet was issued, Bernard Coard, who by then had returned to the Caribbean, would be part of the New Jewel Movement's successful overthrow of Eric Gairy's oppressive regime in Grenada. At a lecture titled "The New School" given at the University of London's Institute of Education in July 1983 (later published in Coard, 1983), just a few months before the revolution's catastrophic implosion and the US invasion that followed, Coard emphasized that a central plank in the Grenadian government's efforts to transform independence into meaningful economic, political, cultural, and spiritual decolonization was the overhaul of the education system. He ended his talk with a quote from the Cuban philosopher José Martí: "The new world requires the new school."

I close by foregrounding this other geography, this different yet connected and as yet tragically unrealized horizon, as a way of reminding us perhaps of what is ultimately at stake in the work that we must keep doing, and how challenging anti-Black racism in our schools is part of the ongoing work of bringing entire new worlds into being. Education – both *as* and *for* liberation – is insurgent work. In the contexts so painstakingly elaborated upon in this important text, we ask: What is the long game and how do we get there?

REFERENCES

Ahmed, S. (2012). *On being included: Racism and diversity in institutional life.* Durham, NC: Duke University Press.

Baldwin, J. (1992). My dungeon shook: Letter to my nephew on the one hundredth anniversary of emancipation. In *The fire next time* (pp. 1–10). New York, NY: Vintage Press. (Original work published 1963)

Coard, B. (1971). *How the West Indian child is made educationally sub-normal in the British school system*. London, UK: New Beacon Books.

Coard, B. (1983). The new school. In *Revolutionary Grenada: A big and popular school* (pp. 9–24). London, UK: Spider Web.

Gilmore, R.W. (2007). *Golden gulag: Prisons, surplus, crisis, and opposition in globalizing California*. Berkeley: University of California Press.

Maynard, R. (2017). *Policing Black lives: State violence in Canada from slavery to the present*. Halifax, NS: Fernwood.

Sinai Health System, Human Rights & Health Equity Office. (2017). *Black experiences in health care: Symposium report*. Toronto, ON: Author. https://www.mountsinai.on.ca/about_us/human-rights/pdfs/SHS-BEHC-report-FINAL-aoda-final.pdf

Taylor, D., & Richards, D. (2019, May 15). Triple jeopardy: Complexities of racism, sexism, and ageism on the experiences of mental health stigma among young Canadian Black women of Caribbean descent. *Frontiers in Sociology*. https://doi.org/10.3389/fsoc.2019.00043

Walcott, R. (1997). *Black like who? Writing Black Canada*. Toronto, ON: Insomniac Press.

Wynter, S. (1992, Fall). No humans involved: An open letter to my colleagues. *Voices of the Black Diaspora: The CAAS Resarch Review, 8*(2): 13–16. https://www.newframe.com/long-read-knowledge-must-mutate-be-fully-human/

Introduction: Exploring the Social and Educational Experiences of Black Canadian Youth over Time

While people of African descent have been living in Canada for centuries, their numbers became substantial only after changes in Canadian immigration laws culminated in the removal of the last explicitly racist and discriminatory provisions in 1967. Thousands of Black people arrived in Canada from the Caribbean starting in the 1970s, and smaller numbers came from Africa in subsequent years. The immigration of the late twentieth century not only increased the size of Canada's Black population but also changed its composition, with people of Caribbean heritage representing the largest group. The most common destination for these immigrants was Toronto.

The social and educational experiences of Black youth in Toronto have been a concern I have explored in much of my professional work since the 1980s, first as a youth worker in one of Toronto's most marginalized communities and subsequently as a professor, researcher, and equity advocate at York University. In the early days, the youth I worked with were almost all born in the Caribbean. Today, many Black youth are likely to be the children or grandchildren of Caribbean immigrants. Enough time has passed in the evolution of Toronto's Black community, as well as in the evolution of my own work, that we can look back and take stock.

A common understanding of immigration to Canada is that while the immigrant generation may struggle, things will be better for their children, and by the third generation substantial signs of social mobility and success in Canadian society will have begun to be evident. What emerges clearly from the studies referenced in this book is that this understanding has in large measure not held true for Black people in Canada. The reason it has not held true is the persistence of anti-Black racism, which Black youth experience in relation to gender, class, sexual identification, generational status, and area of residence, among other factors. Political, economic, cultural, social, and educational forces sustain racism as part of the inequitable structure of society. As a result, writings about Black youth years ago continue to be relevant today, and cumulative accounts of their experiences over generations make for helpful understanding of their lives.

Theoretical Guides

Neoliberalism and Multiculturalism

A prevailing framework for understanding individuals' lived experiences and life prospects is *neoliberalism*. We have a generally accepted notion that individuals can attain the education they desire, make choices, freely pursue employment opportunities, become wealthy, and take responsibility for their lives as they see fit. The neoliberal ethos, which informs these "common-sense" notions, also holds that competition constitutes an important "social good" and the "least restrictive way" of addressing and redistributing inequitable resources (Braedley & Luxton, 2010, p. 8). Neoliberalism represents "a transnational political project" (Wacquant, 2008), based on the principles of a market economy in which individuals are free to pursue wealth without the constraints a welfare state might impose (Braedley & Luxton, 2010; Wacquant, 2008). In this context, individuals and families must take responsibility for their own care and social outcomes (Braedley & Luxton, 2010, p. 15).

Because the hegemonic neoliberal ideology of individualism and competition places responsibility for the circumstances of one's life on the individual, individuals tend to attribute their social or economic circumstances to having made poor choices rather than to the limited, problematic, or "bad" choices available to them. According to Luxton (2010), liberalism's "perverse form of individualism – an obstinate and persistent belief that blames the victim by privatizing social problems" – immobilizes individuals as they become resigned to the inevitability of their situation, failing to see that they have been formed by and subjected to the prevailing values and practices of the larger economic, social, and political structures (p. 172).

Despite neoliberalism's emphasis on individual choice, in a context of structural inequity, the resources and opportunities that individuals can access, and concomitantly their freedom and choices, are inevitably circumscribed by economic and social conditions over which they have little or no control (Braedley & Luxton, 2010; Porfilio & Malott, 2008; Tabb, 2003). The sustained attempts by neoliberal advocates "to promote competition, choice, entrepreneurship, and individualism" constitute what Connell (2010) calls a *sociocultural logic* (pp. 26, 27) that (theoretically) offers formerly excluded individuals access to opportunities without changing the existing "systems of inequality or the ideologies that sustain them" (p. 35).

In examining how youth are incorporated into "a global, neoliberal economic system," Sukarieh and Tannock (2008) argue that today's youth are caught in a capitalist system that has led to large populations of unemployed, working-class, poor, and racialized youth, typically residing in urban settings, with world views, identities, and ways of life that are oppositional or peripheral to the existing social order (p. 304). Educators and other youth service workers then set about to make them "fit functionally" into society, socializing them into a culture of responsibility and entrepreneurship, premised on white middle-class "standardized and universalized notions" of youth development. They learn that if they cannot "make it" in the existing employment market, it is because they "lack the skills of employability," and need to work harder on themselves "to better make it in the system" (p. 309). They also learn about the "ever-increasing educational requirements for jobs," which as Bills and Brown (2011) contend, amount to a practice of "credential inflation" (p. 2).

In Canada, the neoliberal ethos is both complemented and somewhat contradicted by the rhetoric of *multiculturalism*, which has been enshrined in both official policy (1971) and legislation (1988). The multicultural claim is that Canada promotes "inclusive citizenship" and guarantees the "value and dignity" of all citizens, "regardless of their racial and ethnic origins" and "their language or religious affiliation." From this perspective, Canada's promotion of cultural freedom, democracy, and equality enables "cultural groups" to preserve and maintain their culture. Canadian society is seen as "culturally neutral" and "colour-blind"; hence, race is believed not to have any effect on individuals' educational, social, and economic circumstances and opportunities.

However, recognition of "cultural groups" (i.e., minoritized groups) comes up against neoliberal insistence on individual responsibility and choice. And minoritized group members continue to experience educational, social, civic, and economic marginalization and exclusion (Basu, 2011, p. 1308; see also Reitz, Breton, Dion, & Dion, 2009). Indeed, Canadian multiculturalism has been criticized for leading "to the hardening of ethnic and 'racial' stereotypes" (Satzewich & Liodakis, 2010, p. 161), which also functions to position people targeted by those stereotypes at the margins of the society, preserving "the cultural hegemony of the dominant white cultural group" (Henry & Tator, 2010, p. 39). And as Walcott and Abdillahi (2019) observe, in Canada's prevailing colonial paradigm, the dynamism of "the cultural arm of neoliberalism" is used to rationalize the inequitable situation in which Black youth exist, and the "moral regulation, guilt and self-blame" that constitute the ways in which they are racialized (p. 40).

Critical Race Theory and Cultural Analysis

To portray Canadian society in a way that is closer to the lived experience of its Black members, and Black youth in particular, a system of power relations in which race operates as a primary part of economic considerations – what Cedric Robinson (2000) refers to as "racial capitalism" – needs to be acknowledged. Rooted historically in European colonialization and the associated enslavement of African peoples, racism and discrimination towards Black people have been things that Black people have long resisted and against which they continue to struggle. In this regard, any analyses of Black people's experiences necessarily involve employing theoretical frameworks that centre race and draw attention to the agency that Black people have exercised in challenging the structural barriers and hurdles of inequity and racism in their bid to foster and maintain optimism and hope (Crenshaw, 2011; Gillborn, 2015; Howard, 2008; Ladson-Billings & Tate, 1995; Nash, 2019).

Two such frameworks are critical race theory and cultural analysis. *Critical race theory* situates the experiences of people of colour at its centre and thus highlights how seemingly race-neutral and colour-blind practices and policies disproportionately affect minorities (Aylward, 1999, p. 34). According to Howard (2008), critical race theory holds that experiences and opportunities are significantly shaped by race and that "any attempt to eradicate racial inequalities has to be centred on the sociohistorical legacy of racism," which also means challenging the prevailing ideas of meritocracy, fairness, and objectivity that sustain societal discriminatory and exclusionary practices (p. 73; see also Charles, 2011; Gillborn, 2008; Stovall, 2008; Trevino, Harris, & Wallace, 2011).

Critical race theory, as Zamudio, Russell, Rios, and Bridgeman (2011) write, "focuses on the all-encompassing web of race to further our understanding of inequality" (p. 3). It is "concerned with disrupting, exposing, challenging and changing racist policies that work to disenfranchise certain groups of people" and in the process "maintain the *status quo*" (Milner, 2008, p. 333). In today's context, that *status quo* is maintained through a pernicious *new racism*, which Balibar (2007) defines as

> a racism whose dominant theme is not biological heredity but the insurmountability of cultural differences, a racism which, at first sight, does not

postulate the superiority of certain groups or peoples in relation to others but "only" the harmfulness of abolishing frontiers, the incompatibility of life-styles and traditions. (p. 84)

All types of racism – from the individual to the institutional to the structural (or societal), which are all *interlocking and reciprocal* – make for a system of racism by which a process of *racialization* is maintained. This involves categorizing individuals into groups according to their physiological characteristics (specifically skin colour) and attributing abilities, cultural values, morals, and behaviour patterns to these characteristics (Henry & Tator, 2010). Racialization serves to essentialize, homogenize, and generalize about the characteristics of minoritized group members, thereby ignoring group diversity and intragroup differences, and in the process, decontextualizing and dehistoricizing their experiences (Celious & Oyserman, 2001). In relation to schooling and education, Howard (2008) writes that critical race theory

examines racial inequalities in educational achievement in a more probing manner than multicultural education, critical theory, or achievement gap theories by centering the discussion of inequality within the context of racism ... [Critical race theory] within education also serves as a framework to challenge and dismantle prevailing notions of fairness, meritocracy, colorblindness, and neutrality in the education of racial minorities. (p. 963)

Critical race theory as a framework serves to guide investigations, interpretations, and understandings pertaining to the saliency of race and concomitantly anti-Black racism evidenced in, among other concerns, deficit thinking about Black youth (and their families), and their treatment in schools, workplaces, neighbourhoods, and on the streets. In chronicling the voices, experiences, agencies, and ambitions of Black youth, this work provides critical insights into their world as they see it, and as they wish their world and their lives to be understood. Such understanding is critical to the construction of the needed counter-narratives that must be told about why and how Black youth remain marginalized and disenfranchised members of Canadian society.

An important aspect of any critical scholarship in education is its use of "history as both a starting point and roadmap to navigate the contested terrain of race and White racism over time and geographic space" (Donnor, 2019, p. 20). To address the material condition of Black youth is, as Donnor (2019) points out, "not simply to articulate the continuity of White racism in education through voice, counter-storytelling and counter-narrative," but to reveal the nuances of the Negrophobia held by whites. Negrophobia, Donnor writes, is "the politically motivated and culturally informed sense of fear held by a majority of White people that their overall well-being will cease to exist" if Black people are "accorded a semblance of social, political, legal and material equality" (p. 16).

Cultural analysis gives attention to the structures and traditions that we all help to create, which in turn help to produce the circumstances in which individuals find themselves. McDermott and Varenne (2006) make the point that to fully understand and address the issues being investigated, we need to consider the cultural processes that underlie human interactions rather than merely focus on the individual. The idea, then, is to conceive of individuals' problems not simply as a product of their own making but as a product of the cultural worlds they occupy. As McDermott and Varenne assert,

> Cultural analysis, like school reform, requires that we take persons seriously while analytically looking through them – as much as possible in their own terms – to the world with which they are struggling. It is not easy, but it is the best way to see them in their full complexity; anything less delivers a thin portrait of their engagements and leaves them vulnerable to being labeled, classified, diagnosed, blamed, charged, and found lacking without any consideration of how they have been arranged, misheard, unappreciated, set up, and denied by others. (p. 7)

Taking individual complexity into account requires moving beyond the individual, the school, and the dichotomies (such as success/failure, male/female, white/Black) into which we tend to place individuals; we need also to consider the culture of society, which shapes and is shaped by individuals. Indeed, as McDermott and Varenne (2006) proffer, "We have no choice but to study that which we also make" (p. 23). Categories such as race and gender are more than simple terms we use to identify and differentiate individuals – they mediate students' experiences and educational outcomes. In some cultural contexts, gender and race are used "to notice, regulate, and even distort individuals' points of order," making situations "dangerous enough to require constant vigilance" (p. 20).

Both cultural analysis and critical race theory foster a discussion about the intersection of race, gender, and class as they are lived, performed, experienced, and resisted in stratified societies where the culture is shaped, reshaped, and maintained through mechanisms such as racism, sexism, classism, heterosexism, and stereotyping. In Canada, the national multiculturalism discourse sustains the myth of a colour-blind, racially neutral society where culture is not informed by race (Henry & Tator, 2010). However, we cannot ignore the integral role that race, and concomitantly racism, play in Canadian life.

In the case of Black youth, things such as low educational performance, over-representation in foster care and child welfare services, discriminatory police practices (such as carding), and high incarceration rates call for conscientious and consistent advocacy in the face of anti-Black racism (A. Benjamin, 2003; Lewis, 1992; Tecle, 2016; Walcott, 2017; Walcott & Abdillahi, 2019). This naming points to the specificity of Black people's experiences with racism and is cognizant of the historicized and contextual constructs of race and its intersections with gender, class, sexuality, ability, citizenship, and other identity markers (Crichlow, 2016; McCready, 2010; Walcott, 2017; Walcott & Abdillahi, 2019).

The clash between neoliberal and multicultural discourse on the one hand and the realities of Black life on the other can be seen in the strategies employed by some Black youth to navigate and resist the "web of stereotypes" (Howard, 2008, p. 966), which place them at a considerable disadvantage in the school system, work settings, and society generally. These youth work "twice as hard" to "prove" that they are intellectually "just as good" or even "better than" their white peers. Others work hard to prove that they are just as law-abiding and creditable citizens. This "extra work" – which Rockquemore and Laszloffy (2008) refer to as "race tax," and Ulysse (2015) calls "Black tax" – is considered part of the cost of being Black in a society where white supremacy mediates individuals' daily journeys through life. But in as much as the "extra work" might have helped some youth to attain their academic, athletic, and career ambitions, ironically, their successful achievements often tend to be used as evidence that whether or not an individual succeeds is a function of their hard work, not of inequities in society (Rockquemore & Laszloffy, 2008). In other words, individual successes are used to mask the inequities against which individuals struggle.

Still other youth actively resist and contest the institutional structures, policies, and practices in schools, law enforcement agencies, and social services that hold in place the stereotypes which serve to oppress and pathologize Black people. Through their actions these youth seek recognition that the social system is unfair, making it difficult for them to gain access to the opportunities to which they are entitled like their white peers. The inevitable risk to these youth's resistive actions is that their "failures" or lack of "success" come to be used as justifiable "truths" about Black youth (James, 2019). And the possible fear that might be generated by their doing "extra work" and/or resisting the oppressive societal structures – because they seek not to confirm, but to act against, the stereotype – have led to not only intragroup differences among the youth but also inaction, thereby leaving the system and related inequities intact.

Gendered Lives: The Particular Concerns for Black Boys and Young Men

Throughout the years, starting with when I was a youth worker in downtown Toronto in the 1980s and since then as an educator and community-based researcher, students, parents, community members, youth workers, and educators have been drawing my attention to their concerns about the situation of Black male youth. These concerns have been consistent and today are seemingly more urgent. In an attempt to help address these concerns, in my research I have given particular, although far from exclusive, scrutiny to the situation of young Black men. This accounts for the number of chapters in this volume that take up issues and concerns pertaining to their social and educational situation, marginalization, and racialization. Indeed, the situation of Black female youth is not of any less interest or importance.

Clearly, it is necessary to give attention to how gender, race, and class create, perpetuate, and even determine social and educational pathways and outcomes of students, and to the related textured narratives, paradoxes, and complexities of their lived experiences. And notwithstanding the interlocking relationship of gender, race, ethnicity, class, sexual identity, and immigrant/citizenship status in a "White supremist, capitalist, patriarchal" society (hooks, 1992; see also Dua, 1999; Hill Collins, 2006), the ways in which gender operates to inform, structure, and configure Black youth's social and educational lives cannot be homogenized or generalized to the whole group. So, at times it becomes useful and necessary to centre the experiences of males or females to fully grasp, as Annette Henry (1993) writes, "the diverse historical, political, and economic forces within which Black lives are embroiled" (p. 214).

It is the intersection between race and gender that must be taken into account when theorizing Black masculinities. While Black males may be privileged by gender, that privilege is greatly mediated by the hegemonic structures of white masculinity which operates to subordinate and oppress them (McCready, 2010). On the basis of her study of Caribbean youth in New York City, López (2002) found that there were "differing race-gender outlooks [which] arise due to differences in experiences, perceptions and responses to racialization and gender(ing) processes, not biology" (p. 69). In Toronto as in New York City, young Black men have to contend with the general stereotypes of Black males as athletically rather than academically oriented, as low achievers, as troublemakers, and as behaviour-problem students. In "troubled" neighbourhoods, they face the additional stereotypes of Black young men as gang members, drug dealers, and gun users.

Both the statistical data from the Toronto District School Board 2011 Student Census analyzed in chapter 2 and the specific concerns examined in other chapters reveal the ways in which gender complicates the racialization of Black males. For example, the Student Census data revealed that 68 per cent of Black female high school graduates were confirmed in an Ontario postsecondary institution, compared to only 50 per cent of Black male graduates. More recent analysis of Toronto District School Board data indicate that one of the fastest growing and more successful group of students who are excelling in their academic work are Black females, while Black boys continue to be among the students with the lowest academic performance (Cameron, 2020).

Athletics figure prominently in several of the chapters, and are the main focus of chapter 6. While both boys and girls participate in athletics, it is largely for boys that they come to occupy a central position during adolescence. For Black male youth, athletics are seen as a primary arena for the performance of Black masculinity. They are also held out as a fast track to a postsecondary education, especially in gaining entry to a university in the United States, and an escape route out of poverty. However, for the vast majority of young Black men these promises are illusory, and participation in athletics has the effect of diverting them from academic pursuits.

It should be noted that the ongoing concern with the educational and social conditions of young men has contributed, to some degree, to a dearth of scholarship on Black girls' experiences with schooling (George, 2020; A. Henry, 1993). In this regard, my attempt here is neither to overemphasize the conditions of males at the expense of females nor to have us generalize from the experiences of Black males. Rather, my goal is to use the research work in which I have engaged to provide extensive insights gained over a period of time about the lives of Black youth – much of which pertains to Black young men. And while anti-Black racism manifested towards and experienced by Black young women is similar, at some level and in some respects, to that experienced by young men, there are important differences that need to be accounted for. To this end, I invited colleagues with feminist scholarship and expertise to be part of this conversation through their responses.

In terms of athletics, for instance, in research I conducted on "the gendered experiences of female students in sports" (James, 2005, chap. 4) – in which I undertook a gendered analysis of Alicia, a twenty-four-year-old Black student athlete of Caribbean descent who went to university in the United States on an athletic scholarship – I concluded:

> Given the structured gender inequity within society, and by extension within educational and athletic institutions, females do not have the same access and opportunities to educational and athletic opportunities as males. In reality, gender (in addition to the other demographic factors) helps to determine both the form and nature of females' participation and achievement in sports. Furthermore, sports, maintained as part of the male system of hegemony, will continue to be an arena in which females will be marginalized and undervalued. So, it is not merely a matter of individual females' choice, abilities, skills, or ambitions that determine their limits or possibilities, but the educational and athletic systems in which they participate, and the supports and encouragements they receive along the way. (p. 131)

The troubling schooling experiences of Black girls and young women and the costs to their educational and social trajectory – even as they outperform boys and young men in school – are addressed in the chapters about the social and historical schooling contexts of Black students (chapter 1), the significance of generational differences (chapter 2), the social and educational costs growing up in the suburbs (chapter 9), and what schooling is like for Black students in the early twenty-first century (chapter 10). The narrative that can be gleaned about Black girls and young women from these chapters is that they are subjected to anti-Black racism in which the interlocking relationship of Blackness and femaleness operates to inform how as students they are academically engaged, disciplined, and supported to graduation. As with their male peers, the academic abilities, schooling interests, and social ambitions of Black females are undervalued and underestimated by many of their white teachers (Annamma et al., 2019; Gaymes, 2006; George, 2020; Wood, 2011). All of this contributes to their inadequate school engagement, academic performance, and educational achievements, sustained by harsher disciplinary practices on the part of teachers. For instance, in their participatory action research which examined the schooling experiences of African-American females, Evans-Winters (2017) and her young researchers, Girls for Gender Equity, seeking an explanation for the punitive discipline to which their participants were subjected, found:

> School officials viewed girls of color as a threat to the school environment itself. In particular, the girls reported that they were targeted for their style

of dress, their hair, their attitude or character. In the words of the girls, they are viewed as "Dangerous Bodies." As non-White people, they are perceived as inherently violent; as nonwealthy youth, they are viewed as in need of discipline and control; and as girls of color, they are believed to be lacking morals and values. Thus, the body of a Black or Brown girl is seen as simultaneously an inherent threat to school officials and other students as well as a threat to her own safety and well-being. (p. 418)

Accordingly, just like their male peers, Black females are subjected to stereotypes that contribute to perceptions of them as disobedient, defiant, loud, having a bad attitude, and acting "ghetto" (Annamma et al., 2019; Gaymes, 2006; George, 2020; Linton & McLean, 2017; Wood, 2011). And there is, as Kearie Daniel (2020) mentions – quoting Tanya Hayles, founder of Toronto-based Black Moms Connection – teachers' "adultification of our daughters."

Studying Black Youth from Adolescence to Adulthood

I have always wanted to know about the lives of participants I have studied beyond the single interaction I have had with them through one interview. To this end, I have often done longitudinal studies, in which I have interviewed participants at various points in their lives from adolescence though to adulthood. These studies provide insights into their life trajectories and the evolution of their thinking, often through their own words. Here, for example, is "Megan" (all of the names of participants here and elsewhere in the book are pseudonyms), whom I first interviewed in 1984 when she was in her third year at university:

> You have to overcome [discrimination]. Not because it exists, I am going to lay down and die and don't bother trying. I know that it exists ... and I know what I have to do to overcome it. It calls for working hard. (Megan, age twenty-one, 1984)

> I am as optimistic ... maybe now I am more realistic and I think it is possible [to make it] but with a big *but* [and that is] you have to take certain strategies to get there. It is not going to be easy ... but I can do it because I understand the hurdles and what you have to do to get over them. (Megan, age twenty-eight, 1991)

> I wanted to make sure that I had everything that there was – nothing that the potential employer could look at to discount me. I heard the saying that Black people had to work twice as hard to get half as far. There was

always that sense that you couldn't just be equal, you had to be better than. (Megan, age forty-three, 2006)

Like most of the other participants in the study, Megan referred to racism and discrimination as "hurdles" rather than "barriers." The participants preferred to think of them as mechanisms that might be overcome, sidestepped, or jumped over (to use an athletic metaphor) through their education, self-confidence, determination, and hard work. Megan's reflections tell of the impact of these "hurdles" in terms of attaining the career to which she aspired. Over the years, she remained determined, and as she said in 1991, "optimistic" but, with age, "a little more realistic." By 2006 she was married with children, living in a house in the suburbs, receiving a good salary, and holding a job in human resources in a large corporate firm in a downtown Toronto office tower. So, one would think Megan would have concluded that her strategy of determination and optimism had paid off and she had "made it," and hence that racism was not the "hurdle" she had feared. Nonetheless, Megan, like the seven others (two males and five females) who participated in the follow-up study I conducted in 2006, was resolute that race and racism were factors in their "struggles" to negotiate and attain their current jobs, and were realities about which they were constantly reminded and had to take into consideration as they journeyed through life (S. Benjamin, 2006).

The longitudinal study (1984–2006) in which Megan participated started with 60 youths between the ages of 17 and 22 years.[1] Many of the participants (25 of the 60 or 42 per cent) aspired to professional and white-collar careers such as medicine, law, business, teaching, and social work, and were optimistic that even in the face of racism they would realize their career aspirations. And while race was generally perceived to be one "hurdle," gender, for females, was another. Thus

---

1 I interviewed 33 males and 27 females. At that time, they were high school students and graduates, school stop-outs and dropouts, college and university students, and full- and part-time employees. About 60 per cent of them were born in the Caribbean, 20 per cent in Toronto, 5 per cent in Halifax and fewer than 2 per cent in Britain to Caribbean parents. Among them, 15 per cent could be described as being of middle-class background (i.e., having parents in professional or white-collar jobs). They lived in the city's downtown area, the in-between suburbs, and the outer suburbs. I also conducted observations of youth gatherings at public and community events where I had informal conversations with Black youth and other attendees. These included youth programs, political demonstrations, student forums, Caribana activities, and Black Liberation Month events.

Sharon, a participant in the 1984–5 study, stated, "Being a Black woman means that I have two strikes against me to start with, but that makes things challenging." So, for many of the youth, racism was taken to be a challenge by which they were invigorated or inspired to pursue their career goals – something they carried from their youth into their forties. The optimism of many of the participants seemed to be nurtured by their commitment to "represent" their community through their hard work. They worked, as Sharon also stated, "really, really hard" to be examples of what they were capable of doing and attaining.

Participants' optimism was supported by the self-confidence they had cultivated. They believed that they had what it took, and were doing what was necessary, to surmount the hurdles and struggles that they had come to accept as part of their everyday life. Larry, for example, who had just started work as a tool and die maker when he was interviewed in 1984, claimed that he was optimistic and confident that he would become "a foreman at [his] shop," and as he later added:

> Another ten years I will have my own business even though there is discrimination, because I'm a hard worker ... There is always going to be discrimination but there is always someone out there who is going to stand by your side. They don't necessarily have to be Black.

As adolescents, participants held confidently to the idea that they had ample qualities to achieve their aspirations: their education, hard work, skills, and tenacity. They also mentioned that they would "always have to be on guard, be extra careful and extra polite." These strategies, especially those relating to education, were meant, in the words of one participant, "to prove to white people that we can do something." In addition, they believed in their own agency, and the recognition they expected to receive from people who, as Larry said, would stand by them. However, by their late twenties, when I reconnected with 22 of the original 60 participants (then 24 to 29 years old) to conduct a follow-up study (1991), many had started to think that they could not achieve the opportunities and occupations they sought by themselves. They needed to work, as Sonia said in 1991, "in concert with other people of like minds because you can't take on the system by yourself even if you prove to be the brightest or best" (cited in James, 1993, p. 16). In my 1991 study, participants confessed their "naivety" and indicated that they were shifting their focus from exclusively individual efforts to addressing issues in the society. Nevertheless, they remained confident that their knowledge and understanding of the system as well as their education and abilities were sufficient to enable their success in a system they accepted as "not perfect."

I have followed the life journeys of many other Black youth over the years, and some of their stories are told in the chapters that follow. These stories help us discern to what extent the trajectories of subsequent generations of Black youth have differed from that of the 1980s generation and to what extent they have remained the same, as well as whether the harmful narrative of the underachieving, sports-minded, undisciplined, and troublesome Black youth, especially male Black youth, has persisted or changed over time.

About the Essays

This book brings together ten essays that I have written over a period of more than two decades. They cover various topics relating to the lives of Black youth (with a closer scrutiny of Black males) in the Greater Toronto Area, ranging from immigration to education to athletics to mentorship to encounters with the police. Several of the essays probe the lives of specific Black youth, in some cases tracing their journeys from high school through to adulthood, noting the ways in which, in the words of a research participant, "colour matters."

The essays have been edited for style, and in some cases shortened or expanded, but they have not been updated. Each essay reflects the time in which it was written. Taken together, as a collection written over time, the essays give rise to the question: What has changed in the lives of Black youth, and what has remained the same?

The book contains another element as well. Each essay is followed by a brief response from another scholar. These responses engage the topics I explore in the essays through different lenses: first of all, the lens of today rather than that of the time each essay was written. There are also different geographical lenses, as the respondents write from Britain, the United States, and other parts of Canada (Vancouver, St. Catharines, Ottawa, and Montreal) as well as Toronto. That most of the responses to the essays are by women scholars helps to deepen the discussion of the gendered lives of Black young people. Furthermore, each respondent brings their own scholarly interests, concerns, perspectives, and interpretations to understanding the differences, paradoxes, and contradictions of the lived experiences and circumstances of Black Canadian youth. In doing so, they provide insightful observations, thoughtful criticisms, alternative viewpoints, and provocative questions for us to consider. Their contributions alert us to what more might be said, or said differently, about the social, cultural, educational, political, and occupational worlds of Black youth.

Introduction   xxix

In addition to the responses to individual essays, Alissa Trotz's foreword and Michele Johnson's epilogue engage the collection as a whole, including the responses.

In this way, the book takes on the character of a conversation. My hope is that it will engender a wider conversation about the lives of Black youth, their prospects (or lack thereof) in Canadian society, and the structural barriers they face.

In chapter 1, "Historical and Social Context of the Schooling and Education of African Canadians," I outline the historical and social contexts of education from the 1970s to the first two decades of the twenty-first century, as well as the major policies, programs, and activities (and the events that led to them) initiated over the years in a bid to address Black students' schooling and educational issues. The chapter also documents the long-standing efforts of parents, educators, and community members to advocate effectively for Black students.

Chapter 2, "Generational Differences in Black Students' Education Pursuits and Performance," uses the Toronto District School Board (TDSB) 2011 Student Census data to examine the schooling and educational situation of Black students, focusing on intragroup generational and gender differences in terms of diversity. Findings indicate that third-generation students had lesser educational outcomes than their first-generation peers did, and that the differences between the various Black groups can be largely explained in terms of immigration patterns and experiences with inequity in the society. Continuing to explore the experiences of Black youth in relation to generational status, chapter 3, "'To Make a Better Future,'" presents the narrative of a 1.5-generation Caribbean-Canadian young man who immigrated to Canada in his early high school years and is now in his late thirties. The account is based on interviews with him conducted over an eighteen-year period, as well as his responses to the two versions of his story.

On the question of school disengagement, undisciplined behaviour, and educational underachievement of Black male students, chapter 4, "Students 'at Risk': Stereotypes and the Schooling of Black Boys," examines how stereotypes of Black male youth as *immigrant, fatherless, troublemaker, athlete,* and *underachiever* operate in the social construction of these youth as "at-risk" students. Continuing with the theme of education and Black males, in chapter 5, "More than Brains, Education, and Hard Work: The Aspirations and Career Trajectories of Two Young Black Men," I use case studies of two young African-Canadian men from the same stigmatized Toronto neighbourhood to critically discuss the commonly accepted claim that through education, intellectual ability, and hard work, individuals are able to attain the education and careers to which they aspire. While both of these young men are ambitious and well-schooled in the discourse of meritocracy, hard work, and dedication, one successfully attained his career goals while the other struggled to surmount the confounding obstacles of inequity.

Chapter 6, "Class, Race, and Schooling in the Performance of Black Male Athleticism," points to the ways in which race, class, and gender – as marginalizing and racializing demographics – intersect in the construction of Black males as athletes, and in turn, the assumptions and expectations teachers and coaches have of them. Black males, as this essay discusses, are perceived to exist in a culture in which athletics define their Blackness, academic performance, career aspirations, and relationships with coaches and other role models. In chapter 7, "Troubling Role Models: Seeing Racialization in the Discourse Relating to 'Corrective Agents' for Black Males," the framework of new racism is used to interrogate the notion of mentorship and role models as "corrective agents" for Black youth, particularly males. Within the Canadian context of inequities, marginalization, and racialization in society, the need for strong mentors and role models for Black youth tends to be driven by the assumption that individual disposition or community cultural practices are responsible for the negative life circumstances experienced by Black youth.

Chapter 8, "'Up to No Good': Black on the Streets and Encountering Police," originally published in 1998, examines the nature of Black youth's encounters with police in public spaces and on the streets in particular. I argue that police and security personnel discretion and action (such as Stop, Search, and Question) are manifestations of patriarchal, colonial, and racist discourses employed to protect whiteness by symbolically containing the perception of the "dangerous Other." In chapter 9, "'Colour Matters'": Suburban Life, Social Mobility and Its High Cost for Black Youth," I analyse the findings from research with youth and parents of Caribbean descent who are living in outer suburban areas of Toronto. While suburban neighbourhoods have come to represent desirable outcomes such as social mobility, safety, increased opportunity, and possibilities for success for those moving there, I note the "cost," in social, economic, cultural, and psychological terms, for Black youth of growing up in the suburbs.

By way of providing an update on the schooling and education of Black students, chapter 10, "Towards Equity in Education for Black Students," presents an abbreviated version of a report, *Towards Race Equity in Education: The Schooling of Black Students in the Greater Toronto Area*. Using Toronto District School Board data as reference, a team of us conducted investigative sessions in the Greater Toronto Area. The report documents what more than 300 parents, educators, community members, school administrators, and board trustees had to say about Black students' disengagement from school, poor academic performance, encounters with racial stereotyping, excessive surveillance, and educational underachievement, as well as about the streaming of Black students into nonacademic educational paths and how the racism of low expectations operated in their racialization and disenfranchisement.

This final chapter provides a context for understanding what one Black Toronto school administrator emailed to us about the fatal shooting of one of her Black male students two days after she participated in one of our sessions:

> His death reminds me why it is so important to do something now. He was a bright young man who just needed a place to belong. We are losing too many of our young men to the streets and the violence that surrounds them. Hopefully creating an education system that does not negate or demonize Black bodies is a small but powerful request. (Personal communication)

Shortly after the report was released, the *Toronto Star* carried an editorial titled "Academic Streaming Harms Black Students" (2017). The editorial ended with an echo of this teacher's appeal: "This can't wait another twenty-five years. The school system should be a tool for redressing inequities, not compounding them."

Finally ...

The collection of essays tells about the experiences, optimism, ambitions, hopes, and challenges of generations of Black youth, many of them males, living in the Greater Toronto Area. The insights provided by the youth about their lives – told, captured, and reported largely in their own words – reveal the extent to which their educational and career aspirations have been realized, how their respective strategies effectively served them, and how much has changed or remained the same over the years. What is clear is the roles that enablers such as parents, peers, teachers, coaches, and others played over time in the life trajectory of Black youth as they negotiated and navigated the systems of racism and discrimination sustained by social and economic structures of inequity.

Until government and institutional leaders acknowledge anti-Black racism, and put in place structures – not just temporary programs – to address the situation of Black youth, then the optimism and hope that characterize this pivotal stage of life will likely wane. There needs to be widespread acceptance that in an interrelated world the situation of Black youth affects society generally. In other words, the social, economic, cultural, emotional, and health cost of Black youth and their communities is also borne by the entire society. If indeed we are to respond productively to the needs, experiences, and aspirations of Black youth and their parents and communities, then all of society must become acquainted with their lived realities and agency to create and reimagine the needed counternarrative that will lead to their "making it" in terms of achieving success and living healthy, meaningful lives. The novel coronavirus has exposed the dangerous cost of inequity. In fact, the pandemic, COVID-19, has not only highlighted the inequities and the inherent barriers to productive lives but also exacerbated the problems by adding another layer to the marginalization and racialization of Black youth. Therefore, there is an urgent need for changes in societal and institutional regulations, policies, programs and practices if Black youth are to gain the opportunities and privileges in society to which they are entitled.

REFERENCES

Academic streaming harms black students. [Editorial]. (2017, April 30). *Toronto Star*. https://www.thestar.com/opinion/editorials/2017/04/30/academic-streaming-harms-black-students-editorial.html

Annamma, S.A., Anyon, Y., Joseph, N.M., Farrar, J., Greer, E., Downing, B., & Simmons, J. (2019). Black girls and school discipline: The complexities of being overrepresented and understudied. *Urban Education, 54*(2), 211–42. https://doi.org/10.1177/0042085916646610

Aylward, C.A. (1999). *Canadian critical race theory: Racism and the law*. Halifax, NS: Fernwood.

Balibar, E. (2007). Is there a "neo-racism"? In T. Das Gupta, C.E. James, G-E. Galabuzi, & C. Andersen (Eds.), *Race and racialization: Essential readings* (pp. 83–8). Toronto, ON: Canadian Scholars' Press.

Basu, R. (2011). Multiculturalism through multilingualism in schools: Emerging places of "integration" in Toronto. *Annals of the Association of American Geographers, 101*(6), 1307–30. https://doi.org/10.1080/00045608.2011.579536

Benjamin, A. (2003). *The Black/Jamaican criminal: The making of ideology* (unpublished doctoral dissertation). Toronto: Ontario Institute of Studies in Education, University of Toronto.

Benjamin, S. (Director). (2006). *Making it* [Film]. Canada: National Film Board of Canada, CitizenShift. https://www.nfb.ca/film/making_it

Bills, D.B., & Brown, D.K. (2011). New directions in educational credentialism. *Research in Social Stratification and Mobility, 29*(1), 1–4. https://doi.org/10.1016/j.rssm.2011.01.004

Braedley, S., & Luxton, M. (2010). Competing philosophies: Neoliberalism and the challenges of everyday life. In S. Braedley & M. Luxton (Eds.), *Neoliberalism and everyday life* (pp. 3–21). Montreal, QC: McGill-Queen's University Press.

Cameron, D.H. (2020). *Black student experience in TDSB schools*. Toronto, ON: Toronto District School Board, Research Department.

Celious, A., & Oyserman, D. (2001). Race from the inside: An emerging heterogeneous race model. *Journal of Social Issues, 57*, 149–65. https://doi.org/10.1111/0022-4537.00206

Charles, H. (2011). Toward a critical race theory of education. *Contemporary Justice Review, 11*(1), 63–5. https://doi.org/10.1080/10282580701850413

Connell, R. (2010). Understanding neoliberalism. In S. Braedley & M. Luxton (Eds.), *Neoliberalism and everyday life* (pp. 22–36). Montreal, QC: McGill-Queen's University Press.

Crenshaw, K.W. (2011). Twenty years of critical race theory: Looking back to move forward. *Connecticut Law Review, 43*(5), 1253–352. https://opencommons.uconn.edu/law_review/117

Crichlow, W. (2016). *Human rights, intersectionality and Black LGBTQ institutional invisibility*. Racial Profiling Policy Dialogue, Ontario Human Rights Commission. Toronto, ON: York University.

Daniel, K. (2020, April 22). Being a tiger mom is an act of love – and necessity. *Flare*. https://www.flare.com/identity/tiger-parenting-style-black-tiger-mom/

Donnor, J.K. (2019). Understanding the why of whiteness: Negrophobia, segregation, and the legacy of white resistance to Black education in Mississippi. In J.T. DeCuir-Gunby, T.K. Chapman, & P.A. Schutz (Eds.), *Understanding critical race research methods and methodologies: Lessons from the field* (pp. 13–23). New York, NY: Routledge.

Dua, E. (1999). Canadian anti-racist feminist thought: Scratching the surface of racism. In E. Dua & A. Robertson (Eds.), *Scratching the surface: Canadian anti-racist feminist thought* (pp. 7–31). Toronto, ON: Women's Press.

Evans-Winters, V.E. (with Girls for Gender Equity). (2017). Flipping the script: The dangerous bodies of girls of color. *Cultural Studies, 17*(5), 415–23. https://doi.org/10.1177/1532708616684867

Gaymes, A. (2006). *Making spaces that matter: Reflections on the experiences of female students in a Toronto school* (Unpublished master's thesis). Faculty of Education, York University, Toronto, ON.

George, R.C. (2020). Holding it down? The silencing of Black female students in the educational discourses of the Greater Toronto Area. *Canadian Journal of Education, 43*(1), 32–58.

Gillborn, D. (2008). *Racism and education: Coincidence or conspiracy*. London, UK: Routledge.

Gillborn, D. (2015). Intersectionality, critical race theory and the primacy of racism: Race, class, gender and disability in education. *Qualitative Inquiry*, 21(3), 277–87. https://doi.org/10.1177/1077800414557827

Henry, A. (1993). Missing: Black self-representation in Canadian educational research. *Canadian Journal of Education*, 18(3), 206–22. https://doi.org/10.2307/1495383

Henry, F., & Tator, C. (2010). *The colour of democracy: Racism in Canadian society* (4th ed.). Toronto, ON: Nelson Education.

Hill Collins, P. (2006). A telling difference: Dominance, strength, and black masculinities. In A.D. Mutua (Ed.), *Progressive Black masculinities* (pp. 73–98). New York, NY: Routledge.

hooks, b. (1992). *Black looks: Race and representations*. Boston, MA: South End Press.

Howard, T.C. (2008). Who really cares? The disenfranchisement of African American males in preK–12 schools: A critical race theory perspective. *Teachers College Record*, 110(5), 954–85.

James, C.E. (1993). Getting there and staying there: Blacks' employment experience. In P. Axelrod & P. Anisef (Eds.), *Transition: Schooling and employment in Canadian society* (pp. 3–20). Toronto, ON: Thompson Educational Publishing.

James, C.E. (2005). *Race in play: Understanding the socio-cultural worlds of student athletes*. Toronto, ON: Canadian Scholars' Press.

James, C.E. (2019). Adapting, disrupting and resisting: How middle school Black males position themselves in response to racialization in school. *Canadian Journal of Sociology*, 44(4), 373–97. https://doi.org/10.29173/cjs29518

Ladson-Billings, G., & Tate, W.F. (1995). Toward a critical race theory of education. *Teachers College Record*, 97(1), 47–68.

Lewis, S. (1992, June 9). *Report on race relations in Ontario*. Toronto, ON: Government of Ontario.

Linton, R., & McLean, L. (2017). I'm not loud, I'm outspoken: Narratives of four Jamaican girls' identity and academic success. *Girlhood Studies*, 10(1), 71–88. https://doi.org/10.3167/ghs.2017.100106

López, N. (2002). Race-gender experiences and schooling: Second-generation Dominican, West Indian, and Haitian youth in New York City. *Race Ethnicity and Education*, 5(1), 67–89. https://doi.org/10.1080/13613320120117207

Luxton, M. (2010). Doing neoliberalism: Perverse individualism in personal life. In S. Braedley & M. Luxton (Eds.), *Neoliberalism and everyday life* (pp. 163–83). Montreal, QC: McGill-Queen's University Press.

McCready, L.T. (2010). *Making space for diverse masculinities: Difference, intersectionality, and engagement in an urban high school*. New York, NY: Peter Lang.

McDermott, R., & Varenne, H. (2006). Reconstructing culture in educational research. In G. Spindler & L. Hammonds (Eds.), *Innovations in educational ethnography* (pp. 3–31). Mahwah, NJ: Lawrence Erlbaum Associates.

Milner, H.R. (2008). Critical race theory and interest convergence as analytical tools in teacher education policies and practices. *Journal of Teacher Education*, 59(4), 332–46. https://doi.org/10.1177/0022487108321884

Nash, J.C. (2019). *Black feminism imagined after intersectionality*. Durham, NC: Duke University Press.

Porfilio, B., & Malott, C. (Eds.), *The destructive path of neoliberalism: An international examination of urban education*. Rotterdam, Netherlands: Sense Publishers.

Reitz, J.G., Breton, R., Dion, K.K., & Dion, K.L. (2009). *Multiculturalism and social cohesion: Potentials and challenges of diversity*. New York, NY: Springer.

Robinson, C.J. (2000). *Black Marxism: The making of the Black radical tradition*. Chapel Hill, NC: University of North Carolina Press.

Rockquemore, K., & Laszloffy, T. (2008). *The Black academic's guide to winning tenure without losing your soul*. Boulder, CO: Lynne Rienner.

Satzewich, V., & Liodakis, N. (2010). *"Race"and ethnicity in Canada: A critical introduction*. Toronto, ON: Oxford University Press.

Stovall, D. (2008). Forging community in race and class: Critical race theory and the quest for social justice in education. *Race Ethnicity and Education*, 9(3), 243–59. https://doi.org/10.1080/13613320600807550

Sukarieh, M., & Tannock, S. (2008). In the best interests of youth or neoliberalism? The World Bank and the new global youth empowerment project. *Journal of Youth Studies*, 11(3), 301–12. https://doi.org/10.1080/13676260801946431

Tabb, W.K. (2003). Du Bois vs. neoliberalism. *Monthly Review*, 55(6), 33–40. https://doi.org/10.14452/MR-055-06-2003-10_4

Tecle, S. (2016, Winter). Anti-Blackness: Official myths aside, Canadian anti-Black racism is alive and deadly. *Canadian Dimension*, 50(1). https://canadiandimension.com/articles/view/anti-blackness

Trevino, A.J., Harris, M.A., & Wallace, D. (2011). What's so critical about critical race theory? *Contemporary Justice Review*, 11(1), 7–10. https://doi.org/10.1080/10282580701850330

Ulysse, G.A. (2015, December 7). Pedagogies of belonging. *Huffington Post*. http://www.huffingtonpost.com/gina-athena-ulysse/pedagogies-of-belonging_1_b_8693286.html

Wacquant, L. (2008). *Urban outcasts: A comparative sociology of advanced marginality*. Cambridge, UK: Polity Press.

Walcott, R. (2017). *Queer returns: Essays on multiculturalism, diaspora, and Black studies*. Toronto, ON: Insomniac Press.

Walcott, R., & Abdillahi, I. (2019), *Blacklife: Post-BLM and the struggle for freedom*. Winnipeg, MB: ARP Books.

Wood, M. (2011). *Banking on Education: Black Canadian females and schooling* (unpublished doctoral dissertation). Faculty of Education, York University, Toronto, ON.

Zamudio, M.M., Russell, C., Rios, F.A., & Bridgeman, J.L. (2011). *Critical race theory matters: Education and ideology*. New York, NY: Routledge.

COLOUR MATTERS

Essays on the Experiences, Education, and Pursuits of Black Youth

1 Historical and Social Context of the Schooling and Education of African Canadians[1]

Education has long posed a major concern for African-Canadian students, parents, educators, and administrators. Much of this concern relates to claims that the education system has failed – and continues to fail – to meet the needs of African-Canadian students. Accordingly, a strong belief persists that the formal education system, in its current form, either cannot or will not accommodate their needs and interests.[2] Some youth become so disillusioned with their schooling that they drop out (R.S. Brown, 1993; Dei, Holmes, Mazzuca, McIsaac, & Zine, 1997); others physically remain in school but become psychologically disengaged from the process (Brathwaite, 1989; James, 1990, 1994; Solomon, 1992). In response to the experiences of many of our young people, parents and other members of African-Canadian communities have both initiated their own programs and advocated consistently to school boards and provincial governments for changes to the education system, but with inadequate results.

In this chapter, I explore African Canadians' experiences and concerns with the education system over the last five decades, using the 1970s[3] as a point of departure. While I make extensive reference to

---

1 An earlier, and shorter, version of this chapter was published in 1996. See James and Brathwaite (1996). Permission for republication granted by publisher. This version has been significantly revised, updated, and expanded.
2 Issues around African Canadians' successful participation in the education systems in Canada have been a problem since our recorded presence here dating back to the seventeenth century. Ever since then, Africans have contested the ways in which education has been used in our marginalization, limiting our full participation in society.
3 I use the 1970s as my reference since in this period the significant increase in immigrants from the Caribbean brought a correspondingly large number of Black/African Canadian students into the educational system.

Ontario, and metropolitan Toronto in particular, I suggest that these issues and concerns are not unique to this region of Canada. Indeed, there is ample evidence to indicate that similar experiences and concerns exist for African Canadians in Nova Scotia, Alberta, Manitoba, Saskatchewan, and Quebec (Black Learners Advisory Committee, 1994; Calliste, 1996; Codjoe, 2001; D'Oyley, 1994; D'Oyley & James, 1998; Kelly, 1998; Kakembo & Upshaw, 1998).

In addressing these concerns, we see that community members seem to be persuaded or guided by hope – specifically, "critical hope" – which inspires dreams and possibilities (Freire, 1994; hooks, 2003; Weingarten, 2000). As Freire (1994) contends, "there is no change without dream, as there is no dream without hope" (p. 91). Hope, as bell hooks (1999) notes, comprises a life force that can help to sustain those living in a world of pain by pulling them back from "the edge of despair" (p. 8); it can also move them towards action that grows out of solidarity with others and "shared vision" (p. 115). The value of hope lives in the fact that it motivates individuals to engage in the struggle for change, convinced that doing so opens opportunities and possibilities for a future they hope to construct – a future founded on social justice and equity.

I highlight the 1970s as a particularly important and dynamic period in the struggle for representation and equity in education. For instance, it was at this time that we saw a significant increase in the Black population in Canada, and Ontario in particular; the proclamation of a Canadian multiculturalism policy; the introduction of provincial multicultural education policies and later race relations policies (James, 2001); and the observance of the renamed "Black History Month."[4]

It was also the period in which a number of community education projects were established in Toronto, including the Black Education Project (BEP), the Black Liaison Committee (BLC) at the Toronto Board of Education, the Harriet Tubman Youth Centre (HTYC), African-Canadian Heritage Programmes (ACHP), and others. Community members also played a significant role in the establishment of the Transitional Year

---

4 The precursor of Black History Month in Canada dates back to 1957 when the Canadian Negro Women's Association first celebrated Negro History Week. Following the United States, in the 1970s Negro History Week was expanded and renamed Black History Month. In 1979, the one-year-old Ontario Black History Society petitioned the mayor of Toronto to issue the proclamation making February "Black History Month." The tradition continues today with the name Black History Month; but many in the community use and prefer the name "African History Month," as this more accurately represents the heritage that is being recognized.

Program at the University of Toronto (see K. Allen, 1996, 2003; Brathwaite, 2003; Calliste, 1996). Similarly, in Halifax, organizations such as the Nova Scotia Association for the Advancement of Coloured People (NSAACP), the Afro-Canadian Liberation Movement (ACLM), the Black United Front (BUF), and the Negro Education Committee (NEC) mobilized "to improve the quality of life in the African–Nova Scotian community" – one outcome being the establishment of the Transitional Year Program at Dalhousie University (Foyn, 1998). Since these experiences inform our knowledge and understanding of African-Canadian education in Canada, and in Toronto in particular, I will weave them into our discussion.

The 1970s and 1980s: A Reference for the Decades Ahead

Over many years, research has been conducted to assess the low achievement or underachievement of African students in Canadian schools. In the 1970s, for example, research was carried out by several school boards – Toronto (Schreiber, 1970; Stewart, 1975), York (Roth, 1973), and North York (Fram, Broks, Crawford, Handscombe, & Virgin, 1977) – in an attempt to understand what was then characterized as the adjustment problems and needs of Black Caribbean students. Independent researchers such as Ramcharan (1975), W. Anderson and Grant (1975), and Beserve (1976) also contributed towards our understanding of the problems Black Caribbean students were facing in the school system. Without exception, these studies showed that the students' difficulties stemmed not only from their experiences of trying to adjust to a new society (for those who had recently arrived), but also from their experiences with discrimination based on race and cultural differences.

The studies' findings offered a major source of information about Black youth, primarily those from the Caribbean, and reflected the social conditions of the 1970s – a time when Black immigrants from the Caribbean were entering Canada in large numbers and enrolling their children in a school system that was unprepared for them. Some school authorities at the time maintained that the Black students' performance resulted from their adjustment problems. Other explanations tended towards the pathological (see Christensen, Thornley-Brown, & Robinson, 1980) – that is, the youth had psychological problems related to their familial, cultural, and social adjustments. They were also labelled slow learners, learning disabled, hyperactive, or suffering from attention deficit. On the basis of these assessments, many students were placed in special education classes, where it was further established that their educational performance stemmed primarily from their lack of ability and social condition – in which parents played a significant part – and not the school system or its educators.

However, the identified educational problems could not account for the similar school experiences of *Canadian-born* Black youth, who were also not doing well in school, including those whose parents actively supported their educational endeavours and aspirations. Indeed, during the 1970s, research showed that regardless of their social class background, Black students tended to have high educational and career aspirations (Calliste, 1982).[5] It has been well established that Black parents and students place a high value on education because they see education as making it possible for them to get ahead in Canadian society (Brathwaite, 1996; Calliste, 1982; Head, 1975; D'Oyley & Silverman, 1976). As Calliste (1982) explains, education may be the most important, if not the only, mobility channel for Caribbean students. For this reason, Black students are likely to be more highly motivated, achievement-oriented, and concerned about high grades than their Anglo-Canadian counterparts. But the social construction of Black students as academically incompetent presented a barrier to realizing their educational goals.

Research from the 1970s and 1980s showed that Black students were regularly streamed into lower-level or vocational classes within Ontario schools. For example, Toronto Board of Education[6] studies over those two decades revealed that Black students were second to Indigenous students as the most highly represented in basic-level programs of study (Cheng, 1995; Cheng, Tsuji, Yau, & Ziegler, 1987; Cheng, Yau, & Ziegler, 1993; Deosaran, 1976; Wright, 1971; Wright & Tsuji, 1984).

Many Black community organizations (e.g., the BLC at the Toronto Board of Education, BEP, Organization of Parents of Black Children [OPBC], African Heritage Educators Network [AHEN], and Canadian Alliance of Black Educators [CABE]), along with community members, generally saw placement of Black students into vocational classes as a deliberate and discriminating practice by some educators who identified Black students, especially those from the Caribbean, as slow learners (Head, 1975). These organizations and Black community members

---

5 Calliste (1982) suggests that Caribbean people in Canada, while characterized by low social class status, were less entrenched in their class position than other Canadians of similar status.
6 The Toronto District School Board (TDSB) was created in 1998 following the merger of six school boards – Board of Education for the City of York, East York Board of Education, North York Board of Education, Scarborough Board of Education, Etobicoke Board of Education, and Toronto Board of Education.

advocated for changes to the practice of streaming. A 1988 report by the Toronto Board of Education Consultative Committee on the Education of Black Students in Toronto Schools (CCEBSTS) noted that stereotyping, streaming, educational assessment, irrelevant curriculum, and lack of "role models" – in short, discrimination – were responsible for the poor level of educational performance by many Black students in that Board. As one parent expressed it, "Students are forced into non-academic courses leading to dead-end jobs. The school expects the students to be low achievers. The school focuses on the failures of Black students" (CCEBSTS, 1988, Appendix, p. 1). In the words of two students, "Black students with ability and ambition are discouraged and turned off by Guidance," and "Counsellors show us all the negatives" (CCEBSTS, 1988, p. 20).

Evidently, streaming Black students had a significant impact not only on their academic achievement but also on how they perceived the educational and occupational possibilities that their schooling provided them (Coelho, 1988; Curtis, Livingstone, & Smaller, 1992; Deosaran, 1976; Mata, 1989). In fact, researchers at that time indicated that Black students tended to become ambivalent and discouraged with the school system because they did not believe the reward system afforded them opportunities to realize their educational goals (D'Oyley & Silverman, 1976; Head, 1975; James, 1990; Solomon, 1992). In struggling against their marginalization, some students actively resisted by challenging school authorities and disengaging from the academic process (Solomon, 1992), while others held onto their high educational goals, despite their experiences (D'Oyley & Silverman, 1976; Head, 1975; James, 1990).

In their study of Grade 8 students within the Toronto Board of Education, Larter, Cheng, Capps, and Lee (1982) found that Black students and those with origins in the Caribbean were the only two groups who rated education as "most important"; however, these two groups also had the largest representation (35 per cent Blacks and 19 per cent Caribbean) in special education classes. The researchers noted that with parental support, these students aspired to reaching advanced levels of formal education, which they viewed as an avenue for self-realization (Larter et al., 1982, p. 53). The value that Black students attach to education made it difficult for them to drop out. As Oliver (1972) writes:

> The anguish that often accompanies the decision to drop out of school for the Black students is most excruciating. They face feelings of inadequacy and guilt on the one hand, and on the other, the realization that because they are Black their opportunities are far more limited. (p. 221)

Even with this realization, high dropout rates among Black students persisted well into the 1990s, despite the importance that students, their parents, and the community placed on education (Dei et al., 1997).

Evidence indicates that Black students' educational participation and performance within the Canadian school system does not stem from lack of parental encouragement or low educational aspirations but rather from factors inherent in the structure of the broader society and the school system in particular. By examining the school system and the people charged with educating students, therefore, we will find evidence of the barriers to their achievement.

Earlier research indicates that some teachers were instrumental in discouraging students' academic interests, directing them instead into vocational classes and athletic activities. For instance, one of the respondents in Head's (1975) study reported that

> when discussing his desire to become an engineer, the teacher commented that he was not suited to the field. "You are a good basketball player, and the school needs basketball players. Why don't you become a professional and forget about the engineering?" (p. 89)

Young people who participated in a study that I conducted in the late 1980s expressed similar sentiments (James, 1990).

The consistent failure by schools to support the academic interests and aspirations of students was reason enough for Black parents and students to become convinced that "cultural adjustment" to the education system was not causing students' low educational achievement. Rather, it was the inherent racism embedded in the education system, manifested both in the curriculum and through school practices (i.e., treatment by teachers, counsellors, and administrators), that alienated Black students (CCEBSTS, 1988; D'Oyley & Silverman, 1976; Head, 1975; James, 1990; Ramcharan, 1982). As indicated earlier, these practices included streaming Black students into vocational, technical, and behavioural classes and encouraging them into athletic careers. Left unaddressed, systemic racism and discrimination, which inevitably contribute to alienating Black students from the schooling process, continue to have a significant impact on their education. In writing about what she calls "a Canadian dilemma," Keren Brathwaite (1989), who was a member of the CCEBSTS, points out:

> In listening to the stories which Black students and parents tell about the school system, it is impossible to deny that racism is an active part of it. Indeed, racism is a theme of Black students' school experience and the

source of their disenchantment with it. It is an integral part of the course content, classroom atmosphere, discipline procedures, and the philosophy of streaming, which sends our students in large numbers to inferior schools and programs. It is the most serious barrier to their progress in that it affects their self-esteem and sets up limitations around them in the form of expectations, which, as self-fulfilling prophecy, they meet. (pp. 212–13)

Despite the seemingly insurmountable barriers that racism and discrimination posed for Black students through the years, they continued to hold onto the belief that they could effectively negotiate the barriers and succeed. Their belief related to their perception that education was instrumental to their success in Canadian society; ironically, they believed that education would enable them to overcome racism and discrimination (Calliste, 1982; Head, 1975; James, 1990). These sentiments were well represented through research during the 1970s and 1980s. For example, in a study by Head (1975), a young man is quoted as saying, "With a university degree, options increase, and the feeling is there are 'good' and even 'very good' opportunities for employment" (p. 97). And in the study I conducted (James, 1990), two young men stated:

> GREG: If you graduate from high school with good marks and get into university and graduate from there, you can pretty well get a good job, if you just keep on working hard ...
> RICHARD: I feel that I should go to university because without going I don't think I'm going to get too far in society. Without that piece of paper that shows you have been educated, you're not going to get too far in the workforce. Like I don't want to end up working at McDonald's or Eaton's all my life. (pp. 64–5)

Ever conscious of racism posing a barrier to their success, these youth, as well as many others, held onto the belief that, once they were armed with their education, the significance of colour would diminish and "nothing would stop them if they are willing to try."

But not all young people agreed that the avenue to success ran through academic activities. Some, albeit a minority and predominantly males, believed that sports offered a more viable option than education for making it in Canadian society (Head, 1975; James, 1990). These youth valued sport because it helped them to cope with an alienating and discriminatory school system through the recognition they received from teachers, coaches, and peers, which in turn helped to "boost their ego," build their "self-confidence," and develop "pride in themselves" (James, 1990).

Referring to the Black student athletes in his late 1980s study who used sports (e.g., basketball) as a way of resisting the school system, Solomon (1992) writes, "For the jocks, sports serves three main functions: it helps in the formation of Black culture and identity; it preserves machismo; and it is pursued as a viable channel for socio-economic advancement" (p. 76). Noting the significance of sports to Black student athletes, one study participant said to me that a number of his peers could not relate to school, and that they found school boring and difficult. So they looked to basketball as a means of obtaining a scholarship to universities – "so you can say it is our ticket out of school because a lot of us do not have the money to pay tuition fees" (James, 1990, p. 45).

Further, in addition to education, the youth in my study figured that they could overcome obstacles through such strategies as working hard, being determined, relying on their own abilities and skills, having the "right" attitude, holding onto high career aspirations, believing that nothing would stop them, and aspiring to become "the best" (p. 113). For some Black youth, particularly those unable to navigate the white, Eurocentric, middle-class school system effectively, racism and discrimination presented insurmountable barriers. As a result, they disengaged from the schooling process, believing that education offered little help towards their ability to achieve in Canadian society (Head, 1975; James, 1990; Solomon, 1992).

To address the consequences of students' disengagement from schooling – their low educational attainment, low self-concept, and feelings of being second-class citizens (Oliver, 1972) – African-Canadian parents and community members consistently focused on the root cause – systemic racism[7] – and not "cultural adjustment." Many felt that the "psychological deprivation" of Black children, as Jules Oliver (1972) argues, did not result from their living in an impoverished community, but rather from their existence "in an environment which perpetuates white values and white dominance" (p. 221). With this conviction, parents and community members advocated for schools to identify race as a factor in the students' experiences and to recognize that these racialized experiences within schools created a barrier to the students' participation, ultimately resulting in their academic underachievement.

---

7 *Systemic racism* is understood to be different from individual racism. It refers to how established school and societal policies, rules, regulations, and related or resultant values, norms, and practices systematically reflect and produce differential treatment and outcomes for students, in this case Black students (James, 2010).

Several community organizations[8] worked both independently and in collaboration with other parent groups connected to various school boards to put their convictions into action. These groups were instrumental in seeking policies and programs to change the educational situation for Black students. Grade 9 streaming constituted one very important issue the groups addressed, and there is little doubt that tireless efforts by parents, students, educators, and community members contributed to government dismantling the practice in Ontario schools (1992–3).

Parents and community members have also maintained that the multicultural education policies adopted by school boards following the establishment of Canada's multiculturalism policy (1971) were inadequate in addressing the educational needs and situation of African-Canadian students. In Ontario, the Ministry of Education initiated policies and programs in the mid-1970s aimed at fostering sensitivity, relevant school materials, respect for cultural difference, and "integration of minority students" (McAndrew, 1991, p. 135).

With help from federal funding, school "multicultural programs" consistently focused on languages. These programs relied on the assumption that competence in their "heritage language" would help students build their self-confidence and sense of belonging (thus reversing feelings of alienation from society and school), and in turn improve their learning and academic performance. Through such programs, therefore, students mainly learned their mother tongues. African Canadians, however, particularly those who were not from the African continent, did not fit the criteria for funding, so it was left to community members to advocate for other types of programs that could benefit all African-Canadian students.

The resulting Black/African heritage programs were used to educate students about the contributions of Africans to Canadian society in particular and to world development in general. It was also a space to teach students about Africa, to counter – according to Oliver (1972) – the negative "Tarzan and poverty images" to which African students had grown accustomed, and to address the "mentally genocidal" effects of racism (p. 220). Continuous work by parents, students, educators, and community members resulted in some schools incorporating African heritage classes into the school day or as a course in a few high schools.

---

8 For example, the Black Experience Project (BEP), the Canadian Alliance of Black Educators (CABE), the Organization of Parents of Black Children (OPBC), the Black Liaison Committee – Toronto Board (BLC), the Harriett Tubman Youth Centre (HTYC), the African Canadian Heritage Programme (ACHP), the African Heritage Education Network – North York Board (AHEN).

Critics of the "multicultural" approach to educating an increasingly diverse student population argued that these educational policies and programs emphasized cultural differences while failing to acknowledge race and racism. They contended that Eurocentric bias remained evident not only in the curriculum, which promoted conformity or assimilation to Anglo-Canadian values and norms, but also in teaching methods and student assessments – resulting in racialized and immigrant peoples being represented as "other" (foreigners with peculiar culture) through stereotyping evinced in "song and dance" and "museum culture." Parents, community members, and educators maintained that multicultural education policies and programs failed to address both subtle and blatant forms of racism, particularly structural and systemic racism, that remain inherent in the educational system, affecting interactions between parents, students, teachers, and administrators (see CCEBSTS, 1988; James, 2001). Antiracism practitioner, Enid Lee (1994), writes:

> One can organize a unity and diversity club, and deal with cultural holidays, and host a Multicultural Week, and yet not deal with racism. These events may present some information about cultural groups and focus on the exotic and leave many people with a nice feeling but do nothing to address the schools' response or lack of response to the languages and faiths of students of colour. They may leave intact the Eurocentric curriculum which students consume daily. (p. 24)

In response to criticism by Black community members and others, some boards of education initiated race-relations policies and programs. In these cases, race was acknowledged in terms of physical differences but not as a political and social construct of society that affected interactions with and treatment of students (in essence, a multicultural framework; see Gregg, 2006). Racism was seen to be a consequence of ignorance. In this regard,

> To address this problem of racism, educators believe that students' experiences in racially mixed groups provided awareness of, and sensitivity to, each other. Understandings gained through such interactions were expected to prevent racism, therefore creating a school and classroom atmosphere in which racial minority students could participate and become successful. For this reason, we would often hear teachers insisting that racial minority students must mix ... and racial minority "successful" role models would be brought into schools to demonstrate that success is possible in this society irrespective of race. (James, 1995, p. 37)

One very common "multicultural/race relations" activity that became quite prominent in the 1980s was the Black/African History Month program. At that time, many parents, students, and community members welcomed the recognition that Black History Month afforded them.[9] And as Althea Prince (1996) would later write, they participated in the celebration "in the name of community and history, for our children, for ourselves, for our society. We want to see our faces, hear our voices, read our words, speak them. We want our children to do those things" (p. 167). But the seemingly favourable reception to celebrating Black History Month in schools had its limits; for as Prince's essay suggests, students, parents, and community members were adopting a wait-and-see approach – waiting to see if systemic changes that would help address Black students' alienation from their schooling and education would follow.

While waiting, several school and community collaborations established educational programs geared towards addressing the needs of Black students. One such program was established in the mid-1970s at the Harriet Tubman Centre, a YWCA facility. Here, Zanana Akande, a teacher with the City of York School Board (CYSB), helped set up and provide resources for a special education class for Black Caribbean students, but the program was short-lived. So too was another program – the Afro-Caribbean Alternative Secondary School (ACASS) – initiated about ten years later by Jackie Wilson, with help from Veronica Sullivan and Afua Cooper. The ACASS opened in fall 1985 in response to parents' request for a program to support kids who were leaving school. According to Dale Shuttleworth, assistant superintendent of programs for the board, "We have a tradition of helping people who have a need, and there was a need here" (Bailey, 1985, p. A6). Justifying the need for the school, Jackie Wilson was quoted in the *Toronto Star* as saying:

Many kids complain about a certain hostility and an assumption that there's something wrong with them instead of the system ... Our recruitment efforts are for dropouts or parents who want their kids out of the system because of unsolved problems in school ... Our plan isn't to water down courses ... They will actually be harder, but there will be more support in a non-intimidating environment. (Bailey, 1985, p. A6)

---

9 Prince (1996) also makes the point that going from "Black History Week" to "Black History Month" was taken by some people as evidence of "progress": twenty-eight whole days – and twenty-nine in each leap year (p. 167).

In his "special report" to the *Toronto Star* newspaper the day the school was opened (15 October 1985), Ian Bailey, writing under the headline "Black Parents Open School to Combat Dropout Rate," indicated that "an expected 90 students 16 years and older" were to be enrolled in the school, where they would be offered "full-credit courses at the advanced and general academic levels" (p. A6). There were courses "on Black culture and the developing world" through which students were able to fulfil "the standard requirements" and receive "regular credits and a standard high-school diploma" (Wallace, 2009, p. 3).[10] The school lasted eighteen months at D.B. Hood School before it was moved to George Harvey Collegiate, where it received fewer resources, "its status demoted to simply a program," and after an additional year "it was unceremoniously shut down" (Wallace, 2009, p. 3).

Reporting on the debate some twenty-four years later (2008–9) about establishing an Africentric Alternative School in the Toronto District School Board (TDSB), Wallace (2009) writes that "the announcement of the school was met with official skepticism and unease"; and while a few board members (specifically, a superintendent and trustee) supported the school, others, including the then coordinator of multicultural services "maintained reservations ... [contending] that isolating any specific group ran counter to integrationist policy." He is quoted as saying that "there are a lot of people [at the board] who are leery of it ... [and] there isn't anyone who isn't saying, 'if this experiment works, great.'"

The educational experience of African Canadians in the 1970s and 1980s parallels that of Black people in Britain, many of whom shared similar backgrounds as second-generation Caribbean Canadian immigrants (Beserve, 1976; Carrington, 1983; Coard, 1971; Fuller, 1983; Lovell, 1991; Mirza, 1992). Studies of that population also draw our attention to gendered differences related to academic and athletic engagement and achievement. For example, with reference to the situation of African-Caribbean young women in Britain, Fuller (1983) writes:

> Schooling and education provided them with an alternative and less undermining possibility in their search for greater freedom and control. Concentration on education as a way out was something which all Black girls whom I interviewed stressed, though ... as they pointed out, this strategy had its drawbacks, in particular the vocational aspects of schooling and

---

10 Wallace (2009) also reported that students "as old as 35" attended the ACASS, and that "the school offered daycare for students with young children" (p. 3).

further education was attractive and their achievement in these areas were thought to lead to better prospects of a "good" job. Being aware of both sexual and racial discrimination, the girls did not assume that good educational performance was the sufficient requirement for obtaining such jobs, but they did believe it was a necessary one. (p. 172)

From her study, which reported similar findings, Mirza (1992) concluded that social class had an influence on the occupational choice of second-generation Caribbean immigrant young women. Further, while the racially and sexually segregated labour market provided limited opportunities, "schools were seen to play an important role in both structuring and restricting Black female occupational aspirations and expectations" (p. 192).

The 1990s: The Struggle Continues

In the 1990s, a number of school boards developed what were referred to as antiracism policies and programs. Through professional development sessions put on by boards of education and courses offered by faculties of education that attempted to address racial, ethnic, class, gender, language, and sexual identities of the student population, it was anticipated that educators would become conversant with and skilled in antiracism activities and pedagogy. In Ontario, in particular, the New Democratic Party government's Ministry of Education initiated the "common curriculum" (requiring a destreamed Grade 9),[11] and the Anti-Racism and Ethnocultural Equity policy, requiring all school boards across Ontario to undertake an antiracism approach to education. A ministry document (Ontario Ministry of Education and Training, 1993) specified the guidelines for developing and implementing "anti-racism and ethnocultural equity policies":

> The intent of anti-racism and ethnocultural equity education is to ensure that all students achieve their potential and acquire knowledge and information, as well as confidence in their cultural and racial identities. It

---

11 The Common Curriculum was designed to cater to the educational needs of students in Grades 1–9. It was expected that all students would attain a common set of prespecified learning outcomes by Grades 3 and 6. These were linked to a set provincially defined standards. It was thought that the curriculum would be able to cater to the students' differences (developmental and otherwise) and needs. The NDP government was defeated before the full implementation of this curriculum (see S.E. Anderson & Ben Jaafar, 2003, p. 8).

should equip all students with the knowledge, skills, attitudes and behaviours needed to live and work effectively in an increasingly diverse world, and encourage them to appreciate diversity and reject discriminatory attitudes and behaviours. (p. 5)

To oversee the implementation of this policy, the government created the position of assistant deputy minister and hired an African-Canadian educator, Ouida Wright, to fill it. During this period, lobbying efforts by African-Canadian educators and community members, under leadership provided by the Black Educators Working Group (BEWG), unquestionably contributed to the government establishing such anti-racism initiatives.

By the 1990s, one would think that the unrelenting and consistent efforts of African Canadians to bring the educational conditions facing their community – conditions well established by research – to the attention of government and official bodies would have brought about, or at least started to bring about, the necessary institutional changes. But this was not the case – not even after inquiries such as Stephen Lewis's (1992) *Report on Race Relations in Ontario*, the independent report of the Four-Level Government/African-Canadian Community Working Group (1992), and the Royal Commission on Learning in Ontario (1994).

In fact, after "more than 70 meetings" with Black youth, parents, community members, representatives of social service and educational institutions, and Torontonians in general, Stephen Lewis (1992) put into writing the concerns, issues, and problems that were repeatedly communicated to him about the alienation and related disillusionment of Black students and their parents. In his "Dear Bob" report to then-premier Bob Rae, he wrote:

> Everywhere, the refrain of Toronto students, however starkly amended by different schools and different locations, was essentially the refrain of all students. Where are the courses in Black history? Where are the visible minority teachers? Why are there so few role models? Why do our white guidance counsellors know so little of different cultural backgrounds? Why are racist incidents and epithets tolerated? Why are there double standards of discipline? Why are minority students streamed? Why do they discourage us from University? Where are we going to find jobs? What's the use of having an education if there's no employment? How long does it take to change the curriculum so that we're a part of it?
>
> The students were fiercely articulate and often deeply moving. Sometimes angry. They don't understand why the schools are so slow to reflect the broader society. One bright young man in a Metro east high school

said that he had reached Grade 13, without once having a book by a Black author on the curriculum. And when other students, in the large meeting of which he was a part, started to name the books they had been given to read, the titles were "Black Like Me" and "To Kill a Mockingbird" (both, incredibly enough, by white writers!). It's absurd in a world which has a positive cornucopia of magnificent literature by Black authors. I further recall an animated young woman from a high school in Peel, who described her school as overwhelmingly multiracial, and then added that she and her fellow students had white teachers, white counsellors, a white principal, and were taught Black history by a white teacher who didn't like them. There wasn't a single non-white member of the staff. (pp. 20–1)

In response to Stephen Lewis's report, a *Globe and Mail* editorial, "A Blinkered Report on Race" (1992), likely reflecting the sentiments of many if not most Torontonians and Canadians, questioned Lewis's premise "that racism is deep and systemic" and was operating in all institutions and areas of our society. After conceding that the problems experienced by Black youth "are unquestionably real," the editorial went on to say:

> But racism – though it is real too, and must be confronted – is only part of the cause. Canada is not a deeply racist society. Nor are our institutions riddled with racism. That many black youths do poorly in school cannot be blamed, as Mr. Lewis suggests, on the shortage of black history courses, or white guidance counsellors' ignorance of black culture. If racism in the schools is the problem, how is it possible to explain the scholastic success of other visible minorities such as Chinese- and South Asian–Canadians? Similarly, the disproportionate number of blacks in some Toronto jails cannot be attributed principally to discriminatory treatment by police or the courts. And the high unemployment rate among young blacks is not mainly the result of bigotry, or even systemic discrimination, on the part of employers. (p. A16)

The editorial continued to speculate (in the form of questions) that "family breakdown, poor quality of life, and lack of good role models" might be responsible for the "problems" of Black youth. But it also suggested that the answers would "never" be known "as long as people like Mr. Lewis put guilt [and] self-flagellation over intellectual rigour, and musty preconceptions over the search for facts" ("Blinkered Report on Race," 1992, p. A16).

To the extent that the Lewis report, and the reports and research of many scholars and commissioners before him, failed to persuade members of the mainstream society (as represented by the *Globe and Mail* editorial) of the significant impacts caused by systemic racism, corrective measures to address and remove racism seemed not to be forthcoming – even in response to the "Yonge Street incident" (or "riots," as characterized) of May 1992, which had prompted the Stephen Lewis investigation and later the Four-Level Government/African Canadian Community Working Group. In such a context, the Working Group's findings, which reiterated the concerns raised in the Lewis report, did little to advance the perspective that the experiences or problems of Black youth were rooted in the economic, political, and educational system[12] as opposed to individual inadequacy. The Four-Level Working Group (1992) reported:

> A review of the number of reports and presentations before the Working Group makes it clear that, for at least one generation, the African-Canadian community has been crying out in anguish over the poor performance of its youth in the Ontario School system. The dropout rate, the truancy rate, the failure rate, the basic-streaming rate: all these pointed inexorably to the fact that, where Black kids are concerned, something is terribly wrong. (p. 77)

It was also recommended that the TDSB undertake a five-year "Focused Schools" project that would include, among other things, a high proportion of Black educators, an antiracism curriculum, community-based culturally specific services, school clubs that support a positive self-image for Black students, and youth leadership programs.

A short two years later, the Ontario government established the Royal Commission on Learning to study students' educational needs and present "a vision and action plan." The plan would guide educational reform to ensure that students "are well-prepared for the challenges of the 21st century." The commissioners reported:

> Black students, parents, and community leaders came to the Commission and expressed serious concerns about the achievement levels of their young people. They expressed frustration over lack of improvement over the years, during which time they have voiced their concerns to school boards and to the Ministry. They are concerned about the future of young Blacks who, without a secondary school diploma (let alone a college diploma or university degree), face limited job prospects, social marginalization, and

---

12 One presenter at a Working Group session is quoted as saying: "The school system seems to have a built-in deafness; it doesn't hear what it doesn't want to hear" (Four-Level Government/African Canadian Community Working Group, 1992, p. 75).

personal defeat. These presenters argued forcefully that the educational system is failing Black students, and that there is an educational crisis in their community. (Royal Commission on Learning, 1994, p. 92)

In response to this "crisis," the report went on to recommend that in areas with large numbers of Black students, "innovative strategies" be used and "special programs" be established that would address the "urgent" need to substantially improve the academic performance of Black students. In making this recommendation, the Commission signalled that "based on success stories elsewhere," it was worth trying (or the will should be there) to develop African-centred education – something that parents and community members had called for (Royal Commission on Learning, 1994, p. 44).

The New Democratic government at that time established a Discussion Group on "Focused Schools" (facilitated by Ouida Wright) within the Ministry of Education but did little more than that. Then, in 1998, the newly amalgamated TDSB established N'ghana, a Black-focused school for high school students. The school initially operated in a community centre and was staffed by qualified teachers; however, it was soon moved to "a less than hospitable host school" and in the process lost the support needed for it to continue – today, there is hardly any reference to its existence.

Interestingly, just as Black people in Ontario were taking stock of the situation facing their youth, in Nova Scotia the Black Learners Advisory Committee (BLAC) released a report in December 1994 that similarly established that African Nova Scotian students were experiencing, in the words of the chair, Mr. Castor Williams, "a discordant education system that is devoid of any effective policies essential and sympathetic to their needs." In introducing the report, he wrote:

> Clear deficiencies that exist include the shortage of policies affecting race relations at the board and school levels; the need for school curriculum and policies to accommodate cultural diversity; the need to realign the relationship between the home and the school; the lack of any development of creative and resourceful programs for teachers' professional training, maturation and growth in a multicultural and multiracial society; scarcity of Black role models in the systems, methods to respond to racial harassment and the assessment of students for placement; the lack of effective process to evaluate textbooks for bias and the absence of materials to engender more positive attitudes in the African Nova Scotian student. Programs to ensure early childhood education and access to postsecondary education are also in short supply. (BLAC, 1994, p. 13)

Williams's introductory comments get to the core of the debate over the causes of African-Canadian students' poor performance: curriculum concerns, teacher training, staff role models, policies regarding race relations, antiracism, bias in textbooks, parent involvement in education, early childhood education, and access to postsecondary education.

The school curriculum has consistently been identified as a barrier to Black students' success. Certainly, curriculum can either open up or limit learning opportunities and possibilities for students, as well as assist teachers in addressing their students' needs. But as Annette Henry (1994) contends, for Black students in the 1990s, as in earlier decades, the lessons taught in schools did not enable them to make sense of their "blackness in positive, affirming ways." Citing her own experience as an example, she writes: "My teachers never taught in ways that helped me critically understand a larger Black community ... As a young Black girl growing up in England and Canada, my school lessons were often acts of violence" (p. 298).

So even after years of "celebrating" Black/African History Month, the curriculum still failed to provide students with knowledge about themselves and their communities. Indeed, as Prince (1996) contends, very little is achieved through the observance of this "great Canadian multicultural myth" in which "many self-respecting African-Canadian educators, artists, parents – children, many of *us* – have participated" (p. 167). And while community members and parents see the month as providing the space and "opportunities to share who we are, explore where we came from, discuss where we are going," it is not "sufficient," declares Prince:

> Clearly, the history of African-Canadian people needs to be dealt with within the schools. A month is not the way. An inclusive curriculum is not only desirable, but clamours to be developed. It feels sometimes as if we are in a bind. For if we continue to enable the ghettoized version of our history as a people, allowing it to be relegated to one month, then we are complicit in the perpetuation of a hegemony that denies our existence. Yet if we do not take this Black History Month crumb that is offered, we may find that our children, and all children, for that matter, have no access to even the ghettoized version of the history of African peoples ...
>
> Black-History-Month-kits simply cannot redress these historical distortions in one fell swoop. Twenty-eight days is not sufficient time to rewrite history. Hence, psychological band-aids of stories of kings and queens and stories of the slaves' journey on the Underground Railroad to freedom in Canada will fail every time to empower our children. Pretending that Black History Month is able to redress historical atrocities and provide

succor for the souls of African-Canadians is an act that the school can no longer be allowed to practice. (pp. 169, 177)

The Early Years of the Twenty-First Century: Hopeful Signs?

Towards the end of the first decade of the twenty-first century, students, parents, and community members expressed the same refrain: schools were continuing to fail to meet the educational and schooling needs of Black students. The consequences of this failure were not only evident in the high dropout and "stopout" rates of Black students and their low academic achievement during their grade-school years,[13] but also in their lack of viable employment skills and limited life opportunities outside of school.

Dropping out of school was not the only cause of an interrupted education and limited life opportunities for Black students. It was not only Black students' taking a stand and *dropping out* of school that determined their life conditions, but their being suspended or expelled as a consequence of the Safe Schools Act (Bill 81, 2000). The act promoted a discourse of "zero tolerance" and altered students' life conditions, for under this regime Black students were suspended and expelled from school in substantial numbers. Although school boards maintained that they did not keep statistics by race – hence, they were unable to confirm the claim by Black parents and community members that Black students, especially males,[14] were being suspended and expelled from schools at higher rates than other students – the media told another story. One *Globe and Mail* article by Joe Friesen (2006), for example, reported that one public middle school with a large number of Black students handed out eighty-one suspensions over a six-month period, while another handed out ninety-five.[15]

---

13 On 23 June 2006, the *Toronto Star* carried an article (L. Brown, 2006) which indicates that it is largely teenage boys living in Toronto's "horseshoe of poverty" that were dropping out of school. Of students born in the English-speaking Caribbean who started Grade 9 in 2000, 40 per cent had dropped out by 2005, compared to 37 per cent of those born in Central and South America, 35 per cent of those born in southern and western Europe, and 32 per cent of those born in eastern Africa. In contrast, only 14 per cent and 23 per cent, respectively, of those born in East Asia and Canada had dropped out of school.
14 While Black female students have experiences similar to those of their male counterparts, there are differences.
15 In the same schools, some 39 per cent of the students (most of them Black) going on to high school had failed Grade 8. It should be noted that according to the board policy students do not repeat grades (Friesen, 2006).

Mike Malcolm, an educator in the Toronto area, contended that "some students become pawns in the designation of a 'high-needs' school" – the means by which money and concomitantly more resources, including teachers, teacher assistants, and in some cases an additional vice principal, are assigned to the school. He continues:

> Teachers are required to document the students who are recommended for specialized support. Therefore, students who may receive detentions or conferences with teachers for misbehaviour will now receive frequent formal suspensions. Students who may require remedial support in schools would now receive failing grades on their report cards ... These actions take place in schools to provide a paper trail behind all students who are deemed to have high needs academically or socially. This paper trail justifies the need for more money for special programs ... in areas such as school safety, literacy, English as a Second Language, and/or behavioural needs ... And the more defined the high needs image or profile of the school, the more readily additional funding will be given ... The result for many schools is lower expectations of students in certain schools, more suspensions and more stringent enforcement of consequences. (Malcolm, personal communication, August 2005; see also Malcolm, 2006)

Thus, the educational funding structure contributes to the identity construction, schooling situation, educational outcome, and subsequent marginalization of students. And, as this teacher observes, in many cases Black students are the ones labelled "at risk" because of so-called behavioural problems and academic and social needs. In such a context, therefore, the perception of Black students, especially males, as underachievers, troublemakers, and less academically inclined is sustained (James, 2009).

Indeed, much of the discussion regarding the Black student experience tends to be about Black males. Of course, we mostly hear of males being "troublemakers," being suspended and expelled, and dropping out of school. In part, the experience of Black males reflects the "masculinization" that takes place within the heterosexist male hegemonic structure of the schooling system.

Within such a system, Black females not only have to negotiate a classed and raced schooling structure like their male counterparts, they also have to deal with their social construction as females (Gaymes, 2006; Wood, 2011). Alison Gaymes (2006), a middle school teacher in the TDSB, pointed out that Black females have "unique battles" to fight as a result of their marginalization and "absent presence" within the male-centric schooling environment. And while their responses to these battles might be seen as "inappropriate behaviour," as they told Gaymes, "you've got to be rude to be Black" (p. 73). Undoubtedly, the complicated, interlocking relationships of race and gender – Blackness and femaleness – inform these students' responses, resulting in their determination to re-construct and control their images (including images of beauty) as creative and talented students and athletes.

In an effort to address the situation, parents, community members, and scholars in the 1990s, and again in the early 2000s, advocated collecting data by race or at least disaggregating ethnicity and immigrant data that school boards had been collecting. For the most part, school boards rejected the idea of collecting race data on the basis that race has nothing to do with schools' treatment of students, students' participation in schools, or their educational outcomes. Many scholars and community members countered that to understand the Black student experience, students' racial identity must be ascertained since the birthplace (or immigrant) variable does not fully tell the racial background, as most Black students today are born in Canada.

The TDSB is the only board that seems to be taking the value of data by race seriously. Following the recommendation of a board committee, it has started to collect the data, and in the process, disaggregate ethnicity and immigrant data. But we have yet to see the full use of data to inform student programs. It is worth noting, however, that data by race is not new; the former Toronto Board of Education had been collecting and using such data to report on students' participation and achievement in school through the "Every Student Survey."

Through the 1970s, 1980s, and 1990s, a number of community forums were held in downtown Toronto on the topic "Making the Grade: Are We Failing Black Youth?" A similar gathering took place in February 2005, as a large crowd of mostly Black people heard a panel of Black scholars and community members affirm that indeed Toronto schools were failing Black students. They applauded Professor George Dei when he suggested that "alternative schools for Black students were the only way to prevent them from being pushed out of the system" (Kalinowski & Brown, 2005, p. A15).

The government's response was to say that racially segregated schools aren't in the cards. And when the TDSB's newly appointed (and first) Executive Officer for Equity was quoted in the newspaper as saying that it would be worth exploring the idea of a Black-focused school for students who were not doing well in the public system, the school board distanced itself from the statement, saying there were no plans to establish such a school. Ironically, an advisory committee on Black-focus schools comprising community members and educators had been meeting since fall 2004 within the TDSB under the initiative and leadership of Trustee Stephanie Payne. The committee's work seemed to have dissipated when, in late fall 2007, the Board of Trustees was asked to vote on a motion to establish a Black-focused school within its Alternative School Program. The motion was carried and was revisited in January 2008, after a number of community meetings through the fall of 2007.

The school board's policy allowed, upon the request of parents, for the establishment of alternative schools designed for students who are not performing well or whose academic and/or nonacademic needs are not being met in their current schooling situation.[16] Having obtained needed – but certainly not unanimous (which would of course be unrealistic) – community support, the Board of Trustees voted in January 2008 to initiate a program under the theme "Improving the Success of Black Students," and reaffirmed this motion in June 2008. The motion called for establishing an "Africentric Alternative School" for Kindergarten to Grade 5 students by September 2009. The program of study was expected to integrate "the histories, cultures, experiences, and contributions of people of African descent and other racialized groups into the curriculum, teaching methodologies, and social environment of the schools" (Toronto District School Board, 2008, p. 12).

Reaction to the recommendation – including by Ontario Premier Dalton McGuinty, Education Minister Kathleen Wynne, school administrators, educators, and African Canadians – was expressed as disappointment with the trustees. Premier McGuinty told newspaper reporters, "I don't think it's a good idea. I think our shared responsibility is to look for ways to bring people together. One of those most powerful agents of social cohesion is publicly funded education" (Wallace, 2009, p. 5). He encouraged Torontonians, if "they really feel strongly about this," to "speak to their duly elected representatives and tell them how strongly they are opposed to this proposal." Opposition Leader John Tory also condemned the recommendation, while Education Minister Wynne said, "We don't want to see kids separated from each other. We don't think the board should be moving in this direction or the school" (Benzie, 2008, p. A1).

The politicians' sentiments in turn reflected those of Canadians as a whole. Negative reactions to the initiative from Torontonians and

---

16 Such requests for a particular education program (e.g., social justice) that would meet the needs and interests of students are reviewed by the board's Alternative School Committee, and a decision is made after a number of community meetings in which support is solicited and attained.

Canadians generally (Bradshaw & Alphonso, 2008) were reflected in media reports and commentaries. The *Toronto Star* branded the program as "segregationist." "The idea smacks of segregation," said the *Globe and Mail*, "which is contrary to the values of the school system and Canadian society as a whole." The *Globe and Mail* referred to the establishment of Africentric schools as being "as insulting as they are ridiculous." The *National Post* commented that the "concept of special schools for black students is one of those terrible ideas that refuses to die" (cited in Wallace, 2009, p. 5).

But establishing a school with a program specially geared to meet the educational needs and interests of a particular group of students is not without precedent. There are public or government-funded religious schools (Catholic schools) and same-sex schools (girls). Indeed, the TDSB had nearly forty alternative schools, including a lesbian, gay, bisexual, transgender, and queer (LGBTQ) school,[17] as well as six "Specialized Schools" – four Arts Focus (for visual and performing arts), one Entrepreneurship, and one Integrated Technology school. There are also schools with specialized programs such as Gifted; High Performing Athletes; Cyber Arts; Media Arts; Mathematics, Science, and Technology; International Languages; and International Baccalaureate. The existence of such schools and programs indicates recognition that things such as religion, gender, sexuality, and students' interests in arts, drama, technology, or athletics play a role in their lived experiences and schooling needs, interests, and aspirations. On the basis of similar principles related to the cultural values and needs of students who choose to attend existing focused schools and alternative schools, African Canadians were appealing for an Africentric schooling program (James, 2011).

So why the particular concern about an Africentric school as "segregationist" – especially as a solution for students who were not realizing their potential in mainstream schooling? As argued elsewhere (James, 2011), the idea of "segregated" schooling goes against Ontario's 1977 commitment to multicultural education – a program that is believed to foster integration of immigrant and racialized students (in this case,

---

17 A colleague who worked with the Triangle school, as it is called, pointed out that this school "is a satellite of a larger alternative school," and went on to say: "Don't kid yourself, there was incredible controversy when Triangle began. It was a backroom deal because they knew it would never pass if made public. We had to protect the students from the media frenzy that took place for several years. There was a particularly offensive article that came out in the first year – 'Reading, 'Riting, and Rimming'" (Personal communication, May 2011).

African Canadians), accommodate all their differences, educate them in ways that affirm their culture, and maintain the notion that the school system is culturally neutral, thereby providing equal opportunity for all students. Supporting an Africentric school would call into question the Ontario government's commitment, and that of educators, to multicultural education; it would also challenge the concomitant belief that student failure is a product of cultural values and individual effort rather than the education system.

Refusal to accept that an Africentric schooling program would serve African Canadians – and others who choose to attend – the same way that religious (e.g., Catholic) and alternative schools and specialized school programs serve students stems in part from a reluctance to concede that race matters in Canada. Such an admission would mean acknowledging that racism operates as a barrier – both in the school system and in society generally (systemic racism) – to students' educational participation and achievement. This would challenge the efficacy of multiculturalism and its capacity to reduce dissension among Canada's minoritized citizens (James, 2011). As the *Globe and Mail* claimed in 1992, "Canada is not a deeply racist society" ("Blinkered Report on Race," 1992, p. A16); and in 2007, its editorial condemning the idea of an Africentric School called on Canadians to reject the "school by skin colour," insisting that it would be better to focus on the "real causes" of poor achievement by Black students (see also Gulson & Webb, 2013). But as Levine-Rasky (2014) argues, the debates pertaining to the benefit of the school to students and Black communities can be read as "white fear" – a dynamic that serves to reinforce the need for such a school (p. 214).

It bears noting that African Nova Scotians also called for a Black-focused school in 2006, but as in Ontario, the Halifax School Board and the media rejected the idea as "racial segregation." And just as African/Black Canadians, many of them of Caribbean origin, have long been demanding that the school system respond to their children's educational needs, so too have their compatriots in Britain (see John, 2006/2010). In fact, reports coming from Britain have noted that "no single cause" accounts for the "underachievement" of Black students in British schools,

> but rather a network of widely differing attitudes [racism was identified as a "major reason"] and expectations on the part of teachers and the education system as a whole and on the part of West Indian parents, which lead the West Indian child to have particular difficulties and face particular hurdles in achieving his or her full potential. (Aston, 2003, p. 4)

The situation of Black males was repeatedly noted, with one commentator stating, "Although poorly qualified school-leavers face problems, these Afro-Caribbean young people face extra problems of prejudice in schools and discrimination in the labour market" (Aston, 2003, p. 6). In this regard, there have been calls in Britain for "separate" school programs for Black boys, asserting, as the head of Britain's Commission for Racial Equality, Trevor Phillips, did in 2005, that it might be "the only way to break through the wall of attitude that surrounds black boys" ("Call for Separate Classes for Black Boys," 2005). As in Canada, politicians and citizens alike responded by saying such a program would be "counter-productive and even illegal" ("Black Boys Separate Classes Idea," 2005).

Also during the first decade of this century an unusually large number of violent incidents involving young people in Toronto prompted Ontario's Liberal government to commission Roy McMurtry and Alvin Curling to explore the social conditions that formed the root causes of the violence. Their report, *The Roots of Youth Violence*, released in 2008, identified education as the "root of the immediate risk factors," specifically: safe schools policies, curricula, approaches taken to guidance and counselling, composition and training of the teaching force, and the way the education system contributes to the criminalization of youth. The commissioners raised concerns about the long-term consequences of the Mike Harris government's (1995–2001) zero tolerance policy, writing: "And we are also very concerned that Ontario will have to deal with the long-term consequences of the previous policies, in force from September 2001 to early 2008" (McMurtry & Curling, 2008, p. 53).

The Roots of Youth Violence also notes that suspensions and expulsions contributed to what is now referred to as the "school-to-prison pipeline." The report referenced community workers' claims that suspended and expelled students were more likely to drop out of school entirely, often got involved with criminal activity, and, because they were not in school during the day, came under increased scrutiny by police. Quoting a report from the United Kingdom Department for Education and Skills, the report goes on to say:

> Exclusion from school is widely recognized as a driver for wider social exclusion. It is highly correlated with unemployment and involvement in crime. In the words of Martin Narey, Director General of HM Prison Service (2001): "The 13,000 young people excluded from school each year might as well be given a date by which to join the prison service some time later down the line" (United Kingdom Department for Education and Skills, 2006, p. 16). (McMurtry & Curling, 2008, p. 56)

With reference to findings from various other reports, including the TDSB's 2008 School Community Safety Advisory Panel,[18] *The Roots of Youth Violence* report also drew attention to the need for curriculum reform to reflect the diversity of the student population, the negative history of Canada's interaction with Indigenous people and slavery, and acknowledgement of the historical contributions of racialized people. It went on to mention the negative messages that a Eurocentric school curriculum sends to racialized students, including the lack of Black teachers and the low expectations and streaming practices applied by teachers and guidance counsellors. It was said that these continue to alienate Black students and discourage them from pursuing postsecondary education.

In 2009, the Ontario government introduced the *Equity and Inclusive Education Strategy* to identify and remove discriminatory biases and systemic barriers, thus supporting students' achievement and well-being. While the strategy required school boards to review or develop equity and inclusive education policies, it did not go further and mandate school boards to take an antiracism approach to curriculum and teaching, collect disaggregated race-based student data, or implement employment equity programs to ensure a diverse teacher population. These requirements were only instituted in 2017, following the establishment of the Anti-Racism Directorate in February 2016, and antiracism legislation in 2017 by Premier Kathleen Wynne's Liberal government.

The directorate was tasked with promoting policies, programs, and practices that would help to "eliminate systemic racism" in government institutions and "increase awareness and understanding of systemic racism," that would in turn "lead to racial equity" (Government of Ontario, 2017). Its three-year action plan document, *A Better Way Forward*, released 7 March 2017, identified collection of race-based data as a strategy in the government's bid to fight systemic racism.

In a September 2017 announcement that schools across the province would be collecting race-based data, the government noted that this would serve as its "roadmap to identifying and eliminating discriminatory practices, systemic barriers, and bias from schools and classrooms to support the potential for all students to succeed" (Bascaramurty, 2017). A report we (James & Turner, 2017) completed calling for ministry-mandated collection of race-based data, Black community members in Peel, York, and Durham regions expressed concern

---

18 This report called for the school curriculum to be reformed to reflect the diversity of the student population.

that their school boards were not collecting disaggregated race-based student data. They felt that because the TDSB is the only board to collect this data the focus remains on the TDSB, allowing the same issues to go unacknowledged and unaddressed at the other school boards. (p. 38)

Following the Liberal government's announcement, between November 2018 and May 2019, the Peel District School Board, York Region District School Board, and Durham District School Board engaged in their initial data collection efforts. Following the election of a Conservative government in May 2018, however, Ontarians wait to see how this government would proceed in addressing education inequity and racism.

School boards in the Greater Toronto Area have also undertaken other initiatives to address equity issues. The TDSB instituted a revised Integrated Equity Framework and Action Plan 2016–19, with a goal of ensuring that procedures are in place at all levels of the system for developing, implementing, and reviewing policies that promote equity and inclusion (see Malloy, 2016). It also established a Black Student Achievement Advisory Committee (BSAAC) – approved by the Board of Trustees in June 2016 – with a mandate to "examine and make recommendations to the Board ... on strategies to address persistent achievement, opportunity and participation gaps experienced by Black students, and ensure learning environments are safe, nurturing and welcoming" (Toronto District School Board, 2016, p. 1). And in spring 2020, TDSB established the Centre of Excellence for the Education of Black Students.

In response to a report on schooling and the educational challenges facing Black students (Gray, Bailey, Brady, & Tecle, 2016), the Peel District School Board (2016) developed an action plan, *We Rise Together*, with the "overarching purpose" of identifying, understanding, minimizing, and eliminating the marginalization experienced by Black males. The plan, which was initially designed for male students, included females in the third year of programming and focused on integrating the experiences of Black Canadians into the curriculum; providing bias and antiracism professional development to teachers; engaging with Black parents and community; and inspiring Black student leadership and engagement. A study of the Black student experience since the introduction of the *We Rise Together* program concluded that for these students, navigating school was "just life" and something they have to "just deal with." As such they seemed to hold on "to optimism and hope that if they continued to consistently complain about the 'double standards' of the school and do their mobilizing/organizing, eventually the changes they seek or desire would result" (James, 2019, p. 35).

After the release of the *We Rise Together* research report, a review of the Peel District School Board was established in November 2019 "to review the performance of the PDSB in dealing with allegations of systemic discrimination, specifically anti-Black racism; human resources practices; Board leadership; and governance issues" (Chadha, Herbert, & Richard, 2020, p. 2). The reviewers, Ena Chadha, Suzanne Herbert, and Shawn Richard (2020), reported:

> Many students told us about feeling undervalued and being mis-tracked by teachers because of teachers' perceptions about their ability based on their race. What we consistently heard during the course of this Review tells us that too many educators and administrators do not have high expectations for Black students. Many Black students receive inadequate advice on their academic choices and pathways, and by no means are encouraged to realize their full potential. (p. 12)

But despite the findings, community members – including parents and teachers – were dissatisfied with the recommendations of the reviewers, saying that they should have gone further and called for the removal of the existing leadership at Peel. As at the TDSB (see Wilson, 2015), the Peel board's leaders created and maintained an endemic "culture of fear." Hence, the expectation was that, given the damning report, the reviewers would have concluded, as the TDSB review did in 2015, that "too many were pessimistic about the Board's ability to change course, and they felt that someone would have to come in and 'fix it.' They wanted a supervisor, or a group, with the power to change things ... and do whatever the Board has been unable, or unwilling, to do on its own" (Wilson, 2015, p. 31). In summer 2020, a new Director, Colleen Russell-Rawlings,[19] a Black women, was appointed to help bring about the necessary anti-racism changes in the board.

In 2017, the York Region District School Board established a human rights office and developed an Equity Strategic Plan. These initiatives came in response to directives issued by the then-minister of education, Mitzie Hunter, after a ministry review of the board. Headed by Patrick Case and Suzanne Herbert, the review was initiated after two high-profile allegations of anti-Black racism and Islamophobia within the YRDSB – "one in which a school trustee used a racial slur when

---

19 Russell-Rawlings was one of three Black women directors of Ontario's largest school boards – Peel, Toronto, and Ottawa – something which was much talked about in the media and among community members.

referring to a black parent, and another in which a principal posted offensive material on Islam and refugees to her Facebook page" (McGillivray, 2017). In their submission letter to Minister Hunter, Case and Herbert (2017) noted:

> We heard extensively and from multiple perspectives on each of the issues within the scope of our review. Regretfully, we heard far too much that was distressing, and a paucity of anything encouraging. Our overriding observation is that the issues stem from dysfunction and deficit of leadership capacity on both the elected and administrative sides of the organization. We wish to underscore our concerns that the capacity is lacking not only with respect to proper governance but equally, if not more importantly, with their understanding of, and responsibility for equity. (p. 1)

In Durham Region, local news reports in 2015 revealed parents' concerns with Black students being "racially profiled" in local schools (James & Turner, 2017, p. 17). By 2017, the Durham District School Board (DDSB) released its Equity and Diversity Strategic Framework (Follert, 2017) and, the following year, its three-year Equity and Diversity Strategic Plan, which aimed to "cement [its] commitment to the elimination of discrimination and discriminatory barriers that may exist" (DDSB, 2018b, p. 4). The plan included such initiatives as creating more inclusive curriculum resources; launching student advisory councils; diversifying staff complement through an equitable recruitment framework; and incorporating Indigenous ways of knowing in the classroom. Acknowledging the need "to be specific and intentional" in supporting the success of its Black students, the board went a step further, creating a companion resource to its strategic plan – the *Compendium of Action for Black Student Success* (DDSB, 2018a). Using the recommendations from the Community Voice Forums led by Justice Donald McLeod in 2016, as well as the data collected in and recommendations from the *Towards Race Equity in Education* report (James & Turner, 2017), the *Compendium of Action* "lays out a specific plan to remove barriers, reduce frustration for families, and ultimately improve the success of Black/African Caribbean students" in the DDSB (DDSB, 2018a, p. 7).

Black-Focus Schools in "Multicultural" Toronto: What Has Changed or Will Change?

The TDSB's narrowly approved motion to establish an Africentric Alternative School in Toronto became a national concern. As in earlier years, it generated contentious debates and widespread opposition because of, as Levine-Rasky (2014) proffers, "white fear" and a perception that such "segregated" schooling is contrary to the "multicultural mosaic" and integration narrative of which Canada boasts. Opposition to such a school also conforms to the deeply held multicultural belief that society and, by extension, schools are "culturally neutral" and "colour-blind"; hence, colour is seen to have no effect on individuals' educational, social, and economic circumstances and opportunities. Logic would dictate, however, that in a culturally diverse, racially stratified society, the opposite is true – race, intersecting with other characteristics, operates in a variety of ways to privilege and/or limit individuals' integration into the society, as well as their access to opportunities and equality of outcomes (see Sleeter & Grant, 2005).

If either multicultural education or antiracism education[20] is to deliver on promises of recognizing cultural diversity, equalizing access to schooling opportunities, confronting racism, and providing educational remediation, structures must be set up to address and/or remove existing barriers to equitable education for racialized students. Such structures must provide opportunities for student-centred programs using curriculum and pedagogy that critically engage students in teaching/learning processes that interrogate the hegemony of the middle-class Eurocentric schooling system, which tends to alienate racialized students (see Howard & James, 2019).

It might take a focused-schooling structure to effectively respond to the needs, interests, and aspirations of some students. Concomitantly, the existence of a focused school can further the development and implementation of inclusive curriculum that would benefit all students and teachers. In this way, focused schools can be regarded as a means by which multicultural education, premised on principles of equity and inclusivity, is operationalized. The idea is that with time, once the needs of *all* students are genuinely met in "mainstream" culturally diverse classrooms, the focus of such a school would shift.

Obviously, we would wish that Black students could learn and succeed academically in the current schooling system. But that has not been happening; hence there has been – and remains – a need to seek alternative strategies to make this possible. If the solution requires having

---

20 Antiracism education was introduced as a policy in Ontario in 1993 but, as I have argued elsewhere, the pervasiveness of the colour-blind multicultural discourse stifled efforts to implement an educational program that addresses race and racism. So, what was considered antiracism education was in fact a form of multicultural education in which racialized students were identified and treated as having culture "from away" (James, 2001).

them in an environment with students who share similar experiences, needs, interests, values, and aspirations, as many community members and researchers have argued, then creating an Africentric Alternative School seems worthy of a try. In such a context, educators might be able to talk directly to students about issues they consider "for insiders only," and students can learn from one another and build the necessary confidence to become the academic scholars that we would want them to be. In addition to gaining from a learning environment with students "like them," they would have additional educational opportunities for cross-cultural exchanges, engaging and learning with more of their non-Black peers about African people's contributions to Canada, North America, and the world, and being able to challenge and problematize the stereotypes and myths about African peoples held by others.

There is no doubt that all students need to experience diversity and learn through an inclusive curriculum that provides information about themselves and others. But in reality, all schools are not diverse as a result of factors related to structures, choices, and preferences. As indicated earlier, gifted students are placed in classes with other gifted students and athletes attend schools with other athletes; so too, middle-class and working-class students attend schools in their respective communities, and in many cases these schools and programs are populated by students who share a race and/or ethnicity. We do not worry about the "segregation" of these schools; we seem to think that somewhere in these young people's socialization or journeying through our diverse society, they will mix with others. Evidently, the same could be said about Black and other students who choose to attend a Black-focused school.

Toronto's Africentric Alternative School should be regarded as one strategy among others that seeks to address the educational situation of Black and other youth who feel alienated in the current educational system (see also A.M.A. Allen, 2010; Dei, 2006; James & Samaroo, 2017; Thompson & Wallner, 2012). I say other youth, for I do not think that only Black youth will or can benefit from a school that critically engages students in an education willing to explore Canada's colonial history, the place of Indigenous peoples, plurality in settlement history, race privilege, and the variations, complexities, contradictions, and tensions in ethnoracial identities.

One cannot expect that all students or educators will be of the same racial group, for it is not biology that determines educational aptitude, interests, or aspirations, but rather the possibilities afforded through interactions with structures in which young people live, learn, and play. Therefore, even within a Black-focused school, differences and diversity must be recognized if it is to be inclusive – that is, differences in learning styles, and in the social and cultural capital that each student brings to the educational and schooling process. Indeed, all students can benefit from any curriculum that has social justice at its centre.

A study resulting from a three-year collaboration between the Africentric Alternative School, the TDSB, and York University's Centre for Education and Community found that various aspects of the school, such as a culture of high expectations, integration of African-centred knowledge and practices, community and parent involvement, and the development of positive Black identity, have had positive influences on the students (Howard & James, 2019; James & Samaroo, 2017). But the school has faced ongoing challenges, including no school bus service and declining enrolment (Teotonio, 2019). Ultimately, if Black and other students who attend the Africentric Alternative School are to realize the desired outcomes, then the school will need the support and commitment of financial and other resources from government, policymakers, administrators, and educators. Lacking such resources and supports, as the current debate over the proposed school demonstrates, leaves in doubt the possible successes that such schools might provide.

Conclusion

In highlighting the issues and approaches to African-Canadian students' education during the 1970s, 1980s, 1990s, and the first two decades of the twenty-first century, I have attempted to scan the path we have travelled in recent history. Today, Black Canadians continue to advocate for educational change in the hope that school board policies and antiracism programs, including teacher education and student-centred programs, will eventually result in educational change – one that will address the systemic racism responsible for underachievement and alienation of Black students in Canadian schools. Enough school board reviews (see Case & Herbert, 2017; Chadha et al., 2020) have reported on the inequitable and discriminatory treatment of Black students, particularly with regard to streaming, surveillance, suspension, expulsion, absence from curriculum, and other measures. Hence it is time that, as the recent Peel District School Board review (Chadha et al., 2020) concluded, educators, school leaders, and elected leaders in Ontario (and of course Canada as a whole) need to "face the evidence of systemic inequity" (p. 39) that exists within the schooling system and which they have consistently failed to address.

The continuing efforts of parents, educators, and community members generally to address the myriad of issues facing Black students in

Canadian schools requires commitment to an education reform process in which all stakeholders – parents, educators, school boards, ministries of education, and faculties of education – are collectively engaged. With little government or board support and few material resources, initiatives such as Africentic school (elementary and secondary) programs that are supposed to be geared to addressing the situation of Black students have become lost in the educational and financial shuffle and eventually eschewed. Nevertheless, despite a history of frustrated projects and initiatives, African-Canadian parents and community members remain committed to educational reform – in fact, they are desperate for it. Their abiding confidence and optimism, hope and determination, activism, and shared struggles have kept them focused on possible change and transformation within the education system that will one day serve the needs of their young people. They remain confident about the capacity of education to provide Black youth with the skills and knowledge to fully participate and succeed in Canadian society – and they expect that the struggles waged to make their beliefs a reality will not be in vain.

Many African Canadians hold on to this view despite their experiences, in which the education system to date has been unable to respond to the needs, interests, and expectations of a large number of our students. Nevertheless, we continue to live with hope, optimism, and an expectation that sooner, rather than later, our activism will breathe life into the principles of inclusivity, equity, and democracy – and once these take hold, Black students will have access to innovative and student-centred educational programs. To achieve this, we need multiple approaches to educating young people; African-centred schooling represents one important such alternative and a worthy option for African-Canadian students who find the existing school structure and cultural context alienating and unresponsive to their learning/teaching needs, interests, and aspirations.

REFERENCES

Allen, A.M.A. (2010, Spring). Beyond kentes and kwanzaa: Reconceptualizing the Africentric school and curriculum using the principles of anti-racism education. *Our Schools/Our Selves 19*, 327–41.

Allen, K. (1996). The transitional year programme at the University of Toronto: A life-line for Blacks seeking university education. In K.S. Brathwaite & C.E. James (Eds.), *Educating African Canadians* (pp. 234–50). Toronto, ON: Our Schools/Our Selves & James Lorimer.

Allen, K. (2003). University access and educational opportunity: A Canadian perspective. In K.S. Brathwaite (Ed.), *Access and equity in the university* (pp. 79–91). Toronto, ON: Canadian Scholars' Press.

Anderson, S.E., & Ben Jaafar, S. (2003). Policy trends in Ontario education 1990–2003. Working Paper #2. Toronto, ON: Ontario Institute of Studies in Education / University of Toronto.

Anderson, W., & Grant, R.W. (1975). *The new newcomers*. North York, ON: York University.

Aston, C. (2003). *Towards a vision of excellence – London schools and the Black child: 2002 conference report*. London, UK: Greater London Authority.

Bailey, I. (1985, October 15). Black parents open school to combat dropout rate. *Toronto Star*.

Bascaramurty, D. (2017, September 7). Ontario schools to collect race-based data in effort to reduce educational disparities. *Globe and Mail*. https://www.theglobeandmail.com/news/national/education/ontario-schools-to-collect-race-based-data-in-effort-to-reduce-educational-disparities/article36207570/

Benzie, R. (2008, February 1). McGuinty turns up the heat on trustees: Pressure school board to reverse decision, Premier tells citizens. *Toronto Star*, p. A.1.

Beserve, C. (1976). Adjustment problems of West Indian children in Britain and Canada. In V.R. D'Oyley & H. Silverman (Eds.), *Black students in urban Canada*. Toronto, ON: Ontario Ministry of Culture and Recreation, TESL Talk.

Black boys separate classes idea. (2005, March 7). *BBC News*. http://news.bbc.co.uk/2/hi/uk_news/education/4323979.stm

Black Learners Advisory Committee (BLAC). (1994, December). *BLAC report on education: Redressing inequality – empowering Black learners*. Halifax, NS: Author.

A blinkered report on race. (1992, June 11). *Globe and Mail*, p. A16.

Bradshaw, J., & Alphonso, C. (2008, January 31). Multiple Afrocentric schools suggested; Cash-strapped board could be promising more than it can deliver, critics say. *Globe and Mail*, p. A11.

Brathwaite, K.S. (1989). The black student and the school: A Canadian dilemma. In S. Chilungu & S. Niang (Eds.), *African continuities/L'héritage africain* (pp. 195–221). Toronto, ON: Terebi.

Brathwaite, K.S. (1996). Keeping watch over our children: The role of African Canadian parents on the education team. In K.S. Brathwaite & C.E. James (Eds.), *Educating African Canadians* (pp. 107–30). Toronto, ON: Our Schools/Our Selves & James Lorimer.

Brathwaite, K.S. (Ed). (2003). *Access and equity in the university*. Toronto, ON: Canadian Scholars' Press.

Brown, L. (2006, June 23). Dropout, failure rates linked to language. *Toronto Star*.

Brown, R.S. (1993). *A follow-up of the Grade 9 cohort of 1987 Every Secondary Student Survey participants*. Toronto, ON: Toronto Board of Education, Research Services.

Call for separate classes for black boys. (2005, March 7). *The Guardian*. https://www.theguardian.com/education/2005/mar/07/schools.uk

Calliste, A. (1982). Educational and occupational expectations of high school students. *Multiculturalism, 5*(3), 14–19.

Calliste, A. (1996). African Canadians organizing for educational change. In K.S. Brathwaite & C.E. James (Eds.), *Educating African Canadians* (pp. 87–106). Toronto, ON: Our Schools/Our Selves & James Lorimer.

Carrington, B. (1983). Sport as a side-track: An analysis of West Indian involvement in extra-curricular sport. In L. Barton & S. Walker (Eds.), *Race, Class and Education* (pp. 40–65). London, UK: Croom Helm.

Case, P., & Herbert, S. (2017). *Review of the York Region District School Board*. Submitted to Hon. Mitzie Hunter, Minister of Education. Toronto, ON: Government of Ontario. http://www.edu.gov.on.ca/eng/new/2017/YRDSB_review_report_2017.pdf

Chadha, E., Herbert, S., & Richard, S. (2020) *Review of the Peel District School Board*. Submitted to Hon. Stephen Lecce, Minister of Education. Toronto, ON: Government of Ontario. http://www.edu.gov.on.ca/eng/new/review-peel-district-school-board-report-en.pdf

Cheng, M. (1995). *Black youth and schooling in the Canadian context: A focus on Ontario*. Unpublished manuscript, Department of Sociology, Ontario Institute for Studies in Education / University of Toronto, Toronto, ON.

Cheng, M., Tsuji, G., Yau, M., & Ziegler, S. (1987). *Every Secondary Student Survey, #191*. Toronto, ON: Toronto Board of Education, Research Services.

Cheng, M., Yau, M., & Ziegler, S. (1993). *Every Secondary Student Survey, Parts 1, 2 & 3*. Toronto, ON: Toronto Board of Education, Research Services.

Christensen, J.M., Thornley-Brown, A., & Robinson, J. (1980). *West Indians in Toronto: Implications for helping professionals*. Toronto, ON: Family Services Association.

Coard, B. (1971). *How the West Indian child is made educationally subnormal in the British school system*. London, UK: New Beacon Books.

Codjoe, H.M. (2001). Fighting a "public enemy" of Black academic achievement – the persistence of racism and the schooling experiences of Black students in Canada. *Race, Ethnicity and Education, 4*(4), 343–75. https://doi.org/10.1080/13613320120096652

Coelho, E. (1988). *Caribbean students in Canadian schools*. Toronto, ON: Carib-Can.

Consultative Committee on the Education of Black Students in Toronto Schools (CCEBSTS). (1988). *Final report of the consultative committee*. Toronto, ON: Toronto Board of Education.

Curtis, B., Livingstone, D.W., & Smaller, H.J. (1992). *Stacking the deck: The streaming of working class kids in Ontario schools*. Toronto, ON: Our Schools/Our Selves.

Dei, G.J.S. (2006). Black-focused schools: A call for re-visioning. *Education Canada*, 46(3), 27–31.

Dei, G.J.S., Holmes, L., Mazzuca, J., McIsaac, E., & Zine, J. (1997). *Reconstructing "drop-outs": A critical ethnography of the dynamics of Black students' disengagement from school*. Toronto, ON: University of Toronto Press.

Deosaran, R.A. (1976). *The 1975 Every Student Survey: Program placement related to selected countries of birth and selected languages, #140*. Toronto, ON: Toronto Board of Education.

D'Oyley, V.R. (Ed.), for National Council of Black Educators of Canada. (1994). *Innovations in Black education in Canada*. Toronto, ON: Umbrella Press.

D'Oyley, V.R., & James, C.E. (Eds.). (1998). *Re/Visioning: Canadian perspectives on the education of Africans in the late 20th century*. Toronto, ON: Captus Press,

D'Oyley, V.R., & Silverman, H. (Eds.). (1976). *Black students in urban Canada*. Toronto, ON: Ministry of Culture and Recreation, TESL Talk.

Durham District School Board (DDSB). (2018a). *Compendium of action for Black student success*. Oshawa, ON: Author. https://www.ddsb.ca/en/about-ddsb/resources/Documents/Equity/Black-Students-Compendium.pdf

Durham District School Board (DDSB). (2018b). *Equity & diversity strategic plan 2018–2021*. Oshawa, ON: Author. https://www.ddsb.ca/ddsbfiles/EquityFlipbook/4/

Follert, J. (2017, September 25). *Durham school board's new equity plan aims to give everyone a chance at success*. https://www.durhamregion.com/news-story/7574707-durham-school-board-s-new-equity-plan-aims-to-give-everyone-a-chance-at-success/

Four-Level Government/African Canadian Community Working Group. (1992). *Towards a new beginning: The report and action plan*. Toronto, ON: City of Toronto.

Foyn, S.F. (1998). A troika of programs: African Nova Scotian education at Dalhousie. In V.R. D'Oyley & C.E. James (Eds.), *Re/Visioning: Canadian perspectives on the education of Africans in the late 20th century* (pp. 187–97). Toronto, ON: Captus Press.

Fram, I., Broks, G., Crawford, P., Handscombe, J., & Virgin, A.E. (1977). "I don't know yet" – West Indian students in North York Schools: A study of adaptive behaviours. North York, ON: North York Board of Education.

Freire, P. (1994). *Pedagogy of hope: Reliving pedagogy of the oppressed*. New York, NY: Continuum.

Friesen, J. (2006, June 23). Grade expectations: One neighbourhood, three schools, and a world of difference for students. *Globe and Mail*.

https://www.theglobeandmail.com/news/national/one-neighbourhood-three-schools-and-a-world-of-difference-for-students/article711403/

Fuller, M. (1983). Qualified criticism, critical qualifications. In L. Barton & S. Walker (Eds.), *Race, Class and Education* (pp. 66–78). London, UK: Croom Helm.

Gaymes, A. (2006). *Making spaces that matter: Reflections on the experiences of female students in a Toronto school* (Unpublished master's thesis). Faculty of Education, York University, Toronto, ON.

Government of Ontario. (2017). *A better way forward: Ontario's 3-year anti-racism strategic plan.* Toronto, ON: Queen's Printer for Ontario. https://www.ontario.ca/page/better-way-forward-ontarios-3-year-anti-racism-strategic-plan

Gray, E., Bailey, R., Brady, J., & Tecle, S. (2016, September). *Perspectives of Black male students in secondary school: Understanding the successes and challenges.* Mississauga, ON: Peel District School Board.

Gregg, A. (2006, March). Identity crisis: Multiculturalism: A twentieth-century dream becomes a twenty-first century conundrum. *The Walrus, 3*(2), 38–47.

Gulson, K.N., & Webb, P.T. (2013). "Raw, emotional thing": School choice, commodification, and the racialized branding of Afrocentricity in Toronto, Canada. *Education Inquiry, 4*(1), 167–87. https://doi.org/10.3402/edui.v4i1.22067

Head, W. (1975). *The Black presence in the Canadian mosaic: A study of perception and the practice of discrimination against Blacks in Metropolitan Toronto.* Toronto, ON: Ontario Human Rights Commission.

Henry, A. (1994). The empty shelf and other curricular challenges of teaching of children of African descent – implications for teacher practice. *Urban Education, 29*(3), 298–319. https://doi.org/10.1177/0042085994029003004

hooks, b. (1999). *Teaching to transgress: Education as the practice of freedom.* New York, NY: Routledge.

hooks, b. (2003). *Teaching community: A Pedagogy of Hope.* New York, NY: Routledge.

Howard, P.S.S., & James, C.E. (2019). When dreams take flight: How teachers envisage and implement change through transformative pedagogy at an Africentric school in Toronto. *Curriculum Inquiry, 49*(3), 313–37. https://doi.org/10.1080/03626784.2019.1614879

James, C.E. (1990). *Making it: Black youth, racism and career aspirations in a big city.* Oakville, ON: Mosaic Press.

James, C.E. (1994). "I don't want to talk about it": Silencing students in today's classrooms. *Orbit, 25*(2), 26–9.

James, C.E. (1995). Multicultural and anti-racism education in Canada. *Race, Gender & Class, 2*(3), 31–48.

James, C.E. (2001). Multiculturalism, diversity and education in the Canadian context: The search for an inclusive pedagogy. In C. Grant & J. Lei (Eds.), *Global constructions of multicultural education: Theories and realities* (pp. 175–204). Mahwah, NJ: Lawrence Erlbaum Associates.

James, C.E. (2009). Masculinity, racialization and schooling: The making of marginalized men. In W. Martino, W. Kehler, & M.B. Weaver-Hightower (Eds.), *The problem with boys' education: Beyond the backlash* (pp. 102–23). New York, NY: Routledge.

James, C.E. (2010). *Seeing ourselves: Exploring race, ethnicity and culture*. Toronto, ON: Thompson Educational Publishing.

James, C.E. (2011). Multicultural education in a color-blind society. In C.A. Grant & A. Portera (Eds.), *Intercultural and multicultural education: Enhancing global connectedness* (pp. 191–210). New York, NY: Routledge.

James, C.E. (2019, March). *We rise together: A report to the Peel District School Board*. Toronto, ON: York University, Faculty of Education, Jean Augustine Chair in Education, Community & Diaspora.

James, C.E., & Brathwaite, K.S. (1996). Assessing the educational experiences of African Canadians. In K.S. Brathwaite & C.E. James (Eds.), *Educating African Canadians* (pp. 13–31). Toronto, ON: Our Schools/Our Selves & James Lorimer.

James, C.E., & Samaroo, J. (2017). Alternative schooling and Black students: Opportunities, challenges and limitations. In N. Bascia, E. Fine, & M. Levin (Eds.), *Alternative schooling: Canadian stories of democracy within bureaucracy* (pp. 39–54). New York, NY: Palgrave Macmillan.

James, C.E., & Turner, T. (with George, R., & Tecle, S.). (2017, April). *Towards race equity in education: The schooling of Black students in the Greater Toronto Area*. Toronto, ON: York University, Faculty of Education, Jean Augustine Chair in Education, Community & Diaspora. http://edu.yorku.ca/files/2017/04/Towards-Race-Equity-in-Education-April-2017.pdf

John, G. (2006/2010). *Taking a stand: Gus John speaks on education, race, social action and civil unrest 1980–2005*. Surrey, UK: Gus John Books.

Kakembo, P., & Upshaw, R. (1998). The emergence of the Black Learners Advisory Committee in Nova Scotia. In V.R. D'Oyley & C.E. James (Eds.), *Re/Visioning: Canadian perspectives on the education of Africans in the late 20th century* (pp. 140–58). Toronto, ON: Captus Press.

Kalinowski, T., & Brown, L. (2005, February 4). Province rules out Black-only schools. *Toronto Star*, pp. A1, A15.

Kelly, J. (1998). *Under the gaze: Learning to be Black in a white society*. Halifax, NS: Fernwood.

Larter, S., Cheng, M., Capps, S., & Lee, M. (1982). *Post-secondary plans of grade eight students and related variables*. Toronto, ON: Toronto Board of Education.

Lee, E. (1994, May). On any given Saturday [Paper presentation]. Association of African Studies Conference, Toronto, ON.

Levine-Rasky, C. (2014). White fear: Analysing public objection to Toronto's Africentric school. *Race Ethnicity and Education, 17*(2), 202–18. https://doi.org/10.1080/13613324.2012.725043

Lewis, S. (1992, June 9). *Report on race relations in Ontario*. Toronto, ON: Government of Ontario.

Lovell, T. (1991). Sport, racism and young women. In G. Jarvie (Ed.), *Sport, racism and ethnicity* (pp. 58–73). London, UK: Falmer Press.

Malcolm, M. (2006). *Toronto schools and the creation of the deviant school profile and identity: The implications of the social construction of the deviant identity on student success* (Unpublished major research project). Faculty of Education, York University, Toronto, ON.

Malloy, J. (2016, July 29). TDSB's plan to tackle racial disparity. *Toronto Star*. https://www.thestar.com/opinion/commentary/2016/07/29/tdsbs-plan-to-tackle-racial-disparity.html

Mata, F.G. (1989, December). *The Black youth of Toronto: Exploration of issues*. Ottawa, ON: Canada, Multiculturalism & Citizenship: Policy & Research.

McAndrew, M. (1991). Ethnicity, multiculturalism, and multicultural education in Canada. In R. Ghosh & D. Ray (Eds.), *Social change and education in Canada* (pp. 130–41). Toronto, ON: Harcourt Brace Jovanovich.

McGillivray, K. (2017, April 11). Review of York Region District School Board finds "culture of fear," "systemic discrimination." *CBC News*. https://www.cbc.ca/news/canada/toronto/york-district-school-board-probe-1.4065304

McMurtry, R., & Curling, A. (2008). *The review of the roots of youth violence* (Vol. 1). Toronto, ON: Government of Ontario.

Mirza, H.S. (1992). *Young, female and Black*. London, UK: Routledge.

Oliver, J. (1972). The Black child and white education. In N. Bryne & J. Quarter (Eds.), *Must schools fail?* (pp. 218–27). Toronto, ON: McClelland & Stewart.

Ontario Ministry of Education and Training. (1993). *Anti-racism and ethnocultural equity in school boards: Guidelines for policy development and implementation*. Toronto, ON: Queen's Printer for Ontario.

Peel District School Board. (2016, October). *We rise together: The Peel District School Board action plan to support Black male students*. Mississauga, ON: Author.

Prince, A. (1996). Black History Month: A multi-cultural myth or "Have-Black-History-Month-kit-will-travel." In K.S. Brathwaite & C.E. James (Eds.), *Educating African Canadians* (pp. 167–78). Toronto, ON: Our Schools/Our Selves & James Lorimer.

Ramcharan, S. (1975). Special problems of immigrant children in the Toronto school system. In A Wolfgang (Ed.), *Education of immigrant students* (pp. 95–106). Toronto, ON: Ontario Institute for Studies in Education.

Ramcharan, S. (1982). *Racism: Nonwhites in Canada*. Toronto, ON: Butterworth.

Roth, J. (1973). *West Indians in Toronto: The student and the schools*. Toronto, ON: York Board of Education.

Royal Commission on Learning. (1994). *For the love of learning: Report of the Royal Commission on Learning.* Toronto, ON: Ontario Ministry of Education.

Schreiber, J. (1970). *In the course of discovery: The West Indian immigrants in Toronto schools.* Toronto, ON: Toronto Board of Education.

Sleeter, C.E., & Grant, C.A. (2005). *Making choices for multicultural education: Five approaches to race, class and gender.* San Francisco, CA: John Wiley.

Solomon, R.P. (1992). *Black resistance in high school: A separatist culture.* Albany, NY: State University of New York Press.

Stewart, A.M. (1975). *See me yah: Working papers on the newly arrived West Indian child in the downtown school.* Toronto, ON: Toronto Board of Education.

Teotonio, I. (2019, July 28). Canada's only Africentric school was launched amid calls to better support Black youth. Ten years on, has it fulfilled its promise? *Toronto Star.* https://www.thestar.com/news/gta/2019/07/28/canadas-only-africentric-school-was-launched-amid-calls-to-better-support-black-youth-ten-years-on-has-it-fulfilled-its-promise.html

Thompson, D., & Wallner, J. (2012) A focusing tragedy: Public policy and the establishment of Afrocentric education in Toronto. *Canadian Journal of Political Science/Revue canadienne de science politique,* 44(4), 807–28. https://doi.org/doi:10.10170S000842391100076X

Toronto District School Board. (2008). *Urban diversity strategy: Focus on student achievement.* Toronto, ON: Author.

Toronto District School Board. (2016). *Black Student Achievement Advisory Committee (BSAAC) terms of reference.* https://www.tdsb.on.ca/Portals/0/Community/Community Advisory committees/BSAAC/BSAAC%20Terms of Reference.pdf

Wallace, A. (2009, January/February). The test: Africentric schools could be the key to success for a generation at risk (just don't call it segregation). *This Magazine,* p. 4.

Weingarten, K. (2000). Witnessing, wonder, and hope. *Family Process,* 39(4), 389–402. https://doi.org/10.1111/j.1545-5300.2000.39401.x

Wilson, M. (2015). *Review of the Toronto District School Board.* Submitted to Hon. Liz Sandals, Minister of Education. Toronto, ON: Government of Ontario. http://www.edu.gov.on.ca/eng/new/2015/TDSBReview2015.pdf

Wood, M. (2011). *Banking on education: Black Canadian females and schooling* (Unpublished doctoral dissertation). Faculty of Education, York University, Toronto, ON.

Wright, E.N. (1971). *Programme placement related to selected countries of birth and selected languages #99.* Toronto, ON: Toronto Board of Education.

Wright, E.N., & Tsuji, G.K. (1984). *The grade nine student survey, fall 1983.* Toronto, ON: Toronto Board of Education.

Response to Chapter 1

Complicating Gender and Racial Identities within the Study of Educational History

FUNKÉ ALADEJEBI
Department of History/Gender and Women's Studies, University of New Brunswick, Fredericton, New Brunswick, Canada

In this chapter, Carl James documents the history of educational access for African Canadian students and describes the advocacy efforts of parents, teachers, and community members in responding to institutional barriers within Canadian schooling systems. James charts the social and institutional forms of discrimination that have existed within school systems and their contemporary implications. Situating his conversation around the idea of *critical hope*, James argues that, despite the positive educational orientation and aspirations of Black Canadians, discrimination and limited educational opportunities have continued to shape their experiences in Canada. James contends, however, that even though contradictions have existed, African Canadians have sustained their demands for culturally relevant curriculum and inclusive teaching practice in their local school boards.

James's analysis of educational programs and policies from the 1970s to the early 2000s highlights the continuity of anti-Blackness in Canadian schools. Even as multicultural policies gained traction, systemic forms of discrimination coexisted alongside these "inclusive" school practices. School boards and administrative officials have a documented history of often responding to community requests for change with limited engagement and reluctance. The result has been the sporadic, underfunded, and difficult-to-sustain programs serving Black and other racialized students. Included in James's reflection upon ministry and board responses to African-Canadian students are the undocumented and more subtle practices of racial exclusion. Hence, this chapter calls on us to consider the ways that unconscious and culturally biased attitudes create spaces of difference for Black Canadian students. Scholars like Frances Henry (1994) call this the *hidden curriculum* where misconceptions around fixed intelligence and racial difference shape patterns of interaction and teacher expectations within schools (p. 140). This "common-sense" form of racism and discrimination helps to explain how both Caribbean- and Canadian-born Black students experience disengagement and disillusionment in schools.

Through school board records and community-based resources, James focuses largely on Toronto as well as parts of Nova Scotia. An expanded emphasis on other areas such as Chatham, Windsor, and Montreal would help to discern the boundaries of a national education system that has been unable to deal with its Black student populations, and would broaden the focus of education studies to reconsider the landscape of inequality as happening both inside and outside of schooling institutions. In particular, there is a richness of sources in the history of separate schooling and educational experiences of Canadian-born Black students that not only highlights community activism and achievement in Canada but also reveals the processes of racialization within various school systems. Even though Canadian-born Black student populations were demographically smaller than their Caribbean counterparts, similar stories of underfunded educational programs, biased teachers and counsellors, and the streaming of students into special education programs document the uneven but systematic processes of racial exclusion and anti-Blackness happening across Canadian schools.

Similar considerations apply to the lives of continental-born African students, whose experiences have not always been addressed in educational reports and programming. Martha Kumsa (2006) theorizes that Black Africans are often constructed as the "African other" and considered strangers within their own nation. Kumsa's argument asks us to consider as well how the label of *refugee* has stood alongside global conversations about displacement, dislocation, and violence in ways that have structured schooling experiences differently (p. 241). These experiences complicate constructions of Blackness in relation to broader state and institutional forces that homogenize and limit Blackness as linear and unchanging. We are challenged to examine the diversity of Black life in Canada and the multiple and diverging possibilities of Black schooling experiences.

The narrow representations of Black educational experiences in Canada offer limited available data exploring categories of class, gender, and ethnicity in archival and community sources. The consequences of this oversight are a focus that is almost exclusively on Black male youth as a way of understanding the problems of schooling in Canada. While James begins to map out the study of inequality from a gendered lens, limited sources exist that document the lives of Black girls in Canadian schools. In her school-based ethnographic study of Black girls in London, England, Heidi Mirza (1992) found that Black girls left school and often gravitated to jobs and careers as welfare officers, probation and social workers, nurses, and teachers. This focus on career choice shaped the educational decisions Black girls made and reflected broader socioeconomic circumstances that influenced their school experiences. Mirza contends that the focus on Black male learners in schools shifted the conversation away from gender and racial discrimination within institutional environments and emphasized cultural determinants of economic success or failure (p. 2). According to Mirza, the neglect of young Black girls in educational research has led to the myth of Black females' "tradition of self-reliance" that ignores the structural racism and sexual discrimination that they face in British schooling institutions (p. 14). Similarly, the overlooked assumptions regarding Black female participation within Canada's education system speaks to broader social issues that structure education.

My own work concerning Black female educators in Ontario seeks to continue this conversation by examining the various ways in which Black women have disrupted mainstream notions of education in Ontario and challenged Canadian nationhood more broadly. Reviewing the community and professional work practices of Black women teachers in Ontario schools from the 1940s to the 1980s, my research has found that Black women teachers have created resistive pedagogies that have served to bring cultural and community knowledge into the classroom. These educators maintained high expectations of their students, implemented "othermothering" practices that considered the history and needs of Black Canadians, and used their positions within schools to better prepare Black pupils for the social and systemic oppression they might face both inside and outside of school settings. Viewing schooling as community praxis, Black women's experiences as school teachers in the twentieth century reveal complex stories of social justice activism that began in the nineteenth century but continued into contemporary schooling practices. For example, Black educators continued to support antiracist educational programs by joining curriculum-writing committees, participating in and conducting research on the experiences of Black students in schools, and outlining practical ways to implement equitable practices within Canadian classrooms. Similar to the Afrocentric focus

James outlines in this chapter, Black women educators taught in various Ontario schools and created pedagogical practices that both borrowed from provincial curriculum mandates and also challenged their overarching Eurocentric focus by emphasizing the contributions of African-descended peoples as producers of knowledge (Aladejebi, 2015).

My examination of the stories and historical legacies of Black schooling experiences in Canada points to how Black women, in their professional teaching roles, were part of a longer and far more complex trajectory within the history of education in Canada. Any examination of the education of Black students and the struggles that communities, parents, and teachers have waged against the structural constraints surrounding educational inequality must give attention to the roles played by female teachers as active participants in the teaching and learning process.

This chapter provides a comprehensive analysis of the ways Black students have had few or limited opportunities for educational equity within Canadian schooling systems. Its strongest contributions are in the ways James encourages us to consider the multifaceted possibilities for exploring an Afrocentric approach to teaching and learning. Given the systemic forms of discrimination that affect minorities within education systems, a reimagining of school and educational space becomes part of the process of decolonized and inclusive education. Finally, at the heart of James's analysis is his reflection on African-Canadian students as active in their own educational experiences. Whether it was through seeking better educational opportunities, dropping out, or reaffirming their educational beliefs, students, parents, and community workers did not and could not wait for boards to respond. Their experiences and the institutional policies discussed in this chapter document a complex history of Canada's changing and multiracial classrooms and an education system struggling to deal with these challenges.

REFERENCES

Aladejebi, F. (2015). "We've got our quota": Black female educators and resistive pedagogies, 1960s–1980s. *Ontario History*, *107*(1), 113–31. https://doi.org/10.7202/1044330ar

Henry, F. (1994). *The Caribbean diaspora in Toronto: Learning to live with racism*. Toronto, ON: University of Toronto Press.

Kumsa, M.K. (2006). "No! I'm not a refugee!" The poetics of be-longing among young Oromos in Toronto. *Journal of Refugee Studies*, *19*(2), 230–55. https://doi.org/10.1093/jrs/fel001

Mirza, H.S. (1992). *Young, female and Black*. New York, NY: Routledge.

2 Generational Differences in Black Students' Education Pursuits and Performance

We must avoid the tendency to disregard the many nuances and differences among Black students and, aside from gender, talk about them as if they were a homogeneous group; indeed, a range of factors influence their individual educational situations. In addition to gender, these include social class background, parents' country or region of origin, and immigrant and/or generational status (i.e., how long their families have been in Canada). Among Black students, this latter factor has important significance for their educational achievement.

Using the Toronto District School Board's (TDSB's) 2008–11 cohort data, this chapter examines the intergroup and intragroup differences among students by generation, gender, and school activities (i.e., educational programs, graduation, and postsecondary pursuits), showing how Black students rank among or resemble their TDSB peers. The data used for this analysis come from the TDSB 2011 Student Census; as Canada's largest school board, the TDSB conducts a census every four years. The exercise is designed to facilitate discussion of how race and generational differences might account for Black students' educational achievements and outcomes.

The Black student population data are disaggregated by parental birthplace – Canada, Caribbean, Africa, and elsewhere. Intergroup comparisons pertain to Black, white, and other racialized students (e.g., of the 62,328 secondary school students counted that year, 7,289 self-identified as Black, 18,613 as white, and 36,426 as members of other racialized groups).[1] Highlighting this web of identification can further our understanding of the dynamic ways racial inequity – inherent in school

---

1 The data were made available through special runs by the TDSB research department. The numbers used for the analyses may not add up exactly to these totals because of some missing data.

policies and practices – disenfranchises Black and other racialized students, thereby preserving the status quo (Milner, 2008; Zamudio, Russell, Rios, & Bridgeman, 2011).

Data that track TDSB students who went on to York University are also used to show graduation and postsecondary attainment. In the tradition of critical race theory, this intersectional analysis highlights institutional and societal structures that sustain cultural norms and values that in turn foster the subordination, marginalization, and racialization of Black students (Allen, 2017; Gillborn, 2015; Yosso, 2005). Such data-related analysis helps identify the multilayered and diverse factors we must consider when developing strategies to effectively address gaps in schooling opportunities and thus improve educational outcomes for Black students.

TDSB Student Population 2008–2011: Generational Differences in Programs of Study, Graduation, and Educational Pursuits[2]

Figure 1 shows that almost half (48 per cent) of the total 2008–11 student cohort fit the category "second-generation" (born in Canada to immigrant parents), a third (31 per cent) are "first-generation" (born outside the country), and about a fifth (21 per cent) are "third-generation-plus" (born in Canada to Canadian-born parents).[3] When we examine the breakdown for white, Black, and other racialized students, however, we see significant differences, reflecting each group's pattern of immigration.

Specifically, the largest proportion of Black students were second-generation Canadian (71 per cent) – the children of Caribbean immigrants who arrived since changes to Canada's immigration policies in the 1960s. A smaller proportion, 22 per cent, were first-generation – likely a mixture of mostly African-born students and a smaller number of Caribbean-born – while only 7 per cent fell into the third-generation

---

[2] The data are taken from the TDSB cohorts who started Grade 9 between fall 2008 and fall 2011. These students would have been between Grade 9 (the fall 2011 cohort) and Grade 12 (the fall 2008 cohort). Each cohort was followed for five years. For example, the five-year outcomes of the fall 2008 cohort refer to the time between fall 2008 (Grade 9 for this cohort) and fall 2013 (five years later). The five-year outcomes of the fall 2011 cohort refer to the time between fall 2011 (Grade 9 for this cohort) and fall 2016 (five years later). These four cohorts, representing the Grades 9 to 12 students who wrote the 2011 Student Census, are combined to provide greatest detail on key subgroups.

[3] Third-generation-plus, comprising students with Canadian-born parents, is hereafter referred to as "third-generation."

Figure 1. Generational Status for Black, White, and Other Racialized Students

Group	First generation	Second generation	Third generation
All Students (n = 62,328)	31%	48%	21%
Other Racialized (n = 36,426)	42%	55%	4%
White (n = 18,613)	14%	28%	59%
Black (n = 7,289)	22%	71%	7%

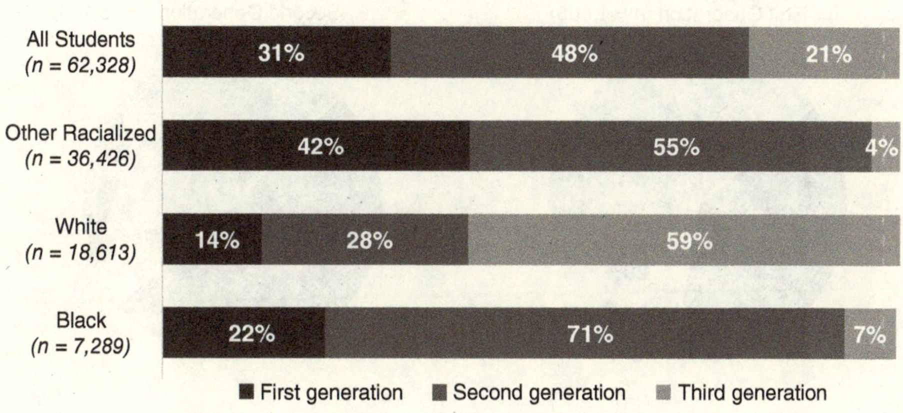

plus category – children of Canadian-born parents, and grandchildren of Caribbean immigrants who would have come to Canada in the 1960s and 1970s.

For white students, by contrast, the largest proportion were third-generation plus Canadian (59 per cent), with only 14 per cent first-generation and 28 per cent second-generation Canadian. For other racialized students, 42 per cent were first-generation, 55 per cent second-generation, and only 4 per cent third-generation plus Canadian.

When we disaggregate the 71 per cent second-generation Black students into regional groupings based on parental birthplace (English-speaking Caribbean, East or West Africa, and Other), we observe, as Figure 2 shows, the following:

- Caribbean students were more likely to be second-generation (51 per cent) than first-generation (39 per cent).
- Students of East or West African descent were about equally likely to be first-generation (44 per cent) or second-generation (41 per cent).
- Other Black students (those whose parents' birthplace is neither Caribbean nor East/West Africa) were much more likely to be first-generation (20 per cent) than second-generation (only 4 per cent).

Programs of Study

Students' Program of Study (POS) – Academic, Applied, or Essential – clearly reflected differences in relation to race and social

Figure 2. Family Birthplace of Black Students by Generational Status

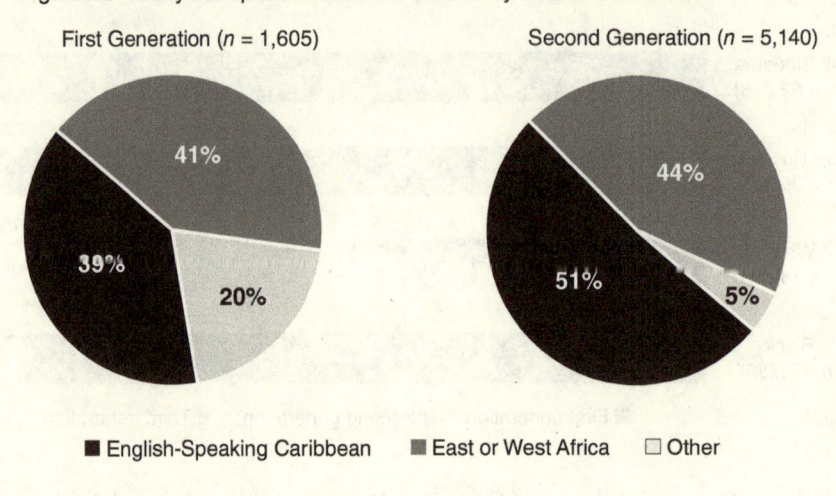

First Generation (*n* = 1,605)
- 41% East or West Africa
- 39% English-Speaking Caribbean
- 20% Other

Second Generation (*n* = 5,140)
- 44% East or West Africa
- 51% English-Speaking Caribbean
- 5% Other

■ English-Speaking Caribbean   ■ East or West Africa   □ Other

class.[4] *Academic* comprises courses which help to develop students' knowledge and skills through the study of theory, concepts, and abstract problems that incorporate practical applications. *Applied* courses "focus on the essential concepts of a subject" through which students are able to develop their knowledge and skills through practical applications, concrete examples, and opportunities for hands-on experience. *Essential* – now referred to as "locally developed" – are courses created by a board for students in a particular school or region to accommodate educational and/or career preparation needs that are not met through courses within the provincial curriculum policy documents. The Academic POS serves as a pathway to university, whereas the Applied POS leads to community college, and the Essential or Locally Developed POS leads directly to the workforce.

Studies have shown that being streamed into the Applied or Essential POS is associated with poorer educational outcomes, such as lower graduation rates (Clandfield et al., 2014; Hamlin & Cameron, 2015). These studies have also indicated that students from lower socioeconomic backgrounds and Black students were more likely to be

---

4 Students for whom no clear POS could be identified, including those with special education needs, those taking noncredit courses, and students entering the TDSB in Grade 11 or 12, are not included in this analysis.

Generational Differences in Black Students' Education 51

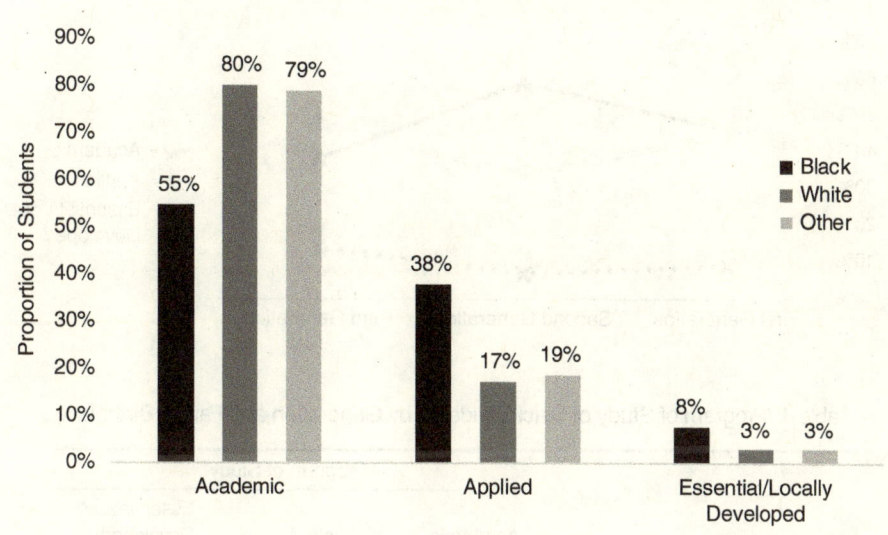

Figure 3. Program of Study of Black, White, and Other Racialized Students

[Bar chart showing:
- Academic: Black 55%, White 80%, Other 79%
- Applied: Black 38%, White 17%, Other 19%
- Essential/Locally Developed: Black 8%, White 3%, Other 3%]

placed in the Applied POS. Figure 3 demonstrates this, showing that compared to 79 per cent of white students and 80 per cent of other racialized students, only 55 per cent of Black students were enrolled in the Academic Program of Study. Conversely, smaller proportions – 17 per cent of white and 19 per cent of other racialized students – were enrolled in the Applied Program of Study, while only 3 per cent of each group was in the Essential Program of Study. In the case of Black students, 38 per cent were enrolled in the Applied and 8 per cent in the Essential Program of Study.

Figure 4 shows that about the same proportion of first-generation Black students were in an Academic or Applied POS (46 per cent and 45 per cent), and only 9 per cent of them were enrolled in an Essential POS. On the other hand, there was a noticeable difference between the proportions of first- and second-generation students (46 per cent and 59 per cent, respectively) taking Academic courses. This means that compared to their first-generation counterparts, second-generation students were more likely to be taking courses that gave them more postsecondary opportunities. Third-generation Black students were least likely to be taking an Academic POS (38 per cent) and most likely to be taking an Applied POS (48 per cent), or an Essential POS (14 per cent).

When we examine differences by parents' birthplaces, as shown in Table 1, we find that both first- and second-generation African students

Figure 4. Program of Study of Black Students by Generational Status

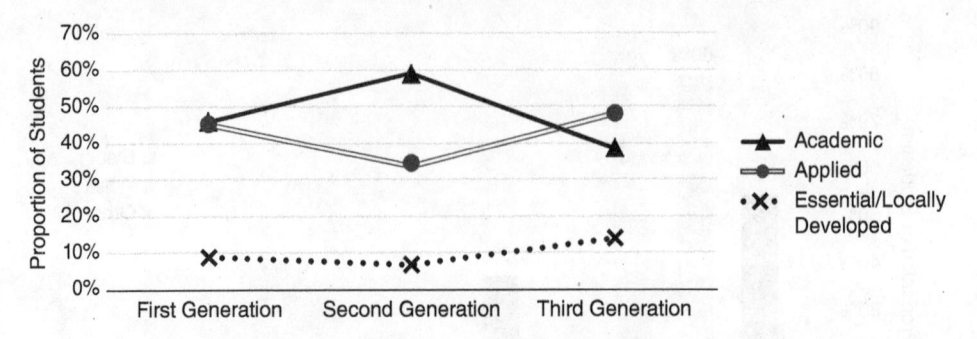

Table 1. Program of Study of Black Students by Generation and Family Birthplace

	Program of Study		
	Academic	Applied	Essential/Loc. Developed
First Generation			
English-Speaking Caribbean	178 (29%)	352 (57%)	85 (14%)
East or West Africa	379 (59%)	240 (37%)	25 (4%)
Other	168 (53%)	124 (39%)	27 (9%)
Second Generation			
English-Speaking Caribbean	1,133 (43%)	1,211 (46%)	265 (10%)
East or West Africa	1,728 (77%)	469 (21%)	60 (3%)
Other	138 (62%)	68 (31%)	15 (7%)
Third Generation			
Canada	201 (38%)	251 (48%)	72 (14%)

were much more likely than their Caribbean counterparts to be enrolled in an Academic POS. Regarding first-generation Black students, 59 per cent of African and 29 per cent of Caribbean students were enrolled in an Academic POS. Of the second-generation population, 77 per cent of African students compared to 43 per cent of Caribbean students attended the Academic program. Both first- (14 per cent) and second-generation (10 per cent) Caribbean students were the most likely of all groups to be enrolled in an Essential or "locally developed" POS.

In terms of gender, Table 2 shows that for all students, regardless of race, there is a noticeable difference in enrolment patterns between male and female students pertaining to POS. Female students (81 per cent) were more likely to be found in an Academic POS than males (72 per

Table 2. Program of Study of Students by Gender

	Program of Study			
	Academic	Applied	Essential/Loc. Developed	Total
All Students				
Female	24,101 (81%)	5,056 (17%)	654 (2%)	29,811 (100%)
Male	23,070 (72%)	7,555 (24%)	1,350 (4%)	31,975 (100%)
Black Students				
Female	2,101 (61%)	1,173 (34%)	180 (5%)	3,454 (100%)
Male	1,824 (49%)	1,542 (41%)	369 (10%)	3,735 (100%)

cent), and males were twice as likely to be in the Essential/Locally Developed POS (4 per cent of males compared to 2 per cent of females). These patterns highlighting gender differences also existed among Black students. Specifically, a larger proportion of Black females (61 per cent versus 49 per cent males) were enrolled in the Academic POS. By contrast, more Black males were enrolled in the Applied POS (41 per cent compared with 34 per cent females) and in the Essential/Locally Developed POS (10 per cent of males and 5 per cent of females).

Special Education Identification

Figure 5 shows that white students (6 per cent) were twice as likely as other racialized students (3 per cent) and six times as likely as Black students (1 per cent) to be identified as gifted. This means that of the 7,289 Black students in the TDSB data set, only sixty-three were identified as gifted. If Black students were identified as gifted at the same rate as their white counterparts (6 per cent), then 437 Black students would have been in TDSB's gifted programs. On the other hand, Black students were more than twice as likely as other racialized students (15 per cent versus 6 per cent), and almost twice as likely as white students (8 per cent) to have been identified as having nonspecified special education needs and to be receiving an Individual Education Plan (IEP).

Note that identification as a special education student helps to determine the educational programs into which students are placed. Table 3 shows the special education identification statistics for Black, white, and other racialized students by generation, revealing that the rates at which Black students were identified as having exceptionalities (excluding gifted) or nonidentified special education needs surpassed that of their white and other racialized counterparts in each generation.

Figure 5. Proportion of Students Identified in Special Education by Race

Non-identified Special Needs or IEP: Black 15%, White 8%, Other Racialized 6%
Exceptionality (Excluding Gifted): Black 14%, White 12%, Other Racialized 7%
Gifted Exceptionalities: Black 1%, White 6%, Other Racialized 3%

■ Black   ■ White   ■ Other Racialized

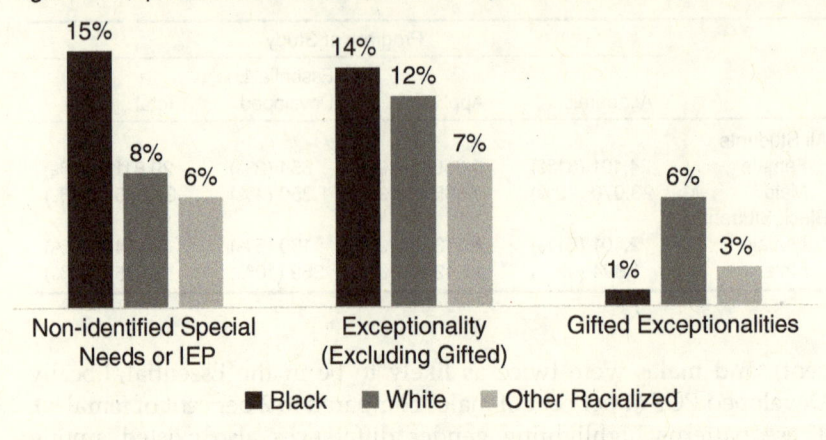

Table 3. Students Identified in Special Education by Generation and Race

	Gifted Exceptionalities	Students without Special Education Needs	Exceptionality (Excluding Gifted)	Nonidentified Special Needs or IEP
First Generation				
Black	***	1,254 (78%)	140 (9%)	204 (13%)
White	125 (5%)	2,144 (85%)	125 (5%)	122 (5%)
Other Racial Categories	486 (3%)	13,327 (88%)	601 (4%)	733 (5%)
Second Generation				
Black	54 (1%)	3,639 (71%)	690 (13%)	757 (15%)
White	328 (6%)	3,925 (76%)	530 (10%)	383 (7%)
Other Racial Categories	660 (3%)	16,252 (82%)	1,594 (8%)	1,380 (7%)
Third Generation				
Black	***	289 (53%)	157 (29%)	96 (18%)
White	677 (6%)	7,785 (71%)	1,563 (14%)	906 (8%)
Other Racial Categories	53 (4%)	963 (69%)	221 (16%)	156 (11%)

***Not reported because less than minimum cell count.

Conversely, white students in all generations were more likely than their counterparts to have been identified as gifted, as 5 per cent of first-generation white students and 3 per cent of other racialized first-generation students were identified as gifted. While we are unable to provide information on gifted Black students in the first and third generations (because their numbers were below the minimum threshold required for reporting), indications are that Black students,

Table 4. Black Students Identified in Special Education by Generation and Family Birthplace

	Students without Special Education Needs	Exceptionality (Excluding Gifted)	Nonidentified Special Needs or IEP
First Generation			
English-Speaking Caribbean	437 (70%)	77 (12%)	110 (18%)
East or West Africa	559 (85%)	39 (6%)	57 (9%)
Other	258 (81%)	24 (8%)	37 (12%)
Second Generation			
English-Speaking Caribbean	1,654 (63%)	494 (19%)	470 (18%)
East or West Africa	1,832 (82%)	158 (7%)	254 (11%)
Other	153 (68%)	38 (17%)	33 (15%)
Third Generation			
Canada	289 (53%)	157 (29%)	96 (18%)

regardless of generational status, were very unlikely to be identified as gifted. As well, they were most likely to be identified with a special need (with an IEP) compared to first-generation white and other racialized students. Moreover, Table 3 shows that of the Black students identified as gifted within the TDSB, almost all were second-generation. That is, of the sixty-three Black students, fifty-four, or 86 per cent, were second-generation.

When we examine special education identification of Black students both by generation and by parents' birthplace, we find that first- and second-generation African students were more likely than their Caribbean and other Black counterparts to have been identified as *not* having special education needs (Table 4).[5] Also, first- and second-generation African students were least likely to be identified with an exceptionality (excluding gifted).

Gender differences were also evident among Black students: Figure 6 shows that double the number of males as females were identified with special education needs other than gifted; specifically, 18 per cent of Black male students, compared with 9 per cent of Black female students, were identified as having an exceptionality (excluding gifted). Similarly, 16 per cent of Black males, compared with 13 per cent of Black females, were found to have nonidentified special education needs. By contrast, the data reveal no gender differences among Black students with respect to the likelihood of being identified as gifted.

---

5 Since so few Black students have been identified as gifted to begin with, regrouping them by family birthplace will not provide any meaningful insights. Thus, we excluded that information in Table 4.

Figure 6. Proportion of Black Students Identified in Special Education by Gender

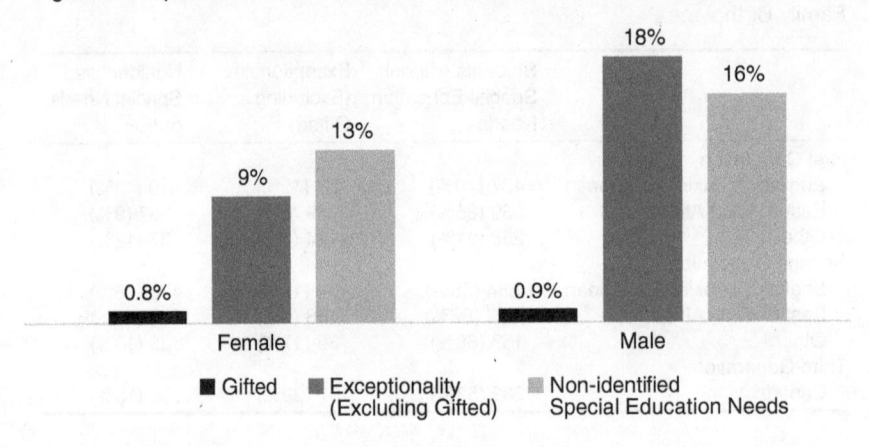

	Female			Male		
Gifted	0.8%			0.9%		
Exceptionality (Excluding Gifted)		9%				18%
Non-identified Special Education Needs			13%			16%

Graduation Status after Five Years in High School

With regard to graduation status, the data in Figure 7 indicate that over a five-year period, other racialized students (90 per cent) were more likely to have graduated or accumulated sufficient credits to graduate than their white (87 per cent) and Black (79 per cent) counterparts. At a rate of 8 per cent, Black students were twice as likely as white (4 per cent) and other racialized (3 per cent) students to indicate that they would be returning to TDSB schools in the following school year and more likely to have dropped out of school (13 per cent versus 8 per cent of white and 6 per cent of other racialized students).

Generational differences among Black students for the same census period indicated that compared to first- and second-generation Black students, the third generation had lower educational outcomes. Specifically, as Figure 8 indicates:

- 77 per cent of all first-generation Black students graduated or had accumulated thirty or more credits, while 15 per cent had dropped out, and 8 per cent were returning to high school in the following year.
- 82 per cent of all second-generation Black students graduated or had accumulated thirty or more credits, while 12 per cent had dropped out, and 7 per cent were returning to high school in the following year.

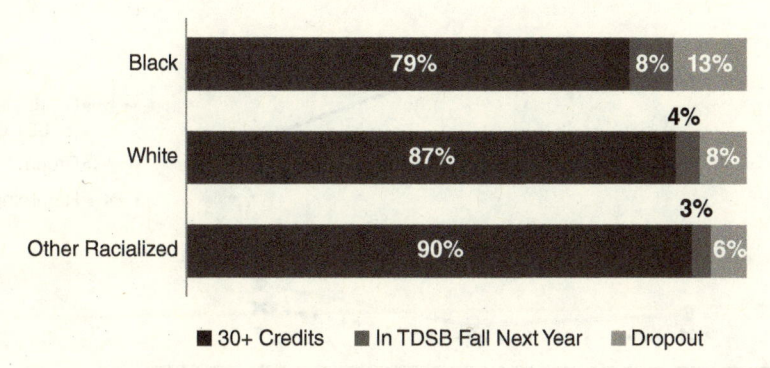

Figure 7. Proportion of Students by Graduation Status and Race

Race	30+ Credits	In TDSB Fall Next Year	Dropout
Black	79%	8%	13%
White	87%	4% / 8%	
Other Racialized	90%	3% / 6%	

- 61 per cent of all third-generation Black students graduated or had accumulated thirty or more credits, while 23 per cent had dropped out, and 16 per cent were returning to high school in the following year.

According to the data in Table 5, which are organized by family birthplace, first- and second-generation Caribbean students had poorer outcomes compared to their African-origin counterparts, with fewer Caribbean students graduating or having sufficient credits to graduate after five years in high school. Worse still were the outcomes of third-generation Black students – a smaller proportion (61 per cent) had graduated or had sufficient credits to graduate; just over a fifth (23 per cent) had dropped out of high school, and few (16 per cent) indicated that they would return to high school in the following year.

In terms of gender, the findings in Table 6 indicate that Black female students were more likely to have graduated or have thirty or more credits (84 per cent) than their male counterparts (63 per cent). Conversely, Black male students were more likely to be returning in the fall (14 per cent) than Black females (9 per cent) and were more likely to have dropped out (24 per cent) than their female counterparts (16 per cent).

Students' Confirmation in Postsecondary Educational Institutions

We also looked at plans for postsecondary education of Black, white, and other racialized students. Figure 9 indicates that compared to white (49 per cent) and Black (31 per cent), a larger proportion of racialized students

58 Colour Matters

Figure 8. Graduation Rates of Black Students by Generation

— Graduated (or 30+ Credits)
— Dropout
••• Returning

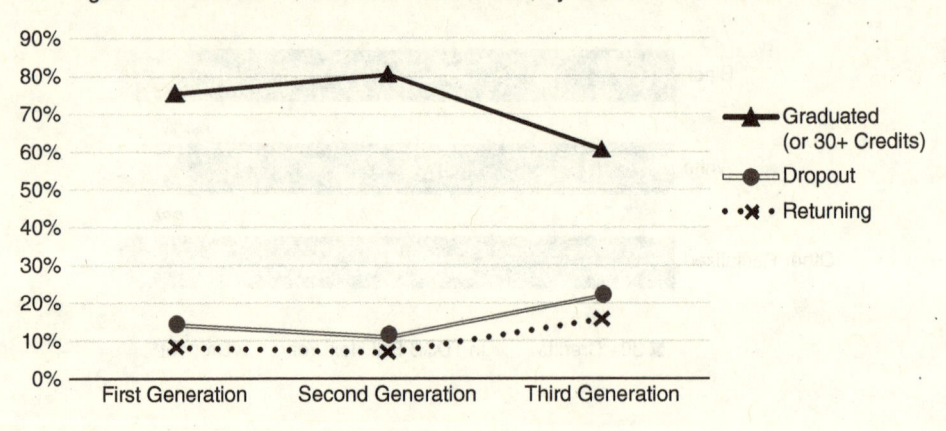

Table 5. Graduation Status of Black Students by Generation and Family Birthplace

	Program of Study		
	Grad or 30+ Credits	In TDSB Fall Next Year	Dropout
First Generation			
English-Speaking Caribbean	367 (68%)	60 (11%)	117 (22%)
East or West Africa	492 (83%)	37 (6%)	62 (11%)
Other	230 (81%)	22 (8%)	32 (11%)
Second Generation			
English-Speaking Caribbean	1,868 (77%)	213 (9%)	352 (15%)
East or West Africa	1,863 (87%)	92 (4%)	183 (9%)
Other	161 (78%)	19 (9%)	26 (13%)
Third Generation			
Canada	298 (61%)	78 (16%)	110 (23%)

(62 per cent) were confirmed as having been accepted in an Ontario *university*. Black students (28 per cent) were more likely than other racialized (17 per cent) and white students (16 per cent) to have been confirmed in an Ontario *college*. Further, Black students were more likely than either of the other groups (32 per cent) not to have applied to either an Ontario college or a university. Finally, the proportion of Black students (32 per cent) who did not apply to postsecondary education was nearly 50 per cent less than their racialized (79 per cent) and white (77 per cent) peers who had confirmed places in Ontario universities and colleges.

Table 6. Graduation Status of Black Students by Gender

	Grad or 30+ Credits	In TDSB Fall Next Year	Dropout
Female	2,712 (84%)	185 (6%)	333 (10%)
Male	2,567 (74%)	336 (10%)	549 (16%)

Figure 9. Proportion of Students Confirmed in Postsecondary Education by Race

	Confirmed University	Confirmed College	Applied to Postsecondary	Did Not Apply to Postsecondary
Black	31%	28%	10%	32%
White	49%	16%	13%	23%
Other Racialized	62%	17%	8%	13%

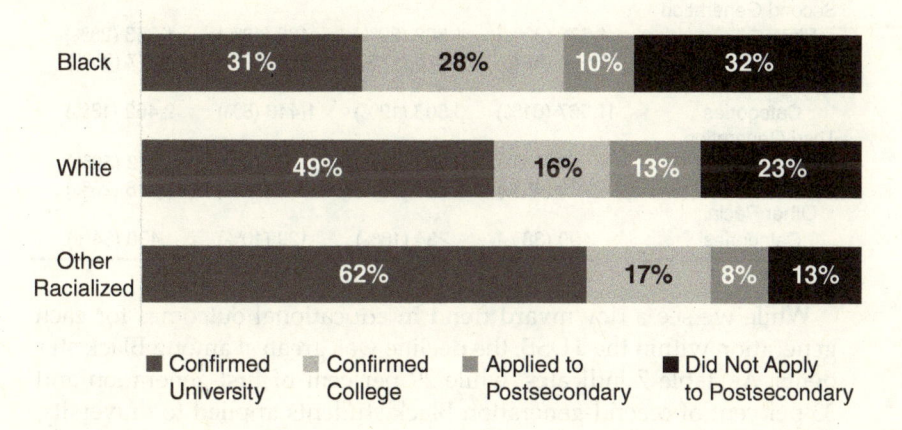

Table 7 shows the racial and generational breakdown of postsecondary confirmations. Specifically, the third generation of each group was less likely to go on to an Ontario university. Moreover, third-generation Black and other racialized students were much more likely not to have even applied to a postsecondary institution than their first-generation counterparts. Among first-generation students, fewer than a third (29 per cent) of Black students confirmed university attendance, compared to more than half (55 per cent) of white students and two-thirds (65 per cent) of other racialized students. On the other hand, first-generation Black students (35 per cent) were more likely not to have applied to an Ontario postsecondary institution than their white (19 per cent) and other racialized (11 per cent) counterparts. This pattern of post–high school pursuits continued to be the case for second- and third-generation students, with Black students being the least likely of all groups to have attended an Ontario postsecondary institution and the most likely not to have applied for admission.

Table 7. Students Confirmed in an Ontario Postsecondary Institution by Generational Status and Race

	Confirmed University	Confirmed College	Applied to Postsecondary	Did Not Apply to Postsecondary
First Generation				
Black	411 (29%)	381 (27%)	135 (10%)	492 (35%)
White	1,239 (55%)	330 (15%)	263 (12%)	416 (19%)
Other Racial Categories	8,958 (65%)	2,141 (16%)	1,155 (8%)	1,569 (11%)
Second Generation				
Black	1,576 (33%)	1,362 (29%)	486 (10%)	1,353 (28%)
White	2,524 (52%)	816 (17%)	576 (12%)	977 (20%)
Other Racial Categories	11,567 (61%)	3,503 (19%)	1,446 (8%)	2,462 (13%)
Third Generation				
Black	63 (13%)	113 (23%)	37 (8%)	273 (56%)
White	4,769 (46%)	1,649 (16%)	1,353 (13%)	2,518 (25%)
Other Racial Categories	499 (38%)	234 (18%)	129 (10%)	438 (34%)

While we see a downward trend in educational outcomes for each generation within the TDSB, the decline was greatest among Black students. As Table 7 indicates, while 29 per cent of first-generation and 33 per cent of second-generation Black students applied to university, this percentage dropped to 13 per cent for third-generation Black students. Conversely, while 35 per cent of first-generation and 28 per cent of second-generation Black students did not apply to pursue postsecondary education, this percentage increased to 56 per cent for third-generation Black students.

The data reveal similar declines in educational outcomes for subsequent generations of white and other racialized students. For white students, the decline was relatively small for the second and third generations – 52 per cent of second-generation and 46 per cent of third-generation white students were confirmed in an Ontario university, compared with 55 per cent of the first generation. Conversely, while only 19 per cent of first-generation white students did not apply to go on to postsecondary education, this figure increased to 20 per cent of second-generation students and 25 per cent of the third generation.

For other racialized students, the decline in the proportion of those who applied to continue on to postsecondary education was small in the second-generation group but large in third-generation – 65 per cent of first-generation and 61 per cent of second-generation students were confirmed in an Ontario university, compared to only 38 per cent of the

Table 8. Students Confirmed in an Ontario Postsecondary Institution by Generation and Family Birthplace

	Confirm University	Confirm College	Applied to Postsecondary	Did Not Apply to Postsecondary
First Generation				
English-Speaking Caribbean	66 (12%)	148 (27%)	55 (10%)	275 (51%)
East or West Africa	244 (41%)	161 (27%)	55 (9%)	131 (22%)
Other	101 (36%)	72 (25%)	25 (9%)	86 (30%)
Second Generation				
English-Speaking Caribbean	460 (19%)	789 (32%)	214 (9%)	970 (40%)
East or West Africa	1,055 (49%)	511 (24%)	245 (12%)	327 (15%)
Other	61 (30%)	62 (30%)	27 (13%)	56 (27%)
Third Generation				
Canada	63 (13%)	113 (23%)	37 (8%)	273 (56%)

third generation. On the other hand, 11 per cent of the first- and 13 per cent of the second-generation of other racialized students did not apply to pursue postsecondary education; this percentage more than doubled to 34 per cent for the third generation of that group.

When we disaggregate the data for Black students, as shown in Table 8, we see that African students were more likely than their Caribbean or other Black counterparts to go on to an Ontario university. This holds true for both first- and second-generation students. Specifically, 41 per cent of first-generation African students went on to an Ontario university, compared to 12 per cent of first-generation Caribbean students and 36 per cent of first-generation students from other regions. Meanwhile, 51 per cent of first-generation Caribbean students, 22 per cent of first-generation African students, and 30 per cent of first-generation Black students from other regions did not apply to go on to postsecondary education of any kind. African students (49 per cent) were more than twice as likely as Caribbean students (19 per cent) and about two-thirds more likely than other Black students (30 per cent) to go on to an Ontario university.

It is worth noting that even though about 59 per cent of first- and 77 per cent of second-generation African students were enrolled in an Academic POS (see Table 1), only 41 per cent of first-generation and 49 per cent of second-generation African students confirmed that they attended an Ontario university. In fact, about a quarter of first-generation and 15 per cent of second-generation African students did not even apply to attend postsecondary education.

Table 9. Black Students Confirmed in an Ontario Postsecondary Institution by Gender

	Confirm University	Confirm College	Applied to Postsecondary	Did Not Apply to Postsecondary
Female	1,222 (38%)	960 (30%)	305 (9%)	743 (23%)
Male	828 (24%)	896 (26%)	353 (10%)	1,375 (40%)

The highest proportions of students who did not apply for postsecondary education were first-generation Caribbean students (51 per cent) and third-generation Black students (56 per cent); they also represented the lowest proportion (12 per cent and 13 per cent, respectively) of students going on to an Ontario university.

When we examine the data by gender, as Table 9 shows, Black females (38 per cent) were more likely than Black males (24 per cent) to be confirmed in an Ontario university; females were also more likely to be confirmed in an Ontario college (30 per cent compared to 26 per cent). Meanwhile, Black males were more likely not to have applied to go on to postsecondary education – specifically, 40 per cent of Black males, compared to 23 per cent of Black female students, did not apply to attend postsecondary education.

University Entry Patterns and Graduation

According to Brown, Davies, and Chakraborty (2019), between 2004 and 2016 an estimated 15,206 TDSB students (or 17 per cent of all graduating TDSB students) entered the University of Toronto. Of these students, 30 per cent were East Asian, 80 per cent of whom graduated; 23 per cent were South Asian, 71 per cent of whom graduated; 18 per cent were Middle Eastern, with a 71 per cent graduation rate; 17 per cent were Southeast Asian, with 66 per cent graduating; and 15 per cent were white, 70 per cent of whom graduated. But of the 8 per cent Black students who entered the University of Toronto, only 51 per cent graduated.

In the case of York University (Figure 10), an estimated 11,414 students from the TDSB (or 13 per cent of graduating TDSB students) attended York during the same period (2004–16) (see Parekh, Brown, & James, 2020). As Figure 10 indicates, only 13 per cent of the students who entered York university during that time were Black, compared to 28 per cent South Asian, 25 per cent white, 16 per cent East Asian, and 19 per cent other.[6]

---

6 The 19 per cent other includes Southeast Asian (4 per cent), mixed-race (5 per cent), Middle Eastern (8 per cent), and Latin American (2 per cent).

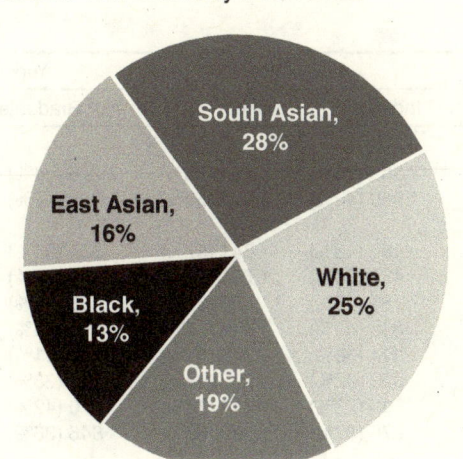

Figure 10. Who Goes to York University from TDSB?

- South Asian, 28%
- East Asian, 16%
- Black, 13%
- Other, 19%
- White, 25%

Overall, more students entered York University directly out of high school, compared to those who entered the University of Toronto, but as Table 10 shows, differences emerge among gender, race, and generational status categories in terms of direct versus indirect entry. For example, slightly more females than males entered directly out of high school, and Black students were among those least likely to enter university directly out of high school (57 per cent). Black students were found mostly in the faculties of Liberal Arts and Professional Studies, Environmental Studies, and Health (13–19 per cent each). Interestingly, fewer than 10 per cent were in each of Education, Fine Arts, Law, Science, and Engineering, and fewer than 2 per cent were in the business school. Essentially, compared to their East Asian, South Asian, and white counterparts, Black students represented very small percentages in most faculties.

In terms of graduation rates, Table 10 shows that Black students had the lowest outcomes with a 50 per cent graduation rate, similar (1 per cent difference) to their graduation rate at the University of Toronto. All other racial groups had higher graduation rates at York than Black students, just as they did at the University of Toronto. However, within each racial group other than Black students, the graduation rate was higher at the University of Toronto than it was at York. For example, East Asian students had an 80 per cent graduation rate at the University of Toronto (Brown et al., 2019) but only a 65 per cent graduation rate at York.

Table 10. Postsecondary Outcomes of Students by Gender, Race, and Generational Status

	Entry into York		York Graduation	
	Indirect	Direct	Not Graduated	Graduated
Gender				
Female	2,503 (38%)	4,165 (63%)	2,276 (34%)	4,392 (66%)
Male	1,969 (42%)	2,778 (59%)	2,254 (47%)	2,493 (53%)
Race				
Black	489 (43%)	641 (57%)	569 (50%)	561 (50%)
East Asian	453 (30%)	1,074 (70%)	532 (35%)	995 (65%)
Latin American	65 (43%)	88 (58%)	66 (43%)	87 (57%)
Middle Eastern	314 (43%)	412 (57%)	316 (44%)	410 (57%)
Mixed	174 (38%)	282 (62%)	189 (41%)	267 (59%)
South Asian	829 (32%)	1,737 (68%)	967 (38%)	1,599 (62%)
Southeast Asian	93 (23%)	317 (77%)	170 (42%)	240 (59%)
White	875 (37%)	1,488 (63%)	846 (36%)	1,517 (64%)
Generational Status				
First	1,364 (36%)	2,405 (64%)	1,394 (37%)	2,375 (63%)
Second	1,310 (33%)	2,660 (67%)	1,618 (41%)	2,352 (59%)
Third	624 (40%)	955 (60%)	642 (41%)	937 (59%)

As Figure 11 indicates, in all of the racial groups, female students were much more likely than male students to graduate. Specifically, on average, female students were about 13 per cent more likely to graduate than male students (66 per cent compared to 53 per cent). Black male students, compared to other male students, had the lowest graduation rates at 37 per cent. Compared to other female students, Black female students also had the lowest graduation rates, at 57 per cent. These numbers fall significantly below the average male and female graduation rates for all students.

When we look at the entry pattern and graduation rates of Black students by generation, as Table 11 reveals, about 50 per cent of first-generation male and female youth tended to enter York University directly from high school (the remaining half would have done other things, for example, gone to work, before entering). Second- and third-generation youth, on the other hand, tended to enter directly from high school at a somewhat higher rate (about 55–63 per cent), still with no significant differences between males and females.

In terms of overall graduation from university, compared to first-generation Black males, second-generation Black male students were about 12 per cent less likely to graduate; only 35 per cent of second-generation Black male students graduated compared to 47 per cent in the first generation (descriptive statistics were not available with

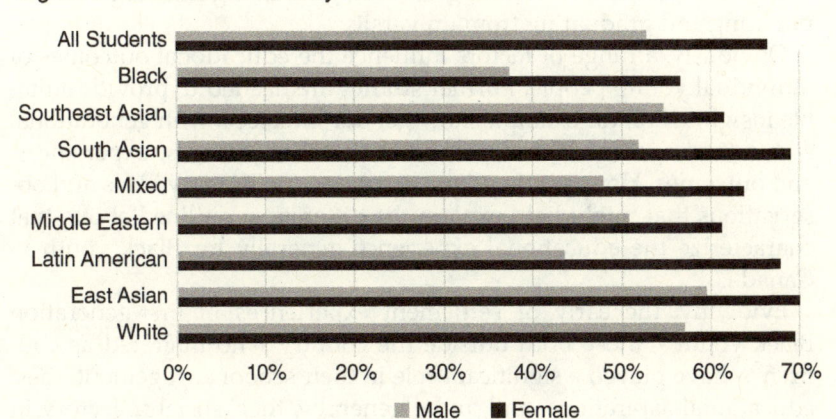

Figure 11. Graduation Rates by Race and Gender

All Students, Black, Southeast Asian, South Asian, Mixed, Middle Eastern, Latin American, East Asian, White — Male, Female (0%–70%)

Table 11. Postsecondary Outcomes of Black Students by Generation and Gender

	Direct Entry	Indirect Entry	Graduated
First Generation			
Female	101 (48%)	109 (52%)	115 (55%)
Male	58 (49%)	60 (51%)	55 (47%)
Second Generation			
Female	288 (63%)	168 (37%)	264 (58%)
Male	148 (55%)	121 (45%)	94 (35%)
Third Generation			
Female	29 (63%)	17 (37%)	23 (50%)
Male	***	***	***

***Not reported because less than minimum cell count.

respect to third-generation Black males due to insufficient observation). Overall graduation rates for Black female students increased slightly from the first to the second generation (from 55 per cent to 58 per cent), but then dipped down to 50 per cent with the third-generation cohort.

Discussion: The Educational Differences among Black Students

The TDSB data show that Black students of all backgrounds and generations have lower levels of educational attainment than their white and other racialized counterparts. Disturbingly, third-generation students – especially males – had the weakest educational record on every metric:

being in an academic POS in high school, graduating from high school, pursuing and graduating from university.

Obviously, a range of factors influence the educational outcomes of individual young people. Further studies are needed to provide suitable insights into, for example, how gender intersects with generational status to shape Black students' educational trajectories, experiences, and outcomes. However, I will present some preliminary ideas and observations that might help explain the differences outlined above that characterize the educational experience generally for Black youth in Canada.

Evidently, the early or settlement experiences of first-generation Black youth – those born outside the country who migrated as children[7] – have played a significant role in their school engagement, their educational aspirations, and, more generally, their social trajectory in Canada (Fuligni, 2001). It is possible that having spent their formative years in predominantly Black societies – surrounded by Black peers, teachers, and community leaders, and a variety of Black role models and sponsors – first-generation youth (especially the 1.5 generation) developed healthy, positive racial identities and a strong sense of self, and by extension self-confidence, which enabled them to buttress the assaults of racism in their schooling and social interactions generally once in Canada.[8]

It is also possible that some of these children internalized their immigrant parents' ambitions and aspirations and committed themselves to their schooling in ways that enabled them to realize their parents' dreams for them (or allowed their parents, through them, to vicariously realize their own dreams). Observing their immigrant parents' struggles in employment[9] and in Canadian society more generally might also have influenced these children's own aspirations. These first-generation Canadian children seem to have come to see and appreciate their parents' sacrifices and hard work as an investment in them, and in return dedicate themselves to do their part to make their parents'

---

7 Individuals who immigrated prior to high school are to be considered *1.5 generation* (see James, 2005; Louie, 2001; Taylor & James, 2015).

8 It is quite possible that, coming into Canadian white supremacy and racism with their enhanced self-confidence, first-and 1.5-generation students might have a naïveté and/or skills that helped them to effectively navigate the educational system.

9 Some of these parents might have had problems finding employment commensurate with their credentials, skills, and experiences – in some cases, credentials that might have enabled them to gain entry into Canada.

ambitions a reality through them. In other words, they endeavour to "pay back" their parents by pursuing postsecondary education, despite the obstacles, believing it represents the means by which their high career and social aspirations can be attained (James & Taylor, 2008). These children's sense of commitment and obligation – to "pay back" their parents or simply live up to their parents' dreams and aspirations for them – might also stem from close family relationships forged through their settlement experiences and the cultural values and norms that carried over from their home countries.

We cannot discount that there may be youth for whom the inequitable societal structure actually serves as a motivator – blunting whatever hopelessness and alienation they may experience and instead driving their high educational and social aspirations.

Many of these first-generation youth offer useful insights into what it might take for Black youth to successfully participate in the Canadian educational and social system and reach their goals. Unlike their Canadian-born peers, the immigration process might have provided them with the social and cultural capital or "community cultural wealth" (Yosso, 2005) to apply themselves to their education and exercise agency in ways that help them to successfully navigate our flawed educational and social systems. Research has shown that in some cases, to "get ahead," some first-generation students distance themselves from their peers; this helps them to resist stereotyping that constructs them as immigrants, fatherless, troublemakers, athletes, and underachievers (see chapter 4 of this volume).

Many high-achieving Black youth draw on their pragmatism, cautiousness, and sense of obligation to "give back" to their family and community (James & Taylor, 2008). These young people insist on being known for contradicting stereotypes, exercising agency, and not being stymied by individual and systemic racism. They are not oblivious to racism, but they do not consider it an insurmountable barrier. They seem to possess a peculiar sense of, as Du Bois (1994) would say, "double-consciousness." This enables them to cope with racism by looking at themselves "through the eyes of others" and feeling "a twoness" (p. 3) – Black and Canadian – that serves to strengthen them. Perhaps this duality will help young Blacks get ahead in Canadian society.

As we have seen, the data indicate gender differences in educational outcomes among various generations of Black students, with many of them underachieving, especially males of Caribbean descent. But we must recognize the complex interrelationship of generational status, gender, and the social, economic, neighbourhood of residence, and political context into which Caribbean and African youth and their parents immigrated and have been living in Canada. That more students of Caribbean descent tend to be second- and third-generation Canadians reflects the fact that their parents and grandparents immigrated one or two generations earlier. Many came as service (or domestic), education, and economic migrants before the introduction of today's point system, under which potential immigrants are selected on the basis of, among other factors, their education, work experience, official language ability, and capacity "to fit in" (James, 2010).

The social and economic context into which Caribbean immigrants came and settled in the 1960s and 1970s (prior to and in the early days of multiculturalism) differed greatly from Canadian society in the 1980s and 1990s, when more Africans came to Canada – many of them economic immigrants from West Africa and refugees from East Africa. Naturally, these two different entry patterns affect the ways parents and their children fashion their lives in Canada – a society in which multiculturalism and employment equity (in place for over fifty and thirty years, respectively) play a role. These policies were believed (or hoped) to serve as evidence that "immigrants" (read: racialized people) are welcomed and can successfully live, learn, work, and play in a "colour-blind" Canada, where "their cultures" are supposedly accepted.

We see from the data that first- and second-generation Black students (especially females) enter university and graduate at higher rates than their third-generation counterparts and at rates not much different from their white and other racialized group peers. This situation might suggest that third-generation Black youth, whose parents were born in Canada and grew up encountering our inequitable educational system, may have decided not to trust the education system – because the educational programs, curriculum content, pedagogical approaches, and disciplinary practices are not culturally relevant and responsive to the needs, interests, and aspirations of racialized students, Black students in particular. These contextual factors contribute to the reality that second- and third-generation Black Canadian youth – predominantly those of Caribbean descent – are unlikely to do as well as their parents and grandparents (Reitz, Breton, Dion, & Dion, 2009).

Conclusion

Irrespective of gender, generation, and family birthplace, in all but a few measures, Black students tend to have lower educational outcomes than their white and other racialized peers. As the data have shown, Black students are significantly less likely to be enrolled in an Academic POS, less likely to be identified as gifted but more likely to be placed in special education classes, and less likely to have graduated from high school after five years, and by extension, from university in later years.

But this profile does not apply to all Black students. Thus we need to pay attention to the diversity and related differences within the Black student population, noting how the cultural differences in their respective homes and communities, along with the lack of relevant educational curriculum content, culturally conscious teachers, and inclusive pedagogy, might account for their school participation, academic attainment, and eventual educational outcomes. The finding here invites further examination of the relatively high educational attainment of first- and second-generation African students. While there may be a positive immigrant effect that supports educational attainment by Black students, we need to examine why they are not capitalizing on this by pursuing postsecondary education.

We might hypothesize that for some Black students, distancing themselves from their immigrant parents' and grandparents' messages regarding the promise of education as the primary means to gain access to employment and career opportunities (Gosine, 2012; James & Taylor, 2008; Plaza, 2006; Taylor & James, 2015; Wood, 2011) – and in turn, upward social mobility – might account for their diminished confidence, faith, and trust in the educational system (Berns-McGown, 2013; Gosine & Islam, 2014; Tecle & James, 2014). Inadequate school participation, poor educational performance, and low academic achievement offer strong motivation for parents, community members, and others concerned with educating Black students to forcefully and consistently advocate to school boards, governments, and other educational agencies (many of which receive government and foundation funding) for changes to the system (see James, 2012). We cannot simply explain the situation as a reflection of hopelessness and pessimism among Black students; we can also see in this their understanding of their educational and social needs and their exercise of agency – in effect they are asserting that, like their non-Black peers, they are entitled to education that is responsive to and inclusive of their needs, interests, expectations, and aspirations.

REFERENCES

Allen, Q. (2017). "They write me off and don't give me a chance to learn anything": Positioning, discipline, and Black masculinities in school: Black male resistance. *Anthropology & Education Quarterly, 48*(3), 269–83. https://doi.org/10.1111/aeq.12199

Berns-McGown, R. (2013). *I am Canadian: Challenging stereotypes about young Somali Canadians*. IRPP study no. 38. Montreal, QC: Institute for Research on Public Policy.

Brown, R.S., Davies, S., & Chakraborty, N. (2019). *The University of Toronto – Toronto District School Board cohort analysis report 1: Introductory findings*. https://www.oise.utoronto.ca/depelab/wp-content/uploads/sites/41/2019/05/U-of-T-TDSB-Report-1-Final-May-8.pdf

Clandfield, D., Curtis, B., Galabuzi, G. E., Gaymes San Vincente, A., Livingstone, D., & Smaller, H. (2014). Restacking the deck: Streaming by class, race, and gender in Ontario schools [special issue]. *Our Schools/Our Selves, 23*(2).

Du Bois, W.E.B. (1994). *The souls of Black folk*. New York, NY: Dover.

Fuligni, A.J. (2001). A comparative longitudinal approach to acculturation among children from immigrant families. *Harvard Educational Review, 71*(3), 566–78. https://doi.org/10.17763/haer.71.3.j7046h63234441u3

Gillborn, D. (2015). Intersectionality, critical race theory and the primacy of racism: Race, class, gender and disability in education. *Qualitative Inquiry, 21*(3), 277–87. https://doi.org/10.1177/1077800414557827

Gosine, K. (2012). Accomplished Black North Americans and antiracism education: Towards bridging a seeming divide. *Critical Sociology, 38*(5), 707–21. https://doi.org/10.1177/0896920510380077

Gosine, K., & Islam, F. (2014). "It's like we're one big family": Marginalized young people, community and the implications for urban schooling. *School Community Journal, 24*(3), 33–62. https://files.eric.ed.gov/fulltext/EJ1048618.pdf

Hamlin, D., & Cameron, D. (2015, April 13). *Applied or academic: High impact decisions for Ontario students*. Toronto, ON: People for Education.

James, C.E. (2005). "I feel like a Trini": Narrative of a generation-and-a-half Canadian. In V. Agnew (Ed.), *Diaspora, memory, and identity: A search for home* (pp. 230–54). Toronto, ON: University of Toronto Press.

James, C.E. (2010). *Seeing ourselves: Exploring race, ethnicity and culture*. Toronto, ON: Thompson Educational Publishing.

James, C.E. (2012). *Life at the intersection: Community, class and schooling*. Halifax, NS: Fernwood.

James, C.E., & Taylor, L. (2008). "Education will get you to the station": Marginalized students' experiences and perceptions of merit in accessing university. *Canadian Journal of Education, 31*(3), 567–90. https://files.eric.ed.gov/fulltext/EJ809261.pdf

Louie, V.S. (2001). Parents' aspirations and investment: The role of social class in the educational experiences of 1.5- and second-generation Chinese Americans. *Harvard Educational Review, 71*(3), 438–74. https://doi.org/10.17763/haer.71.3.lv51475vjk600h38

Milner, H.R. (2008). Critical race theory and interest convergence as analytical tools in teacher education policies and practices. *Journal of Teacher Education.* 59 (4), 332–46. https://doi.org/10.1177/0022487108321884

Parekh, G., Brown, R.S., & James, C.E. (2020, January). *Who comes to York? Access, participation and graduation trends.* Toronto, ON: Faculty of Education, York University, and Toronto District School Board.

Plaza, D. (2006). The construction of a segmented hybrid identity among one-and-a-half and second generation Indo- and African-Caribbean Canadians. *Identity: An International Journal of Theory and Research, 6*(3), 201–30. https://doi.org/10.1207/s1532706xid0603_1

Reitz, J.G., Breton, R., Dion, K.K., & Dion, K.L. (2009). *Multiculturalism and social cohesion: Potentials and challenges of diversity.* New York, NY: Springer.

Taylor, L., & James, C.E. (2015). Living up to expectations: 1.5 and 2nd generation immigrant students' pursuit of university education. In G. Man & R. Cohen (Eds.), *Engendering transnational voices: Studies in families, work, and identities* (pp. 175–92). Waterloo, ON: Wilfrid Laurier University Press.

Tecle, S., & James, C.E. (2014). Refugee students in Canadian schools: Educational issues and challenges. In C.A. Brewer & M. McCabe (Eds.), *Immigrant and refugee students in Canada* (pp. 147–60). Edmonton, AB: Brush Education.

Wood, M. (2011). *Banking on education: Black Canadian females and schooling* (Unpublished doctoral dissertation). Faculty of Education, York University, Toronto, ON.

Yosso, T.J. (2005). Whose culture has capital? A critical race theory discussion of community cultural wealth. *Race Ethnicity and Education, 8*(1), 69–91. https://doi.org/10.1080/1361332052000341006

Zamudio, M.M., Russell, C., Rios, F.A., & Bridgeman, J.L. (2011). *Critical race theory matters: Education and ideology.* New York, NY: Routledge.

Response to Chapter 2

It's the Same with Black British Caribbean Pupils

SHIRLEY ANNE TATE

Director, Centre for Race, Education and Decoloniality, Carnegie School of Education, Leeds Beckett University, UK[1]

The data and discussion in this chapter raise very many important questions about the continuation of racism within the education system even in countries like Canada which see themselves as "colour-blind," and the UK which sees itself as "post-race." Of course, it is clear that "colour-blindness" does not exist in reality and, for Eduardo Bonilla-Silva (2010), racism still exists without racists, which can also be seen to apply to claims of nations being "post-race" (Goldberg, 2015). This chapter shows the disparity in academic achievement, most notably the continuing segregation of Black students into the less academic rungs of the school system which prepare them for low-paid jobs in the labour market as well as lower rates of entry to university. That is, Black students continue not to be seen as gifted and are less likely to be in the Academic Program. We also see that, generationally, achievement can go down, especially if the student is a Caribbean boy, while continental African students continue to do better but less well than white students. Class could explain these differences without doubt, but we should also consider the racial differentiation of access to education and retention within education systems, which exists across generations, and the schooling towards labour which occurs for Black students overall as opposed to their white counterparts.

---

1 In June 2019 Shirley Anne Tate became Professor of Sociology at the University of Alberta in Edmonton.

The discussion presents some possible explanations of white versus African and Black Canadian success differentials: double-consciousness, drawing from W.E.B. Du Bois (1994); the complex interrelationship of generational status, gender, and the social, economic, and political context into which Caribbean and African youth and their parents immigrated and have since lived their lives in Canada; and what is occurring in the school and classroom (for example, lacks in the areas of relevant curriculum content, culturally skilled teachers, and inclusive pedagogy).

The analysis and data from which this discussion draws is very reminiscent of the English debates on Black underachievement in schools, low access rates to universities, a Black attainment gap while at universities, and lack of access to graduate jobs compared to white students. It is also the case that Black girls continue to achieve more than boys, and that there is a difference within the African-descent group, with Caribbean-descent students faring less well than those with origins in the continent. One can indeed wonder at the lack of success of Caribbean-descended boys because, if other racialized pupils can succeed irrespective of irrelevant curriculum content, lack of culturally skilled teachers, and noninclusive pedagogy, why can't they?

This is not a new question; it has been with us since Bernard Coard's (1971) *How the West Indian Child Is Made Educationally Subnormal in the British School System*. We have also seen a repetition over the decades of the same reasons for the lack of success – curriculum, teachers, pedagogy – but nothing has been done to ameliorate the parlous situation of the Black child in the UK education system. Instead, the situation is still judged as appropriate for the purpose of educating the population along racial lines, where education positions whites to run the economy and get the best-paid jobs and Black women and men to be in the worst-paid occupations. Like Canada, the UK still has a colonial system of education in place – just as it did in the Caribbean, where the Black population was only educated to occupy jobs working for or under the management of whites during colonialism. This racialized ordering of the labour market is so ingrained that we take it for granted. That is just how it is; it is the natural order of things. Seeing this as the natural order means that we need not look at the institutional racism of the education system at all levels and the colonial legacy embedded within it.

The institutional racism of the UK schooling system has been repeatedly posited as the reason for the underachievement of pupils of African-Caribbean descent, especially boys. Its persistence has led to its being also taken as a given within the education system, so that if, against all odds, Black boys achieve, they are exceptions and performing above the expectation for their group. There has been a lack of political will to rectify this, and neoliberal education policies exacerbate inequalities (Wright, 2013). According to Feyisa Demie and Christabel McLean (2017), over the past four decades research has shown that the achievement of pupils of Black British Caribbean descent – especially boys – lags behind the average achievement of their peers, and the gap increases at the end of primary and secondary school (Gillborn & Mirza, 2000). Further, UK Department for Education (2014) data show that Black Caribbean pupils are three times more likely to be excluded permanently or temporarily than their white peers (Demie & McLean, 2017). Only 16 per cent of Black Caribbean men in the UK go to university, and they are also more likely to be in jail and mental health institutions than any other group. As is the case in the United States, there is a pipeline from cradle to jail or a mental health institution, with school acting as a sifting agent. There has been failure to address underachievement for at least three generations of Black British Caribbean–descent pupils (Demie & McLean, 2017). There are seven main reasons for underachievement, according to Demie and McLean:

1 Head teachers' poor leadership on equality issues
2 Institutional racism
3 Stereotyping
4 Teachers' low expectations
5 Curriculum relevance and barriers
6 Lack of workplace diversity
7 Lack of targeted support

Nothing much has changed since the 1950s, as this roll call of issues shows, and Black children continue to languish in British schools without a strong national government lead to address the fact that Black British Caribbean–descent children "are not sharing the higher educational standards achieved over the last decade in England" (Demie & McLean, 2017, p. 4).

REFERENCES

Bonilla-Silva, E. (2010). *Racism without racists: Color-blind racism and the persistence of racial inequality in America* (3rd ed.). London, UK: Rowman & Littlefield.

Coard, B. (1971). *How the West Indian child is made educationally subnormal in the British school system.* London, UK: New Beacon Books.

Demie, F., & McLean, C. (2017). *Black Caribbean underachievement in schools in England*. London, UK: Lambeth Education and Learning, Schools' Research Statistics Unit.

Du Bois, W.E.B. (1994). *The souls of Black folk*. New York, NY: Dover.

Gillborn, D., & Mirza, H.S. (2000). *Educational inequality: Mapping race, class and gender*. London, UK: Office for Standards in Education.

Goldberg, D.T. (2015). *Are we all postracial yet?* Cambridge, UK: Polity Press.

Wright, C. (2013). Understanding black academic attainment: Policy and discourse, educational aspirations and resistance. *Education Inquiry*, 4(1), 87–102. https://doi.org/10.3402/edui.v4i1.22063

3 "To Make a Better Future": Narrative of a 1.5-Generation Caribbean Canadian[1]

October 2001

> CARL: *How do you identify, as Trinidadian or Canadian?*
> MARK: Definitely Trini.
> CARL: *Why?*
> MARK: I think it has to do with the way I was raised and the different values I have – the way I see life. And I think my whole perspective on life and education is all different. So, I can't really say I am Canadian in that sense.

June 2002

> CARL: *So how has Canada been for you so far?*
> MARK: Canada has been great. But I think that living here I am not yet fully submerged into the Canadian culture.
> CARL: *Do you like it here?*
> MARK: Yeah, I like it here.
> CARL: *Would you move back to Trinidad?*
> MARK: I don't think I could build a good future there; only if I could have, like, the same type of life. So, I am kind of enjoying the best of both worlds.

December 2007

> MARK: This is my home. Trinidad is the place where I would go for vacation, but I'm used to this society now. I see myself being a

---

1 The first part of this chapter was originally published in 2005. See James (2005a). Reprinted with the permission of the publisher. It has since been revised, updated, and expanded with data from further interviews with the respondent.

productive member of the society here. I think there's a lot of benefits to being in Canadian society, and I feel a lot of positives with regard to my growth in this country.

June 2013

MARK: We knew that it was going to be a harder time for us because of our skin colour.

Born in Trinidad, Mark (a pseudonym) is one of twenty 1.5- and second-generation Black youth who participated in a study we conducted in 2000–2. The study, titled *Product of Canada*,[2] explored the settlement experiences and the educational and occupational outcomes of Caribbean-Canadian youth aged eighteen to twenty-nine. We sought to understand how, in the face of a public discourse that considered them "foreigners," these young Black Caribbean-Canadian males constructed, understood, and articulated their identity as Canadians. We wanted to know about their sense of belonging (see Boyd & Grieco, 1998; Foner, 1997; Handa, 2003; Minichiello, 2001; Norquay, 2000; Park, 1999; Statistics Canada, 2003; Waters, 1999; Zhou, 1997), their experiences in and expectations of the societal and educational institutions they navigated, and the role of parents (or guardians) in their lives.

We defined 1.5-generation or generation-and-a-half Caribbean-Canadians as youth who immigrated to Canada between the ages of eight and twelve years, with or without their parents (I will return to a discussion of this concept in a later section). We perceived that while many of the experiences of the 1.5 generation were likely to be similar

---

2 Professor Dwaine Plaza was the co-investigator on this study. Of the twenty participants, ten (five males and five females) were second-generation and the same number were generation-and-a-half Caribbean Canadians. The study was funded by the Centre for Excellence in Research in Immigrant Settlement (CERIS) in Toronto. Its title is taken from a *Toronto Star* headline of 8 December 1999, which read, "Their Fair Day in Court: Born in Jamaica, the Three Men Accused in the Death of Georgina Leimonis Were a Product of Canada" (Mascoll, 1999). Two weeks later, Adrian Humphreys in the *National Post* (23 December 1999) reported on the deportation of a twenty-two-year-old Guyanese male who was classified as a "danger to the public." The federal court judge noted that the accused had been living in Canada since he was eleven years old and had spent all of his youth and early adulthood in Canada; hence, he appropriately could be described as a product of his environment in Canada rather than that of Guyana.

to those of second-generation (born in Canada) Caribbean Canadians, there would also be differences. The defining aspect of the 1.5 generation's experience involved the early parenting and schooling that these Canadians received in the Caribbean and the fact that, as immigrants, they went through an adjustment process as they settled in Canada.

My initial interview with Mark – then twenty years old – took place during the first semester (fall 2001) of his first year in university. Having established early in the interview that Mark had immigrated to Canada in March 1995 at age thirteen, I asked about how he identified (see above), seeking to learn where he stood on the question of national identity. A variant of this question is often posed to Black people (immigrants and nonimmigrants alike), especially by white Canadians (Agnew, 2003; James, 2001; Palmer, 1997; Shadd, 2001). Mark's response was unequivocal: "Definitely Trini." With that short, nostalgic, and colloquial expression, he asserted his sense of kinship with his home country. He went on to explain that his values and perspective on schooling, education, and life generally were "different" from those of his Canadian-born peers; hence he didn't see himself as Canadian.

In subsequent interviews, however, Mark revealed that he considered Canada "home" (December 2007), and that he "feels Canadian" (June 2013). What are the perceived values and norms that Mark at first believed he did not possess and which therefore made him "different"? Whatever they were, the early schooling and parenting that he, like other 1.5-generation Caribbean Canadians, received in the Caribbean, and the adjustment process he and his family went through as they settled into Canada, would no doubt have played a significant role.

I maintained contact with Mark for more than ten years, interviewing him three additional times (June 2002, December 2007, and June 2013) to hear about his experiences, his sense of belonging (and/or his identity as Canadian), his educational and career aspirations, and the role his mother and other family members played in shaping and/or directing his aspirations and achievements.

This longitudinal approach to learning about Mark's early life in Canada is important. As Fuligni (2001) asserts, the acculturation of children from immigrant families (i.e., the process of adjustment and integration that occurs when individuals enter a new society) involves "a process of individual change over time" (p. 567), and hence must be studied accordingly. He argues that there is a need "for studies that track the same children as they encounter and navigate the potential differences between their cultural traditions and those of the host society" (pp. 567–8).

A longitudinal study and case study approach (Flyvbjerg, 2011; Gilgun, 2005; van Manen, 1990) provide opportunities to ascertain what happens in the course of an individual's development and life journey. For instance, does the value Mark places on education decline as he gains more exposure to Canadian society, schools, and school peers (see Fuligini, 2001)? Specifically, after he enters Canadian society with high educational aspirations, do Mark's educational interests and aspirations decline as he proceeds through high school; and do they begin to align with those of his Black Caribbean-Canadian peers? How does Mark combine his academic and athletic interests as a Black/African-Canadian male? Does he prioritize athletics over academics, as is usually the case among Black student athletes (James, 2005b)?

As a young Caribbean diasporic male, Mark provides insights into the circumstances and factors that shaped his life, informed his educational and career aspirations, and structured his perceptions of the opportunities and possibilities that Canada afforded him. Particularly interesting was the role that sport played in Mark's adjustment to life in Canada. Research has shown that many Caribbean-Canadian youth use sport to navigate high school in an effort to both attain an education and develop their athletic abilities and competence. These young people believe that by excelling at sports, they will be able to win athletic scholarships to American universities and colleges and eventually "make it" in the sport world and in society generally (James, 2003, 2005b; Solomon, 1992; Spence, 1999).

Sport was central to Mark's adjustment to life in Canada and to his career plans. However, in contrast to his Caribbean-Canadian peers, it was Trinidad that provided the opportunities for him to showcase his talent and gain the inspiration and satisfaction he needed to maintain his ambitions. Canada was where he lived, received his education, "found his athletic talent," and developed his athletic skills, but Trinidad provided the foundation for his values, self-confidence, and aspirations. In fact, both countries have made him the person he is, expects to become, and is becoming.

This interpretive account of Mark's youth and early adult years in Canada reveals the complex, pragmatic, sentimental, and contradictory ways this stage of life is conceptualized or imagined. Thinking of what is presented here as "interpretive" is germane, since Mark's story is layered by his interpretations (not mere descriptions) and analyses of events, as well as the social, political, economic, and cultural contexts of the societies that have shaped and structured his life (Denzin, 1996;

Munro, 1998). It is also layered by my own interpretation and experiences as a Black Caribbean-Canadian educator and researcher. Mark's story cannot be considered a static representation of his life at a particular point in time. Rather, his story captures the developing processes and changing pictures of his life journey (Coleman, 1991), as well as the confusions, contradictions, ambiguities, fluctuations, and transitions that comprise his lived experiences (James, 2002).

The many tensions and contradictions inherent in how individuals construct their stories signify the racialization structures and practices against which they write their lives (see Munro, 1998). In such a context, the personal stories of racialized group members like Mark can be an effective source of counterhegemonic insights – they expose the viewpoint embedded in a dominant ideology, and in doing so reveal the reality of life for racialized youth, thereby defying and contradicting essentialist constructs. In exploring Mark's story I seek to provide, as Lincoln (1993) writes, an "active counterpoint by describing historical and social contexts in which silenced groups have traditionally found themselves" (p. 35). In the section that follows, I elaborate on the notion of the 1.5 generation and its significance to the lived experiences of immigrant youth.

1.5 Generation

Scholars such as Louie (2001), Myers and Cranford (1998), and Park (1999) emphasize the unique experiences of this generation that immigrated prior to high school or during early to mid-adolescence. Park (1999) notes that "immigration between the ages of six and ten places one as 1.75 generation; between eleven and twelve, 1.5 generation; and between thirteen and fourteen, 1.25 generation. After graduating from high school, one is classified as the first generation" (p. 140). Louie (2001) similarly defines 1.5 generation as foreign-born children who immigrated at about eleven years old.

In her article "'I Really Do Feel I'm 1.5!': The Construction of Self and Community by Young Korean Americans," Korean-American scholar Kyeyoung Park (1999) makes the point that "although biologically the notion of a '1.5' generation is absurd, the sociocultural characteristics and psychological experiences of the pre-adult immigrant are distinct from either the first or second generation ethnic American" (p. 140). With reference to W.E.B. Du Bois's concept of "double-consciousness" among African Americans, Park posits that Korean Americans similarly live a dual existence in the United States. This duality, Park argues, is especially evident among 1.5-generation young people who "are neither Korean, American, nor Korean American, while they are, at the same time, all three. The simultaneity of their being 'neither/nor' and 'both/all' distinguishes the 1.5 generation from both immigrant Koreans and American-born Korean Americans" (p. 142).

In reference to her Somali-born respondents who arrived in Canada before their fifth or sixth birthdays and who have had long years of socialization in a Canadian diasporic context, Berns-McGown (2013) writes that, assuming newcomers are willing to "embrace their new home," the adjustment process for immigrants is a "two-way street" involving both internal and external integration (p. 3). Internal integration

> involves an individual's weaving of a belief set acquired in the birth country or parental household with that of the adoptive home in an on-going renegotiation of identity and re-evaluation of beliefs, attitudes, and perspectives on everything from food to clothing to friendship to religion. (p. 5)

External integration "involves the willingness of the adoptive home to open up and promote participation of the newcomer in every aspect of civic life" (p. 5) by removing "barriers to participation and to ease the process of becoming a productive member of one's adopted home" (p. 3). Equitable access to education, healthcare, housing, jobs, and so on, as well as being open to the perspectives of the newcomers is necessary for "the (re)negotiating of identity on the part of the diasporic individual and community" (p. 6). Berns-McGown also makes the point that 1.5-generation youth

> live in an imaginative space [not imaginary, but rather one's understanding of multiple, complex stories] where multiple connections and multiple narratives affect one's sense of self as an individual and as a citizen in a world of increasing intersections. It means to have connections to an imagined place of origin – as well as to the adoptive home. (p. 5)

The notion that 1.5 youth and/or other immigrants live with dual identities is common, as Park (1999) notes above. However, given the complex nature of identities, which can be fluid, pragmatic, contradictory, and transitory, I contend that immigrants' identities cannot be accurately represented simply as dual. In the Canadian context, for example, someone like Mark does not enter Canadian society to find a common or unitary Black/African-Canadian cultural identity – given the composition of its population, with Black people having come from all regions of the world, bringing their respective languages.[3] Add to that the African-American influence transmitted through music, education, sport, and other media. We can therefore more accurately say that Black youth's cultural identity constructs are multiple, shifting, and ongoing.

Below, I present Mark's narrative based on my interviews with him over the years. Part 1 comes from the first published essay (James, 2005a), which uses findings from the initial interviews (October 2001 and June 2002). Part 2 consists of a short conference paper (James, 2013) that drew on follow-up interviews (December 2007 and June 2013) to build on the initial narrative.

Part 1: Early Years in Canada, Education, and Sport

Here I explore Mark's (a) early life in Canada, and what moving to Canada meant for him; (b) high school experiences with teachers, coaches, and peers; (c) educational and career aspirations (and the pivotal role of his mother and grandparents in cultivating his faith in education as a mechanism for success); and (d) perception of a career in sport as a viable option.

I conclude with a discussion of how Mark's early years in Canada – his experiences, identification, aspirations, opportunities, and sense of belonging or home – were marked by the "duality" (Park, 1999) of a 1.5-generation Caribbean Canadian. I also examine his attempts to avoid the racialization that has blunted his Black Caribbean-Canadian peers' achievements. In an addendum following the conclusion, I reflect on Mark's response to the essay before its publication.

The Move to Canada: "To Give Us an Opportunity to Get a Better Education"

Mark came to Canada to join his mother, who had immigrated here five years earlier, leaving Mark and his younger brother to live with their maternal grandparents. According to Mark, his mother "moved from Trinidad with the plan to bring us here, to set up a home and stuff, and give us an opportunity to get a better education." The idea of emigrating from the Caribbean to North America to ensure a better life for one's children is well documented (F. Henry, 1994; James, 2002; Plaza

---

3 For example, Somali-Canadian youth in Toronto are known to adopt a "Black identity" that is constructed as Jamaican using language expressions, dress, and other such symbols.

& Simmons, 1998). Strong evidence exists to show that young people can and do attain the better education that their parents had hoped for when immigrating to Canada. Nevertheless, for Mark, who at thirteen was attending "the second best" school in Trinidad (having passed the entrance examination) and "was enjoying school there," it took some persuasion from his mother to convince him to immigrate:

> Well, she had us pretty convinced that it's a better standard of living, and basically the main reason is to look out for your future. She wanted us to have an opportunity. It's sort of like a rat-race in Trinidad, where even students with great grades and high marks are not getting the high jobs that they want, so they have to settle for the jobs they get. But it's a different situation up here. So, I wanted to come for two reasons: to live with her, and to make a better future for myself.

For Mark and his brother, Canada was not merely an escape from the Trinidadian "rat-race," but a place where a better future was possible because of the opportunities he would have to get jobs commensurate with his level of education.

Mark admitted to weighing what he would gain by immigrating to Canada against the fact that he was leaving his grandparents, with whom he had "a closer relationship," and his friends. "It was tough," he said:

> My father was never around, so my grandfather was basically my father. My grandma was much more loving [and] comforting ... I didn't really want to leave them, but I wanted in the same sense to come with my mom because I was missing her as well. She would come back and forth from Canada to Trinidad. So, she was moving back and forth, and it was kind of emotional. Like I would see my mom for a couple of weeks, and then she is going back to Canada. Yeah, it's a fine balance there too.

In Canada, Black children are more likely to grow up in mother-only homes than the rest of the population (Statistics Canada, 2020). In fact, in his Statistics Canada 2020 report on Black youth in Canada, Turcotte (2020) writes that "for several decades, being a single parent has been proportionally higher among the Black immigrant and non-immigrant populations" (p. 4). And while the same census data showed that living in two-parent families was the most common situation for Black children (34 per cent), just as it was for others in the population, "the proportion of persons in a lone-parent family was at least two times higher in the Black population than in the rest of the population (19 per cent and 8 per cent, respectively)" (Statistics Canada, 2020, p. 11).

It would appear that, having decided to immigrate, and despite what he was leaving behind, Mark was confident and satisfied that in return he was coming to Canada to establish a family life with his mother and secure a "future" for himself. But at the time of the interview, Mark, who had been living in Canada for more than seven years, conceded that he had a strong allegiance to Trinidad

> because, I guess the effect that being raised there has on me, and you are taught to be basically loyal; and all my values remain the same, I can say. Maybe my accent has changed, but if I were to go back down there it wouldn't take two days before you would hear me talk in the same way again.

Hearing this comment, I sought to establish the factors that kept Mark from claiming a Canadian instead of a Trinidadian identity. Was it because he was repeatedly asked, "Where are you from?" Or because he was told that he "had an accent"? As Palmer (1997), a Caribbean Canadian, writes, "This probing of our ancestry keeps us forever foreign, forever immigrants to Canada ... Their faulty [or racist] premise assumes that because you are not white you could not be Canadian" (pp. v–vi; see also Agnew, 2003). Were experiences with racism the reason for Mark's assertion that he was Trinidadian? Again, Palmer contends that "systemic racism in all its many guises ensures that no matter how long non-white Canadians are here, we will always be treated differently. No matter how much we assimilate, we will never be accepted as being Canadian" (p. viii). In light of these questions, I proceeded:

CARL: *Are you a Canadian citizen?*
MARK: Yes.
CARL: *So why don't you consider yourself Canadian?*
MARK: Why the difference? I think that living here I am not fully submerged into the Canadian culture because there are many Trinidadian people who I meet here, who cling strongly to their values as well, and to their own heritage, especially at [this university].
CARL: *So how has Canada been for you so far?*
MARK: Canada has been great.
CARL: *Do you like it here?*
MARK: Yeah, I like it here.
CARL: *Would you move back to Trinidad?*
MARK: Yes, I would, but I don't think I could build a good future there – only if I could have, like, the same type of life. So, I am kind of enjoying the best of both worlds. (October 2001)

At this point, Mark perceived that he had not changed his values nor made the cultural shift that would make him a Canadian. He felt this was not necessary, nor did he wish to do so because he was "enjoying the best of both worlds." He was taking advantage of the educational and athletic opportunities that Canada provided while remembering and using his Trinidad-inspired and socialized values and aspirations to keep him focused on his educational and career ambitions. Furthermore, not being Canadian meant that he would be different from his Canadian peers and hence should not be expected to fit the existing social culture and educational profile or stereotype of Black Caribbean-Canadian youth. His idea, then, was to keep distancing himself from such characterization – that is, to purposely *not* assimilate – because to the extent assimilation was possible, the result was not going to be in his favour (see Garrod, Smulyan, Powers, & Kilkenny, 2002, p. 64; see also Minichiello, 2001; Noguera, 2003; Norquay, 2000; Park, 1999; Waters, 1999).

Alternatively, being Trinidadian meant he had a commitment to doing well academically, and had the personal and familial values and aspirations that gave him the confidence and optimism he needed to succeed in Canadian society. So, pragmatically speaking, "both worlds" constituted Mark's imagined home. With his cultural construct of Canada – the society where he resided – he had access to the educational and occupational opportunities he desired and believed his aspirations could be realized. Meanwhile, with his imagined Trinidad, he knew he had the social and cultural capital to take advantage of the opportunities in Canada. In a way, then, physical residency aside, Mark's "home" involved a fluid mixture of both Trinidad and Canada, for he resided emotionally in both places and sought – through a network of supportive individual and structures in both countries – to sustain his values, understanding of life, and ambitions, particularly as he made his way through high school.

School, Teachers, Coaches, and Peers: "I Found My Talents Through High School Here"

Having arrived in March, Mark was initially placed – or, as he said, "dropped" – into Grade 8 in a Toronto school; he then proceeded to high school the following September. His use of the word *dropped* hints at his dissatisfaction with being placed in an elementary school when he already had been attending high school in Trinidad. During his short time in Grade 8, however, he "met a teacher from Trinidad" who, as Annette Henry (1998) would say, functioned like his "other mother" and ensured that he stayed focused on his education. He explained,

She saw me starting to change a bit, trying to fit in with the crowds and stuff. She saw my change in attitude and my focus shifting away from schooling because I thought it was not as difficult as Trinidad at that point in time. And she would always give me pep talks and try to keep me on the right track, and really that was very supporting.

In high school Mark met "other Black teachers" who were also supportive, and in his words, "always looked for me, told me ... not to undermine your talents, try to achieve and fulfill that potential."

As part of his adjustment to school life in Canada, like many Caribbean youth who enter the Toronto school system, Mark started participating in sports upon entering high school. "I had coaches [all of them white] pushing me on, trying to help me recognize my talents." Like many Caribbean students, he started with basketball, a sport with which he, like many others, was unaccustomed (see James, 2005b). Despite his ability "to jump pretty high and block shots," he did not excel because of his limitation in "size," (he was five feet eleven inches), and lack of "handling skills to be a guard."[4] He therefore switched to track and field, something he was also doing for the first time. Mark explained that in Trinidad the emphasis in school was to "get as high marks as you can," but in Canada the emphasis was more "on sporting life." He continued, "That's where I kind of filtered into sports, and I found my talents through high school here. So, in that sense I was very lucky to be able to recognize my talents and focus in on some sports" (October 2001).

Mark recounted with satisfaction the "motivation" he received from both his white and Black teachers, who saw him as "really special" and having lots of "potential." He insisted that the potential his teachers and coaches saw in him related to his competence just as much in sports as in academics. He noted that sports did not play a central role in his school life; he considered them "extracurricular activities." Hence participating in sports did not prevent him from maintaining an "overall A average" while also doing "well on the playing field." According to Mark, "school was a breeze until OAC [the last year]," commenting that the teachers "respected me as an athlete and student." He also pointed out that the size of the school helped him gain recognition and support: "I was lucky enough to go to a small school where I was the one who was making an impact on the school. So, if I went to a bigger

---

4 Mark also pointed out, "I quickly realized that you needed to start younger in order to have the sort of handling skills with the ball" (October 2001).

high school, nobody would have really known your name. You would just be one of many who are talented" (October 2001).

According to Mark, friendships did not distract him from his academic work during high school. In fact, he said,

> I didn't really have a chance to form many significant relationships in high school. I think partially because of racial differences, there just weren't that many Black Caribbean people. Most of them were either born here or have been here for a long time. So, they were different from me when I came. I couldn't really relate to them in any way ... I couldn't relate to many of the white kids either, so I pretty much stuck to myself.

Mark perceived the cultural differences between himself and the other Black and Caribbean students as being just as significant as the racial differences between him and white students, hence his inability to relate to either group (see also Garrod et al., 2002, pp. 65–73; Park, 1999). The "only person" to whom he could relate and with whom he mostly associated was his brother (two years his junior), who obviously shared and supported his ideas and aspirations.

Thus, during high school, Mark's social network – his Black Caribbean teachers and his brother – helped him sustain his perceived Trinidadian cultural values and his ambition as an immigrant to get a good education. From Mark's perspective, being a Trinidadian and an immigrant contributed to his cultural difference, which set him apart from his peers; this distance seemed to help him keep his perceived values and aspirations intact. Sport, then, was merely, as he put it, "an extra something" that occupied his time, since he did not find the schoolwork as demanding as it had been in Trinidad.

Here Mark was identifying yet another difference between himself and his peers: the academic work to which he was accustomed in Trinidad was seen as "very intense" because of strictly enforced discipline compared to what he experienced in Canada.[5] In this regard, Mark perceived that he was better prepared than his Canadian peers to deal with the academic workload. Thus, the sound academic foundation he believed Trinidad had provided him likely contributed to his continuing fondness for, and identification with, the country.

---

5 This explanation came in our follow-up conversation (2 March 2004) in which Mark "retracted" his earlier statement in which he claimed that his schooling experience in Canada was "easier" than in Trinidad. "In retrospect," he said, "the main difference in schooling was the discipline [which] was strictly enforced in Trinidad."

Mark's claim to liking Canada reflected his belief that in Canada he would be able to realize his educational and other aspirations without "becoming Canadian" like his peers; doing so would mean fitting a stereotype in which school was not considered a priority. Mark noted,

> I would say that stereotype doesn't fit me because I was doing well in school. I wasn't responding to any stereotype; I was making my own decisions. If school were suffering because of that, then I would have to give up the sports.

Aspirations and Parental Influence: "Education ... That's What I Came Here For"

Confident that he could participate in sports and maintain high academic standing in high school and now university, Mark participated in track and field and also swimming for a short time while in high school. He aspired "to get into sports medicine, but if that doesn't work out, then definitely the career in running will." To this end, he was pursuing "a double major in psychology and kinesiology," having received an academic scholarship to a university in Toronto.[6]

Mark's choice to study in Canada is significant, for African-Caribbean Canadian athletes tend to seek athletic scholarships to American universities and colleges (James, 2003, 2005b), a practice as popular among 1.5-generation Caribbean Canadians as among their second-generation peers. Mark proved atypical in that, while he wished to attain a scholarship to an American university, he was more focused on his education than the opportunity to advance his athletic career. He would only accept scholarships from "big schools" (universities) for, as he reasoned:

> The type of level of education that you are getting from these smaller schools, it wouldn't be accepted; it wouldn't be respected as much as a degree here [in Canada]. And you are working your butt off running every weekend with somewhat of a non-guarantee. There is no guarantee with regards to having four years of education there. So, it was a more simple decision I made.[7]

---

[6] Mark reported that he received an entrance scholarship to the university based on his "high eighties" high school grades, and it was renewable annually if he maintained the high grades.

[7] Having been encouraged by some of his other coaches to try for a scholarship from an American university, Mark admitted that he "sent packages" to two big-name universities, but "they didn't work out" – he never did hear from them.

That simple decision was to accept the academic scholarship from a Canadian university rather than either one of the two "athletic scholarships" he was offered by two "small" American universities.

In deciding not to accept the US scholarships, Mark was following advice from his mother and coach. Although other school coaches had said to him, "Why don't you? It seems like a good school," Mark indicated, "I already had my mind convinced that it's a small school, and you are not going to get a respectable degree, and my mom was saying the same thing."

As Mark saw things, going to an American school, at least the ones that offered him scholarships, would have been at the expense of his academic success – something on which he was not prepared to gamble.

It is not surprising that Mark's thinking was informed by his mother's expectation that he remained focused on his education and not just on sport:

> My mom was, like, why would you go away and have to be running every single week? Your marks would suffer, plus you don't come back here with a respectable degree. Why not just go to [a Canadian university] and still be able to train and get a good education at the same time? So just that alone, with my mom not pressuring me into having to go away to get a so-called free scholarship, was very good for me because I was able to still focus on the education. That's what I came here for and that's what I am doing.

That Mark gave such considerable attention and credit to his mother's advice relates to his belief that his mother, and not his peers, had the necessary insights and wisdom about what it would take to successfully negotiate societal structures. After all, she was an immigrant who, like him, had had to learn how to survive in the system. In contrast, his peers did not have to learn to survive; they were "Canadians," as he put it. In reiterating that he came to Canada for an education, Mark also signalled the centrality of education to his existence in Canada. He saw education as his security – something to which he could revert if his athletic career did not materialize, particularly in the long term. Convinced that the scholarship did not really mean obtaining a "free education," he was not prepared to take any chances:

> CARL: *You said "so-called free scholarship." You don't believe that scholarship is free?*
> MARK: No way, I hear too many of my own teammates who went down there come back in two years because they all run out, they have injuries,

they are off the team. And they get sent back as soon as they are not able to run and perform for the school anymore. They are sent back. I know that my body would most likely not respond all the time, so it's not worth the risk, wasting time out of school. Having to meet new coaches, having to have new people understand your body, the way you perform, what works for you. It's too complex. I just decided to stay here. (October 2001)

From my other research on Black student athletes, I have found that these students mostly listen to their coaches, and are less critical and discriminating about accepting scholarship offers. They feel they can "bounce back" and do well athletically after injuries (in fact, they tend not to consider or talk about injury as a possibility), and they rarely consult or take advice from their parents (James, 2003). By contrast, Mark "educated" himself and critically assessed the "many options available" to him, by listening to people's good and bad athletic stories, talking with coaches, and forming his "own opinion" – with his mother's guidance. As noted earlier, this difference in the way Mark cautiously approached his athletic, educational, and career ambitions is largely informed by his experience as a 1.5-generation Caribbean Canadian, one who was still very strongly connected to his mother and grandparents. He looked to them for guidance, willingly complied with their expectations of him, and was comfortable with their living vicariously through him:

Both my grandparents always talked about not being able to achieve because they had to work from when they were younger in order to build this. So, they built something, and then my mom moved a step forward. She was able to build something, but she didn't get her university education either. And she is encouraging me because she sees it every day in her workplace, where, as long as you have that piece of paper, you are able to get more money and are able to make decisions. Although she has the brains to do things, they just don't respect you unless you have that, so that's my encouragement, that's what I remember, and that's what I am doing right now. (October 2001)

Like his parents and many other immigrants (see Anisef & Kilbride, 2003; Gitlin, Buendia, Crosland, & Fode, 2003; Li, 2001), Mark was convinced that having "brains," as he did, and education – with "that piece of paper" as evidence – would ultimately enable him to make money and gain respect in society. He made this point repeatedly throughout the interview, demonstrating how he was taking agency and implementing a plan of action.

A Plan of Action and Opportunities for Success: "I Cling to My Roots"

While Mark made pursuing his university education a priority, he also had a short-term plan to pursue a career in track and field, especially since he had been "doing well [in track] at the national and international levels." Mark had also been participating in an athletic club while in university, and his achievements and the support he was receiving made him feel confident that devoting about eight years to a career in athletics was a possibility. As he said: "We reach our peak at the age of, say, around twenty-eight, and I am twenty years old."

It seems somewhat contradictory that Mark would talk about investing so much time in sports, especially when he understands the precarity of an athletic career. Is it possible that he is like the other Black Caribbean-Canadian youth who see sport as their ticket to success (James, 2003) – those from whom he had previously distanced himself? Perhaps not. Through sport, Mark was able to stay connected to his "roots," become nationally and internationally known, and gain respect. Reflecting on the supports he received from Trinidad, Mark stated,

> This past summer [2002], I competed as a junior, meaning under twenty, at the national level here. I won Canadian junior nationals, and I was in contact with one of the coaches in Trinidad ... And I was asking him if I could be a part of the Trinidad team to compete at the Pan Am Junior games in Argentina. I wanted to compete for Canada, but Canada was charging ... So, you had to come up with [money] to run for Canada, and Trinidad was going to pay for me to go for free. So, after telling him that I achieved this and this, and these were my PBs [personal best] before, they were very grateful to have me on the team. They did a whole story in the newspaper; I had a whole big article on me in the newspapers there. I went down and travelled with the team and I was there with the team, and I saw some of my friends from here who were competing for Canada, and it was kind of weird. This year I'm going to the Commonwealth Games for Trinidad and to another competition in the States.[8]

It is worth noting that I interviewed Mark in the fall following his participation and success in the Pan American Junior games and the publicity he received in Trinidad. With his enhanced reputation, it is understandable that Mark would feel confident that a career in track

---

8 In our follow-up conversation (March 2004), Mark reported that he was injured and was unable to go to these competitions.

was a possibility and within his reach. This success might help explain his passionate identification as a Trinidadian – not the fact that he had only been living in Canada for seven years. For him, Trinidad might not have been able to provide the education he sought, but it gave him the opportunity to pursue his athletic career – one based on a talent uncovered in Canada, ironically, as he adjusted to school life there.

Given that gaining a position on a national sport team was more achievable in Trinidad than in Canada, it made sense for Mark to use his Trinidadian contacts to seize the opportunity to run for that country. Mark had expressed a similar logic earlier, when he spoke of the benefits he gained from having attended one of the smaller high schools in Canada. He said then that he was known at the school and was "not just one of many [students] who are talented."

Ostensibly, Mark accepted that Trinidad and Canada were both useful and important to his ambitions. It was not that he did not feel some affinity to Canada or rejected Canada as home – indeed, he admitted feeling "weird" upon seeing his friends compete for Canada while he competed for Trinidad. Instead, his comments reflect his practicality, pragmatism, and criticism of the way Canada treated athletes like him. He reasoned,

> If Canada was to support their athletes the way that other countries do, then people would want to compete for them [Canada]. But if you have other options, you should explore them. Similar to what Ato Boldon did, he was American, and he decided to run for Trinidad, and that was my decision. And Ato just happens to be one of my role models.

I asked Mark, if Canada offered the same opportunities as Trinidad, would he then run for Canada? He replied,

> It's a very, very tough question, but I already know that Canada doesn't have the finances to do that, and they never will. So, I would stay with Trinidad. You are asking me to totally blank out the fact that I know that Canada cannot do it. I would still run for Trinidad if it was even. [*Why?*] Because I cling more to my roots there.

I pursued this line of questioning, seeking to ascertain whether racism was a factor in why Mark "clung to his roots" or why he might reject Canada as home. He said, "I think both societies are almost the same with multiculturalism and stuff like that. The white culture here is more dominant obviously, but I haven't experienced any racism here, so I can't say that." Later, to a series of questions, he added:

MARK: I don't see colours when I see people, I see people. So, I look at the way people react to me. Sometimes you see, like, say, you're walking down the street at nighttime, you see the differences or reactions. I don't really see racism as a factor in Canada; at least not in my neighbourhood or where I was raised.

CARL: *And do you ever see in the future that race could possibly influence your life chances?*

MARK: No.

CARL: *Do you think racism could make it difficult, or become a barrier for you in the future?*

MARK: Not in the field of sports, no.

CARL: *Why?*

MARK: Because in the field of sports, we all follow the same rules, and it's a level playing field. That's why Jesse Owens was able to showcase his talents.

CARL: *And you think Canada compared to the US could give a Black person the same opportunities as the US gave to Jesse Owens?*

MARK: The US gives more financial support to their athletes, and that's a known fact. But I think Canada can make something out of you, but they can easily put you down just as Ben Johnson was. They can lift you up to making a lot of money and being a well-known figure as Donovan Bailey, but they can easily put you down the same way.

CARL: *So, do you have any fear of that?*

MARK: No. I need to make my right decisions. I'll make the right decisions when they come up.

CARL: *You sound very confident. Why are you so confident?*

MARK: You can't beat destiny. (October 2001)[9]

Like many Canadians, Mark understood Canada to be multicultural, and as he put it, "almost the same" as Trinidad. This thinking likely stems from his belief that after six years in Canada, he had managed to maintain his "Trinidadian" culture. Such imagined cultural maintenance is consistent with the premise of the multicultural discourse, which holds that assimilation to Canadian culture is not necessary, and that racial and ethnic minoritized group members are "free" to indulge in "their" cultural practices. The idea that culture is static and demarcated by such things as the national, racial, and

---

9 In the follow-up interview (March 2004), Mark noted, "I wouldn't be so confident if asked this question again. Let's just say, if you have talent, you should use it to the best of your abilities."

ethnic affiliation and origins of minoritized group members underlies this premise.

At the same time, we have the claim that in Canada individuals are not identified by race or skin colour, nor are their opportunities and achievements mediated by these characteristics (Dei & Calliste, 2000; James, 2003). Mark's "colour-blindness" and belief that racism will have no effect on his ability to realize his ambitions are consistent with Canada's multicultural discourse, something he has obviously incorporated into his belief system as a Canadian resident (see also Minichiello, 2001).

Mark's belief that equal opportunity existed in sport[10] matches his coached sport values; it is also informed by the broader multiculturalism discourse and the related notion of colour-blindness, which permeate Canadian society (Reitz, Breton, Dion, & Dion, 2009). Like many other athletes, especially marginalized young people looking to make it big in sport, Mark displayed his optimism, faith, and belief that he would be assessed and rewarded with opportunities to compete solely on the basis of his skills, abilities, and competence in track. Accordingly, Mark believed that regardless of skin colour, his success in sport is possible because he "made the right decisions" and it is his "destiny" (see James, 2005b).

Ironically, while Mark claimed to be colour-blind, and to not "really see racism as a factor in Canada," the individuals he mentioned when discussing equal opportunities – Ben Johnson and Donovan Bailey – were Black young men who, like himself, were of Caribbean origin. Furthermore, while saying that opportunities exist in Canada for athletes to "make something" of themselves – that is, make "a lot of money" and become "well known" – he also admitted that "they [implying non-Black Canadians] can easily put you down the same way." With these illustrations, Mark was actually alluding to the fact that structurally, race does matter in Canada. Thus, contrary to his own stated view, Mark was indeed "seeing" colour and was alluding to the racialized ways structures operate in affecting individuals' outcomes.

On the surface, Mark's assertions that he did not "see colour" and had not "experienced any racism here" can be considered contradictory. In fact, his "blindness" to colour and racism allowed him to maintain – and expect to continue maintaining – his self-confidence and conviction

---

10 In making this point, Mark asserted that "it's a level playing field," and that is why it was possible for Jesse Owens, a Black American, to succeed in his sport. In referencing Owens, Mark was indicating that race was not a barrier because athletes "all follow the same rules."

that he could achieve what he sought in Canada. Mark was expressing confidence that he understood how the system works and was therefore able to effectively navigate racist structures that would otherwise bar his success. He was not actually colour-blind; rather, with his youthful optimism, immigrant drive, Trinidad-referenced, 1.5-generation Caribbean-Canadian identity – like many other immigrant, marginalized Black youth – Mark believed he could *sidestep* the structural barriers created by racism, and with his high performance in education and athletics, he would be able to realize his ambitions *despite* the barriers. After all, as he said, "You can't beat destiny" (see Anisef, Axelrod, Baichman, James, & Turrittin, 2000; Desai & Subramanian, 2003; James, 2003, 2005b; Seat, 2003).

Summing Up: "You Can't Beat Destiny"

> Growing up, my mom would always encourage me not to follow people, first of all not to follow this group, not to follow this person because they are doing something. Do what you think is right. So, in that sense I was sort of pushed into being one who makes my own decisions and doesn't like to follow. In another sense, I always liked the thought of being somebody who is known for something, who is notable and who can be recognized, so I am forming my own destiny, and I like that idea. (October 2001)

After more than six years in Canada, Mark proffered that he is Trinidadian – "I feel like I am a Trini" – but that he liked being in Canada: "Canada has been great." His Trinidadian identification seemed to be related to what Trinidad had offered him: a good grounding in and respect for education, and the opportunity to participate in national and international athletic activities as he worked towards realizing his athletic aspirations. He also noted that during his formative years in Trinidad, he learned the fundamentals of discipline, respect, and politeness, which he claimed his Canadian peers did not have. His treasured skills and mindset, established in Trinidad, appear to explain his feelings for the country.

Seemingly then, Mark's identification with Trinidad stems from the sense of self and accomplishments that Trinidad offered him and does not necessarily reflect a rejection of Canada. After all, Canada enabled him to escape the "rat-race of Trinidad"; attend a school where his latent athletic talents were revealed, tested, and nurtured; and attend university, where he was able to pursue the necessary education for his career in "sports medicine." And in 2000, just as his "role model" Ato Boldon did in the United States, Mark enrolled in university in

Canada, where he is training to compete in both national and international sport arenas.

Mark's seeming reluctance to identify as a Canadian likely relates to what he does *not* wish to become. He does not want to be like his Canadian-born (second-generation) peers of Caribbean origin, whom he viewed as fitting a stereotype: putting sport before their education, doing poorly in their academic work, and paying more attention to their coaches' advice than to that of their parents, with whom they tended to have strained relationships. For Mark, pursuing his interest in sport was never going to come at the expense of his academic work, for he wanted his mother and grandparents to be proud of him. It did not matter to him that his mother did not "have the time to come and watch" him run: "I'm not one of those who would be angry. She is a busy woman. She is trying to handle all the finances and be responsible for everything. So, she is proud, and she supports me anyway" (October 2002).

In taking his mother's advice not to accept athletic scholarships to US universities, Mark was showing how much he appreciated the time, effort, and money that she and his grandparents had invested in him and demonstrating that he felt morally obligated to meet their expectations. Mark presented as a practical, pragmatic, careful, and cautious young man who wanted to be known not because he fit the stereotypes but because he broke the stereotypes, exercised agency in establishing his own meaning in life, and demonstrated leadership. As he said,

> Well, I think most people are searching for their own meaning and essence in life. They want to be noted for something, whether it be in your studies or in your field or profession. I want to be noted for my athletic career, or if that doesn't work out, then at least people can remember me as being able to achieve in school and achieve on the field.

That Mark recognized the stereotypes and essentialism that apply to Black youth and took steps to contradict and challenge them indicate that he was certainly not oblivious to individual and systemic racism as they might affect him. Here the "double-consciousness" about which Du Bois (1994) writes in relation to Black Americans could be applied to how Mark, as a Black Canadian, understood and dealt with racism, knowing it could pose a barrier to achieving his career ambitions. This double-consciousness is a "peculiar sensation, a sense of always looking at one's self through the eyes of others," and a feeling of "twoness – an American, a Negro; two souls, two thoughts, two unreconciled strivings; two warring ideals in one dark body, whose dogged strength alone keeps it from being torn asunder" (Du Bois, 1994, p. 3).

The duality and "dogged strength" that Mark revealed could be understood as his consciousness that racism exists, while simultaneously pretending that it would not stand as an obstacle to his success. Such a conceptualization must be understood in relation to Mark's experience as a 1.5-generation Caribbean Canadian who has not yet become cynical about the opportunities available in Canada. Mark's confidence and optimism that racism does not present an insurmountable barrier might be explained by the fact that, at the time of writing, he had lived in Canada for only about seven years, had the support and example of his immigrant mother, siblings, and grandparents, with whom he had a close relationship, and had achieved some successes. Hence, Mark viewed his future in Canada as secure, because it is his destiny.

The double-consciousness is also evident in Mark's sense of home. If home is the place where comfort and confidence are nurtured, where safety, security, and stability are provided, and where a world perspective is formulated and sustained, then for Mark, as a diasporic Canadian, and specifically as a 1.5-generation Caribbean Canadian, home necessarily involves a combination of his "two worlds" – Trinidad and Canada. We must understand Mark's constructed story/ies of his life, identity/ies, and aspirations through his understanding and imagination of both societies. The "twoness" or duality is represented in his perception of Trinidad as his birthplace, or "roots," a place that provided the foundational values upon which he had built his life and aspirations, a place of belonging and cultural reference; and Canada as his place of residence, a place he "likes" that "has been great" to him, a place that has provided and continues to provide the opportunities on which he can base his future.

This conceptualization means that home is not a fixed entity, space, or place with boundaries or borders, but a fluid construction that informs and mediates an individual's life-stage, context, and situation. Within this context, Mark's identification as a "Trini" representing his Trinidadian roots and his Canadian existence should not be seen as confusing, erroneous, or irreconcilable. The strength of this duality gives him sustenance and nurtures his ambitions and his sense of home, as demonstrated in the comfort, confidence, stability, and security he expressed in his "feelings" about his life and future.

Addendum 1

In March 2004, more than three years after I first interviewed him, I showed Mark the earlier version of this essay for his comments on my reading of his life narrative. I also wanted him to further consider his consent for me to tell his story, since his subsequent national profile in sport along with his unique status as a 1.5-generation Caribbean Canadian would make it difficult to strictly maintain his anonymity. As Sparkes (2000) points out, it is difficult in a biographical study "to disguise somebody when they have a national profile in a specific sport" and at the same time provide the necessary and sufficient details or "thick description" for the individual to be recognizable to himself and to others (p. 20).

When he returned the essay a day later on his way to track practice, Mark and I talked at length about its content and his many notes, which explained or rationalized his earlier comments and updated his activities further. He stated that he was comfortable with the essay's content and agreed to my submitting it for publication. We then spoke about his education and athletic activities. He reported that he was doing well in university and still working towards his degree in psychology and kinesiology, with the expectation of going into medicine afterwards. His mother by then had moved to Europe, and he continued to live with his siblings who were also in university. He revealed that he visited Trinidad annually to see his grandparents and had recently competed in the OUA (Ontario University Athletics) indoor track meet and won his event. He figured that making the Canadian team would be "out of reach" for him given the standard here.

In his notes on the essay and the points he reiterated in our conversation, Mark pointed out that he identifies as a "Trini" because he thinks that "there is no real Canadian identity." He continued:

> I think Canada is about two or three generations away from a true national identity. Many people you speak with in Toronto rarely say they are Canadians. They're born somewhere in Europe, and family is from somewhere in Asia or the Caribbean. Canada is different from the US where national identity is firmly established.

He emphasized that it was not that he did not like Canada; in fact, he said he does not think he would return to live in Trinidad, except "maybe just to vacation for a month." Thus, Canada, a country where he believes he will be able to realize his dreams while identifying as a "Trini," remains home for Mark. The imagined culture and identity he insisted he has retained can be regarded as representative of the Canadian cultural value system. Given the complexity and elusiveness of culture, Mark, like many Canadians, will continue to live his Canadian "imagined Trini" existence while culturally participating and integrating successfully into our society. He showed this by his keen knowledge of Canada's societal structures and how to navigate them, as well as his questioning of the existence of a national cultural identity. In essence, despite his insistence otherwise, Mark has learned to be culturally Canadian, and he lives as such.

Part 2: Life as a Young Adult with Work and Family

Using data from follow-up interviews with Mark (December 2007 and June 2013), I examined his account of his achievements to date and his explanation of how he negotiated Canada's educational, athletic, social, and economic systems to become the person he is today. And as I had done with earlier essays about him, I sent Mark the essay for his comment.

Recall that a major theme that emerged from Mark's earlier interviews is that he came to Canada "for two reasons: to live with [my mother] and to make a better future for myself" (June 2002). For Mark, as he said in his third interview (December 2007), this meant having a "second chance" at schooling, because just before emigrating he was not applying himself to his education in Trinidad. He reasoned: "Either I do what I did in Trinidad and fail or turn things around ... Immigration motivated me to take advantage of the opportunities I knew I had here" (June 2013). With this commitment to make his "second chance" prove valuable for him, and with a commitment or obligation to his mother, Mark applied himself to his school work – taking advantage of the educational and athletic opportunities that his Canadian schooling provided while remembering and using his Trinidad-inspired and socialized values and aspirations to keep him focused on his educational and career ambitions. He stated, "My history in Trinidad made me seek out excellence; and Canada has given me opportunities and a greater perspective on the world" (June 2013).

Further, Mark continued to point out how he is "different" from his Canadian-born peers, in that he was more committed to his academic work than they were, he was not going to excel in sport at the expense of his academic work, and his personal and familial values and aspirations gave him the confidence and optimism he needed to succeed in Canadian society.

Mark again cited his earlier decision not to accept an athletic scholarship to a US university – especially one that was not "respected" – since doing so would not have been to his benefit. Mark justified his decisions by citing his family's social and economic situation – one that meant he had to work during his high school and university years to help his mother "pay the utility bills." He maintained that his commitment to his education was premised on not wanting to struggle financially as an adult (December 2007). Mark echoed the same sentiment in his subsequent interview (June 2013), noting that he could not afford to take his schooling opportunities for granted because

> my mother had two sons and was making $30,000 a year. I saw her struggle, and I decided that I wasn't going to have to struggle that way. I was going to work hard knowing that I was always representing my race.

He continued:

> My mother ... expressed to me and my brother that we were always to do the right thing; [and she] made sure we knew that it was going to be a harder time for us because of our skin colour ... She said, you have to work double hard; and that was something that we accepted; and we took it as a personal challenge. She made us aware that ... I was always to be maybe one step ahead of my competition. (June 2013)

In addition to doing "the right thing" and working "double hard" to keep "ahead of [the] competition," Mark had support from his teachers and coaches, who became his role models and mentors. In earlier interviews, Mark talked of his Black Caribbean-Canadian female teacher who would "give [him] pep talks and try to keep [him] on the right track" and his Black male teacher who was the coach who introduced him to sport and would insist on Mark taking his academic work seriously. In the third interview Mark also mentioned his math teacher, an "Italian man" whom he credited with his success in mathematics; and after graduating with a degree in kinesiology, Mark now teaches mathematics at a high school with a special sport-focus program. Similarly, he credited his hurdles coach for his success in sport and his coaching career today.

Mark affirmed that these teachers – in particular, the males – played a significant role in his life. They were not only teachers and coaches, but also life coaches who provided support and guidance so that he developed a healthy demeanour by focusing on his educational and athletic career ambitions. For as Mark admitted in the fourth interview: "I was an angry, very angry and aggressive kid. My father was not around. I wanted support like what I saw my friends getting. I had a real attitude." He conceded that these teachers and coach and his mother helped him to harness his aggression "and channel my anger in the right way" (June 2013).

While Mark never said it directly, we can assume that, for him, sport offered a way to manage his anger and aggression in an appropriate and legitimate space where his coach – fittingly, a Black male coach – seemingly served as a substitute father (James, 2005b). These adults – his coach and his other teachers and mother and grandparents – were people whom, as Mark would come to admit, he wanted "to impress." Speaking mostly in the second person, his words were: "You should have somebody in my life that you do not want to disappoint or who you want to impress" (June 2013).

Mark willingly complied with the expectations that these significant adults had for him, and he has kept in touch with them. As for his mother and grandparents, whose aspirations and belief in what was possible in Canada Mark seemed to have internalized, he remained immensely loyal. Mark understood that, ultimately, they were the ones, like many immigrant parents, whose efforts were pivotal to the agency he has been able to exercise, the plan of action he established, and the path to his achievements he has followed (James & Taylor, 2008).

Conclusion

By our last conversation, Mark – by then an employed teacher, husband, and father of a seven-month-old daughter – declared: "I feel Canadian. Canada has been good to me." Nevertheless, he remained cognizant of the fact that because of racism he had to "work double hard" to stay "one step ahead of [his] competition" to realize his ambitions. He credited his achievements to date to his knowledge of how "the system works" and his ability to effectively navigate the racist structures that operate as barriers for people like him.

In keeping with his belief in education as a primary means by which he will stay ahead of his competition and attain his aspirations, at the time of the interview Mark was pursing his master's degree in education. Interestingly, while he did not "get into sports medicine" as he originally desired – a career to which many youth aspire, frequently with parental encouragement because of its prestige (James, 2010; James & Taylor, 2008) – Mark continued in a sports-related career. That Mark was able to map out his career trajectory in his early high school years and attain it in some form reflects his foresight, self-knowledge, adaptability, and determination to "make something" of himself.

Addendum 2

Upon completion of this final version of his narrative, I sent it to "Mark" for his comments. Here is his email response.

From: "Mark"@gmail.com
Sent: Tuesday, January 15, 2019 11:11 AM
To: Carl Everton James CJames@yorku.ca
Subject: Mark's thoughts Jan 15, 2019

Hi Carl,

WOW! What a journey it has been. I remember our first interview in the early 2000s. I had no doubt I would be an Olympian. I was a very confident athlete. Haha! While I didn't quite make the Olympic standard, I took everything that I could from the sport. I travelled to different parts of the world, worked with international coaches, made great contacts, and learned the intimate details of my sport. Now as a coach, teacher, and parent, it has all come full circle. My experiences and my knowledge can be shared to impact future generations.

What stood out to me from the essay was my wisdom on knowing that a good education would be the key to my future. I analyzed all the information available to me before deciding to stay in Canada. It was not an impulsive decision. I think my career path benefitted greatly from staying in Canada. I was lucky to have some great role models of all races – teachers and coaches who inspired me to pursue the highest standards and who motivated me to see potential I could not even dream of. The message I share now with students is that sport is a pathway to a better education. In my teaching experience, the Canadian identity hasn't changed in all this time. It's still just a mix of cultures in the mosaic. Immigrant students cling to their cultures and Canadian students always mention their family's cultural backgrounds.

My identity is Trini-Canadian. As mentioned in the essay, my cultural values are mostly because of my upbringing in Trinidad. My drive and work ethic are also part of my Trinidadian experiences in a competitive climate. As a working adult now, I see Canada as this multicultural society, and I embrace everything it has to offer. My three kids were all born here. Canada has given me many opportunities but as a minority, I experience the burden of having to be conscious of my race at all times. I know that I stand out in the workplace, in small rural towns, even in some fancy restaurants. As mentioned many years ago, it is my purpose in life to defy the stereotypes and to continue to break barriers to improve race relations in our society.

Thank you,

"Mark," MEd, ChPC
NCCP Level 4

The pedagogical process is to steer students toward independence and mastery.
– Dan Pfaff

REFERENCES

Agnew, V. (2003). *Where I come from.* Waterloo, ON: Wilfrid Laurier University Press.

Anisef, P., Axelrod, P., Baichman, E., James, C.E., & Turrittin, A. (2000). *Opportunities and uncertainties: Life course experiences of the class of '73.* Toronto, ON: University of Toronto Press.

Anisef, P., & Kilbride, K. (Eds.). (2003). *Managing two worlds: The experiences and concerns of immigrant youth in Ontario.* Toronto, ON: Canadian Scholars' Press.

Berns-McGown, R. (2013). *I am Canadian: Challenging stereotypes about young Somali Canadians.* IRPP study no. 38. Montreal, QC: Institute for Research on Public Policy.

Boyd, M., & Grieco, E.M. (1998). Triumphant transitions: Socioeconomic achievements of the second generation in Canada. *International Migration Review, 32*(4), 853–76. https://doi.org/10.1177/019791839803200401

Coleman, P.G. (1991). Aging and life history: The meaning of reminiscence in late life. In S. Dex (Ed.), *Life and history analysis: Qualitative and quantitative developments* (pp. 124–36). New York, NY: Routledge.

Dei, G.S., & Calliste, A. (Eds.). (2000). *Power, knowledge and anti-racism education.* Halifax, NS: Fernwood.

Denzin, N.K. (1996). *Interpretive ethnography: Ethnographic practices for the 21st century.* London, UK: Sage.

Desai, S., & Subramanian, S. (2003). Colour culture and dual consciousness: Issues identified by South Asian immigrant youth in the Greater Toronto Area. In P. Anisef & K. Kilbride (Eds.), *Managing two worlds: The experiences and concerns of immigrant youth in Ontario* (pp. 118–61). Toronto, ON: Canadian Scholars' Press.

Du Bois, W.E.B. (1994). *The souls of Black folk.* New York, NY: Dover.

Flyvbjerg, B. (2011). Case study. In N.K. Denzin & Y.S. Lincoln (Eds.), *The Sage handbook of qualitative research* (pp. 1–20). Thousand Oaks, CA: Sage.

Foner, N. (1997). The immigrant family: Cultural legacies and cultural changes. *International Migration Review, 32*(4), 961–74. https://doi.org/10.1177/019791839703100407

Fuligni, A.J. (2001). A comparative longitudinal approach to acculturation among children from immigrant families. *Harvard Educational Review, 71*(3), 566–78. https://doi.org/10.17763/haer.71.3.j7046h63234441u3

Garrod, A.C., Smulyan, L., Powers, S.I., & Kilkenny, R. (2002). *Adolescent portraits: Identity, relationships and challenges.* Boston, MA: Allyn and Bacon.

Gilgun, J.F. (2005). Qualitative research and family psychology. *Journal of Family Psychology, 19*(1), 40–50. https://doi.org/10.1037/0893-3200.19.1.40

Gitlin, A., Buendia, E., Crosland, K., & Fode, D. (2003). The production of margin and center: Welcoming-unwelcoming of immigrant students.

American Educational Research Journal, 40(1), 91–122. https://doi.org/10.3102/00028312040001091

Handa, A. (2003). *Of silk saris and mini-skirts: South Asian girls walk the tightrope of culture.* Toronto, ON: Women's Press.

Henry, A. (1998). *Taking back control: African Canadian women teachers: Lives and practice.* Albany, NY: State University of New York Press.

Henry, F. (1994). *The Caribbean diaspora in Toronto: Learning to live with racism.* Toronto, ON: University of Toronto Press.

Humphreys, A. (1999, December 23). Guyana doesn't want dumped deportees. *National Post,* pp. A1, 7.

James, C.E. (2001). Encounters in race, ethnicity and language. In C.E. James & A. Shadd (Eds.), *Talking about identity: Encounters in race, language and identity* (pp. 1–8). Toronto, ON: Between the Lines.

James, C.E. (2002). Achieving desire: Narrative of a Black male teacher. *International Journal of Qualitative Studies in Education, 15*(2), 171–86. https://doi.org/10.1080/09518390110111901

James, C.E. (2003). Schooling, basketball and U.S. scholarship aspirations of Canadian student athletes. *Race, Ethnicity and Education, 6*(2), 123–44. https://doi.org/10.1080/13613320308198

James, C.E. (2005a). "I feel like a Trini": Narrative of a generation-and-a-half Canadian. In V. Agnew (Ed.), *Diaspora, memory and identity: A search for home* (pp. 230–53). Toronto, ON: University of Toronto Press.

James, C.E. (2005b). *Race in play: Understanding the socio-cultural worlds of student athletes.* Toronto, ON: Canadian Scholars' Press.

James, C.E. (2010). Schooling and the university plans of immigrant Black students from an urban neighborhood. In H.R. Milner (Ed.) *Culture, curriculum, and identity in education* (pp. 117–39). New York, NY: Palgrave Macmillan.

James, C.E. (2013). "This is my home": Narrative of a 1.5 generation Caribbean Canadian [Paper presentation]. 15th National Conference of Metropolis, Ottawa, ON.

James, C.E., & Taylor, L. (2008). "Education will get you to the station": Marginalized students' experiences and perceptions of merit in accessing university. *Canadian Journal of Education, 31*(3), 567–90. https://journals.sfu.ca/cje/index.php/cje-rce/article/view/3013/2301

Li, J. (2001). Expectations of Chinese immigrant parents for their children's education: The interplay to Chinese tradition and the Canadian context. *Canadian Journal of Education, 26*(1), 477–94. https://doi.org/10.2307/1602178

Lincoln, Y.S. (1993). I and Thou: Method, voice, and roles in research with the silenced. In D. McLaughlin & W.G. Tierney (Eds.), *Naming silenced lives: Personal narratives and the process of educational change* (pp. 29–50). New York, NY: Routledge.

Louie, V. (2001). The role of social class in the educational experiences of 1.5- and second-generation Chinese Americans. *Harvard Educational Review*, 71(3), 438–74. https://doi.org/10.17763/haer.71.3.lv51475vjk600h38

Mascoll, P. (1999, December 8). Their fair day in court: Born in Jamaica, the three men accused in the death of Georgina Leimonis were a product of Canada. *Toronto Star*, pp. C1, 3.

Minichiello, D. (2001). Chinese voices in a Canadian secondary school landscape. *Canadian Journal of Education*, 26(1), 77–96. https://doi.org/10.2307/1602146

Munro, P. (1998). *Subject to fiction: Some teachers' life narratives and the cultural politics of resistance*. Philadelphia, PA: Open University Press.

Myers, D., & Cranford, C.J. (1998). Temporal differentiation in the occupational mobility of immigrant and native-born Latina workers. *American Sociological Review*, 63(1), 68–93. https://doi.org/10.2307/2657478

Noguera, P.A. (2003). Joaquin's dilemma: Understanding the link between racial identity and school-related behaviours. In M. Sadowski (Ed.), *Adolescents at school: Perspectives on youth, identity, and education* (pp. 19–30). Cambridge, MA: Harvard Education Press.

Norquay, N. (2000). Where is here? *Pedagogy, Culture and Society*, 8(1), 7–21. https://doi.org/10.1080/14681360000200080

Palmer, H. (1997). *"... But where are you really from?": Stories of identity and assimilation in Canada*. Toronto, ON: Sister Vision Press.

Park, K. (1999). "I really do feel I'm 15!" : The construction of self and community by young Korean Americans. *Amerasia Journal*, 25(1), 139–63. https://doi.org/10.17953/amer.25.1.07x6826254g3567w

Plaza, D., & Simmons, A. (1998). Breaking through the glass ceiling: The pursuit of university training among African Caribbean migrants and their children in Toronto. *Canadian Ethnic Studies*, 30(3), 99–120.

Reitz, J.G., Breton, R., Dion, K.K., & Dion, K.L. (2009). *Multiculturalism and social cohesion: Potentials and challenges of diversity*. New York, NY: Springer.

Seat, R. (2003). Factors affecting the settlement and adaptation process of Canadian adolescent newcomers sixteen to nineteen years of age. In P. Anisef & K. Kilbride (Eds.), *Managing two worlds: The experiences and concerns of immigrant youth in Ontario* (pp. 162–95). Toronto, ON: Canadian Scholars' Press.

Shadd, A. (2001). "Where are you really from?": Notes of an "immigrant" from Buxton, Ontario. In C.E. James & A. Shadd (Eds.), *Talking about identity: Encounters in race, language and identity* (pp. 10–16). Toronto, ON: Between the Lines.

Solomon, R.P. (1992). *Forging a separatist culture: Black resistance in high school*. Albany, NY: State University of New York Press.

Sparkes, A.C. (2000). Illness, premature career-termination, and the loss of self: A biographical study of an elite athlete. In R.L. Jones & K.A. Armour

(Eds.), *Sociology of sport: Theory and practice* (pp. 13–32). Harlow, UK: Pearson Education.

Spence, C. (1999). *The skin I'm in: Racism, sport and education*. Halifax, NS: Fernwood.

Statistics Canada. (2003). *Ethnic diversity survey: Portrait of a multicultural society*. Ottawa, ON: Minister of Industry.

Statistics Canada. (2020, February 25). *Canada's Black population: Education, labour and resilience*. Cat. no. 89-657-X2020002. Ottawa, ON: Minister of Industry.

Turcotte, M. (2020, February 25). *Results from the 2016 census: Education and labour market integration of Black youth in Canada*. Statistics Canada cat. no. 75-006-X. Ottawa, ON: Minister of Industry.

van Manen, M. (1990). *Researching lived experience*. Albany, NY: State University of New York Press.

Waters, M.C. (1999). *Black identities: West Indian immigrant dreams and American realities*. Cambridge, MA: Harvard University Press.

Zhou, M. (1997). Segregation assimilation: Issues, controversies, and recent research on the new second generation. *International Migration Review, 31*(4), 975–1008. https://doi.org/10.1177/019791839703100408

Response to Chapter 3

Using Gender to Think Through Migration, Love, and Student Success

AMOABA GOODEN

Chair and Associate Professor, Department of Pan-African Studies, Kent State University, Ohio, USA

Between 1965 and the early 2000s – motivated by desire and love, as well as economic and political disruptions in their homelands – thousands of African-Caribbean migrant women, like Mark's mom, left their homes in search of a better life or to reunite with family members. This large movement of African-Caribbean people into Canada altered Canada's political and cultural landscapes and ultimately changed the face of the country. More than 500,000 Caribbean immigrants arrived in Canada between 1967 and 2001 as "landed immigrants," bringing the Black population to over one million by 2016 (Statistics Canada, 2017).

Unlike other migrant groups to Canada, Black Caribbean women outnumbered Caribbean men (Crawford, 2018). Mark's mother, "Brenda," like the majority of Black Caribbean women, migrated alone and not as an appendage to a male partner. As a result of both the labour demands of the receiving country and a lack of opportunity in their home countries, Caribbean women saw migration as a viable option to overcome poverty. Many women, like Brenda, left behind children with family members and/or "othermothers" as a survival strategy (see Baldwin & Mortley, 2016; Crawford, 2018). According to Baldwin and Mortley (2016), for some Caribbean women, the act of migrating is powered by love.

From Mark's narrative we can see how his mother manifested her love by leaving her children in the loving care of her parents, but this was not the case for many children. After many years, these children, like Mark and his brother, would join their parent(s) once jobs and a place to live were secured, along with enough savings to support a family. This model demonstrates how gender shaped Brenda's migration process – migration, settlement, transnational mothering, reunification. This process influenced Mark's experience of migration, settlement, and identity. Mark's narrative, then, must be understood within the context of his mother's love, her temporary transnational mothering, and her strategy of using migration to seek a better life for herself and her sons.

Mark's settlement in Canada must be foregrounded from this gendered perspective. First, we must centre Mark's experience alongside his mother's, particularly given his mother's racialized and feminized position in the global economy as a woman of colour. Brenda "resisted exploitation and created counternarratives that have contributed to [Mark's] new epistemologies of belonging and citizenship" in Canada (Crawford, 2018, p. 36).

Clearly, given Mark's comment that he knew things would be difficult in Canada because of his skin colour, Brenda taught her sons to be race-conscious and to be aware that race would play a part in how they would be treated. Mark used his mother's racialized and gendered experience to refute Western colonial ideas of racism and to create his own counternarrative, with education serving as a tool to overcome discrimination. For instance, Mark highlights his mother's struggle in the workplace because she lacked a postsecondary degree. His counternarrative was to "win" for himself and his mother. We see this in his decision to prioritize a postsecondary degree over sports, by choosing to attend a recognized Canadian institution rather than a smaller college in the United States, and in his focus on doing well in university. His path highlights how immigrants often navigate existing racialized power structures as they strive to win in spite of these structures (Procter, 2004). Mark intentionally frames his story as both powerless (his mother's lack of a university degree) and powerful (his own degree and success). This is radical in that it foregrounds his agency and ability to overcome forms of discrimination alongside his mother's experiences in the workplace.

Not surprisingly, Mark's narrative pulls us into conversation with feminist scholars such as Patricia Hill Collins (2002) and Mary Chamberlain (2003), both of whom have theorized about the importance of "othermothers" in Black communities. The Pan-African-based practice of "othermothers" emerged out of the colonial era as a tradition that supports family members and/or non-blood relatives caring for a child. "Othermothering" is often practised when women are pushed out of their homes to seek work – evident in the way Mark was raised by his grandmother for about five years after his mother migrated.

Another example of "othermothers" appears in the form of Mark's Grade 8 teacher, herself a migrant from the Caribbean. According to Hill Collins (2002), "othermothering" is a practice embedded within racialized and class formations and speaks to the ways Black women care for or nurture others. Mark clearly recognized his teacher's care as a form of nurturing and welcomed it in shaping his own identity and expectations. While we do not know if this teacher claimed feminism as a radical approach to social transformation, her radical love in a colonial Canadian education setting speaks to the ways Black women often shape caregiving practices and use them as radical extension of a kind of feminist consciousness. They recognize the negative impact that socialization structures can have on the life changes of African-descended people and offer care and love in extraordinary ways.

Reading Mark's narrative and his email response, I reflected on my own experiences as a 1.5-generation immigrant young woman athlete with working-class parents. I also thought deeply on Rhonda George's (2020) article "Holding It Down? The Silencing of Black Female Students in the Educational Discourse of the Greater Toronto Area." I wondered about the differences between my experiences and Mark's. George's research and my own experiences raise some important questions about the knowledge gaps and silence in the academic scholarship relating to the experiences of Black female students. While we know that there are "common" differences, which are grounded in historical complexities, we also know that racialized girls and boys experience migration and settlement differently.

For example, like Black men and boys, Black women and girls in Canada have historically faced and are currently facing a "pervasive violence associated with systems of domination which [views their] Black bodies as less than, deviant, hypervisible and simultaneously invisible" (Mullings, Gooden, & Brown Spencer, in press, p. 1). We see this, for example, when a six-year-old girl in Mississauga, Ontario, was handcuffed in 2017, or when a high school teacher in the late 1980s thought it was funny to throw a golf ball down my friend's top, or in the ways that sporting opportunities were offered primarily to Black boys when I was in high school. As Mullings, Gooden, and Brown Spencer (in press) point out, these systems of domination, which include sexism, racism, and classism, "are part of a long history of colonial violence, and their impact on Black bodies are extensive" (p. 1; see also Stein, 2018). According to Crawford (2018), we understand these experiences as intersectional inequities that occur along gender, race, class, and citizenship lines, and that contribute to devaluing people of African descent.

Although we are both racialized immigrants, my experience as a high school female athlete was very different from Mark's. For example, I was very much aware of the differential treatment given to the young male athletes – they got most of our coaches' attention. My high school coaches spent much more time training and supporting male athletes than they did the female athletes. At co-ed events, such as track and field meets, the boys were coached, encouraged, and cared for in ways the female athletes were not. Boys were given advice on cool-downs, foods to eat after an event, and general guidance on how to keep their bodies at peak performance levels during meets. Most of the female athletes were ignored or treated in ambivalent ways. And there were the inherent tensions and struggles of being female athletes, because as James (2005) notes, quoting his research respondent, Alicia: "on the court you are a basketball player ... off the court [I am expected] to carry myself as a woman" (p. 128). According to James "for males, being an athlete is 'so much easier' [quoting Alicia] and more convenient, whereas for Alicia (and others like her), they have to contend with a dual existence or two 'selves' – athlete and woman – which do not seem to cohabit easily in the same body at the same time" (p. 129).

Along with most of my Black female teammates, I experienced "trickle-down equality" which, as George (2020) explains, occurs "when the level of attention and resources put into Black female students is far less than what is put into their male counterparts" (p. 46). But there are "specific ways that Black students are experiencing their schooling" (p. 50); and while there is specificity – as the ways Mark experienced his schooling and athletic pursuits indicate – there are also commonalities, leading to questions about what experiences are similar across genders for Black boys and girls. What were the differences between my experience and Mark's in relation to sports? What were the similarities? How do class, migration, and place of birth intersect to create different or similar experiences? Answers to these questions will give us a more nuanced understanding of the migratory experiences of the 1.5-generation Caribbean Canadian.

Migration and settlement trajectories (successful or not) of the 1.5 generation must be understood from a nuanced perspective and by centring the subject's full experiences. For example, using gender, we were able to understand Mark's narrative and subsequent settlement experiences, and how his positionality is intimately intertwined with his mother's love and her decision to use migration as a strategy for success. We are also able to see the various ways that Mark was able to hold his mother's voice and her practice of community – her use of "othermothers," for example – to make decisions about his future. Placing my experience alongside Mark's narrative, we can see that gender – along with the settlement, schooling, and aspirational experiences of Caribbean Canadians – all factor into the experiences of the 1.5 generation.

REFERENCES

Baldwin, A.N., & Mortley, N.K. (2016). Reassessing Caribbean migration: Love, power and (re) building in the diaspora. *Journal of International Women's Studies*, 17(3), 164–76. http://vc.bridgew.edu/jiws/vol17/iss3/14

Chamberlain, M. (2003). Rethinking Caribbean families: Extending the links. *Community, Work & Family*, 6(1), 63–76. https://doi.org/10.1080/1366880032000063905

Crawford, C. (2018). Decolonizing reproductive labor: Caribbean women, migration, and domestic work in the global economy. *The Global South*, 12(1), 33–55. https://doi.org/10.2979/globalsouth.12.1.03

George, R.C. (2020). Holding it down? The silencing of Black female students in the educational discourses of the Greater Toronto Area. *Canadian Journal of Education*, 43(1), 32–58. https://journals.sfu.ca/cje/index.php/cje-rce/article/view/3801

Hill Collins, P. (2002). *Black feminist thought: Knowledge, consciousness, and the politics of empowerment* (2nd ed.). New York, NY: Routledge.

James, C.E. (2005). *Race in play: Understanding the socio-cultural worlds of student athletes*. Toronto, ON: Canadian Scholars' Press.

Mullings, D., Gooden, A., & Brown Spencer, E. (in press). Catch me when I fall! Resiliency, freedom and Black sisterhood in the academy. *Cultural and Pedagogical Inquiry*.

Procter, J. (2004). *Stuart Hall*. Routledge Critical Thinkers. London, UK: Routledge.

Statistics Canada. (2017). *Census profile, 2016 census*. Cat. no. 98-316-X2016001. Ottawa, ON: Minister of Industry. https://www12.statcan.gc.ca/census-recensement/2016/dp-pd/prof/index.cfm?Lang=E

Stein, S. (2018). Confronting the radical-colonial foundations of US higher education. *Journal for the Study of Postsecondary and Tertiary Education*, 3, 77–96. https://doi.org/10.28945/4105

4 Students "at Risk": Stereotypes and the Schooling of Black Boys[1]

Parents and educators in Canadian schools share an ongoing concern about disengagement, poor academic performance, and low educational outcomes by Black male students (Abada & Lin, 2011; Caldas, Bernier, & Marceau, 2009; Codjoe, 2006; James, 2009), and the resulting tendency for them to be identified as youth *at risk* who need special educational supports. "In the name of instilling discipline," as Raby (2002) puts it, the at-risk discourse "justifies mechanisms of social control" (p. 431).

Levin (2004) defines an at-risk student as "one whose past and present characteristics or conditions are associated with a higher risk or probability of failing to obtain desired life outcomes" (p. 2). Often, the at-risk identification tends to be less about Black male students' probable learning needs and more about their deficits – which make learning, along with educational engagement and outcomes, problematic (Wotherspoon & Schissel, 2001). As Wotherspoon and Schissel (2001) argue, "the language of risk can serve as a euphemism for racism, sexism, and biases," based on factors such as class, immigrant status, family makeup, residential neighbourhood, cultural assumptions, and other "risk-inducing" constructs (p. 331). Haberman (as cited in Milner, 2007) explains the problem more broadly, noting, "Language is not an innocent reflection of how we think. The terms we use control our perceptions, shape our understanding, and lead us to particular proposals for improvement" (p. 389).

---

1 An earlier version of this chapter was published in 2012. See James (2012a). Reprinted with the permission of the publisher. This version is revised, updated, and expanded.

Kelly (2000) sees the at-risk discourse as "dangerous," for the process of identifying, mobilizing, and designating youth as *at risk* represents an attempt to regulate and recode "institutionally structured relations" of class, gender, and race in ways that serve to hold Black youth and their parents responsible for circumstances, opportunities, options, and life chances over which they have no or little control (p. 468). Indeed, as Fine (1993) writes in her contribution to the book *Children at Risk in America*, risk is not an abstract or rhetorical construct, but one through which people, groups, and communities are assessed, on the basis of dearly held societal values. Therefore, as the notion of risk increasingly permeates our "daily consciousness, educational practices, and bureaucratic policy-making," we must remember that

> the cultural construction of a group defined through a discourse of risk represents a quite partial image, typically strengthening those institutions and groups that have carved out, severed, denied connection to, and then promised to "save" those who will undoubtedly remain "at risk." (p. 91)

Levin and Peacock (2004) examined Canadian "students at risk" using the "vulnerability index" from the National Longitudinal Study of Children and Youth's (NLSCY), Canada's child poverty rate, and high school dropout rates. They estimated that one-quarter of the student population was at "some definite vulnerability to risk." The researchers identified poverty – assessed on the basis of the students' home situation and neighbourhood – as a major contributor to, and indicator of, the children being or becoming at risk. Individual characteristics found to contribute to an at-risk situation included personality traits such as inability to work effectively with others; lacking a sense of efficacy, autonomy, or resilience; and being disobedient or unable to sit still. The researchers observed that parenting practices such as inconsistent routines for children at home, not monitoring school performance, or not encouraging high educational aspirations also contributed to students' vulnerability to risk. Finally, teachers and administrators contributed to risk through their low expectations of students and their failure to provide needed support and assistance (Levin & Peacock, 2004).

We do need to identify students who are at risk because of their failure to attend school, earn passing grades, comply with school discipline, or productively engage with educational expectations. Such identification could be used to help plan needed interventions for these students (Levin, 2004). To date, however, Canada (and Toronto in particular) show little evidence that current intervention measures have a positive impact on students' "risky" practices and circumstances, particularly for African-Canadian or Black male students. In fact, Black youth account for the most at-risk students because of their continued disengagement from school, poor academic performance, and high rates of absenteeism, suspension, expulsion, and dropping out – due in part to schools' *progressive discipline*[2] policies and practices (Bhattacharjee, 2003; Henry & Tator, 2010).

Why does this situation persist for Black males? Might it be because of educational authorities' persistent disregard for, or unwillingness to acknowledge, race and racism as factors influencing students' gendered schooling and educational experiences – a perspective informed by the colour-blind discourse[3] embedded in and perpetuated by Canada's multiculturalism policy? Such disregard might explain why schooling produces and maintains rather than reduces risk.

I take schooling and education to be different though overlapping processes, and as Shujaa (1993) points out, "you can have one without the other" (p. 328). Schooling, Shujaa writes, "is a process *intended* to perpetuate and maintain the society's existing power relations and the institutional structures" that support socially sanctioned values, norms, and patterns of behaviour that members are expected to learn to fully participate in society. In contrast to schooling, education "is the process of transmitting from one generation to the next the knowledge, values, skills, and traditions that will maintain its culture and ensure its survival" (pp. 330–1). Schooling and education could provide Black youth with the required knowledge and skills[4] to fully and equally participate in society. But this becomes difficult when their experience continues to be informed by the prevailing gendered at-risk discourse.

My intent in this chapter is to reflect on the situation of African-Canadian male youth, who are often categorized as "at-risk" students and whose abilities and behaviours are attributed to their culture. I observe the often unstated components of the at-risk designation – that

---

2 In 2007, the Ontario Ministry of Education acknowledged that its zero tolerance policy "could have a disproportionate impact on students from racialized communities," and as a result the policy was replaced with the "progressive discipline" policy which promotes "in-school detentions, peer mediation, restorative practice, referrals for consultation, and/or transfer [to another school]" (Henry & Tator, 2010, p. 213).

3 In the Canadian discourse, culture, and not race or colour, is believed to account for differences and diversity among people. But the irony is that, in practice, culture is read onto the bodies of those who are racially different, or in Canadian parlance, "visible minorities." By default, race or colour is used to represent difference.

4 Shujaa (1993) lists some of these skills as literacy, numeracy, humanities, technology, critical thinking, "understanding of the political system," and historical knowledge of their own society and others (p. 331).

is, stereotyping and cultural attribution in the social construction of these at-risk males. Through the conceptual lens of cultural analysis and critical race theory, I discuss how a "web of stereotypes" (Howard, 2008) or "confluence of stereotyping" (Hernandez & Davis, 2009) racializes and marginalizes these youth and structures their learning process, social opportunities, life chances, and educational outcomes.

Significantly, along with many scholars, educators, parents, and community members, I have observed that African-Canadian students are frequently cited for disciplinary problems, placed (and in some cases, over-represented) in special education classes as a result of behavioural concerns, and often labelled at risk (Bhattacharjee, 2003; Raby, 2002). I reference the stereotypes of African-Canadian males as *immigrants*,[5] *fatherless, athletes, troublemakers,* and *underachievers,* noting how these stereotypes tend to reflexively frame individuals' perceptions of and discourses about Black youth, and in the process contribute to the very educational and social problems that the at-risk identification is expected to address. Although these stereotypes are discussed separately here, they invariably overlap, intersect, and reinforce one another. Indeed, they form a web in which too many Black people are caught. I consider each stereotype following a discussion of the conceptual lens of cultural analysis and critical race theory in the next section.

Conceptual References

As noted in the introduction to this book, cultural analysis and critical race theory are two useful frames for understanding the lives of Black people. Cultural analysis gives attention to the structures and traditions that we all help to create, which in turn help to produce the circumstances in which individuals find themselves. To fully understand and address the issues being investigated, we need to consider the cultural processes that underlie human interactions rather than merely focus on the individual – to conceive of individuals' problems not simply as a product of their own making but as a product of the cultural worlds they occupy (McDermott & Varenne, 2006).

---

5 While the refugee experience is different from that of immigrants, I will not go into this difference since, for the most part, unless students are from known refugee-producing countries like Somalia, Sudan, and Ethiopia, educators and others tend to treat them as immigrants. Moreover, the vast majority of Black youth have parents and grandparents who came as immigrants – in Toronto, they are mostly from the Caribbean.

Critical race theory makes race and its interlocking relationship with gender, class, and other demographic factors central to any social analysis. As Milner (2008) has written, it is "concerned with disrupting, exposing, challenging and changing racist policies that work to disenfranchise certain groups of people" and in the process "maintain the *status quo*" (p. 333). Both cultural analysis and critical race theory foster a discussion about the intersection of race, gender, and class as they are lived, performed, experienced, and resisted in stratified societies where the culture is shaped, reshaped, and maintained through mechanisms such as racism, sexism, classism, and stereotyping. How then can we leave unexamined race-informed policies and practices that account for Black, Indigenous, and Latinx youth being most often identified as students at risk (Toronto District School Board, 2010), and for them to be over-represented in the criminal justice system (Tanovich, 2006)? In one form or another, our society has produced and continues to produce conditions where race matters; any attempts to reverse its significance or consequences requires acknowledgment of its place in our culture.

In a society where all males' lives are structured by Anglo-white, middle-class, heterosexual masculinity – the socially constructed set of ideals, norms, roles, values, and expectations for and of men (Leach, 1994/2009) – it is expected that boys and men demonstrate and live up to the requisite dominance, strength, aggression, competitiveness, athleticism, and control (Anderson & McCormack, 2010; James, 2009; McCready, 2010). In situations where boys and young men are unable to live up to these masculine norms, invariably, they, as Kimmel (2007) asserts, will be "found wanting" (p. 76).

In the case of Black males, the white hegemonic structure of masculinity against which they are measured not only serves to marginalize and racialize them but also leads to what Kimmel (2007) refers to as "chronic terrors of emasculation, emotional emptiness, and gendered rage that leave a wide swath of destruction in its wake" (p. 75). According to Stevenson (2004), the racialized script that Black males are expected to follow is one "designed within white society's projected fears of Black manhood, not the self-determined efforts, experiences, and potential of Black manhood" (p. 13; see also Walcott, 2009). Possibly, therefore, for many adolescent males who find themselves on the margins of schooling and society because of their subordinated racial and class status, the resultant masculinity performance *is* the performance of "at-riskness," as defined, understood, and legislated.

A cultural analysis of student schooling experiences and outcomes directs us to examine how the educational institutions create the many youth who become at risk. The term itself is imbued with cultural values that we must necessarily take into account. The designation of students as at risk is often justified as being merely an indication that they need educational supports, guidance, and mentorship. However, critical race theorists contend that this justification is tied to the prevailing racist discourse within society. The supposed good intentions behind an at-risk designation unfortunately obfuscate the "inconspicuous and covert approach to issues of inequity that ambiguously suggest racial preconceptions" of Black and other racialized students (James, 2021b, p. 81). For Black males in particular, an at-risk designation, supported by the convergence of stereotypes – immigrant, fatherless, athlete, troublemaker, and underachiever – places them at a considerable disadvantage in school and society generally (for further discussion of African-American males, see Howard, 2008; Hernandez & Davis, 2009).

The Stereotypes of Black Boys and Young Men

Immigrant

Africans' presence in Canada dates back to the early seventeenth century, and despite legislative attempts to bar their immigration and settlement for reasons such as "inability to assimilate," they did manage to settle in Canada. In fact, the 1901 census indicates that some 17,500 "Negroes" (0.3 per cent of the population) resided in Canada at that time. By 1971, that number had doubled, and by 1981, with a change in immigration policies, the population had grown to an estimated 289,500.

Today, the African-Canadian population of about 1.2 million (3.5 per cent of Canada's overall population) comprises mostly people who have resided in Canada for more than two generations (Statistics Canada, 2019). They include descendants of former enslaved African people, United Empire Loyalists, and immigrants from the Caribbean, Africa, Britain, and Latin America who came in the 1970s and 1980s. With this profile, one would expect that today's young African Canadians – the majority of whom were born in Canada to Canadian parents – would not be asked the question, "Where are you from?" as a means of establishing their foreign roots. In writing about this (extremely common) practice, Palmer (1998) maintains, "This probing of our ancestral roots keeps us forever foreign, forever immigrants to Canada" (p. v; see also Shadd, 2001).

Understanding those Canadians who are not of English or French European ancestry as "foreign" stems from Canada's immigration and multicultural policies. As noted earlier, until 1971, Canada's immigration policies restricted nonwhite immigration. Bashi (2004) explains that "Canada's anti-black immigration policy" relied on "cultural and biological arguments" to justify the unsuitability of this group to Canada. He writes that Canada was reluctant to admit Blacks because it would mean "the nation was just asking for problems (e.g., race riots) that Britain and the U.S. had to bear for having black residents" (p. 586).

The idea of fixed homogeneous cultural behaviours among immigrants or ethnic and racial minoritized groups is also featured in the federal multicultural discourse, which holds that Canada's promotion of cultural freedom, democracy, and equality enables "cultural groups" – i.e., "Other Canadians" – to preserve and maintain their culture. Having preserved and maintained their culture – the values, beliefs, behaviours, and religious practices from their countries of origin – whatever Blacks and other "foreign" Canadians do that seems inconsistent (in English Canada) with "Anglo-Canadian culture" is typically attributed to their foreign origin.[6]

On the basis of the stereotype of young Black males as foreigners[7] with cultures from elsewhere, their poor educational performance and disciplinary problems are attributed to their lack of Canadian educational values and discipline, due to their inability or unwillingness to assimilate, as well as to their "foreign cultures" that do not value education. Hence, unaware educators will tend to take the position that nothing or very little can be done to help these youth. These educators and others might point to the prevailing statistics showing low test scores, frequent special-needs designations, high dropout rates, school disciplinary problems, and lack of parental involvement in their children's education as evidence that the situation is irreversible (Brown & Parekh, 2010; McKenzie, 2009). Such perceptions are compounded by the reality that many Black youth live in stigmatized, heavily policed low-income urban neighbourhoods populated by a significant number of immigrants with related issues of unemployment, poverty, limited school-community interactions, and negative media reports (Smith, Schneider, & Ruck, 2005; Young, Wood, & Keil, 2011; see also van der Land & Doff, 2010). Their parents' difficult circumstances are seen as evidence of what can be expected for these students in the future.

The tendency to homogenize Black youth and ascribe immigrant status to them means discounting their diversity – in terms of their places

---

[6] State multiculturalism, argues Mackey (2002), "implicitly constructs the idea of a core English-Canadian culture, and that other cultures become 'multicultural' in relation to that unmarked, yet dominant, Anglo-Canadian core culture" (p. 2).

[7] Similarly, Lee (2008) writes that Asian Americans are stereotyped as "perpetual foreigners."

of birth, ethnicities, histories, and parents' national origins. Indeed, while the entire group might identify (or be identified) as African or Black Canadian, in reality their parents and/or grandparents might be from Trinidad, Haiti, Antigua, Ghana, Kenya, Brazil, Eritrea, and many other countries. Many (if not most) Canadians commonly assume that all Black people they meet come from Jamaica; the accompanying stereotype is that they are an undisciplined group (Aguiar, McKinnon, & Sookraj, 2011). Notwithstanding the fact that Jamaicans make up the largest proportion of the African-Canadian population and hence can be found in proportionally large numbers among Canada's legislators, professors, scientists, teachers, and medical practitioners, the stereotype of the Jamaican – and more generally the "Black foreigner" simply based on skin colour – persists. That a significant number of people deported[8] to the Caribbean are sent to Jamaica (understandable given their numbers) further reinforces the stereotype.

The construction of African Canadians as immigrants, as people who are incapable of assimilating and who do not abide by the law, contributes to a sense of temporality that then characterizes how they are dealt with in society generally and within their schooling in particular. This temporality manifests in the fact that mainstream historical accounts, even after four centuries, do not tell of the presence of Black people in Canada, and Black History Month remains in many cases more an annual *event* for and about Black people. It is also reflected in educators' practices – in which the resources used, references made, or stories told are of African Americans and/or Black people living in the Caribbean and Africa. Given their stereotype as immigrants and absence from educational resources and curriculum, it is understandable and unsurprising that many of today's Black youth would eventually become disengaged from school and the educational process.

Simmel's (1908/1950) concept of "the stranger" could also apply here. According to Simmel, strangers occupy a position in society where they are both "near and far *at the same time*"; their interactions with other members of the society are "founded only on generally human commonness." As such, they are "not really conceived as individuals, but as strangers of a particular type: the element of distance is no less general in regard to them than the element of nearness" (p. 407). While many Canadians might say, "except for Indigenous (or Aboriginal) people, we are all immigrants," the same understanding of

---

8 The reasons for deportation are typically related to being in Canada illegally and convictions related to criminal activities. The young people who get deported are often permanent residents and a conviction makes them ineligible for citizenship.

immigrant is not applied to African Canadians (and other racial-minoritized Canadians) as it is to most white Canadians. The tendency is to think of whites, particularly English and French people, as Canadians, and "visible minorities" as members of "cultural groups." What seems to be primary in the social position that African Canadians hold is their "visibility" as African Canadians, and not as "the individual bearer" (Simmel, 1908/1950, p. 408) of an invariable attribute.

In response to the stereotype of African Canadians as immigrants, some youth tend to conform to the expectations, while others reject the stereotype altogether. In conforming, they adopt immigrant identities, the most common of which manifests through their constructed Jamaican language, accent, and demeanour (Ibrahim, 2000). But taking on and performing this identity does not necessarily mean they accept that they are not Canadian; rather they are, in part, demanding that their presence as African Canadians be acknowledged and accepted on their terms, and that space for their expression of that identity be provided. Conceivably, their "immigrant" identities reflect a combination of their parents' aspirations and expectations and their own racialized experiences – socialized by their immigrant parents and/or grandparents, they have high educational aspirations and believe they have to work twice as hard to succeed in the society (Codjoe, 2006; Gosine, 2012; James, 2010).

It seems plausible that as students who have been raised by parents who place great importance on strong academic performance and educational success for social mobility (Fuligni, 2001; James, 2010; Lee, 2008; Suárez-Orozco, Qin, & Amthor, 2008), being classified as at risk would situate them in stark contrast to their parents' expectations. Educators and others must therefore understand the implication of the immigrant/foreigner stereotype, recognizing that even as African-Canadian youth might appear to "conform" to the stereotype, they are in a way resisting it – by using the stereotype to assert their agency within a system that seeks to label and define them as foreign and relegate them to that status.

Fatherless

Related to the stereotype of African Canadians as immigrants, with foreign values and morals, comes the perception of their family structure as one in which single motherhood represents the norm. Insofar as single parenthood does not provide the same level of opportunity (because of limits on income, time, and other resources) to fully engage with children's education and schooling (helping with school work, monitoring school performance, and attending parent-teacher meetings), the children are perceived as lacking needed educational and social skills, aptitudes, discipline, and supports putting them at risk of failing in school.

Single-parent families tend to be disparaged and judged as problematic for their social and economic cost to society (Lawson, 2012). A "kind of social pathology," writes Dowd (1997), characterizes the way single-parent families are presented in popular culture and public policies. In a society that upholds the traditional nuclear patriarchal family as the norm, the term serves as a euphemism for "problem family" and conjures notions of such a family representing some deviant, unstable "underclass." Thus, the rise in the number of single-parent families is equated with social decline and the end of the "real family" (p. 3).

According to Statistics Canada (2009), some 46 per cent of African-Canadian children (compared to a national average of 18 per cent) were growing up in one-parent, typically single-mother, households.[9] That these families are perceived to be "dysfunctional" and "producing damaged children" (Griffith, 2006, p. 129)[10] undoubtedly influences the concerns educators and other institutional agents express about the schooling and disciplinary problems of Black students. In 2007, a radio series produced by the Canadian Broadcasting Corporation entitled "Growing Up without Men" featured a number of investigative reporters, educators, religious leaders, other professionals, and community activists insisting that the "breakdown of the nuclear family" and the "absence" of fathers in the lives of Black boys was responsible for "the Black youth delinquent."[11] A recurring theme emerged – that mothers were unable to provide the appropriate and necessary supports and guidance for their boys. One program guest, David Popenoe, stated,

---

[9] The 2016 census indicates that "2 in 10 Black individuals were in lone-parent families." Specifically, 19 per cent of the Black population – compared to 8 per cent of the Canadian population – were living in lone-parent families, 70 per cent were women, and they "were more likely to be living in a low-income situation" (Statistics Canada 2020; see also Turcotte, 2020).

[10] Drawing on her experience, Griffith (2006) explains that "as single parents, we rarely see ourselves as socially deviant. Rather, our concerns are often about money, how our children are growing and maturing, the kind of adults they are becoming, and so on. Our children's experiences of schools are always a hot topic. We are often puzzled by some of the difficulties our children encounter in school. We speak about school problems with other single parents without necessarily being able to understand or resolve the issues" (p. 128).

[11] Writing of the "criticisms of contemporary forms of black womanhood and manhood" levelled by Boston-based religious leader Eugene Rivers, Walcott (2009) stated, "Rivers' message was well received, given its embeddedness in neoliberalism's individual managerial language of personal responsibility with little recognition of a collective responsibility and a common social good" (p. 79).

"The most widely-reported statistic is that a child growing up without two parents has about twice the risk in life of having serious problems" ("Growing Up without Men," 2007).

Chris Spence, with his experience as director of education of public school boards in Hamilton and Toronto, suggested that in a classroom it was possible to identify students who were growing up in single-parent families because they were often "angry young men with little or no respect for themselves or others, poor academic skills, limited problem-solving skills ... [and] they viewed school as temporary incarceration" ("Growing Up without Men," 2007). The generally accepted "solution" to the "problem" of fatherlessness is for the youth to have Black male mentors as role models.[12] To this end, there has been a significant growth in role-model programs in schools and community organizations.

Accepting the idea that fatherlessness contributes to delinquency among young Black men and that Black sons are not learning about manliness from the person considered best suited to teach them (Fraser, 2011; James, 2012b), also means accepting the corollary – that mothers, who at times are portrayed as authoritarian, strict, and demanding,[13] are incapable of giving their sons the social and cultural capital needed to successfully navigate and negotiate society's social and educational structures. Evidence – in the form of the accomplished men who act as mentors, who promote the virtues and importance of men being there for boys and who were themselves raised by single mothers – challenges this corollary. The truth is, in most cases, even in two-parent nuclear families, mothers are usually most involved in the early, foundational socialization of children and are most involved in their children's schooling, for example, attending parent-teacher meetings (Fraser, 2011; James, 2010). As Lawson-Bush (2004) writes about the participation of Black mothers in their sons' lives, "no aspect or component of Black male life eluded these mothers in their ability to teach lessons that were necessary for manhood or the development of masculinity" (p. 384).

---

12 Elsewhere (James, 2012b), I refer to mentors and role models as "corrective agents," borrowing Patrick Shannon's (1998) term. I concur with Sevier and Ashcraft (2009) who argue that a gender analysis is necessary if we are to avoid the "simplistic sex-role socialization" that a "surrogate-father" is what boys need without paying attention to "what kinds of masculinities we wish to model" (p. 536).

13 Gosa and Alexander (2007) also said this of African-American mothers; and they go on to point out that "there is great diversity in black family life ... and wide variation in the socialization experiences of black children" (p. 295).

That Black men and women, and even single mothers, have come to accept the truism that boys, especially Black boys, need fathers physically present in their homes or lives reflects the hegemonic societal discourse.[14] This internalization of fixed gender roles undermines individuals' attempts to resist their racialization in their aspiration to be "good mothers," and in the case of immigrant parents, their aspiration to attain the immigrant dream of "making it" – if not for them, then for their children (Fraser, 2011; Smith et al., 2005). Black and other racial-minoritized parents, even the absented fathers, look to education as the means by which their children might become academically successful, socially responsible, productive citizens.

We need to shift from the deficit paradigm that blames family deficiencies and look at what schools are not doing and what is lacking in the education they offer to single-parent Black boys. Griffith (2006), who conducted research in Toronto-area schools, noted that the prevalence of single-parent families within an area became one of the criteria used in classifying an "inner-city school" and determining its eligibility for extra funding. She contended that "the single parent family becomes just one of the many problems in the inner-city school – one that can be identified but which has little currency in an educational setting that, by definition, deviates from 'ordinary' school" (p. 134).

Undoubtedly, the absence of fathers in Black boys' lives means they are not learning from their fathers' particular insights, aspirations, and experiences. But claims regarding limitations of their mothers' parenting skills, or overemphasis on such limitations, negates the crucial contributions that mothers have been making in socializing their sons. On this point in his response to the *Globe and Mail*'s series on "Failing Boys," Haille Bailey-Harris (2010), a high school student, said the following:

> Every time I hear about another study telling me that, as a boy, especially a fatherless boy, I may be destined to fail in school, it makes me cringe and more determined to prove the researchers wrong. I'm one of those statistics discussed in the studies ... Raised by my mother alone, I'm a fatherless boy ... Although not discussed in the articles, I have what other studies said is also a risk factor for dropping out of school: I'm black. Hell, I should

---

14 In a *Toronto Star* article "Where Are the Men?" based on observations and interviews with single mothers – mostly Black – in public housing, Linda Diebel (2007) reported that for the most part the women were "raising children on little money, often in public housing where kids are exposed to greater risks, because it's all they can afford" (see also Aggarwal-Schefellite, 2020; Cross, 2019; Lawson, 2012).

throw in the towel! ... Although I don't think the studies are always right, I agree that growing up without a father (especially if your family is also poor) can be a real challenge. And since we know this, we should be working hard to intervene before failing is a done deal. That's what my mother did. And though I have lots of time yet to screw up, today, I'm a happy, well-adjusted 16-year-old who really loves to read, already has a university scholarship waiting and is a published writer. (paras. 1–6)

Evidently, correctives to the at-risk situation of Black youth cannot simply be found through fathers or "surrogate fathers" – as in male teachers and other professionals acting as mentors and role models. The idea that being fatherless is inherent to the problem of underachievement and troublemaking comes close to suggesting, as Sevier and Ashcraft (2009) proffer, "that the presence of men is a necessary corrective to the damaging effects of overexposure to single mothers or other women" (p. 536). The idea can also operate as a self-fulfilling prophecy, thereby reinforcing beliefs pertaining to the efficacy of African-Canadian mothers (see Kim, 2009).

Athlete

Many believe that youth who are deemed at risk can surmount the obstacles and challenges they face in their communities and schools through participation in athletic programs. African-Canadian athletes, who are habitually reduced to their bodies and their talent "attributed to nature" (Ferber, 2007, p. 20),[15] face what Harry Edwards refers to as "double negative label," in that they are constructed as "dumb" athletes and "unintelligent" Blacks (in Harrison, Sailes, Rotich, & Bimper, 2011; see also Singer, 2009). If they are good at sports, the stereotypical assumption dictates that they must also be poor students.

But we know that Black students do not arrive at school with an "anti-intellectual orientation" (Noguera, 2008). Rather, as Hernandez and Davis (2009) mention, Black boys tend to arrive with "high regard for their teachers" and are "very optimistic" about their learning. This positive outlook on their education decreases as they go through school (p. 19). That Black students are expected to do well on the basketball court but not in the classroom in part reflects the messages they receive

---

15 On the other hand, the accomplishments of white athletes are credited to their "fortitude, intelligence, moral character, strategic preparation, coachability, and good organization" (Coakley, 2006, as cited in Ferber, 2007, p. 20).

from their teachers and coaches and the hidden curriculum pertaining to racial stereotypes.

Numerous African-Canadian male student-athletes have told stories of how they were recruited for basketball teams primarily on the basis of race and physicality. For instance, in my essay "Why Is the School Basketball Team Predominantly Black?" (James, 2011), I reference a newspaper report about an up-and-coming student-athlete, Dwayne. The reporter related that upon meeting Dwayne for the first time, the teacher who would become Dwayne's coach, "after seeing his size, encouraged him to take part in sports." About his athletic skills, the coach said, Dwayne is "very athletic, can dunk the ball, has a great vertical leap and seems to be comfortable playing the game"; he was also impressed with Dwayne's "work ethic in sports" (James, 2011, pp. 452–3). Nothing was said of Dwayne's academic performance, but the reporter speculated that he was "on track" to get an "athletic scholarship" to study in the United States.

Kevin, another student-athlete, recalled receiving a call from his older brother's high school basketball coach encouraging Kevin to remain at his current school – where the coach would be moving to become the basketball coach. Kevin indicated that the coach had never met him and mostly knew of his basketball career through his brother and friends. The coach's confidence in Kevin's basketball ability might be explained by his familiarity with Kevin's brother's abilities and skills, as well as an assumption of athletic abilities among siblings – a genetic stereotype that often influences coaches and scouts as they recruit athletes (James, 2011).

Coaches and teachers are known to use racial stereotypes in their consideration of who will make the best basketball players. For example, in the essay referenced above (James, 2011), I mention Amir, a South Asian high school student-athlete, saying that he was not given the same opportunities on the basketball court as his Black teammates because the coach saw him as "very smart or highly intelligent" and expected him to get an academic scholarship. Amir said the coach showed preference for the Black players, seeing them as "natural" athletes and the ones who would win the athletic scholarships. For the coach to be convinced otherwise, as Amir put it, "I had to be extra good, faster, just to prove myself more than the Black players on the team because I was not Black" (James, 2011, pp. 454–5).

The practice of recruiting young Black men for their athletic talents and encouraging them in their athletic pursuits, particularly basketball and track and field, occurs in many Toronto schools and neighbourhoods today and is influenced by historical images of them as natural athletes – a myth that persists (Ferber, 2007). As long as particular sports are perceived to represent the culture of Black young men, as well as their interests, capabilities, and possibilities, these young men – especially those with the stereotypical physical characteristics – will be recruited to sports teams (James, 2011).

In addition to their physicality, what is often even more important than their academic performance in school is their "coachability" (Ferber, 2007; Frey, 2004).[16] Being coachable relates to the extent to which young men internalize the values and characteristics of a "good" reliable athlete, prove their athletic prowess, and remain consistent in their work ethic pertaining to the sport. In return, they will receive the needed support from coaches (especially if they are "star" athletes), who in many cases, working with the stereotype of the fatherless boy, act as "surrogate fathers." Such students' performance, abilities, and skills in the relevant sport become very important – and their interest in mathematics, history, or chemistry not important at all.

Cultural significance is attached to the particular sport. For example, if you are Black, you are not perceived to have the aptitude, skills, and physicality for hockey, Canada's "national" sport. An inability to play or excel in hockey therefore comes to represent – rather than the failure of coaches and others to encourage and train Black youth in the sport – the youths' lack of assimilability into Canadian recreational activities. As a result, they remain "foreign." Once young Black men have been stereotyped as immigrants or cultural outsiders, coaches will more likely assume they lack both the talent and the discipline for hockey. As Blacks, basketball and track and field (particularly within the context of school athletics) are seen as "their" sports, just as these same sports are for their American counterparts.

Black students' success in a particular sport becomes a self-fulfilling prophecy, which of course contributes to shoring up the stereotype. For coaches and teachers, it represents "proof" that athletics provide the most productive opportunities for these students to participate in school. For the youth, the attention, recognition, and adulation they receive from peers, coaches, scouts, parents, teachers, and society generally, as well as the scholarship possibilities and offers from postsecondary institutions, not only inspire them to play sports (James, 2011; Singer, 2009) but also offer sufficient reason to live up to the stereotype.

Some argue that although attributing athletic competence to Black males represents a stereotype, given the genuine opportunities they

---

16 See Singer's (2009) discussion of the role and responsibilities of coaches in helping student-athletes to realize their academic potential (pp. 40–3).

might attain through athletics it can be viewed as a "positive stereotype." The seductive nature of positive stereotyping masks the racism and structural inequity in society, and it can be quite harmful (James, 2011). The case of Dwayne, discussed above, offers an example. The support he received from his coach, teachers, and the newspaper reporter reinforce the idea that he is "on the right track." As a consequence, his focus on basketball to the exclusion of other educational or career pursuits could mean that he is unlikely to develop other skills necessary for a productive social and economic life (see Singer & Buford May, 2010, for a discussion of a similar student-athlete).

In a society and schooling system where sports remain "the bastion of heterosexual masculinity and site of performance," playing sports has meant "fitting in, measuring up, and becoming men" (James, 2011, p. 458). Undoubtedly, many young Black men pay a high cost for living up to the stereotype – for starters, the inordinate amount of time, energy, and dedication given to learning, playing, and mastering their sport at the expense of their academic work.

Overvaluing heterosexual masculinity not only serves to structure acceptable forms of masculine behaviours, traits, and roles (Anderson & McCormack, 2010; McCready, 2010), but also serves to limit the sporting options of Black male youth. More to the point, as Harrison et al. (2011) stress:

> Far too often sport is framed as the red-carpet pathway out of poverty and obscurity and into fame and fortune. While a few do achieve their dreams, the vast majority are rudely awakened at a point where they have forgone their opportunity to secure a valid and valuable education. (p. 100)

Troublemaker

There is a peculiar logic to thinking that because of their immigrant (or perceived immigrant) backgrounds, their fatherlessness, and their inclination to athletic pursuits, students who lack social support and cultural capital are unlikely to do well in school. And in a society and school system structured by individualism, any animated reactions by students that demonstrate dissatisfaction or frustration with the educational system's lack of attention to their needs, interests, and aspirations might be considered disruptive, troublesome, or disorderly.

Consider also the associations made between race, gender, and behaviour, especially in a context where the "immigrant" represents an unfamiliar person with fixed characteristics. Therefore, in the case of young Black men, there will be a normalization of their behaviours – meaning they will be stereotyped as troublemakers and undisciplined.

In their popular text *The Colour of Democracy: Racism in Canadian Society*, Henry and Tator (2010) make the point that stereotypical images of certain racialized communities represented on television, in newspaper articles and photographs, and in "the everyday discourses of politicians, police, and other public authorities" breathe fear into society. The authors argue that

> the myths reinforce stereotypes of crime and criminality as "a Black problem" or "an Aboriginal problem" ... The rhetorical discourses of Black-on-Black crime have no parallel in terms of a matching discourse on White-on-White crime. (p. 15)

Historical and contemporary social images of Black people clearly inform and influence young Black men's schooling experiences. Studies indicate that stereotyping (termed *racial profiling* because of how race leads to a socially constructed view of racialized youth as potential safety and security threats) contributes to many of the problems and struggles students experience in schools, specifically Ontario schools (Dei, 1997; James & Taylor, 2010; Solomon & Palmer, 2004).

The particular urban neighbourhoods where students reside also contribute to the profile of Black youth as problem students. There is a tendency to associate their "problem" behaviours with the fact that they reside in stigmatized neighbourhoods in urban areas – areas that receive disproportionately negative attention in the media, where they are portrayed as deprived, derelict spaces to be feared (Wacquant, 2008, p. 1).[17] Research into the schooling experiences of Black high school students conducted in one such Toronto neighbourhood revealed that the participants were routinely stereotyped as "bad" or "troublemakers" and assumptions were made about their academic abilities and behavioural motives on the basis of their skin colour, their clothing, and their neighbourhood. The students characterized these experiences as "racial profiling" by their teachers and school administrators, who were disrespectful to them, did not take into account their particular circumstances when dealing with their complaints and/or actions, and

---

17 Wacquant (2008) continues to make the point that "owing to the halo of danger and dread that enshrouds [these communities] and to the scorn that afflicts their inhabitants, a variegated mix of disposed households, dishonoured minorities and disenfranchised immigrants, they are typically depicted from above and from afar in somber and monochrome tones" (p. 1).

in some cases "delivered" them to the judicial system (James & Taylor, 2010; Mosher, 2008). According to one Grade 11 male student, "Even at school, teachers treat you differently ... Like if you're a Black kid walking through the hallway ... they're expecting you to cause trouble or be bad" (as cited in James & Taylor, 2010, p. 127).

Referring to police officers who would come to their school, either on routine visits or because the principal called them about an incident, one male research participant surmised:

Once they [police] see what colour skin you have, you are bad news ... I could be walking in the neighbourhood, and they think I am going somewhere bad and they just look at you like you have their shirt on, they just stare at you. They don't look at you as a person; they look at you as where you're from.

This student went on to say that his neighbourhood "might be known as a bad area, but seeing a bunch of guys together" should not lead to "automatically think[ing] gang, or automatically think[ing] we're out there doing something bad with some drugs or smoking or doing something illegal" (James & Taylor, 2010, p. 128). The youth in the study indicated that such stereotyping or racial profiling was so much a part of their lived experiences in the larger society, their communities, and their schools that many of them became resigned to its presence. They took for granted that they would be treated differently and "singled out" by teachers, principals, police officers, and hall monitors because of preconceived ideas about Black youth (James & Taylor, 2010, p. 127).

In many urban schooling contexts, in an effort to thwart students' potential insubordinate and disruptive behaviours, school administrators and teachers take what might be considered a "preemptive" stance by having security cameras, locking outside doors while classes are in session, and requiring school uniforms. They have also enlisted the services of hall monitors, security guards, or police officers. These preemptive responses, according to Farmer (2010), constitute part of the criminalization of schools, which she describes as a "combination of reactive-disciplinary policies, surveillance, metal detectors, unwarranted searching and lockdowns that reflect the contemporary criminal justice system within the school environment" (p. 367). The expectation of student violence or hostility leads to what Farmer describes as a "moral panic" or "racialized moral panic," premised on the notion that African-Canadian youth cannot fit into school norms. Hence their behaviour creates anxiety among teachers and administrators concerned with school and "classroom management," which mainly relates to an emphasis on teachers "always being in control of student behaviour" (Butler, Joubert, & Lewis, 2009, p. 3).

In response to this "moral panic" and resulting anxiety, educators take a "get-tough" approach, evident in zero-tolerance practices – for example, "time out" at the principal's office, detentions, suspensions, expulsions. These in turn produce "deficient narratives about the moral capacity of Black youth ... and constrain the public moral imagination" in regard to them (Farmer, 2010, p. 373). Furthermore, the get-tough approach, fostered by the construction of Black students as troublemakers, facilitates the "school-to-prison pipeline" (Henry & Tator, 2010; Meiners & Winn, 2010; Noguera, 2008; Solomon & Palmer, 2004) – a devastating development in which schools have unwittingly played a role in criminalizing young people through their continuing surveillance of students deemed "at risk."

Underachiever

Despite the evidence that African-Canadian students, encouraged by parents, have high educational and social aspirations (Gosine, 2012; James, 2010; Hernandez-Ramdwar, 2009; Smith et al., 2005), the stereotype of them as underachievers persists. What accounts for this persistence? Studies indicate that typically Black youth, supported by their parents, enter school willing and able to engage in their learning process (Gosine, 2012; James, 2010). But they encounter an inequitable schooling system where a Eurocentric curriculum and approach to learning become impediments to educational success.

The degree to which the stereotype seems to be justified does not result from Black students' lack of intelligence, skills, or interests, or from their immigrant or "Black" culture, which is viewed as antithetical to academic pursuits. The stereotype of Black students as underachievers survives through the social context of schooling, teachers' attitudes and practices, and how Black youth themselves take up or act upon the underachiever stereotype.

In his study of successful educational experiences and attainment by Black youth, Codjoe (2006) points out that most existing studies have focused on their "poor academic performance" (p. 33). He reasons that although these studies may have been prompted by a desire to understand Black students' academic problems, in some cases they reinforce stereotypes of Black students as lazy, dumb, athletic, stupid, intellectually inferior, deviant, dangerous, and mentally incompetent – all presented as relating to their "Black culture" (p. 34). These stereotypes constitute part of the deficit thinking about Black students, against which they must struggle as they try to productively engage with their education process.

Codjoe's (2006) findings address the question of whether it is possible for Black students to succeed in an education system in a society that views them as perpetual academic underachievers. These findings indicate that yes, it is possible, but the students must first build up their defences "against the inevitable psychological insults of racism" (p. 46). According to Codjoe, the resulting "self-identity and pride in African cultural/racial identity positively affects academic success among Black students by serving as an important buffer against racism and devaluation of African peoples, and providing students with requisite coping skills" (p. 48).

Many of today's schools, including those in Toronto, express concern about the "achievement gap" that exists between Black students, particularly males, and others, as reflected in successful completion of high school (Toronto District School Board, 2010). Test scores and other standardized measures are used to gauge students' ability, skill level, and knowledge of educational material – and to identify at-risk students. That tests are also seen as a means of holding teachers accountable begs the question: accountable to whom – which parents, and which students? Overreliance on both schoolwide and individual test scores, rather than a focus on teaching and learning processes, results in stigmatizing schools and reinforcing stereotypes. "Too much testing and not enough teaching," as Milner (2010) argues, will not eliminate the achievement gap. Besides, in school systems that purport to be taking into account the diversity of their students, standardization in terms of tests, educational materials, pedagogy, and content "is antithetical to diversity because it suggests that all students live and operate in homogeneous environments with equality of opportunity afforded to them" (p. 3).

Obviously, teachers play a pivotal role in the construction of students as underachievers and their at-risk designations. Unfortunately, few Canadian studies address the Black parent-teacher relationship. Insights provided by US studies are nevertheless instructive. Lynn, Bacon, Totten, Bridges, and Jennings (2010) conducted a study in which they examined "teachers' beliefs about African-American male students in a low-performing high school." They found a substantial majority of teachers attributed students' academic failure to the students, their parents, or their community, rather than to their own teaching. They write that

> about 80% of teachers argued that African-American students' failure to achieve was primarily shaped by their lack of motivation to learn, their failure to attend classes, their lack of interest in learning, their lack of

preparation for school, their inability to focus, their participation in street culture, and failure to behave appropriately in class. (p. 308)

The teachers identified parents as the "chief source of the problem" because they cultivated in their children "cultural mores and values" that were inconsistent with those of the school (p. 309). Such beliefs among teachers correlate with their practice of not engaging with parents and assuming the "parents do not have the time, interest, money, or energy to support what they are doing" at school (Kim, 2009). This assumption of parents' lack of commitment to their children's schooling is seen as an explanation for their children's underachievement and ultimately their at-risk designation.[18]

For their part, young Black male students either conform to or resist the underachiever stereotype, but we note a complexity in the ways this stereotype is taken up. There are those who conform, having come to internalize the underachiever and at-risk designation, and believe that academic work is not for them. And there are those who conform merely as a coping mechanism – because doing otherwise would pit them against a system that they believe will never accept their ability to perform as competent academic students.

Some of these students present themselves as athletes, whose interest in school is "to play ball" (James, 2009). Those who resist the stereotype set out to challenge it; hence they work "harder" to "prove" that they are not like their peers or to prove their teachers wrong. Ironically, this negative stereotype, combined with seeing their underachieving peers, can motivate some students to do well in school. As one young man said, "You can allow things to govern your life or you can deal with them then, and just kind of move on and prove them [teachers] wrong" (James, 2010, p. 127; see also Howard, 2008).

Conclusion

These stereotypes exist in relation to one another, and they serve to categorize, essentialize, and disenfranchise young Black male students as they navigate and negotiate the school system. The cultural context of schooling – with its Eurocentric curriculum, homogeneous approach

---

18 The assumption of parents' lack of commitment is contrary to the evidence that minoritized and working-class parents seldom question the authority of teachers, and rely on them for direction pertaining to the educational aspirations and needs of their children. The distance that parents keep from school can also be seen as their attempt to avoid the surveillance to which they are subjected (McGhee Hassrick & Schneider, 2009).

to the teaching/learning process, and reliance on culturally inappropriate assessments – functions as an incubator for these deeply rooted stereotypes.

The idea that schools operate on principles of cultural freedom (multiculturalism), democracy, merit, racial neutrality (colour-blindness), and equality of opportunity is not borne out in the experiences of Black male students. Their school and societal experiences generally are affected by constructions of Black masculinities linked to fatherlessness, hopelessness, deviance, low expectations, and poor academic performance (Hernandez & Davis, 2009, p. 19; McCready, 2010).

A "colour-blind" approach to working with students effectively conceals and obscures the preconceived ideas that inform educators' understanding of particular students' learning needs and interests. Hence in the case of Black males, popular media images and their physical appearance, combined with low grades (perceived to stem from a lack of interest in academic work), have been used as "good" reasons to encourage such students to join sports teams. Colour-blindness also serves to negate the social and cultural capital that students bring to school and to their learning (Lynn et al., 2010; Yosso, 2005).

In Canadian schools, stereotyping, including the at-risk designation itself, operates in the context of a multicultural discourse that masks the fact that race matters. Race and racism do inform educational policies and practices, contrary to educators' claims of neutrality and objectivity in their work with, and expectations of, Black male students.

Stereotyping remains a major issue that continues to limit the educational opportunities, possibilities, and successes of these students. That some of these youth actively resist and contest schools' policies and practices that construct and label them tells us that they have encountered structures that invariably caused them to employ or display the very behaviour patterns that earned them the stereotypes in the first place and which they seek to eliminate. The sad irony is that because of these behaviour patterns – for example, poor academic performance and disruptive conduct, which may have led to their at-risk designation – teachers and others come to feel justified in the "truth" of their stereotypes and assessments. Educators need to recognize how hegemonic schooling policies, programs, and practices perpetuate stereotyping that is oppressive to racialized students, who through their paradoxical responses and actions seek to register their needs, concerns, and interests so that their schooling experiences can be meaningful, self-validating, relevant, safe, and empowering for them.

The "web of stereotypes" in which Black students are caught forms part of the cultural structure of the society in which they and their teachers operate. Indeed, as McDermott and Varenne (2006) point out, "it takes a culture full of people to make such a mess" (p. 19). The mess in this case involves a schooling situation where preconceived ideas and formal evaluation measures, supported by an inequitable social structure, contribute to gendered labels from which many Black male students struggle to escape.

According to Noguera (2008), understanding and debunking racial stereotypes and challenging the systems that maintain them should fall not only to teachers, principals, "role models," and education leaders but to the entire society. Rather than making formative or summative evaluation measures and disciplinary management central to our educational policies and programs, perhaps we need a differentiated approach to students' learning – one that pays attention to their problems and lived experiences and to the social context in which they are positioned as Black boys and young men and accordingly expected to learn, understand, and perform their masculinity.

REFERENCES

Abada, T., & Lin, S. (2011). *The educational attainments and labour market outcomes of the children of immigrants in Ontario.* Toronto, ON: Higher Education Quality Council of Ontario.

Aggarwal-Schefellite, M. (2020, January, 16) Why single-parent homes don't affect black children as negatively as white kids. *Phys.Org.* https://phys.org/news/2020-01-single-parent-homes-dont-affect-black.html

Aguiar, L.M., McKinnon, A., & Sookraj, D. (2011). Racialization and the repertoires of racism: Reactions to Jamaicans in the Okanagan Valley. *BC Studies, 168,* 65–79. https://doi.org/10.14288/bcs.v0i168.1575

Anderson, E., & McCormack, M. (2010). Intersectionality, critical race theory, and American sporting oppression: Examining Black and gay male athletes. *Journal of Homosexuality, 57,* 949–67. https://doi.org/10.1080/00918369.2010.503502

Bailey-Harris, H. (2010, October 21). 16-year-old: I'm fatherless, black, but no "failing boy." *Globe and Mail.* https://www.theglobeandmail.com/news/national/time-to-lead/16-year-old-im-fatherless-black-but-no-failing-boy/article1215288/

Bashi, V. (2004). Globalized anti-blackness: Transnationalizing western immigration law, policy, and practice. *Ethnic and Racial Studies, 27*(4), 584–606. https://doi.org/10.1080/01491987042000216726

Bhattacharjee, A. (2003). *Paying the price: The human cost of racial profiling.* Toronto, ON: Ontario Human Rights Commission.

Brown, R.S., & Parekh, G. (2010). *Special education: Structural overview and student demographics*. Research report. Toronto, ON: Toronto District School Board, Research and Information Services.

Butler, B., Joubert, M., & Lewis, C. (2009). Who's really disrupting the classroom? An examination of African American male students and their disciplinary roles. *National Journal of Urban Education & Practice, 3*(1), 1–12. https://files.eric.ed.gov/fulltext/ED511847.pdf

Caldas, S., Bernier, S., & Marceau, R. (2009). Explanatory factors of the black achievement gap in Montréal's public and private schools: A multivariate analysis. *Education and Urban Society, 41* (2), 197–215. https://doi.org/10.1177/0013124508325547

Codjoe, H. (2006). The role of an affirmed Black cultural identity and heritage in the academic achievement of African-Canadian students. *Intercultural Education, 17*(1), 33–54. https://doi.org/10.1080/14675980500502271

Cross, C. (2019). Racial/ethnic differences in the association between family structure and children's education. *Journal of Marriage and Family, 82*(6), 691–712. https://doi.org/10.1111/jomf.12625

Dei, G.J.S. (1997). Race and the production of identity in the schooling experiences of African-Canadian youth. *Discourse: Studies in the Cultural Politics of Education, 18*(2), 241–57. https://doi.org/10.1080/0159630970180206

Diebel, L. (2007, August 19). Where are the men? *Toronto Star*. p. A1

Dowd, N. (1997). *In defense of single-parent families*. New York, NY: New York University Press.

Farmer, S. (2010). Criminality of Black youth in inner-city schools: "Moral panic," moral imagination, and moral formation. *Race, Ethnicity and Education, 13*(3), 367–81. https://doi.org/10.1080/13613324.2010.500845

Ferber, A. (2007). The construction of Black masculinity: White supremacy now and then. *Journal of Sport & Social Issues, 31*(1), 11–24. https://doi.org/10.1177/0193723506296829

Fine, M. (1993). Making controversy: Who's "at risk"? In R. Wollons (Ed.), *Children at risk in America: History, concepts, and public policy* (pp. 91–110). Albany, NY: State University of New York Press.

Fraser, N. (2011). *Guilt trippin' and the mothering of Black boys in Toronto* (Unpublished doctoral dissertation). York University, Toronto, ON.

Frey, D. (2004). *The last shot: City streets, basketball dreams*. Boston, MA: Mariner Books.

Fuligni, A.J. (2001). A comparative longitudinal approach to acculturation among children from immigrant families. *Harvard Educational Review, 71*(3), 566–78. https://doi.org/10.17763/haer.71.3.j7046h63234441u3

Gosa, T., & Alexander, K.L. (2007). Family (dis)advantage and the educational prospects of better off African American youth: How race still matters. *Teachers College Record, 109*(2), 285–321.

Gosine, K. (2012). Accomplished Black North Americans and antiracism education: Towards bridging a seeming divide. *Critical Sociology, 38*(5), 707–21. https://doi.org/10.1177/0896920510380077

Griffith, A. (2006). Constructing single parent families for schooling: Discovering an institutional discourse. In D.E. Smith (Ed.), *Institutional ethnography as practice* (pp. 127–38). Lanham, MD: Rowman & Littlefield.

Growing up without men [radio transcript]. (2007). *Metro Morning*. Toronto, ON: Canadian Broadcasting Corporation.

Harrison, L., Sailes, G, Rotich, W.K., & Bimper, A.Y. (2011). Living the dream or awakening from the nightmare: Race and athletic identity. *Race, Ethnicity and Education, 14*(1), 91–103. https://doi.org/10.1080/13613324.2011.531982

Henry, F., & Tator, C. (2010). *The colour of democracy: Racism in Canadian society* (4th ed.). Toronto, ON: Nelson Education.

Hernandez, K.C., & Davis, J.E. (2009). The other side of gender: Understanding Black masculinity in teaching and learning. In H.R. Milner (Ed.), *Diversity and education: Teachers, teaching and teacher education* (pp. 17–30). Springfield, IL: Charles C. Thomas.

Hernandez-Ramdwar, C. (2009). Caribbean students in the Canadian academy: We've come a long way? In F. Henry & C. Tator (Eds.), *Racism in the Canadian university: Demanding social justice, inclusion, and equity* (pp. 106–27). Toronto, ON: University of Toronto Press.

Howard, T.C. (2008). Who really cares? The disenfranchisement of African American males in preK–12 schools: A critical race theory perspective. *Teachers College Record, 110*(5), 954–85.

Ibrahim, A. (2000). "Whassup homeboy?" Black popular culture and the politics of curriculum. In G.S. Dei & A. Calliste (Eds.), *Power, knowledge and anti-racism education: A sritical reader* (pp. 57–72). Halifax, NS: Fernwood.

James, C.E. (2009). Masculinity, racialization, and schooling: The making of marginalized men. In W. Martino, M. Kehler, & M.B. Weaver-Hightower (Eds.), *The problem with boys' education: Beyond the backlash* (pp. 102–23). New York, NY: Routledge.

James, C.E. (2010). Schooling and the university plans of immigrant Black students from an urban neighborhood. In H.R. Milner (Ed.), *Culture, curriculum, and identity in education* (pp. 117–39). New York, NY: Palgrave Macmillan.

James, C.E. (2011). Why is the school basketball team predominantly Black? In S. Tozer, B. Gallegos, A. Henry, M. Bushell Greiner, & P. Groves Price (Eds.), *Handbook of research in social foundations of education* (pp. 450–9). New York, NY: Routledge.

James, C.E. (2012a). Students "at risk": Stereotyping and the schooling of Black boys. *Urban Education, 47*(2), 464–94. https://doi.org/10.1177/0042085911429084

James, C.E. (2012b). Troubling role models: Seeing racialization in the discourse relating to "corrective agents" for Black males. In K. Moffatt (Ed.), *Troubled masculinities: Reimagining urban men* (pp. 77–92). Toronto, ON: University of Toronto Press.

James, C.E., & Taylor, L. (2010). The making of at risk students: How youth see teachers thwarting their education. In C.C. Smith (Ed.), *Anti-racism in education: Missing in action* (pp. 123–36). Ottawa, ON: Canadian Centre for Policy Alternatives.

Kelly, P. (2000). The dangerousness of youth-at-risk: The possibilities of surveillance and intervention in uncertain times. *Journal of Adolescence, 23*, 463–76. https://doi.org/10.1006/jado.2000.0331

Kim, Y. (2009). Minority parental involvement and school barriers: Moving the focus away from deficiencies of parents. *Educational Research Review, 4*, 80–102. https://doi.org/10.1016/j.edurev.2009.02.003

Kimmel, M. (2007). Masculinity as homophobia: Fear, shame and silence in the construction of gender identity. In N. Cook (Ed.), *Gender relations in global perspective: Essential readings* (pp. 73–82). Toronto, ON: Canadian Scholars' Press.

Lawson, E. (2012). Single mothers, absentee fathers and gun violence in Toronto: A contextual interpretation. *Women's Studies, 41*(7), 805–28. https://doi.org/10.1080/00497878.2012.707903

Lawson-Bush, V. (2004). How black mothers participate in the development of manhood and masculinity: What do we know about black mothers and their sons? *Journal of Negro Education, 73*(4), 381–91. https://doi.org/10.2307/4129623

Leach, M. (1994/2009). The politics of masculinity: An overview of contemporary theory. *Social Alternatives, 12*(4), 36–7. https://xyonline.net/content/politics-masculinity-overview-contemporary-theory

Lee, S.J. (2008). Model minorities and perpetual foreigners. In M. Sadowski (Ed.), *Adolescents at school: Perspectives on youth, identity, and education* (pp. 75–84). Cambridge, MA: Harvard Education Press.

Levin, B. (2004). Students at-risk: A review of research. *Educator's Notebook: Reviews of Research of Interest to Educators, 15*(3), 1–4

Levin, B., & Peacock. K. (2004). *Students at risk.* Progress report on the quality of public education in Canada, no. 2. Toronto, ON: The Learning Partnership.

Lynn, M., Bacon, J.N., Totten, T.L., Bridges, T.L., III, & Jennings, M.E. (2010). Examining teachers' beliefs about African American male students in a low-performing high school in an African American school district. *Teachers College Record, 112*(1), 289–330.

Mackey, E. (2002). *The house of difference: Cultural politics and national identity in Canada.* Toronto, ON: University of Toronto Press.

McCready, L.T. (2010). *Making space for diverse masculinities: Difference, intersectionality, and engagement in an urban high school.* New York, NY: Peter Lang.

McDermott, R., & Varenne, H. (2006). Reconstructing culture in educational research. In G. Spindler & L. Hammonds (Eds.), *Innovations in educational ethnography* (pp. 3–31). Mahwah, NJ: Lawrence Erlbaum Associates.

McGhee Hassrick, E., & Schneider, B.L. (2009). Parent surveillance in schools: A question of social class. *American Journal of Education, 115*, 195–225. https://doi.org/10.1086/595665

McKenzie, K. (2009). Emotional abuse of students of color: The hidden inhumanity in our schools. *International Journal of Qualitative Studies in Education, 2*(22), 129–43. https://doi.org/10.1080/09518390801998270

Meiners, E.R., & Winn, M.T. (2010). Resisting the school to prison pipeline: The practice to build abolition democracies. *Race, Ethnicity and Education, 13*(3), 271–6. https://doi.org/10.1080/13613324.2010.500832

Milner, H.R. (2007). Race, culture, and researcher positionality: Working through dangers seen, unseen, and unforeseen. *Educational Researcher, 36*(7), 388–400. https://doi.org/10.3102/0013189X07309471

Milner, H.R. (2008). Critical race theory and interest convergence as analytical tools in teacher education policies and practices. *Journal of Teacher Education. 59*(4), 332–46. https://doi.org/10.1177/0022487108321884

Milner, H.R. (2010). *Start where you are, but don't stay there: Understanding diversity, opportunity gaps, and teaching in today's classrooms*. Cambridge, MA: Harvard University Press.

Mosher, J.E. (2008). Lessons in access to justice: Racialized youths and Ontario's Safe Schools. *Osgoode Hall Law Journal, 46*(4), 807–51. https://digitalcommons.osgoode.yorku.ca/ohlj/vol46/iss4/4/

Noguera, P.A. (2008). *The trouble with Black boys: And other reflections on race, equity, and the future of public education*. San Francisco, CA: Jossey-Bass.

Palmer, H. (1998). "… But where are you really from?": Stories of identity and assimilation in Canada. Toronto, ON: Sister Vision Press.

Raby, R. (2002). A tangle of discourses: Girls negotiating adolescence. *Journal of Youth Studies, 5*(4), 425–48. https://doi.org/10.1080/1367626022000030976

Sevier, B., & Ashcraft, C. (2009). Be careful what you ask for: Exploring the confusion around and usefulness of the male teacher as male role model discourse. *Men and Masculinities, 11*(5), 533–57. https://doi.org/10.1177/1097184X07302290

Shadd, A. (2001), "Where are you really from?": Notes of an "immigrant" from Buxton, Ontario. In C.E. James & A. Shadd (Eds.), *Talking about identity: Encounters in race, language and identity* (pp. 10–16). Toronto, ON: Between the Lines.

Shannon, P. (1998). *Reading poverty*. Portsmouth, NH: Heinemann.

Shujaa, M.J. (1993) Education and schooling: You can have one without the other. *Urban Education, 27*(4), 328–51. https://doi.org/10.1177/0042085993027004002

Simmel, G. (1950). The stranger. (K. Wolff, Trans.). In K. Wolff (Ed.), *The sociology of Georg Simmel* (pp. 402–8). New York, NY: Free Press. (Original work published 1908)

Singer. J.N. (2009). Preparing African American male student-athletes for post-secondary education: Implications for educational stakeholders. In H.R. Milner (Ed.), *Diversity and education: Teachers, teaching and teacher education* (pp. 31–50). Springfield, IL: Charles C. Thomas.

Singer, J.N., & Buford May, R.A. (2010). The career trajectory of a Black male high school basketball player: A social reproduction perspective. *International Review for the Sociology of Sport, 46*(3), 299–314. https://doi.org/10.1177/1012690210378283

Smith, A., Schneider, B.H., & Ruck, M.D. (2005). "Thinking about makin' it": Black Canadian students' beliefs regarding education and academic achievement. *Journal of Youth and Adolescence, 34*(4), 347–59. https://doi.org/10.1007/s10964-005-5759-0

Solomon, R.P., & Palmer, H. (2004). Schooling in Babylon, Babylon in school: When racial profiling and zero tolerance converge. *Canadian Journal of Educational Administration and Policy, 33*. https://journalhosting.ucalgary.ca/index.php/cjeap/article/view/42713

Statistics Canada. (2009). *Canada's ethnocultural mosaic, 2006 census*. Cat. no. 97-562-X. Ottawa, ON: Minister of Industry. http://www12.statcan.ca/english/census06/analysis/ethnicorigin/pdf/97-562-XIE2006001.pdf

Statistics Canada (2019, February 27). Diversity of the Black population in Canada: An overview. https://www150.statcan.gc.ca/n1/pub/89-657-x/89-657-x2019002-eng.htm

Statistics Canada. (2020, February 25). *Canada's Black population: Education, labour and resilience*. Cat. no. 89-657-X2020002. Ottawa, ON: Minister of Industry. https://www150.statcan.gc.ca/n1/pub/89-657-x/89-657-x2020002-eng.htm

Stevenson, H.C. (2004). Boys in men's clothing: Racial socialization and neighbourhood safety as buffers to hypervulnerability in African American adolescent males. In N. Way & J.Y. Chu (Eds.), *Adolescent boys: Exploring diverse cultures of boyhood* (pp. 59–77). New York, NY: New York University Press.

Suárez-Orozco, C., Qin, D.B., & Amthor, R.F. (2008). Relationships and adaptation in school. In M. Sadowski (Ed.), *Adolescents at school: Perspectives on youth, identity, and education* (pp. 51–69). Cambridge, MA: Harvard Education Press.

Tanovich, D. (2006). *The colour of justice: Policing race in Canada*. Toronto, ON: Irwin Law.

Toronto District School Board. (2010, May). *Achievement gap task force draft report*. Toronto, ON: Toronto District School Board, Student and Community Equity.

Turcotte, M. (2020, February 25). *Results from the 2016 census: Education and labour market integration of Black youth in Canada*. Statistics Canada cat. no. 75-006-X. Ottawa, ON: Minister of Industry.

van der Land, M., & Doff, W. (2010). Voice, exit and efficacy: Dealing with perceived neighbourhood decline without moving out. *Journal of Housing and the Built Environment, 25*, 429–45. https://doi.org/10.1007/s10901-010-9197-2

Wacquant, L. (2008). *Urban outcasts: A comparative sociology of advanced marginality*. Cambridge, UK: Polity Press.

Walcott, R. (2009). Reconstructing manhood; or, the drag of Black masculinity. *Small Axe, 13*(1), 75–89. https://doi.org/10.1215/07990537-2008-007

Wotherspoon, T., & Schissel, B. (2001). The business of placing Canadian children and youth "at-risk." *Canadian Journal of Education, 26*(3), 321–39. https://doi.org/10.2307/1602211

Yosso, T.J. (2005). Whose culture has capital? A critical race theory discussion of community cultural wealth. *Race Ethnicity and Education, 8*(1), 69–91. https://doi.org/10.1080/1361332052000341006

Young, D., Wood, P.B., & Keil, R. (Eds.). (2011). *In-between infrastructure: Urban connectivity in an age of vulnerability*. Kelowna, BC: Praxis (e)Press.

Response to Chapter 4

Black Lives Matter in the USA and Canada

JOYCE E. KING
Benjamin E. Mays Endowed Chair for Urban Teaching, Learning & Leadership, Department of Educational Policy Studies, College of Education and Human Development, Georgia State University, Georgia, USA

Say Their Names: Black Men and Boys Killed by the Police
in the United States and Canada

UNITED STATES

Amadou Diallo, Sean Bell, Trayvon Martin, Eric Garner, Tamir Rice, Clifford Glover, Oscar Grant, Philando Castille, Keith Scott, Michael Brown, Jordan Davis, Laquan McDonald, Freddie Gray, Samuel DuBose, Shem Jean, Akai Gurley, Walter L. Scott, Paul O'Neal, Alton B. Sterling, Keith Lamont Scott, Christian Taylor, Stephon Clark, Terence Crutcher, Tony Robinson, Rumain Brisbon, Antwon Rose, John Crawford, Jemel Roberson, Ahmaud Arbery, Daniel Prude, George Floyd …

CANADA

Albert Johnson, Buddy Evans, Abdirahman Abdi, Pierre Coriolan, Andrew Loku, Alex Wettlaufer, Kwasi Skene-Peters, Jean-Pierre Bony, Ian Pryce, Frank Antony Berry, Michael Eligon, Eric Osawe, Reyal Jardine-Douglas, Junior Alexander Manon, Lester Donaldson, Anthony Griffin, Michael Wade Lawson, O'Brien Christopher-Reid, Jermaine Carby, Ian Coley, Albert Moses, Raymond Lawrence, Nicholas Gibbs, D'Andre Campbell …[1]

---

1 Sammy Yatim, a youth of colour, was killed by a policeman who was convicted of "attempted murder" (W. Campbell & Miller, 2016). See also Gillis (2015), Harper and Mukerjee (2018), Mukerjee (2018), Ontario Human Rights Commission (2017).

> When Black people are killed by the police, white Canada has a ready script of liberalism, multiculturalism, and Canadian fairness that serves to silence any discussion of race and racism. (Barrett, 2017)

> The way that Black children and youth are treated [in Canada] – and the way that their suffering is largely ignored or unseen – makes clear that anti-Blackness determines their experiences within the education system and beyond. (Maynard, 2017a)

This brief reflection is informed by my long view of relevant research (e.g., Henry, 1998), official reports, and my engaged scholarship (King, 1992), including a book that explored "the paradox of dilemma as choice" that Black mothers experience raising our sons – "between a rock and a hard place" in family, community, and school settings (King & Mitchell, 1995, p. 9). In chapter 4, Carl James incisively analyses African-Canadian male students' schooling experiences and outcomes: how they "become at risk" and what cultural meanings this designation reveals about the prevailing racist discourse in Canada. Notwithstanding both real and imagined differences between structural and discursive racism in the US and Canada ("ugly American, quiet Canadian"), anti-Black stereotypes function in both contexts. Another alarming shared reality is likely a consequence of such dehumanizing classifications: police murder Black men and boys with apparent impunity in both the US and Canada (Giamondi, 2017). *The Atlantic* reports:

> According to several different studies, black men [in the US] aged 15–34 are between nine and 16 times more likely to be killed by police than other people. In 2017, police killed 19 unarmed black males, down from 36 in 2015, according to *The Washington Post*. The *Post* analyses also showed that police usually use fatal force against people armed with knives or guns. (Khazan, 2018, para. 5)

Such gendered racial terror (Haley, 2016) also exists in Canada: racialized stereotypes as mechanisms of white supremacy racism are matters of life and death and not just barriers to societal inclusion and equality (Hayes, 2018).

In addition to lecturing in Halifax and Toronto and evaluating academic programs in Toronto universities, I have had arresting personal encounters with the diverse impacts of anti-Black racism in Canada's schools and on Black youth. When I participated in a World Council of Churches Programme to Combat Racism fact-finding delegation to Toronto – visiting schools, witnessing "discipline" practices, and meeting with local Black community leaders – the police shot and seriously wounded an unarmed sixteen-year-old Black youth and there was a vocal protest against a racist museum exhibit on Africa in the city. What seems to have changed since these events in 1989 is the organized capacity of Black Canadians, supported by the kind of research chapter 4 presents, to analyse, agitate, and propose remedies in defence of the diverse African-Canadian communities (see "Royal Ontario Museum Apologizes," 2016).

Anti-Black Racism in Canada

Since chapter 4 appeared in *Urban Education* in 2012, more and more research projects and numerous investigations have documented the impact of anti-Black racism in Canada. This documentation includes the *Report* of the United Nations Working Group of Experts on People of African Descent (2017); Maynard's (2017b) book, *Policing Black Lives: State Violence in Canada from Slavery to the Present*; and the African Canadian Legal Clinic's (2017) report to the UN High Commission on Human Rights Committee on the Elimination of Racial Discrimination (CERD). The UN Working Group of Experts (2017) recommended that the government should "strengthen Afrocentric education curricula" in Canada (p. 19). Further, the African community's report to CERD, "Making Real Change for African Canadians," cites Carl James's research, and these excerpts about education are worth noting:

- By teaching students using a predominantly White, Eurocentric curriculum, Canadian schools epistemically neglect the culture and history of racialized groups in Canadian society. As one of Canada's oldest peoples, this is particularly burdensome for the African Canadian community, which has had a substantial element of its history erased from Canada's national history …
- The absence or minimization of African Canadian culture from standardized Canadian curricula enforces the ideological superiority of European thought patterns. Canada must reflect on the ideological spaces it intends to create for its people; if it generally seeks to form an inclusive identity, then provincial governments must address the ways in which they enforce Eurocentric superiority. (African Canadian Legal Clinic, 2017, p. 26)

Beyond Invisibilizing Stereotypes in the Language of Dominance

Scholars observe that Canada's multicultural discourse (proclaiming tolerance, inclusion, etc.) masks the fact that race matters in the Canadian context. James emphasizes that language is not innocent. Indeed, as the celebrated Black writer Toni Morrison (1993) observed in her Nobel Prize lecture and acceptance speech: "Sexist language, racist language, theistic language – all are typical of the policing languages of mastery, and cannot, do not permit new knowledge or encourage the mutual exchange of ideas" (pp. 16–17).

The cultural analysis in chapter 4 of the invisibilizing stereotypes of Black male students and the dehumanizing "language of risk" is a step towards unmasking the inherent racism in Canada's "ready script" (Barrett, 2017) of multiculturalism. However, using action verbs instead of descriptive adjectives and nouns can take the subtle onus of culpability in this language of Black youth and their families. For example, instead of describing "fatherless" youth and "absent fathers," using the verb *"absented* fathers" reframes the reality and redirects our thinking towards critically uncovering the societal circumstances that maintain white dominance and prevent fathers from being present in their families and in the lives of sons and daughters (Khan-Cullors, 2017). In *Blackening Canada*, Barrett (2015) uses the conceptualization of "absented history" to denote the way Eurocentric curricula omit Canada's history of slavery, segregation, and racism (Bradburn, 2018).

Chapter 4 reveals that Black students whom educators label as "troublemakers" are preemptively *criminalized* by what Milner (2018) argues are punishment rather than disciplinary practices (e.g., the presence of police officers) in schools in Canada and the US, where the "Eurocentric curriculum and the approach of educators to the learning of Black students operate as impediments to educational success." Thus, "underachievers" can be more accurately understood as *impeded* achievers. Likewise, using verbs like *resource-starved* instead of *under-resourced* and replacing *poverty* and *poor* with *impoverishment* and *impoverished* with reference to students and their schools and communities signals human actions and societal mechanisms and not the inevitability of Black people's marginalization or presumed cultural deficits.

Instead of inadvertently promulgating the "inassimilability" stereotype of Black youth, might the alternative conceptualization of *becoming unapologetically Black,* centred within Africana/Black Studies theorizing, illuminate the limiting cultural processes within education that is centred within the Canadian national narrative and that is devoid of African Canadians' history and heritage of cultural capital and resilience (Manzo & Bailey, 2005)? Accordingly, Maynard (2018) recognizes that both "invisibility within curricula and the predominantly white demographic makeup of educators continue to negatively affect Black students."

As a Black American mother explains, keeping young Black American males "physically and emotionally safe" is a matter of avoiding "spirit-murdering" (Arki, 2018, p. 271), as conceptualized by Williams (1991) and elaborated by Love (2014):

> The personal, psychological, and spiritual injuries to people of color through the fixed, yet fluid and moldable, structures of racism, privilege, and power spirit-murdering denies inclusion, protection, safety, nurturance, and acceptance – all things a person needs to be human and to be educated. (p. 302)

This brief reflection on reframing to go beyond the discourse on stereotypes is intended to disconnect the implicit language of dominance, which is emotionally and epistemically connected to white educators' feelings about their Canadian (or American) identity, from a vocabulary that, Wynter (2006) theorizes, ineluctably affirms the supposed inferiority of conceptual Blackness in alter ego relation to conceptual whiteness.

Conclusion

Beyond Stereotypes: From Blackness to Diasporic Subjectivity for Human Freedom

In conclusion, in addition to examining the limits of the prevailing overreliance on testing, we can advance our communities' best interests by defining what it means to "do well in school" from a Black epistemological and ideological position. Woodson (1933/1993) and Du Bois (1897, 1935) represent the Black intellectual tradition that has challenged African Americans to consider what kind of education our people require, not to assimilate but to meet our collective community needs. Scholars/practitioners (Acosta, Foster, & Houchen, 2018; L. Campbell, 2014; Codjoe, 2006; Henry, 1998; Nasir, 2012) have demonstrated that pedagogy and curricula that affirm students' self-identity and pride in their African cultural/racial identity and excellence traditions are essential to our well-being, both as people of diverse African ancestries and the experiences they entail, and as citizens of the countries in which we reside. Wherever people of African ancestry are, we need opportunities to learn about indigenous African knowledge and languages within our excellence traditions (Adeji, 2007; Asante, 2017; Dei, 2000; King & Swartz, 2018; Nobles, 2008). What then constitutes a culturally informed antiracist/anticolonial education for diaspora literacy and human freedom in Canada where, instead of *being* black (Taddese, 2017) – that is, assigned "a stable identity defined by skin or corporeality" (Dei & James, 1998, p. 104) within a racist cultural model – our students instead achieve *diasporic subjectivity* (Cho, 2017), *becoming* Black through collective memory and agency as well as "process, performance, and strategy" (Walcott, 2003, p. 13)? In other words, "Blackness is also a way of being and becoming [human] in the world" on our own terms in our relations with others (Walcott, 2003, p. 125).

REFERENCES

Acosta, M.M., Foster, M., & Houchen, D.F. (2018). "Why seek the living among the dead?" African American pedagogical excellence: Exemplar practice for teacher education. *Journal of Teacher Education, 69*(4), 341–53. https://doi.org/10.1177/0022487118761881

Adeji, P.B. (2007). Decolonizing knowledge production: The pedagogic relevance of Gandhian Satyagraha to schooling and education in Ghana. *Canadian Journal of Education, 30*(4), 1046–67. https://doi.org/10.2307/20466678

African Canadian Legal Clinic. (2017). Making real change happen for African Canadians: Report of the African Canadian Legal Clinic to the Committee on the Elimination of Racial Discrimination (93rd Session). Toronto, ON: Author. https://tbinternet.ohchr.org/Treaties/CERD/Shared Documents/CAN/INT_CERD_NGO_CAN_28173_E.pdf

Arki, S. (2018). Ruminations from the intersections of a #BlackMommyActivist. In E. Moore, Jr., A. Michael, & M.W. Penick-Parks (Eds.), *The guide for white women who teach Black boys* (pp. 270–7). Thousand Oaks, CA: Corwin.

Asante, M.K. (2017). *Revolutionary pedagogy: Primer for teachers of Black children.* Brooklyn, NY: Universal Write Publications.

Barrett, P. (2015). *Blackening Canada: Diaspora, race and multiculturalism.* Toronto, ON: University of Toronto Press.

Barrett, P. (2017, February 24). *In Canada, the killing of Black men never seems to be about race.* rabble.ca. http://rabble.ca/blogs/bloggers/2017-02-24t000000/canada-killing-black-men-police-never-seems-be-about-race

Bradburn, J. (2018, February 26). *The Story of Ontario's last segregated Black school.* TVO. https://tvo.org/article/current-affairs/the-story-of-ontarios-last-segregated-black-school

Campbell, L. (2014). Austin Steward: "Home-style" teaching, planning, and assessment. In J.E. King & E.E. Swartz (Eds.), *"Re-membering" history in student and teacher learning: An Afrocentric culturally informed praxis* (pp. 107–20). New York, NY: Routledge.

Campbell, W., & Miller, A. (2016, January 25). Sammy Yatim: Toronto cop guilty of attempted murder in streetcar shooting. *Global News.* https://

globalnews.ca/news/2465927/sammy-yatim-toronto-police-officer-found-not-guilty-of-2nd-degree-murder-in-2013-streetcar-shooting/

Cho, L. (2017). The turn to diaspora. *Topia: Canadian Journal of Cultural Studies, 17*, 11–13. https://doi.org/10.3138/topia.17.11

Codjoe, H. (2006). The role of an affirmed black cultural identity and heritage in the academic achievement of African-Canadian students. *Intercultural Education, 17*(1), 33–54. https://doi.org/10.1080/14675980500502271

Dei, G.J.S. (2000). Rethinking the role of Indigenous knowledges in the academy. *International Journal of Inclusive Education, 4*(2), 111–32. https://doi.org/10.1080/136031100284849

Dei, G.J.S., & James, I.M. (1998). "Becoming Black": African-Canadian youth and the politics of negotiating racial and racialized identities. *Race Ethnicity and Education, 1*(1), 91–108. https://doi.org/10.1080/1361332980010107

Du Bois, W.E.B. (1897). The conservation of races. *The American Negro Academy Occasional Papers, 2*, 1–15.

Du Bois, W.E.B. (1935, July). Does the Negro need separate schools? *Journal of Negro Education*, 328–35. https://doi.org/10.2307/2291871

Giamondi, M. (2017, August 15). Quiet Canadian, ugly American: Does racism differ north of the border? The Conversation. http://theconversation.com/quiet-canadian-ugly-american-does-racism-differ-north-of-the-border-81388

Gillis, W. (2015, August 16). Killed by Toronto police? We can't know. *Toronto Star*. https://www.thestar.com/news/crime/2015/08/16/how-many-black-men-have-been-killed-by-toronto-police-we-cant-know.html

Haley, S. (2016). *No mercy here: Gender, punishment, and the making of Jim Crow modernity*. Chapel Hill, NC: University of North Carolina Press.

Harper, T., & Mukherjee, A. (2018, March 29). *Remembering the mentally ill people of colour killed by Toronto police*. Vice. https://www.vice.com/en_ca/article/a3y3ek/remembering-the-mentally-ill-people-of-colour-killed-by-toronto-police

Hayes, M. (2018, December 11). Black people more likely to be injured or killed by Toronto police officers. *Globe and Mail*. https://www.theglobeandmail.com/canada/toronto/article-report-reveals-racial-disparities-in-toronto-polices-use-of-force/

Henry, A. (1998). *Taking back control: African Canadian women teachers' lives and practice*. Albany, NY: State University of New York Press.

Khan-Cullors, P. (2017). *When they call you a terrorist: A Black Lives Matter memoir*. New York, NY: St. Martin's Press.

Khazan, O. (2018, May 18). In one year 57,375 years of life were lost to police violence. *The Atlantic*. https://www.theatlantic.com/health/archive/2018/05/the-57375-years-of-life-lost-to-police-violence/559835/

King, J.E. (1992). Diaspora literacy and consciousness in the struggle against mis-education in the Black community. *Journal of Negro Education, 61*(3), 317–38. https://doi.org/10.2307/2295251

King, J.E., & Mitchell, C.A. (1995). *Black mothers to sons: Juxtaposing African American literature with social practice*. New York, NY: Peter Lang.

King, J.E., & Swartz, E.E. (2018). *Heritage knowledge in the curriculum: Retrieving an African episteme*. New York, NY: Routledge.

Love, B. (2014). "I see Trayvon Martin": What teachers can learn from the tragic death of a young black male. *Urban Review, 46*(2), 292–306. https://doi.org/10.1007/s11256-013-0260-7

Manzo, J.F., & Bailey, M.M. (2005). On the assimilation of racial stereotypes among Black Canadian young offenders. *Canadian Review of Sociology, 42*(3), 283–300. https://doi.org/10.1111/j.1755-618X.2005.tb00841.x

Maynard, R. (2017a, November 29). Canadian education is steeped in anti-Black racism. *The Walrus*. https://thewalrus.ca/canadian-education-is-steeped-in-anti-black-racism/

Maynard, R. (2017b). *Policing Black lives: State violence in Canada from slavery to the present*. Halifax, NS: Fernwood.

Maynard, R. (2018, April 24). Over-policing in black communities is a Canadian problem, too. *Washington Post*. https://www.washingtonpost.com/news/global-opinions/wp/2018/04/24/over-policing-in-black-communities-is-a-canadian-crisis-too/

Milner, H.R. (2018, October 25). *Disrupting punitive practices and politics: Rac(e)ing back to teaching: Teacher preparation, and Brown*. 15th Annual AERA Brown Lecture in Education Research, Washington, DC. https://www.youtube.com/watch?v=wBoF5pFHtDM&t=1502s

Morrison, T. (1993). *The Nobel lecture in literature*. New York, NY: Knopf.

Mukherjee, A. (with Harper, T.). (2018). *Excessive force: Toronto's fight to reform city policing*. Madeira Park, BC: Douglas & McIntyre.

Nasir, N.S. (2012). *Racialized identities: Race and achievement among African American youth*. Stanford, CA: Stanford University Press.

Nobles, W.W. (2008). Per Âa Asa Hilliard: The Great House of Black Light for educational excellence. *Review of Educational Research, 78*(3), 727–47. https://doi.org/10.3102/0034654308320969

Ontario Human Rights Commission. (2017). Timeline of racial discrimination and racial profiling of Black persons by the Toronto Police Service, and OHRC initiatives related to the Toronto Police. http://www.ohrc.on.ca/en/timeline-tps

Royal Ontario Museum apologizes for "racist" Africa exhibit it held nearly 30 years ago. (2016, November 10). *National Post*. https://nationalpost.com/news/toronto/royal-ontario-museum-apologizes-for-racist-africa-exhibit-it-held-nearly-30-years-ago

Taddese, Y. (2017, July 28). I didn't know I was Black until I moved to Canada: It's not the story Canada likes to tell about itself. But it's a story that needs to be told. *CBC*. https://www.cbc.ca/2017/i-didn-t-know-i-was-black-until-i-moved-to-canada-1.4219157

United Nations Working Group of Experts on People of African Descent. (2017, September). *Report of the Working Group of Experts on People of African Descent on its mission to Canada.* https://ansa.novascotia.ca/sites/default/files/files/report-of-the-working-group-of-experts-on-people-of-african-descent-on-its-mission-to-canada.pdf

Walcott, R. (2003). *Black like who? Writing Black Canada.* Toronto, ON: Insomniac Press.

Williams, P.J. (1991). *The alchemy of race and rights.* Cambridge, MA: Harvard University Press.

Woodson, C.G. (1993). *The mis-education of the Negro.* Trenton, NJ: Africa World Press. (Original work published 1933)

Wynter, S. (2006). On how we mistook the map for the territory, and re-imprisoned ourselves in our unbearable wrongness of being, of désêtre: Black Studies toward the human project. In L.R. Gordon & J.A. Gordon (Eds.), *Not only the master's tools: African-American studies in theory and practice* (pp. 107–69). New York, NY: Paradigm.

5 More than Brains, Education, and Hard Work: The Aspirations and Career Trajectories of Two Young Black Men[1]

In a 2011 article in *Forbes* magazine, entitled "If I Were a Poor Black Kid," Gene Marks (2011) refers to what he calls an "excellent speech" by President Obama, who spoke about the possibilities of social mobility for working-class people in America. Marks suggests that "everyone in this country has a chance to succeed," and states that prospects are not "impossible for those kids from the inner city." Marks goes on to say, "It takes brains. It takes hard work. It takes a little luck. And a little help from others. It takes the ability and the know-how to use the resources that are available. Like technology." Like Marks and many other Americans (evident from the feedback his article generated[2]), Canadians too have long pondered why "poor black kids" do not take advantage of the educational opportunities and the technological resources available to them.

The idea that equality of opportunity exists, and that all Black youth have to do is use their "brains," work hard, and access the necessary resources is premised on certain foundational concepts and values – individualism, competition, personal responsibility, free choice, accountability, exercise of agency, resiliency, and strategic aspirations – all of which together constitute the ethos of neoliberalism (see Braedley & Luxton, 2010; Porfilio & Malott, 2008), outlined in the introduction to this volume. Influenced by this ethos, particularly through their schooling, Black youth and their parents come to expect that they can realize the educational, social, and material successes they seek. But the path to such realization is contingent on many social, institutional, and structural

---

1 This chapter was originally published in 2015. James (2015). Reprinted with the permission of the publisher.
2 See Emdin (2011), Gandy (2011), Peitzman (2011), and Touré (2011).

factors that fall beyond an individual's control. For young Black men, the neoliberal "success formula" is remarkably precarious when we take into account how race, class, and gender operate in their lives.

In this chapter, I reference the experiences of two African-Canadian men in their late twenties, "Kobe" and "Trevor" (pseudonyms), to show how neoliberal rationalities contributed to forming both their career aspirations and their employment opportunities. While both young men grew up in the same media-branded "troubled" Toronto community and would appear to have made "all the right moves" in terms of their efforts to attain their career aspirations, their achievements differ dramatically. I argue that the difference in outcome cannot be explained simply by intellectual ability, level of education attained, or professional qualification, but – probably more importantly – by the complex ways that opportunities were afforded to them.

I will start by reviewing the principles that underpin neoliberalism, and using critical race theory as a rejoinder, discuss the ways neoliberalism obscures the effects of race, class, and gender for racialized people. Before analyzing the findings, I briefly discuss my theoretical references and research methodology. These are followed by a brief description of the neighbourhood where the two young men grew up.

Theoretical References: Neoliberalism and Critical Race Theory

We have a generally accepted notion that individuals can attain the education they desire, make choices, freely pursue employment opportunities, become wealthy, and take responsibility for their lives as they see fit. The prevailing ethos of neoliberalism, which informs these "common-sense" notions, also holds that competition constitutes an important "social good" and the "least restrictive way" of addressing and redistributing inequitable resources (Braedley & Luxton, 2010, p. 8). In addition, Canada, which has an official multiculturalism policy (1971) and legislation (1988), promotes "inclusive citizenship" and guarantees the "value and dignity" of all citizens, "regardless of their racial and ethnic origins," and "their language or religious affiliation."

Yet minoritized group members continue to experience educational, social, civic, and economic marginalization and exclusion (Basu, 2011, p. 1308; see also Reitz, Breton, Dion, & Dion, 2009). Moreover, today's youth are caught in a capitalist system that has led to large populations of unemployed, working-class, poor, and racialized youth, typically residing in urban settings, with worldviews, identities, and ways of life that are oppositional or peripheral to the existing social order

(Sukarieh & Tannock, 2008, p. 304). Despite the promise of mobility, racialized youth must wrestle with the dynamic, complex aspects of racism. Here critical race theory is particularly useful, for it enables us to understand how youth of colour fare in a neoliberal context. Critical race theory situates the experiences of people of colour at its centre and thus highlights how seemingly race-neutral and colour-blind practices and policies disproportionately affect minoritized people (Aylward, 1999, p. 34).

The "inextricable layers of racialized subordination" (Howard, 2008, p. 73), based on gender, social class, and generational status, play a significant role in determining the opportunities young people will have, the neighbourhoods in which they will live, the schools they can attend, and the educational resources to which they will have access (see chapter 4). Participating in an inequitable education system poses difficulties for students who do not possess or have access to middle-class "cultural capital," which Yosso (2005) defines as "an accumulation of specific forms of knowledge, skills, and abilities that are *valued* by privileged groups in society" (p. 76). Nevertheless, Yosso argues, youth of colour utilize "community cultural wealth" – that is, "an array of knowledge, skills, abilities, and contacts ... to survive and resist macro and micro-forms of oppression" (p. 77) – which enables them "to dream of possibilities beyond their present circumstances," even without the "objective means" to attain their educational, occupational, or social goals (p. 78).

Community resources and supports are crucial to young Black males on their journey through life, for as Walcott (2009) asserts, "under the contemporary regime of the global terms of neoliberal economy and by extension ... its culturally rhetorical disciplinary apparatus" (p. 75), Black masculinity is always constructed as deficient. As a counter to this hegemonic message, Black males subscribe to a masculinity framework that enables them to hold on to their "hopes and dreams for the future" – one that is sustained through aspirational capital, navigational skills, familial supports, and community validation, through which they are able, in Yosso's words (2005), to "challenge (resist) oppressive conditions" (p. 77).

Research Method

I interviewed Kobe and Trevor as part of two different qualitative research studies that I conducted with Toronto youth over a ten-year period. I took a "constructionist" approach to these studies – using the interviews (each lasting one to two hours) to have participants engage in a process of meaning-making or "sense-making work" (Roulston, 2007, p. 16).

I was not a neutral observer simply trying to access and then represent certain truths about my research participants (Stephenson, 2005). The audiotaped interviews were unstructured, enabling me to engage with Kobe's and Trevor's experiences and realities. As critical race theorists encourage, my approach allowed me to capture the stories (and counterstories) of participants in ways that incorporated *their* perspectives on their lives, including how they coped with and responded to their social, educational, and material conditions (Fernandez, 2002; Moore, Henfield, & Owens, 2008). This case-study approach, with its detailed examination of a particular issue, incident, or individual, not only recognizes and addresses issues in the participants' lives, it also enables a range of broad understandings that might otherwise be missed (Creswell, 1994). Notwithstanding the lack of generalizability, scholars assert that case studies can be used "to illuminate the nuanced complexity of social life in a variety of contexts" (Singer & Buford May, 2010, p. 305; see also Lichtman, 2013; Stake, 2000).

Kobe participated in a study with twenty-two other racialized young men and women between eighteen and twenty-five who had grown up in a marginalized Toronto neighbourhood. The study was designed to examine African-Canadian university students of Caribbean origin – their experiences, educational and career aspirations, and perceptions of their occupational opportunities and outcomes. Participants were first interviewed in 2001 or 2002, with follow-up interviews conducted with ten of the original respondents in 2006; Kobe alone was interviewed a third time in 2011. First interviewed in 2002 during his third year of university, Kobe, then twenty-two years old, was one of three participants who had been born in the Caribbean – in his case, Jamaica. He stood out initially from the other research participants not only for his display of self-confidence, tenacity, high achievement, and ways of engaging with his schooling (his teachers specifically) but also for his ambivalent relationship with his community. He recognized that his community could be a liability; hence, he distanced himself from it. At the same time, he used that liability as motivation to achieve his aspirations.

Trevor participated in a study that was first conducted in 2006, and designed specifically to study Black/African-Canadian male basketball players between the ages of eighteen and twenty-eight living in Toronto – their motivations, experiences, and aspirations. This study sought to probe whether playing on their high school basketball team proved to be a liability or an asset for Black student-athletes. Trevor was one of twelve participants in this study and the only one who had grown up in the same neighbourhood as Kobe. I interviewed Trevor initially in 2006, when he was twenty-five and in his fourth year of university, and then again in 2011. During his initial interview, I observed that Trevor, unlike Kobe, had strong ties to his community; this sparked my curiosity and interest in exploring the similarities and differences in their educational and career paths, their ambitions, and the role of the community in their lives.

Despite (among other similarities) having grown up in the same stigmatized Toronto neighbourhood, the two young men exhibited important differences – specifically, the ways they were supported (or not) by the educational system and by educators, and the privileging of particular educational and occupational interests over others. During the follow-up interviews, I asked about their educational achievements and occupational situation up until that point, noting their optimism and satisfaction with how they approached the goals they had set for themselves.

Kobe and Trevor, like the other participants in my studies, represented a growing population of second-generation (and 1.5-generation) Black/African-and Caribbean-Canadian youth who had been motivated by their immigrant parents' expectations to do well educationally in order to achieve success. Canadian studies of Black university students (Gosine, 2012; James & Taylor, 2008) show that their educational aspirations stem from their sense of obligation to their parents and their desire to "give back" to their (Black) community. And although aware of the structural realities of racism and other related barriers, these students maintained that because of their individual efforts and willpower, and on the basis of merit, "education had worked, was working, and would continue to work for them" (James & Taylor, 2008, p. 585). Gosine (2012) contends that such logic is informed by the larger society's neoliberal ethos of meritocracy, individualism, and "the belief that racism can be overcome by way of academic and occupational attainment, hard work, determination, and black solidarity" (p. 9).

In the following section, I discuss Kobe's and Trevor's childhood neighbourhood and then examine their career trajectories, noting similarities and differences in their strategies, levels of familial support, and achievements to date.

Kobe's and Trevor's Aspirations and Career Trajectories

The Neighbourhood

Kobe and Trevor lived and attended school in one of Toronto's "priority" areas, characterized by high rates of poverty, large numbers of low-income earners and public-housing tenants, a high proportion of immigrants, and a racialized population (Hulchanski, 2007; Stapleton, Murphy, & Xing, 2012). Established during the 1960s, the community is commonly referred to as an *urban* or *inner-city* neighbourhood, but Keil and Young's (2011) term *in-between* seems more fitting, in that it is an urban space "couched between the glamour zones of the downtown neighbourhoods and the exploding single-family home in the suburbs and exurbs ... an area that oscillates between unwelcome notoriety (for poverty and crime) and outright invisibility" (p. 1).

About 80,000 people live in this high-density neighbourhood, with a large cluster of high-rise apartment buildings and townhouses. Characteristic of what Myles and Hou (2004) term a *low-income immigrant enclave* (p. 31), it is home to a broad representation of Canada's diverse ethnoracial population. Black/African Canadians – most of them born in Canada to Caribbean parents – make up the largest racial-minoritized group (about 20 per cent), with the next largest racial minoritized being South Asian (about 18 per cent – a 2 per cent difference). The largest racial group in this neighbourhood, however, is white (nearly 30 per cent). It also has "one of the highest proportions of youth, sole-supported families, refugees, and immigrants ... of any community in Toronto" (MacNevin 1999, cited in James, 2012, p. 32). Schooling issues (such as low educational achievements, high dropout rates, and absenteeism) and social issues (drugs, gangs, and violence) draw widespread attention from educators, government policy-makers, police, and the media (Ezeonu, 2008; Lawson, 2014).

Many of the residents maintain a strong sense of loyalty, responsibility, and commitment to the place they consider home. But some residents, weary of the marginalization, stigmatization, and racialization, choose to leave the neighbourhood – often for the suburbs, seeking safety, comfort, and better schooling conditions for themselves and/or their children. These residents, many of them first-generation Canadians, construct going to live in the suburbs as a marker of upward social mobility (see chapter 9; also Myles & Hou, 2004).

Family, Community, and School

At twelve years old, Kobe immigrated to Canada from rural Jamaica with his older sister to join their single mother, who had already been living in Toronto for six years. He recalled that while he was "excited" about leaving Jamaica because of the inevitable changes that would come to his life, he was unsure about what to expect. About two years after settling in Toronto, his family moved to a rented apartment in the neighbourhood that Kobe would call home for the next ten years.

Trevor, on the other hand, was born in that same neighbourhood to a single mother who had grown up in the neighbourhood. He lived with his mother, grandmother, and uncle (a police officer). Trevor's mother had immigrated as a teenager to Canada from London, England, with her mother and brother.

Both young men grew up with working mothers – Kobe's mother worked as a legal secretary, Trevor's mother as a nurse. Both had concerns about raising their sons in the neighbourhood and conveyed these concerns to them, expressing that theirs was a neighbourhood of risk and danger – a place from which they should move as soon as possible. This characterization of the neighbourhood was consistent with the media's portrayal and its general reputation.

It is understandable that Kobe would avoid interactions with peers in the neighbourhood outside of school since he did not want "to get in trouble because of its reputation." He also stated, "I went to school, went to track, and went home and did my homework ... I had no friends in the area ... I didn't really, I guess, associate with a lot of people from the area outside of school." But for Trevor, growing up in the neighbourhood "was a blessing." As he explained,

> Growing up in [the neighbourhood] helped me by allowing me to see and feel what it was like to live in a community which did not have the best reputation. I think it helped make me [become] a critical thinker based on the fact that I was able to experience the positive things that the community had to offer rather than just hear about the negative.

In keeping with their determination to leave the "bad neighbourhood" for the sake of their children, especially their sons, both families did move from the neighbourhood. Kobe moved about three kilometres away during his second year in university, and Trevor moved to the outer suburbs at the end of Grade 7. As Trevor reported, his mother did not want him to "fall into the stereotype" or "become a statistic" – a reference to gang violence, shootings, and police targeting of Black youth in the neighbourhood (Ezeonu, 2008; Lawson, 2014). However, Trevor's mother agreed to his wish to complete middle school in the neighbourhood; as he said, "I didn't think I would be comfortable going to a new school for just one year." This enabled Trevor to spend "a lot of time" in his old neighbourhood and maintain his friendships. But Trevor's transfer to high school in the new suburban neighbourhood was not a welcoming experience. He referred to his early experience in his high school as "a culture shock," at least in part because it was not a "multicultural" neighbourhood like the one he had left – residents were "either white or Asians." In reflecting on his experience in his new school, Trevor said,

> I had a hard time adjusting to the new environment and fitting in with the rest of the students. I felt that I was completely different from everyone else. It seemed that the students and teachers knew about me and where I came from before I was formally introduced to any of them. I felt as if they already had their prejudgments about me before they even got to know me.

In our last interview, Trevor noted, "It seemed that they thought I should be a certain way because of where I grew up. They were expecting to see this thug, or from what some people said, 'someone more Black.'"

Trevor recalled that there were "approximately ten Black students in the entire school" when he was in Grade 9. While he moved in a different academic circle, he "bonded" with them because they were having "the same feelings" about the school. Their bonding was also facilitated by their involvement in the school's sports teams. As Trevor noted, "All of the Black students in the school were on the sports team, whether it was basketball, volleyball, or track and field."[3] Some of them were in special education classes "for behavioural or academic reasons" – classes where Black students tend to be over-represented (see Toronto District School Board, 2010). While Trevor and his Black peers received recognition from their teachers and related support for their athletic prowess, they did not receive the same recognition and support in their academic programs. Trevor observed that among his peers, "Academics became secondary to athletics, and the Black students relied more on their athletic ability than on their academic ability."

That many of the Black students joined athletic teams likely reflects their use of sports as an intervention and preemptive strategy – making it a form of social control and regulation that has become, as Spaaij (2009) would argue, "a substantial aspect of the neoliberal repertoire" (p. 247). In keeping with his mother's desire for him "to have access to the best education" (hence their move to the suburbs), Trevor resisted his coaches' and peers' efforts to sell him on the benefits of athletics as a route towards his educational and career goals. He explained:

---

3 Trevor also added: "It seemed as though a Black student was always the star of the sports teams, usually basketball or track and field."

I remember my basketball coach insisting that we make a videotape to send to schools in the States in hopes that I would receive a scholarship to play basketball at an American university. He also took it upon himself to give me a basketball rim to put up at my house so that I could practise. My mom was offended by this gesture, because she probably felt that me being a Black student, he should have been encouraging me more with academics instead of sports.

Sports also played a role in helping Kobe negotiate and navigate his schooling environment, and acculturate to life in Canada. During his first year in high school, Kobe's gym teacher invited him to try out for the track team – something he gladly did knowing that his school had a reputation for producing students who won athletic scholarships to US universities. Kobe did become a member of his school's track team, and he valued the opportunities that his athletic abilities and skills provided,[4] but he had no interest in trying for an athletic scholarship. What he expected from his schooling – essentially from his teachers and coach – was support for his academic work. As a child with an immigrant mother who had limited understanding of the educational system, Kobe looked to his teachers for help in navigating the school system. This is not to say that his mother did not do her part; she provided, according to Kobe, "a lot of the basic principles of the hard work ethic" required to get through school. In his initial interview, he also attributed the ways in which he applied himself to his schooling and education to "the principles I learned in Jamaica."

Unlike Trevor, Kobe was able to identify "good" teachers to whom he could relate effectively and who worked to address his needs and interests. Aside from his Caribbean-born teachers with whom he "had a good rapport" (given that they were able to understand and appreciate his situation as an immigrant youth from the Caribbean), Kobe credited one teacher, "who is actually … a white teacher," for his generosity and support. Kobe felt that this teacher genuinely cared about him, saw him for who he was, and went out of his way to help him. In expressing his appreciation for this teacher, Kobe mentioned that even though he was "the pickiest teacher [I] ever had," he learned from this teacher "the skills to see my mistakes and that I had the ability to correct them."

---

4 In reflecting on the plausibility of US athletic scholarships, Kobe reasoned that the larger population of Black people in the United States makes possible "more opportunities for … Black students." And he added, "While there is discrimination, I think that there [the US] is better, in terms of community trying to help people that are Black."

Not underestimating "the socio-economic conditions" of the neighbourhood and believing that teachers were influenced by media and other negative representations of it – and by extension the students – Kobe did what he could to show that he was "someone who is pretty smart," and had the "personal drive" and "family support" to do well. Ostensibly, in such a context – an "urban" school with mainly disadvantaged racialized students, many of them Black – being seen as "a Black male who had potential" meant that teachers were willing to go out of their way to help. Indeed, as Kobe reported, he went from being a student with "a very indifferent attitude" towards school to a scholarship student because his teachers saw "promise." He recalled that teachers encouraged him to take advanced-level (as opposed to general-level) courses, which prepared him for university.

Even though, as Kobe suggested, schools such as his were more likely to get "bad teachers" – because only a certain "type of teachers want to go there" – a few committed teachers turned out to be "amazing" because "they care about students" and they recognized the social and cultural capital that the students brought to their education (see Milner, 2010; Moore et al., 2008). In reflecting on the idea that "bad schools get bad teachers," Kobe referred to his experience in university with students from the suburban area where Trevor attended school. Kobe surmised that students who attended suburban schools did better educationally because they had a "better" education system. But Trevor, another Black male with potential who had the necessary family support, missed out on having similar caring teachers to support him in his academic endeavours.

That the most significant help Trevor received from his coach was a basketball net and an offer to make videos to solicit athletic scholarships suggests that the coach, who was also his teacher, could not see past Trevor's six-foot height and physically fit appearance. He saw only a basketball player who could bring him and the school accolades, not a student with academic potential and promise. We might conclude that for Black students, and males in particular, attending an urban, racially diverse school with committed and aware teachers is likely to lead to better educational experiences than attending middle-class suburban schools with uninformed and uncommitted teachers. The situation is even more problematic for Black male students like Trevor whose bodies are persistently read in relation to the reputation or stigma of their former urban neighbourhood – in essence, a racialization process in which they are defined as underachievers, troublemakers, and athletes (see chapter 4), unable to change. We will examine how Kobe and Trevor constructed their aspirations and worked to attain them in the following section.

Career Aspirations, Employment Opportunities, and Achievements

Kobe recalled that upon entering high school he expressed interest in becoming a lawyer. He attributed this career goal to his exposure to lawyers and legal education through his mother, who "went back to school" to become a legal secretary. He admitted that he did not know what career his mother wished for him, but he understood that while she had the attitude, "Do whatever you want to do," she also expected him "to go to school, do your homework, do well" and then go to university. Kobe understood that, to fulfil his mother's expectations, he needed to stay focused on his work, have a career goal, avoid distractions (he did this by isolating himself from his neighbourhood peers), and establish himself as a model student (counter to the stereotype of Black males in the community) who would gain and retain his teachers' support because they recognized his academic potential.

Many Black students, especially males like Kobe, are encouraged by their teachers to become role models for other students. To this end, they are often guided to become teachers and return to work in the community. This concept of returning to work in the community is part of neoliberal thinking regarding teachers' working with Black students. It reinforces the notion that the community's social welfare rests on them – as individuals, they are responsible for and expected to improve neighbourhood conditions. This expectation could limit a young person's aspirations, but fortunately, this was not the case for Kobe. He never said during any of the three interviews that becoming a lawyer was part of his plan to return and work in the community; he also never entertained the idea of becoming a teacher. In fact, in his most recent interview (2011), Kobe declared that he was "careful not to take on the responsibility of a saviour." During his undergraduate years, Kobe accepted invitations from his former teachers to give presentations to students (i.e., be a role model), but he did so out of a sense of civic responsibility, not because he was "taking on the mantle of saving lives."

Having had what might be described as a successful high school experience, Kobe entered university on a scholarship and pursued a four-year degree in business administration. Upon graduation, he worked for one year in marketing, before returning to the same university to pursue his law degree concurrently with a master's degree in business administration. During his seven years of university, Kobe supplemented his scholarships with financial assistance from his mother, his student bursary, and part-time weekend and summer jobs. He also received corporate philanthropic support, including a summer job with a marketing firm that turned into full-time employment when he completed his business degree.

The connection to the marketing firm was organized by a service organization dedicated to preparing and placing "underserved youth," particularly racialized youth, in business or professional organizations. As a resident of an underserved or disadvantaged neighbourhood, Kobe represented an ideal recruit for the corporate world as a lawyer – the kind of Black young man who embodied the neoliberal ethos of individualism, hard work, and entrepreneurship (Braedley & Luxton, 2010). Kobe was someone who, through abilities, skills, and efforts, was able to surmount his disadvantages, thereby showing that career ambitions can be realized.

Since he had moved to the suburbs, Trevor could not benefit from his residential address as Kobe did, even though Trevor shared Kobe's disadvantages and high aspirations. Early in his life, Trevor had aspired to become a police officer, but given his interest in sports, his friendship with athletic peers, and encouragement from his coach, when the time came to apply to university, he thought of entering a program related to sport.

He was admitted into a kinesiology program at the same university as Kobe, but after one year he transferred to sociology because he "was not doing very well in 'Kine." Trevor had planned to complete his honours degree in sociology and then apply to the police force, but in his final year of university his mother and others encouraged him to pursue teaching. He applied to education faculties and was accepted a year after graduation. During the in-between year, Trevor worked as a waiter in a restaurant (where he had worked part time while attending university) so that he "could pay off his student loan." He graduated with his teaching degree, applied to school boards around Toronto, but was unsuccessful in getting a job. In the summer following his graduation, Trevor worked as a youth worker in his old neighbourhood and at the restaurant on the weekends.

Unable to obtain a teaching job in Toronto and encouraged by friends who had taught in London, England, Trevor decided to take a chance and migrated to London in 2009. Since his mother was born there, he was also a British citizen, making his decision to go there easier. In terms of his personal and professional growth, London turned out to be a productive move for Trevor. As he stated, "Teaching in London seemed to be an easier process than teaching in Toronto. There were less hoops to jump through and I found work almost instantly." After just two weeks in London, Trevor found a job at an alternative school "located in a lower socio-economic community" (similar to the one in which he grew up) where he worked for two years. He taught special-needs students,[5] and was able to build relationships with them and help with their social and emotional issues as well as their education. According to Trevor, teaching in London "was extremely challenging and difficult, but rewarding at the same time." He explained that the rewards came from seeing students go from

> selling drugs, fighting, or just negativity in general ... to applying to different colleges, or finding an apprenticeship. The difficulty came from seeing some students sent to prison, a mental hospital, or just give up on their future in general.

Trevor returned to Toronto in summer 2011, hopeful that with his background and experience teaching in London he would be able to get a teaching job, especially having heard about the need for Black male teachers in Toronto-area schools. Six months after returning, however, he was still unemployed, despite many applications to teaching jobs in four different school boards. Running out of money,[6] Trevor had to reconsider his options – apply for jobs as a youth worker or return to his job at the restaurant. But, as he commented,

> once you have made a certain amount of money or have been doing a certain type of work, you become accustomed to it. [Hence] I find it extremely difficult to go back to a part-time job or a service job. To me it feels like a step backwards, and I am trying to move forwards.

Finally, Trevor returned to his earlier career interest in policing, noting, "My uncle was a major influence in me deciding to get into policing when I was younger ... I have always looked up to him and thought that joining the police force would be a natural progression." Trevor applied to police forces in the Greater Toronto Area, "the ones that are hiring." Trevor had grown up with neighbourhood peers who accused the police of racial profiling, which has contributed to police-youth-community relationships filled with tension and conflict (Chapman-Nyaho, James, & Kwan-Lafond, 2012; Ezeonu, 2008). Evidently influenced more by his uncle than his friends, Trevor remained convinced that there were opportunities and possibilities for him as a police officer.

---

5 These were students who were "excluded from mainstream schools due to their behaviour, lack of attendance, or special needs."
6 Trevor said that he did manage to save a significant amount of money from working in London, and living with his parents was helping with his financial situation.

While waiting to hear about his application (which he did not get), he worked part time as a youth worker and afterwards as a full-time city transit driver.

Trevor could be said to have the same determination and level of motivation to attain his career goal as Kobe. Unlike Kobe, he was not fortunate enough (or had not been at the right place at the right time) to receive the necessary institutional help.[7] Well-schooled in the neoliberal ethos of individualism, personal responsibility, and rules of competition, Trevor continued to pursue his career goal, believing that it is up to him to succeed, even though his many attempts – through numerous applications and job interviews – have been unproductive to date.

In trying to understand his failures, and admitting frustration, Trevor directed his attention to "the process" he faced (Luxton, 2010) rather than the opportunity structures he had been up against:

> Some of my frustrations come with the process and time it takes to find a job/career that you want ... Working in England for two years, and having a teaching degree, I believe I have jumped through enough hoops that the process should be somewhat easier.

Clearly, the difference between Kobe and Trevor in obtaining their respective career goals cannot be attributed only to their individual efforts, abilities, and commitment.

Conclusion: "The Climb Is a Lot Steeper"

Apart from their personal efforts and attributes, Kobe's and Trevor's paths towards their career goals have been shaped by how effectively they were able to navigate the layered, multifaceted structures of inequity inherent in the hegemonic ideology and common-sense rhetoric of neoliberalism, which presents confounding obstacles. Their imagination and acceptance of the idea that success in the competitive labour market depends on "the rational choices they make and their own skilled and diligent work" (Luxton, 2010, p. 180) seem to have inspired

---

7 While Kobe might have had the social and educational support of his friends, Trevor did not. In fact, their friendship groups were quite different. Kobe reported that all his close friends have "at least two degrees." And Trevor, in suggesting that the move from his neighbourhood might have been "a good idea," went on to say that a number of the people with whom he grew up and "called friends ... have become victims of murder or have had someone in their family murdered, and others ... have fallen into a life of crime."

their consistent efforts and tenacity. However, these qualities alone proved insufficient (at least for Trevor), without support and sponsorship from individuals and institutions.

Kobe, Trevor, and their families – encouraged by teachers and coaches – dutifully worked with the idea that education is largely (if not singularly) what it takes for them to succeed in this society. This would appear to be the case, if we look at Kobe as an example of someone whose education and intellectual ability enabled him to become the corporate lawyer he is today, working between Toronto and New York City. But his relationship with caring teachers and coaches, and the support he received from them, as well as from charitable service organizations, cannot be underestimated. Indeed, the resources all played significant roles in helping Kobe to navigate the structures and become a role model and example for others to follow. Kobe thus represents the proof that one can escape the conditions of one's childhood.

Trevor, on the other hand, was left to find his way on his own with whatever support his family members could provide. Trevor's move to the suburbs for better schooling and education did not play out as his mother had expected (see Deluca & Rosenblatt, 2010). Ironically, leaving his neighbourhood might have contributed to Trevor's loss of educational, social, and other opportunities to which Black youth living in "troubled" neighbourhoods might have access. In other words, Trevor might have lost his "at-risk" status – a social capital that might have served in building relationships with educators and human service personnel interested in "helping" young Black men with potential to escape delinquency-producing neighbourhoods (Wacquant. 2008). But it is possible that having left the neighbourhood might have inadvertently helped him become the police officer he is today.

Neither Kobe[8] nor Trevor negated the significance of education as a means to attain their career goals. Nor did they challenge the idea that it was up to them to work hard towards this end to succeed. But they recognized that what they have achieved to date, or what anyone is able to achieve, is not totally of their own making. In fact, when asked what they thought of the notion that a person can become whatever they want to be, Kobe submitted,

> Life is much too unkind for that. You control maybe 10 per cent; 50 to 60 per cent depends on winning the birth lottery. While there is no guarantee,

---

[8] In all of the interviews I have conducted with Kobe he admitted to being highly influenced by capitalism.

you're well on your way ... This is the reality of life. Watch the interview process, and see who gets hired.

Kobe concluded by saying that for someone like him, "the climb is a lot steeper." Trevor commented that "if someone works hard at what they want to become in life, eventually it may come true," but then went on to suggest (probably hinting at his coping mechanism):

> What should be said is that even if you work hard and do everything the way you are supposed to do it, your end result may not be exactly what you expected, and your end goal may not happen when you expect it to happen. There are other factors that come into play when trying to become someone or entering into a certain career – factors such as location (the area where you have always wanted to work is not hiring for the career you are interested in) [and] competition for the career you're looking into is high. Although you may be the most qualified for the position, I am a firm believer in the idea that it's who you know that really gets you into a career rather than what you know.

Kobe's and Trevor's stories illustrate how individual agency is mediated by social, economic, and educational structures. They suggest that if young Black boys and men are to maintain confidence in their potential and in the possibilities their education can afford, they will need help from educators and others working in the system to "read," understand, and successfully navigate it. They will need to know how factors outside their control – many of which cannot be anticipated – affect their life goals.

While the rationalized success formula and seductive reasoning of neoliberalism lays out a seemingly reasonable path to success, in reality, it is primarily individuals who have access to and are conversant with "mainstream" social and cultural capital who will ultimately realize their high aspirations through brains, determination, and hard work.

REFERENCES

Aylward, C.A. (1999). *Canadian critical race theory: Racism and the law*. Halifax, NS: Fernwood.

Basu, R. (2011). Multiculturalism through multilingualism in schools: Emerging places of "integration" in Toronto. *Annals of the Association of American Geographers*, *101*(6), 1307–30. https://doi.org/10.1080/00045608.2011.579536

Braedley, S., & Luxton, M. (2010). Competing philosophies: Neoliberalism and the challenges of everyday life. In S. Braedley & M. Luxton (Eds.), *Neoliberalism and everyday life* (pp. 3–21). Montreal, QC: McGill-Queen's University Press.

Chapman-Nyaho, S., James, C.E., & Kwan-Lafond, D. (2012). "We expect much of you": Enlisting youth in the policing of their marginalized communities. *Canadian Ethnic Studies, 43–44*(3–1), 81–98. https://doi.org/10.1353/ces.2011.0048

Creswell, J.W. (1994). *Qualitative and quantitative approaches*. Thousand Oaks, CA: Sage.

Deluca, S., & Rosenblatt, P. (2010). Does moving to better neighborhoods lead to better schooling opportunities? Parental school choice in an experimental housing voucher program. *Teachers College Record, 112*(5), 1443–91.

Emdin, C. (2011, December 20). Five lessons from the "If I were a poor Black Kid" debate. *Huffington Post*. http://www.huffingtonpost.com/christopher-emdin/if-i-were-a-poor-black-kid_b_1159059.html

Ezeonu, I. (2008). Dudes, let's talk about us: The Black "community" construction of gun violence in Toronto. *Journal of African American Studies, 12*, 193–214. https://doi.org/10.1007/s12111-008-9042-9

Fernandez, L. (2002). Telling stories about school: Using critical race and Latino critical theories to document Latina/Latino education and resistance. *Qualitative Inquiry, 8*(1), 45–65. https://doi.org/10.1177/1077800402008001004

Gandy, I. (2011, December 14). "If I were a poor black kid": Really, Forbes? *The Root*. https://www.theroot.com/if-i-were-a-poor-black-kid-really-forbes-1790867391

Gosine, K. (2012). Accomplished Black North Americans and antiracism education: Towards bridging a seeming divide. *Critical Sociology, 38*(5), 707–21. https://doi.org/10.1177/0896920510380077

Howard, T.C. (2008). Who really cares? The disenfranchisement of African American males in preK–12 schools: A critical race theory perspective. *Teachers College Record, 110*(5), 954–85.

Hulchanski, J.D. (2007). *The three cities within Toronto: Income polarization among Toronto's neighbourhoods, 1970–2005*. Toronto, ON: University of Toronto, Cities Centre.

James, C.E. (2012). *Life at the intersection: Community, class and schooling*. Halifax, NS: Fernwood.

James, C.E. (2015). Beyond education, brains and hard work: The aspirations and career trajectory of two Black young men. *Alternate Routes: A Journal of Critical Social Research, 26*, 332–53. http://www.alternateroutes.ca/index.php/ar/article/view/22325/18117

James, C.E., & Taylor, L. (2008). "Education will get you to the station": Marginalized students' experiences and perceptions of merit in accessing university. *Canadian Journal of Education, 31*(3), 567–90. https://www.jstor.org/stable/20466716.pdf

Keil, R., & Young, D. (2011). In-between Canada: The emergence of the new urban middle. In D. Young, P.B. Wood, & R. Keil (Eds.), *In-between infrastructure: Urban connectivity in an age of vulnerability* (pp. 1–18). Kelowna, BC: Praxis (e)Press.

Lawson, E. (2014). Disenfranchised grief and social inequality: Bereaved African Canadians and oppositional narratives about the violent deaths of friends and family members. *Ethnic and Racial Studies, 37*(11), 2092–109. https://doi.org/10.1080/01419870.2013.800569

Lichtman, M. (2013). *Qualitative research in education*. Los Angeles, CA: Sage

Luxton, M. (2010). Doing neoliberalism: Perverse individualism in personal life. In S. Braedley & M. Luxton (Eds.), *Neoliberalism and everyday life* (pp. 163–83). Montreal, QC: McGill-Queen's University Press.

Marks, G. (2011, December 12). If I were a poor Black kid. *Forbes*. Retrieved from http://www.forbes.com/sites/quickerbettertech/2011/12/12/if-i-was-a-poor-black-kid/

Milner, H.R. (2010). *Start where you are, but don't stay there: Understanding diversity, opportunity gaps, and teaching in today's classrooms*. Cambridge, MA: Harvard University Press.

Moore, J.L., Henfield, M.S., & Owens, D. (2008). African American males in special education. *American Behavioral Scientist, 51*(7), 907–27. https://doi.org/10.1177/0002764207311997

Myles, J., & Hou, F. (2004). Changing colours: Spatial assimilation and new racial minority immigrants. *Canadian Journal of Sociology, 29*(1), 29–58. https://doi.org/10.1353/cjs.2004.0011

Peitzman, L. (2011, December 13). If I were a middle aged white man. *Huffington Post*. https://www.huffpost.com/entry/if-i-were-a-middle-aged-w_b_1146790

Porfilio, B., & Malott, C. (Eds.). (2008). *The destructive path of neoliberalism: An international examination of urban education*. Rotterdam, Netherlands: Sense Publishers.

Reitz, J.G., Breton, R., Dion, K.K., & Dion, K.L. (2009). *Multiculturalism and social cohesion: Potentials and challenges of diversity*. New York, NY: Springer.

Roulston, K. (2007). Theorizing the qualitative interview [Paper presentation]. 3rd International Conference of Qualitative Inquiry, University of Illinois, Urbana-Champaign.

Singer, J.N., & Buford May, R.A. (2010). The career trajectory of a Black male high school basketball player: A social reproduction perspective. *International Review for the Sociology of Sport, 46*(3), 299–314. https://doi.org/10.1177/1012690210378283

Spaaij, R. (2009). Sport as a vehicle for social mobility and regulation of disadvantaged urban youth. *International Review for the Sociology of Sport*, 44(2–3), 247–64. https://doi.org/10.1177/1012690209338415

Stake, R.E. (2000). Case studies. In N.K. Denzin & Y.S. Lincoln (Eds.), *Handbook of qualitative research* (pp. 453–4). London, UK: Sage.

Stapleton, J., Murphy, B., & Xing, Y. (2012). *The "working poor" in the Toronto region: Who they are, where they live, and how trends are changing*. Toronto, ON: Metcalf Foundation.

Stephenson, N. (2005) Living history, undoing linearity: Memory-work as a research method in the social sciences. *International Journal of Social Research Methodology*, 8(1), 33–45. https://doi.org/10.1080/1364557032000081645

Sukarieh, M., & Tannock, S. (2008). In the best interests of youth or neoliberalism? The World Bank and the new global youth empowerment project. *Journal of Youth Studies*, 11(3), 301–12. https://doi.org/10.1080/13676260801946431

Toronto District School Board. (2010, May). *Achievement gap task force draft report*. Toronto, ON: Toronto District School Board, Student and Community Equity.

Touré. (2011, December 15). If I were a middle class white guy writing about being a poor black kid. *Time*. http://ideas.time.com/2011/12/15/if-i-was-a-middle-class-white-guy-writing-about-being-a-poor-black-kid/

Wacquant, L. (2008). *Urban outcasts: A comparative sociology of advanced marginality*. Cambridge, UK: Polity Press.

Walcott, R. (2009). Reconstructing manhood; or, the drag of Black masculinity. *Small Axe*, 13(1), 75–89. https://doi.org/10.1215/07990537-2008-007

Yosso, T.J. (2005). Whose culture has capital? A critical race theory discussion of community cultural wealth. *Race Ethnicity and Education*, 8(1), 69–91. https://doi.org/10.1080/1361332052000341006

Response to Chapter 5

What Folks Don't Get: Race and Class Matter

ANNETTE M. HENRY
Department of Language and Literacy, Faculty of Education, University of British Columbia, Vancouver, British Columbia, Canada

In a comedic and satirical letter in response to Gene Marks's (2011a) *Forbes* magazine article "If I Were a Poor Black Kid," Baratunde Thurston (2011) expresses gratitude to Marks for his advice about the ways Black children might be able to succeed in society. Thurston writes: "Thank you Mr. Marks. You have changed everything about my life. Thanks to your article, I worked to make sure I got the best grades, made reading my number one priority and created better paths for myself. If only someone had suggested this earlier." In response, Marks (2011b) confesses, "What do I know about being a 'poor black kid'? Absolutely nothing. I'm a middle-class white guy. But I went to school."

Like Thurston, in his essay "More than Brains and Hard Work," James picks up on Marks's failure to acknowledge the roles that colonialism, race, and racism play in the historical and contemporary lives of Black people and his reliance instead on the pervasive negative societal stereotypes of Black people as lazy, helpless, ignorant, and residing in single-parent families. In doing so, James provides an insightful and moving account of two Black men of Caribbean heritage who lived part of their youth in the same low-income neighbourhood. The essay weaves together several themes that James has explored over the past thirty years regarding Black youth: their career aspirations, their educational experiences, and the role of athletics in their lives. Raising the interplay of race, class, neighbourhood, gender, and age, the essay teases apart some contradictions in Marks's (2011a) article, premised on the neoliberal myth of educational egalitarianism regarding Black youth and the thinking that they reside in a just and compassionate society (see Frank, 2016; Themalis, 2017).

The discussion of the neighbourhood in which Kobe and Trevor grew up reminds me of the comments by two of my African-American colleagues who lived in major northern American urban centres. Several years ago, they said that, if they "had to do it over again," they would raise their children in the South for the sense of community, support, and caring that their children would receive from teachers who understood the needs of Black children. My colleagues longed for the kinds of communities that existed years earlier – and still do – in many Black communities in the United States and Canada (Talbot, 1984; Walker, 1979). Churches, schools, families, and close community networks ensured that someone was always looking out for, or looking after, Black children with a sense of responsibility. Much has been lost in our contemporary individualistic fast-paced capitalist society, where teaching is a "job" rather than a vocation and where we barely know our neighbours.

I wonder how many Trevors there are for every Kobe that we celebrate. Indeed, the countless attempts by Black parents and families to actualize fulfilling future lives for their children turn the argument of hard work and brains on its head. Like Trevor, unable to attain the career to which he aspires, many a Black male youth has become a wavering boat on a windy sea, listening to gusts of reasonable advice from caring peers and family in his pursuits, but to little avail. Often, despite his extraordinary efforts and determination to pursue his dreams and not "become a statistic" – referring to some of the social misfortunes that befall Black male youth – he is positioned as a statistic or anomaly in Canadian society. Some, like Kobe (at times with the help of teachers), are more successful in attaining career goals and societal status, but as Black males from working-class neighbourhoods their climb in pursuit of their aspirations is, as Kobe put it, "a lot steeper." One wonders, nonetheless, at what costs do Black men and women achieve success in a society that bell hooks (1992) terms a "White supremacist capitalist patriarchy" (p. 80).

Schools determine futures; the narratives of Kobe and Trevor show that race, gender, class, and the schooling process intersected as salient social dimensions in their academic outcomes and future participation in society. More specifically, schooling functioned to reproduce particular forms of race and gender which cast young men like Kobe and Trevor into a particular heterosexist biosocial view of Black masculinity. That is, essentialized dominant societal images of Black male muscularity, strength, and speed problematically naturalize Black male students' abilities as less inclined towards academics and more suited to certain sports such as basketball and track and field (Hill Collins, 2004). Black students understand the merits of school sports programs, especially when athletics might be seen as a way to win a university scholarship. But they sometimes become entangled in the racialized dichotomy of either sports or academics, so that their participation in sports often occurs to the detriment of their academic success.

Unfortunately, teachers sometimes act as foot-soldiers in the institutional racialization and deintellectualization of Black youth through lowered expectations, such as envisioning them as athletes rather than as developing scholars. While encouraging young people to participate and excel in sports has many physical, social, and emotional merits and can be a means for them to garner some relevant capital – such as status, admiration, privileges, and exemptions from certain school activities – the support of sports rather than academics can become "a pedagogy of exclusion, denying learners the opportunity to engage in really useful knowledge" (Lusted, 1986, p. 8). Further, steering Black youth into sports *instead of* supporting their academic development as fervently reflects a long legacy of dominant thinking about the Black body as profitable and controllable. White control of the Black male and female bodies has been a prevalent issue from slavery to the present (Hill Collins, 2004). Sports has become a highly racialized pedagogy in a set of practices that transmit messages of Blacks' non-intellectual capabilities and that foster particular views of their potential. Classrooms are, indeed, political spaces (Hill Collins, 2009).

While Kobe and Trevor completed at least two university degrees, their narratives attest to the presence of academic tracking along dimensions of race, gender, and class. These narratives paint a picture of the inaccessibility and lack of educational egalitarianism for many young urban Black males, especially those in certain low-income Canadian communities, and the kinds of choices and curricula that may await them despite their high aspirations. These dimensions of race, class, and gender tend to play out differently for girls and boys. While both sexes share similar school experiences, such as presumed unsuitability for academics, Black girls undergo other gendered specificities.

In my own research into working-and middle-class adolescent girls' experiences in school where they had to contend with the dominance of male classmates, I found their intelligence and emotional needs were overlooked by teachers (Henry, 1998a, 1998b), and they were often deemed to have little of importance to say (Davies & Ogundipe-Leslie, 1995). Indeed, studies show that Black girls tend to be less visible to teachers. They are expected to display traditionally "feminine" behaviours – that is, to be quiet and accommodating (Fordham, 1993; Henry, 1998a, 1998b) – and they are also assessed on external characteristics such as looks, hair, and skin colour (Okazawa-Rey, Robinson, & Ward, 1987). Educators may stereotype Black girls as loud, brash, unfeminine, less innocent, more mature for their age, needing less attention, and hypersexual (Epstein, Blake, & González, 2017). When they speak up confidently and assertively, they are seen as defiant, and thus may be subject to disciplinary measures up to and including suspension (Epstein et al., 2017). In this political moment in which schools are increasingly policed and managed like prisons (Anderson-Zavala, Krueger-Henney, Meiners, & Pour-Khorshid, 2017), the suspension rates of Black female students are disproportionate to their representation, exceeding those of white girls and, in some places, the suspension rates of Black boys (Crenshaw, 2015).

James's essay highlights the multidimensional and complex realities of negotiating inequitable education systems as Black students. The stories of Kobe and Trevor, and the research on Black youth more generally, remind us of the disparities between theory and praxis. The kinds of philosophical discussions, idealized curricula, and pedagogies advocated in our teacher education programs are not always realized in real-world multiracial contexts. In these contexts, "brains and hard work" and, indeed, luck all play roles. In addition, there are multilayered and overlapping personal, social, familial, economic, and societal factors that contribute to students' school experiences and outcomes. Intersecting factors, such as teachers and classroom dynamics, as well as race, gender, immigrant and class backgrounds, neighbourhood, age, and social capital mediate their experiences and opportunities.

REFERENCES

Anderson-Zavala, C., Krueger-Henney, P., Meiners, E., & Pour-Khorshid, F. (2017). Fierce urgency of now: Building movements to end the prison industrial complex in our schools. *Multicultural Perspectives*, *19*(3), 151–4. https://doi.org/10.1080/15210960.2017.1331743

Crenshaw, K.W. (with Ocen, P., & Nanda, J.). (2015). *Black girls matter: Pushed out, overpoliced, and underprotected.* New York, NY: African American Policy Forum & Columbia Law School, Center for Intersectionality and Social Policy Studies. http://www.law.columbia.edu/null/download?&exclusive=filemgr.download&file_id=613546

Davies, C.B., & Ogundipe-Leslie, M. (Eds.). (1995). *Moving beyond boundaries: Vol. 1. Hearing Black women's voices: Transgressing imposed boundaries.* New York, NY: New York University Press.

Epstein, R., Blake, J., & González, T. (2017). *Girlhood interrupted: The erasure of Black girls' childhood*. Washington, DC: Georgetown Law, Center on Poverty and Inequality. http://jjie.org/wp-content/uploads/2016/09/girlhood-interrupted.pdf

Fordham, S. (1993). "Those loud Black girls": (Black) women, silence, and gender "passing" in the Academy. *Anthropology & Education Quarterly, 24*(1), 3–32. https://doi.org/10.1525/aeq.1993.24.1.05x1736t

Frank, R.H. (2016). *Success and luck: Good fortune and the myth of meritocracy*. Princeton, NJ: Princeton University Press.

Henry, A. (1998a) Complacent and womanish: Girls negotiating their lives in an African Centered School in the U.S. *Race Ethnicity and Education, 1*(2), 151–70. https://doi.org/10.1080/1361332980010202

Henry, A. (1998b). Speaking up and speaking out: Examining voice in a reading/writing program with adolescent African Caribbean girls. *Journal of Literacy Research, 30*(2), 233–52. https://doi.org/10.1080/10862969809547997

Hill Collins, P. (2004). *Black sexual politics: African Americans, gender, and the new racism*. New York, NY: Routledge.

Hill Collins, P. (2009). *Another kind of public education: Race, schools, the media, and democratic possibilities*. Boston, MA: Beacon Press.

hooks, b. (1992). *Black looks: Race and representation*. Boston, MA: Beacon Press.

Lusted, D. (1986). Why pedagogy? *Screen, 27*(5), 2–16. https://doi.org/10.1093/screen/27.5.2

Marks, G. (2011a, December 12). If I were a poor Black kid. *Forbes*. http://www.forbes.com/sites/quickerbettertech/2011/12/12/if-i-was-a-poor-black-kid/

Marks, G. (2011b, December 15). Opinion: Forbes' "If I were a poor Black kid" writer Gene Marks responds to Baratunde Thurston. *CNN*. https://www.cnn.com/2011/12/15/us/forbes-if-i-were-a-poor-black-kid-writer-gene-marks-responds-to-baratunde-thurston/index.html

Okazawa-Rey, M., Robinson, T., & Ward, J. (1987). Black women and the politics of skin and hair. *Women and Therapy, 6*, 89–102. https://doi.org/10.1300/J015V06N01_07

Talbot, C. (1984). *Growing up Black in Canada*. Toronto, ON: Williams-Wallace.

Themalis, S. (2017). Education and equality: Debunking the myth of meritocracy. *Educação & Formação, 2*(4), 3–17. https://revistas.uece.br/index.php/redufor/article/view/120

Thurston, B. (2011, December 14). Opinion: Letter from a poor Black kid: Baratunde Thurston responds to Forbes' Gene Marks. *CNN*. https://www.cnn.com/2011/12/14/us/letter-from-a-poor-black-kid-baratunde-thurston-responds-to-forbes-gene-marks/index.html

Walker, J.W.G. (1979). *Identity: The Black experience*. Toronto, ON: Gage Educational Publishing.

6 Class, Race, and Schooling in the Performance of Black Male Athleticism[1]

If not sports, where else to fit in? To belong? Growing up in a predominantly racialized and immigrant community and attending high school in an area with starkly different demographics, there were not many spaces in school in which I felt I belonged. Sport, and I was involved in many, offered a space that was thought to be "inherently" our own. Race had a lot to do with this prevailing ideology. (Dwaine)

It did not seem that you mattered as a Black student in my high school unless you were in sports. Sports gave us status, notoriety, recognition, and purpose in school. As young Black males ... how could we turn down this form of "celebrity"? So, it is clear that, yes, we had to be interested in sports, mainly due to the fact that school wasn't all that interested in us. (Semere)

"Semere" (pseudonym), a participant in one of my studies (James, 2011), recalled that school gained meaning through sports – for him and the other young Black athletes in his "inner social circle." I concluded in that study that it was understandable that many Toronto high school basketball teams would be "predominantly Black." As I argued then, for many Black student-athletes,

sports is seen as a creative, viable, and socially acceptable way to navigate and negotiate the alienating and inequitable schooling environment

---

1 This chapter was originally published in 2012. See James (2012a). Reprinted with the permission of the publisher. I am indebted to Alex Miller, Charles Chapman, Sam Ogbazghi, Alani Prince, and Atiba James for assisting with this research, offering suggestions, and commenting on the various drafts of this chapter.

in which they can attain an education that satisfies their interests and prepares them for the world in which they live. (James, 2011, p. 452)

But as Semere indicates, using sports to "fit in," to feel that he "belonged," and to gain "status, notoriety, recognition, and purpose in school" had to do not only with race but also with social class. He grew up "in a predominantly racialized and immigrant community" and attended high school in "an area with starkly different demographics." I wish to explore this nexus of class, race, and schooling in this chapter.

Much has been written about how sports offer inspiration – even act as an opiate – for Black student-athletes (Branch, 2011; Coakley, 2009; James, 2005; Pitter, 2004), but the role that social and economic class plays in establishing and maintaining the Black male in athletics often gets lost in the discussion. Some scholars have indicated that many working-class Black student-athletes view sport as a means not only to negotiate and navigate the school system but also to achieve social and economic mobility – essentially, as a way out of poverty (Buford May, 2008; James, 2012b). Others (e.g., Pitter, 2004; Singer & Buford May, 2010) indicate that sports actually operate to sustain or reproduce the social and class position of working-class Black male student-athletes – specifically, the intersectionality of class, gender, and race interweaves and structures the experiences, values, practices, and expectations of working-class Black male student-athletes.

I contend that Black student-athlete culture relates to the "performance" of a Black male athleticism, which is based on a set of assumptions about young Black boys or men: that they will (a) have an interest, or ought to be interested, in sports; (b) "play Black"; (c) participate in a "Black athletic culture"; (d) aspire to go "south" on an athletic scholarship; and (e) be best supported by a "role model" coach whom they will come to see as a "substitute father." Before elaborating on these points, let us consider how race, class, and gender operate in the construction of Black male athleticism in Canada.

Class, Race, and Gender in the Construction of Black Male Athleticism

All groups operate on the basis of culture structured by a set of values, norms, expectations, and aspirations that influence participants' lives, organize their experiences, structure their worldview, shape their behaviours, and harmonize their relationships (James, 2010). Cultures, as Kagawa-Singer and Chung (1994) write, function as a *tool* that defines individuals' reality and *purpose in life*, providing them "with some degree of personal and social meaning" for their existence (p. 198); one's culture provides a sense of safety, self-worth, and belonging. Thus, in an alienating, largely white middle-class environment, working-class Black males are likely to gravitate towards others who, like them, are receiving messages about how, when, and where they, as Semere put it, "matter," and with their peers participate in activities that are psychologically beneficial to them; that is, they are likely to embrace a culture that gives them a positive message about who they are and where they belong.

Structural inequities in relation to class, race, and gender inform the creation of a Black athletic culture by which students – in this case, Black male student-athletes – function in their effort to resist their exclusion from their schooling system, assert their presence and interests, and insert themselves into their schooling process (Dunne & Gazeley, 2008; Singer & Buford May, 2010; Warren, 2005). Insofar as class structures shape educators' perceptions – in this case, how they perceive a Black working-class student's academic abilities – it also carries implications for how students feel about themselves and apply themselves to their academic learning (Hempel-Jorgensen, 2009).

On the basis of their investigation into the role that social class plays in high school teachers' perceptions of student underachievement in Britain, Dunne and Gazeley (2008) surmise:

> Although it was seldom explicitly acknowledged, teachers' tacit recognition of pupils' social class positions was a key factor in their constructions of pupil underachievement. Further, teacher reluctance to explicitly acknowledge pupils' social class identities helped to maintain the educational conditions in which middle-class pupils were encouraged to achieve while the underachievement of many working-class pupils was normalized. (p. 452)

Essentially, the practice of positioning students in relation to their social class is "intricately interwoven" with judgments about their potential, capacities, and achievement (Dunne & Gazeley, 2008, p. 459).

By extension, parents become implicated in teachers' views of their students' engagement in schooling and their academic achievements. Teachers largely hold parents responsible for students' educational performance. Middle-class parents support their children's education through what they provide at home, their consultations with teachers, and their visits to school – actions that McGhee Hassrick and Schneider (2009) refer to as "surveillance." As these researchers found, these parents are "primarily understood as interested spectators, external stakeholders, or helpful partners of teachers, mostly interested in the educational outcomes of their individual child, rather than the organizational dynamics that shape the everyday instructional environment in schools" (p. 195). By contrast, working-class parents tend to keep a distance from their children's school, rely on teachers for information and advice about their children, and out of respect for teachers' authority do not question them; this deference to authority leads to the educators' perception that parents are apathetic and have little interest in their children's education (McGhee Hassrick & Schneider, 2009; see also Taylor, 2006). Black students' and parents' experiences with systemic racism contribute to a low level of social trust, which they tend to have for teachers and the schooling system generally (Brathwaite & James, 1996; see also McGhee Hassrick & Schneider, 2009).

We see clear differences in the assumptions and expectations that teachers have of middle- and working-class students and their parents directly related to race, gender, immigrant status, and neighbourhood. Applying white middle-class norms, practices, and taken-for-granted notions that the schooling system is colour-blind, meritocratic, and culturally neutral, teachers attribute low Black student achievement to their lack of interest in education and assume it has nothing to do with teachers' expectations of them as learners – expectations contaminated by stereotypes of Black youth being more likely to do well in applied- and physical-activities classes than academic ones.

In chapter 4, I argue that race, class, and gender come together in the schooling experiences of Black males, in particular through their categorization as "at-risk" students. I make the point that students are subject to a "web of stereotypes" (Howard, 2008) or "confluence of stereotyping" (Hernandez & Davis, 2009). These stereotypes operate together and in relation to one another to "racialize and marginalize these youth and structure their learning process, social opportunities, life chances, and educational outcomes" (see chapter 4). The process becomes oddly circular – situations created by these stereotypes in turn function to preserve and foster them. For example, because Black students are habitually perceived as athletes, sport becomes a tool to redress their "at riskness," enabling them to surmount the obstacles and challenges they face – and *not* drop out (see chapter 4). Consistently reduced to their "bodies," and their talent "attributed to nature" (Ferber, 2007, p. 20), their sport successes match the stereotype (albeit a "positive" one), "proving" that athletics offers a viable and important means by which these boys can best become more productively engaged in school.

In our society and schooling system, sport supports "heterosexual masculinity" (Abdel-Shehid & Kalman-Lamb, 2011), and we use it to socialize young people in society generally, and in community and school. Playing sports means more than *playing the game*; it also means "fitting in, measuring up, and becoming men" (James, 2011, p. 258; see also Martino, Kehler, & Weaver-Hightower, 2009; McCready, 2010). For young Black working-class men, the idea is even more seductive; playing sports is also constructed "as the red-carpet pathway out of poverty and obscurity and into fame and fortune" (Harrison, Sailes, Rotich, & Bimper, 2011, p. 100; see also Singer & Buford May, 2010). Understandably, these young men are attracted to sports and related activities that help them comply with masculine expectations (Anderson & McCormack, 2010; McCready, 2010; Kwan-Lafond, 2011).

Even as young men actively resist the athletic stereotype and refuse to participate in sports, athletics is so much a part of Black masculinity and group identification that it is read onto their bodies. Black youth have little alternative if they want to fit in with their Black peers. Besides, an athletic scholarship offers a strong attraction, particularly for youth who could not otherwise afford a postsecondary education.

Below, I draw from the comments of young Black males in my earlier study (2012b) – "Semere," "Seif," "Dennis," "Dwaine," and "Kani" (pseudonyms) – all former high school athletes between twenty-five and thirty-five years old at the time. I asked them to comment on themes I had developed based on the literature and my empirical research into young Black people's athletic lives and expectations.

Framework for Black Student-Athletes

Must Be Interested in Sports and in Playing Sports

> I experienced this growing up. A significant portion of my identity was tied into not only my interest in playing sports but also being good at the sport of my choice. I also feel that when I grew up, the "Black" sport was basketball. This seemed to attract the most attention from my peers (including the young ladies). Culture has a role in this. I saw this in one of my schoolmates. He came from the Caribbean, and he did not really play basketball. He quickly acclimated to the Toronto scene and focused his efforts on basketball. He went from being a player with poor skill to making our basketball team. To me, that showed effort and focus, and knowing what would make him accepted as a young Black male. I believe in other schools, football may have been more important than in my school since my school did not have a football team. Overall, you have to

be interested in playing sports, but you also have to pick the right sport to play. (Dwaine)

With this comment, Dwaine explains how important he perceived sports to be to his identity, including his heterosexual masculinity (e.g., attracting attention from "the young ladies") and how sports served as an essential mechanism for fitting into the school culture, especially as an immigrant youth. Often the expectation that Black youth play sports manifests in the question, "What do you mean, you don't play sports?" The premise here is that Black males, with no other ways of being and belonging in society or alternative means to succeed in society, must be interested in sports; if not, they should be, because they have some hidden sport talent waiting to be cultivated. Of course, it's not sufficient to just play sports; one is also expected to participate in a sports culture – this means watching sports, talking about sports, reading about sports, collecting sports cards and magazines, knowing sports statistics, and staying current on what is happening in professional leagues (e.g., trades, controversies, and changes in coaches).

Participation in sports also constitutes a means of socialization for young working-class Black males. Given the way they are perceived, based on stereotypes (as immigrants, fatherless, troublemakers, and underachievers), they must be acculturated into the appropriate societal values (see chapter 4) and then disciplined in the ways of society. Beyond the teamwork and democratic ethos, discipline and time-management skills, and values of responsibility and hard work are what young athletes are expected to learn from participating in sports (Eitzen, 2009; Pitter, 2004). And for many young Black men, sports also serve as a mechanism of social policing or surveillance, especially by coaches with the support of teachers. This becomes evident from community and school programs designed for young Black males – often sport looms large in these programs for it is seen as part of their identity and interests.

Will "Play Black"

I was always described as being fundamental or playing fundamentally sound. My coach at the time emphasized continually improving upon these skills but that to take my game "to another level," I would need to be more comfortable with "having fun" and playing with a little more flair – especially if I wanted to get noticed by scouts. It was never explicitly said that I should play more "Black," but this style of play was coded as the "city game" or in other words the inner-city style of play. Again, while it was not explicit, the players I was recommended to watch and model myself after were often Black and from the inner city. (Dennis)

The Black male's athletic identity relies not only in his interest in playing sports but also in his showing adeptness and strength[2] in his sport. This relates to the stereotype of Black people as natural athletes with a body that is genetically built for sport (Buford May, 2008; Ferber, 2007) – particularly basketball, football, track and field, and boxing. Talking about his experience with boxing, Seif (an amateur boxer) said, "There's an automatic assumption that 'Black guys' will be more athletic, faster, slicker, et cetera. And it's a kind of flashy performance that is valued in (white) hip-hop-admiring culture."

Whatever the sport, there is a flashy, crowd-pleasing style of athletic showmanship that is expected of Black players, who often oblige. This style of play is one way that Black athletes build their reputation in school. Take, for example, dunking in basketball. Kani recalls several times in his high school career when a player scored "a particularly nice dunk, and the whole school would be talking about the dunk for the rest of the week. Nothing else could garner that level of instant fame among the Black students at the school."

The "flashy performance" or "flair," as Dennis indicates above, is often constructed in relation to race, and communicated, as Kani puts it, through the "instant fame" status that athletes attain from their peers – with his "nice dunk" he lived up to expectations. The message comes through: it is not enough for the Black athlete just to play well by demonstrating a high degree of proficiency in performing basic skills – he must also add a degree of flair to his good plays and *look good* while doing so. By standing out with his expected "star" performance, he earns support and respect from his peers and coach.

Race correlates with social class in construction of the star athlete – evident in the code words coaches use when working with Black players. As Dennis points out above, the euphemism "inner-city style of play" conveyed how his coach expected him to play basketball. In popular North American discourse, the term describes part of a city that is populated by poor, racialized (often Black) people. It encompasses neighbourhoods from which, it is expected, young people want to escape (James, 2012b). Hence, the expectation is ingrained that young athletes play to be noticed by scouts, who can provide coveted opportunities (including scholarships) to play at universities, colleges, or even

---

2 Dennis suggests that to play strong also means playing "aggressively, physically, and with little fear whether on defence or on offence."

private high schools in the United States or, failing that, postsecondary institutions in Canada.

Reflecting on his student-athlete career, Dwaine, now a basketball coach, says that he would like to say that "Blackness" has nothing to do with how he has approached or played basketball, but this is because he has now "matured" (see also Buford May, 2008). He recalls that when he was growing up,

> there was a stereotype of how a black athlete should play ... Black players were supposed to be quick, be able to jump high, and be very agile (e.g., shake, crossover, rock a man). Therefore, players who were able to dunk and to show agility with the ball were seen to be very good.

But as Dwaine points out:

> As a coach, this has been an annoyance of mine since the popularization of this type of play has made it more difficult at times to develop the fundamental skills that are needed. If I were to be honest, I would have been a more successful basketball player if I focused on developing fundamental things such as shooting and using my left hand. Instead, I had put too much emphasis on stereotypical skills such as spending endless amounts of time developing my jumping and fancy moves (e.g., "killer crossover"). Playing this way gave you more respect among your peers. You were revered as a player. You had style.

Will Participate in a "Black Athletic Culture"

> We all listened to the same/similar music, and if you didn't know something then people would often "put you up on it" (teach you about it). It wasn't explicit, but really just the style at the time was to wear bigger clothes, have your hair braided in cornrows, and wear stud-earrings and a do-rag or fitted hat. It wasn't like you were going to show up to a game in a pair of tight/fitted pants because if you did, you would get laughed at. Having the newest brand-name sneakers and the most expensive (that you could possibly afford) was always a big thing. If you couldn't get them, you would often drool over them in magazines or on the internet. And any time anyone got a new pair, it would be noticed and you would go to investigate the new shoes up close. Shoes are one of the biggest markers of personal style on the court as they point to your style of play or who you might want to play like depending on who endorses that brand/model of shoe. It was also one of the few markers of personal style (aside from headbands, armbands, socks, and hair style) that could set you apart,

considering everyone has to wear the same uniform. When off the court, ball, music, and girls were often main topics of conversation. (Dennis)

Being a Black student-athlete has as much to do with what one does, or how one carries oneself, off the court or field as on it. So how one plays the game and the accolades one receives for athletic prowess are expected to be carried over into the company one keeps and the culture of the group. As Dennis indicates, the group's culture informed how they dressed, the music they listened to,[3] and their topics of conversation. These representations of athleticism – influenced in part by professional players – enabled these young student-athletes to keep up with expectations, cultivate their social and cultural capital, construct their aspirations, and sustain their masculinity (heterosexual, for according to Dennis, "girls" were often part of their conversations).

Psychologically, these characteristics of athleticism served to maintain (or sanction) what it took for them to become or remain good players. As Dennis explained, "It always seemed that those people who played better had the better sneakers. And if you did not wear the more recognized/popular (i.e., expensive) sneakers, then you had better be that much better."

In most cases, the athletes know one another before playing on the same team. Often friends or acquaintances from the community or school choose to play the same sport or join the same team. For example, Semere notes that the members of his basketball team "all hung out, ate, and took classes together," and it was through their association and encouragement that potential players would attend tryouts and eventually become team members. Semere recounts what he refers to as "a very interesting socialization ritual" for new team members. This typically involved students who were new to the school and were not known to team members, but were "good enough to make the basketball team":

Every year there would be one or maybe even two members of the team that literally came out of nowhere ... I remember our coach ... telling us to take the new team members under our wing, to have them hang out with us, and to make them feel "a part of the team." All of what he was suggesting for us [the core members of the team] to do were activities that were off the court, to improve bonding, and ultimately to improve performance, cohesiveness and our functioning as a unit on the court. What

---

3 The music to which many Black athletes listened was hip-hop, reggae, rhythm and blues, and dance hall (Dennis, Semere, Dwaine).

was interesting was that both of these team members were not Black – one was of Asian descent, and the other was Eastern European. It very much served as an initiation into our "group culture" and our socialized mannerisms and behaviours. And these experiences and our outings served as a space for them to *learn* Blackness, our Blackness, and to reaffirm our Blackness, our behaviours, norms, etc. And as new members to a foreign and established group/collective/team, the Asian and Eastern European players did not question this acceptance. They just learned and behaved accordingly, with very little resistance. After all, they did want to be a part of "the team," right?

In terms of their academic work, Semere reveals that his team members had a "cavalier attitude" towards school, particularly towards attending classes and handing in assignments. This approach to their schooling stemmed from their privileged status "as good athletes." So, when the new team members would regularly attend classes, especially during the basketball season, they were encouraged *not* to do so, and to adopt the practices of the established members of the team since it was "tradition" or "the way that we always did things."

In addition to dress and approach to academic work, speech pattern was also mentioned as a significant aspect of the athletic group culture. Bailey (2010) notes that language plays a crucial role in the performance of race and class – for racial identification and also in the connection between certain forms of speech and certain groups. In the case of Black student-athletes, their speech patterns not only stigmatized them but also represented their "resistance to dominant hierarchies in society" and at least a partial rejection of the system that devalues them (p. 82).

Bailey (2010) also contends that the use of a language or speech pattern that does not promote socio-economic mobility "can be self-defeating"; it supports "the dominant ideology that speakers of racially or class-stigmatized varieties of English choose to remain marginal and are undeserving of the prestige and resources afforded other members of the society" (p. 83). Evidently, Black student-athletes' culture is informed by their experiences with and their understanding of racism as a systemic process that constructs them as "athletes" with a related web of stereotypes and expectations. But as Seif contends:

> There is pressure to conform to this stereotype for fear of being considered not really Black. Being mixed-race, this is something I've experienced mostly from white people, but I think it extends to blackness more generally. To be Black is to be a part of the "Black experience," which is admired as cool.

Will Aspire to Go South on an Athletic Scholarship

> I believe that all athletes, particularly basketball and track athletes, both of which I was, demand and expect of ourselves to have this aspiration. To have the desire, or at least publicly state that we ultimately want to aspire to win an athletic scholarship, to "go south." We would constantly check in the stands for scouts, to read in the paper and see which of our athletes were being offered scholarships, from whom, and so on. To do otherwise, i.e., set sights on a Canadian school or not want to go south means that you did not think you were good enough. This is not "cool." To this end, we would constantly play with an eye to where and when the scout would be around, and you'd go to places where you could be seen. (Semere)

An essential aspect of student-athlete culture in Canada involves the aspiration to go south to a US university or college on an athletic scholarship – be it for track and field, basketball, football, or soccer. And while many student-athletes might not have a clear plan about how this might come about, they nevertheless nurture the dream of going south (James, 2005). Some athletes, fearing that in Toronto or elsewhere in Canada they are too far from the indispensable eyes of the US scout, will elect to complete high school or "prep school" in the United States.

Most student-athletes consider going south "a major landmark," "the ultimate prize," which sets them apart from other players and extends the dream, hopes, and possibility of playing professionally.[4] Asked why he so desperately wanted to win an American scholarship, Dwaine responded, "In Canada, we grow up watching American sports. It is what we consume and what we see as 'real' sport." And as Dennis declares, going south would serve to "solidify your status as a respectable ballplayer."

While they might not have known exactly how they would attain their scholarship goal, the athletes nevertheless had what Dennis called a "formula – play at a well-known school, get lots of minutes, accumulate stats, send highlight tapes to coaches, and play at tournaments and camps in the US." To that end, many student-athletes attend camps or play in US tournaments. Some are more successful than others, often with support from their coach – for whom the scholarship win represents a positive reflection of his skills and abilities as a coach and mentor (or father figure). Student-athletes live with optimism and hope that

---

4 While a scholarship to a US postsecondary institution was the preferred prize, an alternative was being recruited for a European league, and as Dwaine said, going "out east to the Atlantic schools was seen to be better than staying in Ontario."

their abilities and skills (which they work at daily), high performance on the better high school teams, experiences in provincial leagues, exposure from travelling, and nurturing sport networks (with help from their coaches and educators) will help them attain the ultimate sports prize. Usually athletes will not consider other options (e.g., junior colleges and prep schools in the US or Canadian colleges and universities) until it becomes clear that a major scholarship to a US university is not forthcoming.

Will Be Supported by a Role-Model Coach Whom He Comes to See as a "Substitute Father"

> Although I already have a father, one of my coaches filled this role in another sense. I had one coach with whom I practised for a significant portion of my adolescent years. He provided a lot of support for me in terms of developing my skills and pushing me to compete at a higher level. I actually remember one summer where he proclaimed his role as a "father." I was at a major basketball camp in the United States with a group of other young men from the GTA [Greater Toronto Area], and this coach had driven us to the camp. At the beginning of the week, as part of a discussion on expectations and behaviour, he also added that he saw himself as our "basketball dad" and that we could see him in this sense. For a good portion of my youth, this is in fact how I saw him. I had my dad who took care of everything at home, but because I spent a substantial amount of time (almost all of my time that I was not at school or studying) engaged in basketball activities and because of his position of significant knowledge and experience on what it took for me to "get to the next level," I saw him by and large as my "basketball dad." (Dennis)

Understandably, given the amount of time that Dennis and his team members spent with the coach, eventually they would develop a "father–son" relationship. But more than time spent together (in practices, games, away tournaments, sometimes tutoring), having a shared interest in something significant to both of them – like winning games and scholarships and getting the related adulation, respect, and recognition – sustained their relationship. Moreover, the coach had the power to make decisions that affected the athlete's current and future possibilities in life.

Unquestionably, working with an adult who shares your interests and life goals, spends time working and talking with you about something in which you are highly engaged, and appears to be similarly invested in your success is quite meaningful. Recalling his experience with his coach, Semere comments,

> He came in with the idea that the role of the basketball coach spanned much farther than the lines dictated by the gym. He offered advice on topics that did not directly fall under athletics or school, but life in general.

Reflecting on his experience as a coach, Dwaine had this to say:

> As a coach now, I understand the attachment that you can develop for your players ... We spend weekends together at tournaments. We support each other. I feel responsible for them off the court. They are my players, my sons. Spending time with each other leads to solid relationships. It is a reciprocal relationship.

This father–son paradigm was not only observed by coaches, but also by teachers who would defer to the coach about the student-athlete's educational and familial life. Semere offers an example of this. He remembers that midway through the school year, one of his Black teammates was doing quite poorly in English class – getting about a 35 per cent average – and hence was in serious jeopardy of failing the course.[5] The English teacher and the staff sponsor, who attended all practices and games and handled the team's administrative duties, chose to contact the coach about the situation, rather than the students' parents. All four – the English teacher, the staff sponsor, the coach, and the student – met to discuss whether the student should continue on the team and what measures should be put in place to address the situation.

This practice of turning to the coach and not the parents to address an educational (and sometimes a social and/or familial) concern demonstrates how minimally the school views the parents' role in the life of these students. In such situations, coaches – exercising their role as substitute "basketball" parents – will use permission to play a game as a punishment or reward. As Semere suggested, such practices likely stem from stereotypes about the Black student-athlete as being both working-class and fatherless (see chapter 4).

In the absence of interventionist parents who would provide the needed discipline and guidance (McGhee Hassrick & Schneider, 2009),

---

5 This is a serious situation, as failing English, a mandatory credit in each year of high school, meant that the student would either have to attend summer school or stay back a grade to make up the credit.

coaches (regardless of race[6]), with the complicity of teachers, feel justified in taking up such matters without consulting the parents. For their part, having accepted the coach as a concerned substitute father with the power to determine their future in life, Black student-athletes defer to their coaches. To resist would mean sacrificing the support of a "parent" and "family" (i.e., team) members, and social mobility. After all, the coach as parent is part of the culture of Black male athleticism.

Conclusion

> Race is the modality in which class is lived.
> – Hall et al., 1979 (cited in Andrews, Silk, & Pitter, 2008, p. 284)

In an earlier essay (James, 2011), I explored the question of why the basketball team is predominantly Black, and what that says about the role educators play in levelling the playing field. I argued that the "over-representation of Black student-athletes on a number of basketball teams in urban Toronto schools" revealed a schooling system in which educators had not yet come to terms with inequities that marginalized and racialized students – in this case, Black students.

In a context of marginalization and racialization, sports become a way to engage Black youth, particularly males, in the schooling process and to offer them a pathway to educational and social success. But which Black boys? In this chapter, I have suggested that this "solution" targets working-class Black male student-athletes. They end up accepting a cultural ethos in which they "regard their bodies as instruments or tools and thus see sports as a legitimate means to the economic stability already enjoyed by the middle class" (Pitter & Andrews, 1997, p. 94).

In fact, race, class, gender, and, in many cases, where one resides, all intersect to inform identification of the Black student-athlete (along with the youth's own athletic identification). Furthermore, young working-class men may be inclined to participate in sports because that enables them to exercise their cultural capital, gain a sense of belonging in the school and society, navigate racist structures, and perform their masculinity (heterosexual, strong, fearless, and aggressive) successfully.

---

6 However, informed by white liberalism and the stereotype or prevailing notion of fatherless Black youth living in dysfunctional homes, the white coach would see his work as nonracist and helpful.

Living out their conception of masculinity – specifically, Black masculinity – through sport is reinforced by peers, school personnel (teachers, coaches, administrators), parents, media reporters, and their young female fans. Middle-class students, by contrast, with their material wealth, economic stability, and cultural capital, are able to appreciate the "health and aesthetic" benefits of participation in sports (Pitter & Andrews, 1997, p. 94) and the cultural advantage of being "well-rounded" individuals physically and intellectually. They know they have other avenues to success and to having an impact on society; hence, they do not need to invest in sports as much as working-class youth.

The extent to which young Black males express an interest in sports; play sports with quickness, flair, and aggression (code for "playing Black"); adhere to group norms, symbols, and practices of a particular Black athletic culture; nurture a single-minded aspiration to go south on scholarship – all these are a product of their own making as much as a product of an inequitable, discriminatory, alienating society and schooling system. As their narratives indicate, socializing agents like coaches, teachers, educational administrators, social service workers, and media personnel operate within this system to construct, maintain, and propagate a culture of Black male athleticism that in the end disadvantages working-class Black males. The Black student-athlete culture does not enable many of them – especially those from working-class backgrounds – to effectively negotiate or surmount the educational, social, and economic barriers to attain success in society. Evidence shows that many still drop out of high school and only a measly few ever make it south on scholarships; even of those who do, many return without either completing their educational programs or making it to the professional leagues.

We need a significant cultural shift through which Black and other racialized student-athletes learn how inequity, structural and institutional racism, and heterosexism operate to disenfranchise them, and we need to develop a culture that socializes them to critically engage with schooling and athletic structures.

REFERENCES

Abdel-Shehid, G., & Kalman-Lamb, N. (2011). *Out of left field: Social inequality and sport*. Halifax, NS: Fernwood.

Anderson, E., & McCormack, M. (2010). Comparing the Black and gay male athlete: Patterns in American oppression. *Journal of Men's Studies, 18*(2), 145–58. https://doi.org/10.3149/jms.1802.145

Andrews, D.L., Silk, M., & Pitter, R. (2008). Physical culture and the polarised American metropolis. In B. Houlihan (Ed.), *Sport and society: A student introduction* (2nd ed., pp. 284–304). London, UK: Sage.

Bailey, B. (2010). Language, power, and the performance of race and class. In K.O. Korgen (Ed.), *Multiracial Americans and social class: The influence of social class on racial identity* (pp. 72–87). Abingdon, UK: Routledge.

Branch, T. (2011, October). The shame of college sports. *The Atlantic.* https://www.theatlantic.com/magazine/archive/2011/10/the-shame-of-college-sports/308643/

Brathwaite, K.S., & James, C.E. (Eds.). (1996). *Educating African Canadians.* Toronto, ON: Our Schools/Our Selves & James Lorimer.

Buford May, R.A. (2008). *Living through the hoop: High school basketball, race, and the American dream.* New York, NY: New York University Press.

Coakley, J.J. (2009). Sport in society: An inspiration or an opiate? In D.S. Eitzen (Ed.), *Sport in contemporary society* (pp. 10–15). London, UK: Paradigm.

Dunne, M., & Gazeley, L. (2008). Teachers, social class and underachievement. *British Journal of Sociology and Education*, 29(5), 451–63. https://doi.org/10.1080/01425690802263627

Eitzen, D.S. (Ed.). (2009). *Sport in contemporary society.* London, UK: Paradigm.

Ferber, A. (2007). The construction of Black masculinity: White supremacy now and then. *Journal of Sport & Social Issues*, 31(1), 11–24. https://doi.org/10.1177/0193723506296829

Harrison, L., Sailes, G, Rotich, W.K., & Bimper, A.Y. (2011). Living the dream or awakening from the nightmare: Race and athletic identity. *Race Ethnicity and Education*, 14(1), 91–103. https://doi.org/10.1080/13613324.2011.531982

Hempel-Jorgensen, A. (2009). The construction of the "ideal pupil" and pupils' perceptions of "misbehaviour" and discipline: Contrasting experiences from a low-socio-economic and a high-socio-economic primary school. *British Journal of Sociology of Education*, 30(4), 435–48. https://doi org/10.1080/01425690902954612

Hernandez, K.C., & Davis, J.E. (2009). The other side of gender: Understanding Black masculinity in teaching and learning. In H.R. Milner (Ed.), *Diversity and education: Teachers, teaching and teacher education* (pp. 17–30). Springfield, IL: Charles C. Thomas.

Howard, T.C. (2008). Who really cares? The disenfranchisement of African American males in preK–12 schools: A critical race theory perspective. *Teachers College Record*, 110(5), 954–85.

James, C.E. (2005). *Race in play: Understanding the socio-cultural worlds of student athletes.* Toronto, ON: Canadian Scholars' Press.

James, C.E. (2010). *Seeing ourselves: Exploring race, ethnicity and culture.* Toronto, ON: Thompson Educational Publishing.

James, C.E. (2011). Why is the school basketball team predominantly Black? In S. Tozer, B. Gallegos, A. Henry, M. Bushell Greiner, & P. Groves Price (Eds.), *Handbook of research in social foundations of education* (pp. 450–9). New York, NY: Routledge.

James, C.E. (2012a). Class, race and schooling in the performance of Black male athleticism. In C.J. Greig & W.J. Martino (Eds.), *Canadian men and masculinities: Historical and contemporary perspectives* (pp. 176–90). Toronto, ON: Canadians Scholars' Press.

James, C.E. (2012b). *Life at the intersection: Community, class and schooling.* Halifax, NS: Fernwood.

Kagawa-Singer, M., & Chung, R.C.-Y. (1994). A paradigm for culturally based care in ethnic minority populations. *Journal of Community Psychology, 22*, 192–208. https://doi.org/10.1002/1520-6629(199404)22:2<192::AID-JCOP2290220213>3.0.CO;2-H

Kwan-Lafond, D. (2011). Racialized masculinities in Canada. In J. Laker (Ed.), *Canadian perspectives on men and masculinities: An interdisciplinary reader* (pp. 221–39). Toronto, ON: Oxford University Press.

Martino, W., Kehler, M., & Weaver-Hightower, M.B. (Eds.). (2009). *The problem with boys' education: Beyond the backlash.* New York, NY: Routledge.

McCready, L.T. (2010). *Making space for diverse masculinities: Difference, intersectionality, and engagement in an urban high school.* New York, NY: Peter Lang.

McGhee Hassrick, E., & Schneider, B.L. (2009). Parent surveillance in schools: A question of social class. *American Journal of Education, 115*, 195–225. https://doi.org/10.1086/595665

Pitter, R. (2004). Midnight basketball: Avoiding the hazards of assimilative reform. In B. Kidd & J. Phillips (Eds.), *From enforcement and prevention to civic engagement: Research on community safety* (pp. 170–83). Toronto, ON: University of Toronto, Centre of Criminology.

Pitter, R., & Andrews, D.L. (1997). Serving America's underserved youth: Reflections on sport and recreation in an emerging social problems industry. *Quest, 49*, 85–9. https://doi.org/10.1080/00336297.1997.10484225

Singer, J.N., & Buford May, R.A. (2010). The career trajectory of a Black male high school basketball player: A social reproduction perspective. *International Review for the Sociology of Sport, 46*(3), 299–314. https://doi.org/10.1177/1012690210378283

Taylor, Y. (2006). Intersections of class and sexuality in the classroom. *Gender and Education, 18*(4), 447–52. https://doi.org/10.1080/09540250600805179

Warren, S. (2005). Resilience and refusal: African-Caribbean young men's agency, school exclusions, and school-based mentoring programmes. *Race Ethnicity and Education, 8*(3), 243–59. https://doi.org/10.1080/13613320500174283

Response to Chapter 6

Basketball's Black Creative Labour and the Mitigation of Anti-Black Schooling

MARK V. CAMPBELL
Assistant Professor, Department of Arts, Culture and Media, University of Toronto, Scarborough, Ontario, Canada

In "Class, Race, and Schooling in the Performance of Black Male Athleticism," James details the ways in which alienating and inequitable school environments are made more bearable for Black male students by their participation in sports. Forms of celebrity are sought and performed by these students within learning environments that are largely hostile to the possibility of Black student academic success. Basketball players, particularly but not exclusively those in school, engage in creative labour in the form of aesthetically pleasing athletic stylings, increasing their social value in the face of blatant anti-Blackness. While playing basketball with flair is nothing new, the embrace of this style of playing, combined with the continuing anti-Black low academic expectations, illuminates a set of codependent relations. Young Black males seek athletic prowess as one way, among others, to mitigate the climates of hostility Black students face in schools. Teachers, cognizant of their students' participation in sports teams, use Black male students' athletic participation as a way to set expectations that are aligned with the dominant society's fabricated rendition of Blackness as unintelligent and ineducable.

Leaning on and extending Clinton Hutton's (2007) notion of a "creative ethos," I suggest we understand Black creative labour as comprising acts of survival that are constitutive of the Black diasporic experience. Such acts are not simply performative measures; they signal a critical desire to live as something other than "units of labour" under Western capitalism (Wynter, n.d.). Hutton (2007) explains how the arts have played a role in the survival of enslaved populations in the Caribbean, allowing for the creation of semi-autonomous zones of self-creation and subjecthood beyond the reach of the colonial authorities. Extending Hutton's creative ethos, I am suggesting that Black creative labour remains a necessary activity and demands a notion of self that exceeds the limited conceptions of Blackness currently allowed within Western mainstream discourses. Unfortunately, Black creative labour is problematized when it is performed outside of the school environment, for it often becomes commodified in highlight reels, the language of sports commentators, video games, and the endorsement of products. The desire to exist as more than a unit of labour becomes a slippery proposition as the sport-industrial complex continues its expansion. If we reflect on the historical trajectory of stylistic basketball performances and examine contemporary examples propped up by the world of social media, we can get a better sense of how school players' adherence to the flair model of play as a way to mitigate the schooling environment actually folds them back into a commodified state within machination of social media.

Since 1976, Black male basketball players have played the game in an excessively stylish manner, innovating new styles of play that audiences crave. Julius Erving's famous cradle dunk in 1983, repeated by Michael Jordan a few years later in the National Basketball Association's slam dunk competition, is a prime example of the kinds of creative labour undertaken to enhance one's status. Endorsement deals – Erving's with Converse and Jordan's with Nike – evidenced their growing and lucrative popularity. Jordan's clearly unnecessary accumulation of gold chains worn in the 1985 dunk competition enhanced not just the popularity of his bestselling sneaker but birthed another generation of players deeply invested in a particular flashy style of play.

For instance, the five freshman starters who formed the "Fab Five" at the University of Michigan in the 1992 and 1993 seasons are among the generation of players who continued Jordan's stylistic innovations. Sporting bald heads like Jordan and excessively large basketball shorts, black shoes (which were banned in the NBA), and black socks, these teenagers' creative labour led to new styles of play, increased college apparel sales, new styles of broadcasting, and an explosion of media coverage (Albom, 1994; Pierznik, 2015). In addition to their style of play, modes of celebration deeply connected to hip-hop music distinguished this generation of basketball players, evidenced by the Fab Five's Chris Webber waving his arms to the crowd as Naughty By Nature's "Hip Hop Hurray" played in the stadium. This kind of Black creative labour appeals to largely white audiences while also impressing Black peers, increasing, in turn, the social value of Black players and signalling that their possible humble beginnings could be overcome or overlooked. Webber, for example, would leave Michigan after his sophomore season for a $90-million NBA contract and an endorsement deal with Nike.

Within schools in the Greater Toronto Area (GTA), the relationships between schooling, race, and Black male athleticism have been influenced by the growth of two new elements: digital media and local basketball infrastructure. Unfortunately, these two elements have not mitigated the ways in which Black students are treated in, and "pushed out" of, their schools, nor have they cleared the minefield of inequities that make the daily navigation of the school system by ambitious Black students treacherous (Dei, Mazzuca, & McIsaac, 1997).

The growth of digital media and their increasing presence in the lives of young people is a relatively recent phenomenon. Some high school basketball stars accumulate millions of views on Instagram and Snapchat, primarily visual platforms through which young people socialize. High-school-aged youth largely ignore older social media platforms such as Facebook and Twitter, seeing them as spaces in which adults might monitor their activities. While the platforms that young people use allow for greater social connectivity, they also allow for a deepening fetishization of the Black athletic body.

Websites and YouTube channels such as Ballislife provide a nonstop feed of short basketball clips that heightens one's awareness of basketball and its subcultures. The videos overwhelmingly focus on the "aggressive" and flashy styles of play that James's interviewees detailed as ones they appreciated or were encouraged to mimic. High-flying slam dunks, alley oops, killer crossovers, and no-look passes litter the basketball online environment, feeding audiences of players and non-players a constant stream of highly digestible and desirable modes of play. Also, on these sites and other news and rumour sites like Slam or Bleacher Report, basketball players can and do maintain a steady diet of information and gossip related to all levels of the sport. Therefore, the arena in which today's aspiring basketball players can craft their identity and playing style has expanded dramatically.

Meanwhile, schools in the GTA have not substantially rearranged their troubled relationships with Black students (Dei, 1997; Poisson, 2014; Schroeter & James, 2015; Shum, 2014). Stereotypes based on racial hierarchies still position Black students as intellectually inferior. Teachers' active engagement of old racial stereotypes manifests itself in acceptance of Black student underachievement and unwillingness to encourage Black students to greater academic success. Black male students' dismal literacy rates positively correlate with low graduation rates and are problematically propped up by teachers who either want to rid their classrooms of these students or accept the lowest level of achievement as a confirmation of the illusion of racial hierarchy.

What this means is that today high school basketball teams can, and at times do, comprise solely boys from special education programs – boys whose chances of attending a postsecondary institution are slim to nil. This has two very significant ramifications. First, for students not in university-bound courses, the dream of "going south" wanes significantly as American schools cannot accept prospective students who do not have high enough SAT scores. Second, the heightened visibility of high school basketball players, in social media as captured by fellow students as well as local media, increases the returns of these students' limited and fleeting "celebrity status." Teachers and administrators become complicit in feeding these students' reputations by bending rules to ensure participation in games despite poor academic performance, often knowing the damage not participating in sports can do to a student's self-esteem.

Class matters deeply in how Black male athletes survive or avoid the trap of low expectations and low achievement that plague both public and Catholic schools.[1] For students with parents who can afford to invest both money and time for elite training, the prep-school route separates those who can from those who cannot succeed in the quest to play basketball professionally. The prep-school route often (although not always) leads to the United States, as can be seen in the journeys of recent Canadian hoop stars Rowan Barrett, who attended Florida's Monteverde Academy, and former number-one draft pick Andrew Wiggins, who went to Huntington St. Joseph Prep in West Virginia. Parents with the resources to send their children to prep school or who choose to enrol them in a local elite basketball program must invest their time and money in weekend tournaments, travel, uniforms, and other miscellaneous costs. Such resource- and time-intensive investments are often incompatible with shift work, seasonal or precarious work, and other undesirable labour arrangements under neoliberal capital.

The increasing number of elite basketball programs in Toronto, like the CIA Bounce Team (which Andrew Wiggins played for) and the Northern Kings program, means that the infrastructure to support local basketball farm systems is growing. The Toronto Raptors' 905 farm team and the success of prep programs like Orangeville Prep means that there are an increasing number of ways Black male students can

---

1 In Ontario, Catholic schools, while publicly funded, are distinguished from "public" (nonreligious) schools. However, the two systems share many similarities in how they overpolice and push out Black youth.

seek success in basketball. Unfortunately, such a plethora of opportunities to participate in the sport means the strategies of playing ball in high school to mitigate the systemic racism and daily dose of anti-Black low-academic expectations may wither away.

For many, staying in school means dealing with being subjected to extreme surveillance on a daily basis and generally ill measured on the basis of white supremacist colonial logic, without the tools of Fanonian discourse to make sense of their socially constructed realities. In his seminal essay "The Fact of Blackness," Frantz Fanon (1952/1967) describes a situation where a little boy on the subway points at him and calls him into subjecthood, "Mama, the nigger is gonna eat me up" (p. 114). Fanon's erudite analyses of social constructions of anti-Blackness allow us to become cognizant of our "crushing objecthood" and our inability to have "ontological resistance" in the white gaze (p. 110). Yet, once the Black male basketball player is deemed "successful" via endorsement deals and media attention, the same strategies of creative labour used in school settings and rewarded in professional settings fold him back into being a commodity, still with low academic expectations but smothered with millions of dollars. A great example is that of recent NBA rookie Jaylen Brown of the Boston Celtics, who was referred to as "too smart to play in the league" as he explained to *The Guardian* newspaper his understanding of sport as a form of social control in America (McRae, 2018).

Black creative labour is found on the football field in end-zone dances, on the basketball court in midair preceding an unimaginable contortion before a slam dunk, or on the ice in the dynamic stick work of former Montreal Canadiens defenceman P.K. Subban. It provides opportunities for enhanced social value for Black athletes – a value that has yet to, and cannot permanently, dislodge the intricate workings of anti-Blackness in our digital-media-infused social space of schooling. With the unfortunate commodification of these forms of cultural innovation, the "crushing objecthood" schools nefariously force upon their Black male ballplayers reasserts itself within larger market-driven scenarios in which views, likes, and endorsement deals do little to disrupt the vestiges of anti-Black life.

REFERENCES

Albom, M. (1993). *The Fab Five: Basketball, trash talk, the American dream*. New York, NY: Warner Books.

Dei, G.J.S. (1997). Race and the production of identity in the schooling experiences of African-Canadian youth. *Discourse: Studies in the Cultural*

Politics of Education, 18(2), 241–57. https://doi.org/10.1080/0159630970180206

Dei, G.J.S., Mazzuca, J., & McIsaac, E. (1997). *Reconstructing "drop-out": A critical ethnography of the dynamics of Black students' disengagement from school*. Toronto, ON: University of Toronto Press.

Fanon, F. (1967). *Black skin, white masks* (C. Lam Markmann, Trans.). New York, NY: Grove Press. (Original work published 1952)

Hutton, C. (2007). The creative ethos of the African diaspora: Performance aesthetics and the fight for freedom and identity. *Caribbean Quarterly*, 53(1–2), 127–49. https://doi.org/10.1080/00086495.2007.11672312

McRae, D. (2018, January 9). Jaylen Brown: Sport is a mechanism of control in America. *The Guardian*. https://www.theguardian.com/sport/2018/jan/09/jaylen-brown-boston-celtics-nba-interview

Pierznik, C. (2015, May 15). Chris Webber, Jalen Rose and the battle for the legacy of the Fab Five. *Medium*. https://medium.com/the-passion-of-christopher-pierznik-books-rhymes/chris-webber-jalen-rose-and-the-battle-for-the-legacy-of-the-fab-five-bd0ef8401304

Poisson, J. (2014, April 24). Somali community split over task force recommendations. *Toronto Star*. http://www.thestar.com/news/gta/2014/04/24/somali_community_split_over_task_force_recommendations.html

Schroeter, S., & James, C.E. (2014). "We're here because we're Black": The schooling experiences of French-speaking African-Canadian students with refugee backgrounds. *Race Ethnicity and Education*, 18(1), 20–39. https://doi.org/10.1080/13613324.2014.885419

Shum, D. (2014, April 24). Somali community fear stigmatization with new TDSB action plan. *Global News*. http://globalnews.ca/news/1289062/somali-community-fear-stigtimization-with-new-tdsb-action-plan/

Wynter, S. (n.d.) *Black metamorphosis: New natives in a new world* [Unpublished manuscript].

7 Troubling Role Models: Seeing Racialization in the Discourse Relating to "Corrective Agents" for Black Males[1]

To respond to educational, social, and cultural concerns and needs of Black youth, particularly males, educational and social service institutions have initiated role modelling and mentorship programs. These programs pair "successful" Black men with their young charges to help them with school assignments, family issues, and social concerns. The assumption behind such programs is that young Black men need male role models and mentors – or "corrective agents," to borrow Patrick Shannon's (1998) term – to steer them to become educationally successful, socially responsible, productive citizens. In this chapter, I use new racism as a framework to interrogate this notion.

Role models and mentors ostensibly know how to take advantage of the opportunities in life through individual efforts. For Black youth, they represent *evidence* that despite the barriers facing them in life, they can still attain their goals. The message: limitations or barriers are merely personal constructs that young people can effectively navigate, negotiate, and even overcome – if they take their mentors' teachings seriously, emulate their values, and take advantage of the extra support. Further, the challenges and other "setbacks" they might face are simply opportunities for building character and strength that will help them become like their mentors and role models, living respectful and successful lives.

I can relate this concept to two of my own experiences. First, a high school teacher invited me to visit his media class, in which approximately one-third of the students were Black. Concerned about their

---

1 This chapter was originally published in 2012. See James (2012). Reprinted with the permission of the publisher.

supposed lack of high educational aspirations and the negative images of Blacks to which they were exposed, he wanted his Black students to meet, as he said, "someone who holds a position in a university." I was a successful Black male who, like his students, has experienced racism. This qualified me to advise them about "how they too [could] be successful by focusing on their academic work" (James, 2000, p. 89).

Second, in a graduate class I taught, we watched a documentary, *Invisible City* (Davis, Lentin, & Flahive, 2009), which told the life stories of two young Black men, Mikey and Kendell – both of whom were only sons who lived with their mothers – and their mentor-teacher, Ainsworth Morgan. The teacher and the two young men all grew up in downtown Toronto, in one of Canada's oldest low-income and racially diverse neighbourhoods. Morgan, a Black male in his late thirties now living in a middle-class suburban area of Toronto, nurtured and supported Mikey and Kendell from when they were in his Grade 7 class until they were eighteen (the film tracks them over this four-year period).

Morgan is shown talking with the young men – sometimes alone, sometimes together – discussing their legal troubles and how to navigate the justice system, their schooling and the importance of paying attention to their schoolwork, and their respect for their mothers. The documentary also shows Morgan's return to his first apartment (in a building now slated for demolition) where he had lived with his younger brother and single mother, who immigrated to Toronto from Jamaica five years before she was joined by her two sons. In the apartment scene, Morgan reminisces about sharing the bedroom with his brother and comments on the small size of the room and the apartment. This comment becomes even more meaningful in another scene with Morgan, his three young children (including two boys under ten), and Mikey and Kendell at Morgan's big house in the suburbs – a long way both physically and socially from his early community.

Morgan's role modelling was quite evident: he was able to show Mikey and Kendall the possibility of success if they applied themselves to their school work, kept out of trouble, and listened to their mothers. He showed sensitivity to the young men's situation, noting that "manhood comes early in the neighbourhood [where] being weak is not an option." Morgan saw himself as being a positive force in Mikey's and Kendell's lives, commenting, "Every child needs to have someone in their world that he or she does not want to disappoint."

In the class discussion following the movie, one young Black woman commended Morgan: "We need more men like you. We need more role models and mentors like you." This comment was motivated in part by the noticeable absence of the boys' fathers in their lives and the lament from one that his father had little time for him. Morgan was seen as a "good man" and an appropriate male figure for Mikey and Kendall to emulate. After all, he played with his sons and daughter, and he would tell Mikey and Kendell "I love you" as they parted. The need for male figures or, more precisely, a father figure for "fatherless" Black boys looms large in this discourse on mentors and role models. We assume that males like Morgan will help to "fix" young men who do not have fathers actively in their lives.

Father-Absent Families and the Link to Violence

In trying to explain violence and poor educational performances among Black youth, Toronto media have suggested these happen because the youth come "from fatherless homes" (Macfarlane, 2006). A *Globe and Mail* article entitled "The Many Fatherless Boys in Black Families" (2005) noted:

> Who is doing the killing and who is being killed in the wave of reckless public violence that has struck Toronto? Black boys and young men with no fathers in their homes. Yet as politicians at all three levels and black community leaders scramble for answers to the anarchy, no one has dared talk about the crisis of fatherlessness in the black community. The silence is inexcusable. Growing up without a father present is now the norm for many black children in Canada, particularly those of Jamaican ancestry. Nearly half of all black children under 14 in Canada have just one parent in the home, compared to slightly under one in five of Canadian children as a whole, census figures from 2001 show. Two in three Jamaican-Canadian children in Toronto are being raised by a single parent. The U.S. trend of "radical fatherlessness" – in which the majority of children in an apartment building, on a street or in a neighbourhood lack fathers – is hitting Toronto like a tsunami. (paras. 1–2)

In a *Toronto Star* article, "Where Are the Men?" based on interviews with single mothers (mostly Black), community groups, and churches, Linda Diebel (2007) reported that these women were "raising children on little money, often in public housing where kids [were] exposed to greater risks, because it's all they can afford" (p. A1). Diebel underscored that a great number of the women interviewed were themselves raised in "fatherless homes," had become teenage mothers, and struggled financially to support their children while also protecting them from the continual threat of violence, drugs, and gangs. Diebel cited the experience of one mother who worked two jobs to support her three children – one of whom, her oldest, went to jail on a gun-related charge. This mother took responsibility for her son's charge and "beat herself up for not spending more time with her son." She was quoted as saying:

> We are single mothers working two and three jobs to keep bread on the table, and they don't care ... The fathers aren't helping, and the kids are turning to crime ... But fathers make a big difference ... I hear the kids, and they're always talking about their fathers, and how they're not there. That's what these fathers have to realize. They must step up to the plate. They must. Because when they're not here, they're replaced by other factors like gangs. Kids need role models, not deadbeat dads. (p. A1)

The notion that Black boys need fathers (and Black male teachers) as role models was also expressed by Johnson (2006) writing about the "Black American condition today." He wrote that "without strong, self-sacrificing, frugal, and industrious fathers as role models, our boys go astray, never learn how to be parents (or men), and perpetuate the dismal situation of single-parent homes run by tired and overworked Black women" (p. 13). Chris Spence, director of education for the Toronto District School Board from 2009 to 2013, would concur. A proponent of a Boys to Men program, structured around role modelling and mentorship for at-risk Black boys, Spence (2002) advocated an all-boys elementary school in response to boys' lower test scores and higher rates of school suspensions and expulsion. On the basis of his teaching experience, Spence suggested that strong mentors for boys can likely offset their "fatherless worlds" (see also Brown & Rushowy, 2009; Talaga, Daubs, & Rushowy, 2009).

The call for mentors and role models rests on the notion that the problems Black boys face stem largely from their individual attitudes, values, actions, and sense of purpose. By extension, their parents share the blame – mothers who cannot provide the appropriate and necessary supports and guidance, and neglectful, irresponsible fathers whose absence results in boys going "astray" and not learning about maleness from the person considered best suited to teach them (see also Lawson, 2012). Media personnel, politicians, educators, social service workers, parents, and community members – white and Black alike – all espouse the merits of mentors and role models. This widespread agreement suggests general acceptance of the idea that our young Black men's problems are best addressed through individual effort, not systemic changes. However, as Lawson (2012) writes: "The telling of stories that frame African diasporic peoples as 'social problems' overlook and/or erase how emotionality, love, sex, and desire complicate how they negotiate parenting roles and responsibilities" (p. 822).

Blaming the Victim, Individualizing the Problems: The New Racism

I believe that the focus on mentorship and role modelling to address the ills that befall young Black males rests on the liberal notion of individualism – a notion that holds these boys and young men, their parents, and their communities responsible for their situation. Their disproportionately poor educational outcomes and worrying social circumstances, which should serve to contradict the assumed equity, democracy, and accessibility of our society, are instead explained by the "common-sense" notion of fatherlessness, understood as the absence of a male father figure from the home. According to this reasoning, if these young men share the common characteristic of being raised by single mothers, then providing them with "substitute fathers" – that is, mentors and role models – would help address the situation.

This approach amounts to blaming the victim and individualizing the problems. The so-called common-sense approach actually constitutes an important aspect of *new racism*, which obscures the systemic or structural impediments facing young Black men and their parents, leaving the status quo intact (Bonilla-Silva, 2003; Ferber, 2007; Henry & Tator, 2004). Under the new racism framework, gender is understood to be central to the working of racism. As Ferber (2007) puts it, "Gender is constructed through race, and race is constructed through gender; they are intersectional and mutually constitutive" (p. 15).

New racism can be defined as an inconspicuous and covert approach to issues of inequity, denying the existence of racism while simultaneously suggesting racial preconceptions pertaining to minoritized group members. "Old-fashioned" racism (Leach, 2005; van Dijk, 2000) can be understood as an overt approach – segregation, educational streaming, antagonism, name calling, and so on. In today's society, under the prevailing understanding that race and racism no longer play pivotal roles in access to society's resources, racism is perceived to be nonexistent. According to Balibar (2007), new racism is

> a racism whose dominant theme is not biological heredity but the insurmountability of cultural differences, a racism, which at first sight, does not postulate the superiority of certain groups or peoples in relation to others but "only" the harmfulness of abolishing frontiers, the incompatibility of life-styles and traditions. (p. 84)

Historical forms of racism explicitly suggested a biological or hereditary basis for individuals' superior and inferior skills and capacity and for their temperament and life situation. But twenty-first-century racism proffers simultaneously a colour-blind ideology and a cultural difference epistemology, or what Balibar (2007) terms the "idea of racism without race" (p. 85). Jorge (2009) would add that the covert attitudes, beliefs, and behaviours of new racism position the Other as deeply different and inferior.

Scholars hold that in both the United States and Canada the post-civil rights era brought a shift in racism. This occurred through outlawing overt practices of white supremacy and recognizing legal claims by minorities, Blacks in particular, to the principles and benefits of liberalism – democracy, equal opportunity, meritocracy, justice, and fairness (Bonilla-Silva, 2003; Ferber, 2007; Henry & Tator, 2004; Hill Collins, 2004). Nevertheless, the new racism that evolved remains firmly rooted in white supremacy while operating through "practices that are subtle, institutional, and apparently non-racial" (Bonilla-Silva, 2003, p. 3).

So, racism cannot be considered a thing of the past, for the racial order of things remains. Henry and Tator (2004) use the term *democratic racism* to reflect on how and why white supremacy remains intact despite claims of postracialism. They write, "Democratic racism results from the retention of racist beliefs and behaviours in a 'democratic' society" (p. 19). Its distinguishing quality remains its "justification of the inherent conflict between the egalitarian values of liberalism ... and the racist ideologies reflected in the collective mass belief system as well as the racist attitudes, perceptions, and assumptions of individuals" (p. 19).

Colour-blindness is a major tenet of new racism; under this discourse, white privilege remains untouched and ideas about its mere existence are deemed fallacious. Indeed, as Bonilla-Silva (2003) writes with reference to the United States (which can be equally applied to Canada):

> Compared to Jim Crow racism, the ideology of color blindness seems like "racism lite." Instead of relying on name calling, color-blind racism otherizes softly; instead of proclaiming God placed minorities in the world in a servile position, it suggests they are behind because they do not work hard enough ... And the beauty of this new ideology is that it aids in the maintenance of white privilege without fanfare, without naming those who it subjects and those who it rewards. (pp. 3–4)

A particularly misleading and troublesome feature of the notion of colour-blindness in the discourse of new racism is the practice of seeking out and then referencing "successful" Black individuals (in dominant-culture terms) like Barack Obama, Oprah Winfrey, Michael

Jordan (of course, athletes are always in the mix), and Michaëlle Jean (a Canadian example), exemplifying the efficacy of our meritocracy. The model thus justifies eliminating programs – equity and affirmative action programs in the United States and employment and educational equity programs in Canada (Bonilla-Silva, 2003; James, 2010). In this way, the failure of individuals to live successful lives is not attributed to racism, but to "the moral shortcomings of minority group members" (Augoustinos, Tuffin, & Every, 2005, p. 317). The message becomes hard work and not privilege determine success. This belief ignores systemic barriers that render many opportunities inaccessible to people of colour, simultaneously absolving whites, and others who operate on their behalf, of any responsibility for preserving white privilege.

Showcasing Black people who have "made it" further reinforces the common-sense notion that individuals create their destiny and opportunities irrespective of structural impediments in society. As Hill Collins (2004) notes about the US context:

> The joblessness, poor schools, racially segregated neighborhoods, and unequal public services that characterize American society vanish, and social class hierarchies ... as well as patterns of social mobility within them, become explained solely by issues of individual values, motivation, and morals. (p. 178)

Further, the historical argument of biological differences – once used to characterize as natural the failures, hostility, or underperformance of minoritized racial-group members – has been replaced with a discourse in which lack of morals or cultural propriety is commonly used as justification for their condition (Bonilla-Silva, 2003; Henry & Tator, 2004). These explanations, or new racism, serve to comfort those who benefit from race privilege as they take solace in believing that "they are not involved in the terrible ordeal of creating and maintaining inequality" (Bonilla-Silva, 2003, p. 26). And as Bonilla-Silvaalso points out, "charmed by the almost magic qualities of the hegemonic ideology," those with privilege take solace in believing that "they are not involved in the terrible ordeal of creating and maintaining inequality" (p. 74). Besides, racialized group members who make it in the society tend to become known as "model minorities"[2] – people who, when placed

---

2 Asians are often referenced in this regard for their educational accomplishments. It is especially noted that they might have been immigrants or had language differences and still succeeded better than long-time residents (see Lee, 2005; Pon, 2000).

against or compared with other racialized group members, serve as "evidence" that individuals are solely responsible for their successes and failures.[3]

Role of Mass Media in the New Racism Discourse

A number of scholars have noted the important role mass media play in routinely manufacturing and recycling common-sense ideas until they become part of the dominant popular imagination (Bonilla-Silva, 2003; Ferber, 2007; Henry & Tator, 2004; Walsh, 2009). Everyday images and representations of minoritized-group members remind individuals of the "truths" behind common-sense notions that depict their level of educational attainment and antisocial activities. The media's role in perpetuating these constructed images of minoritized members is supported by other institutions, such as schools, courts, law enforcement agencies, arts organizations and cultural institutions, human services, governments, politicians, and businesses (Henry & Tator, 2004).

This racist ideology and related racist discourse produce (for some people) a constant tension, resulting from the contradiction between their own lived experiences with stereotyping and racism and the notion (often internalized) that they are the sole architects of their own misfortunes. The tension also relates to the expectation that all members of society will conduct themselves on the basis of morality and values of "individual self-reliance, obedience, discipline and hard work" premised on white European middle-class male norms (Augoustinos et al., 2005, p. 317; see also Hinchey, 2008).

Gordon and Klug (1986) summarize new racism as "a cluster of beliefs which holds that it is natural for people who share a way of life, a culture, to bond together in a group and to be antagonistic towards outsiders who are different and who are seen to threaten their identity as a group" (p. 22). Accordingly, individuals whose language and actions epitomize racism will claim that they are not racist, "nor are they making any value judgements about minority group members, but simply recognizing that they are different" (p. 22). The disadvantages that minoritized-group members experience in relation to their race are perceived to be a consequence of their transgression of the prevailing societal values and norms rather than a natural outcome of structural inequities (Augoustinos et al., 2005, p. 317). So, saying that Black youth

---

[3] In some cases, the model minority construct also serves to undermine the potential, sense of self, and self-confidence of the other racialized groups' members.

need mentors and role models to lead successful lives and develop a healthy sense of what it means to be a "man" means using the language of difference to conceal the systemic racism through which Black males are essentialized on the basis of cultural difference.

The Construction of Black Males as Deficient

In her article "The Construction of Black Masculinity," Abby Ferber (2007) raises the following question in reference to African Americans: "How can a White supremacist nation, which subjects Black men to ongoing racism and demonization, at the same time admire and worship Black men as athletes?" (p. 11). Insofar as Canada is a similar white supremacist nation, the same question can be asked here.[4]

But I prefer to pose another question: How can we explain the support and appreciation of Black student-athletes by coaches, teachers, principals, other students, and the media when their profiles also involve low grades (compared to white student-athletes), temper tantrums, and ferocious behaviours at games and in the community? Often, we read about these athletes as potential scholarship winners to study at American universities (James, 2005). Is it that coaches, educators, and sport reporters agree that the athletic abilities of Black males are "natural" (in contrast to white peers who gained theirs through training and practice), and that this explains their low aptitude for academics, aggressiveness, and violent behaviours (Ferber, 2007; James, 2005)?

From a new racism perspective, the response would be that *natural* does not imply biology, as would have been the perspective years ago, but rather that it is part of their culture – something into which they are socialized. But why would sports be linked to Black people more than other people, when we see other ethnic and racial group members just as involved in sports? Why is it that sports tend to be more often identified with keeping Black students in school compared to other students? Aren't the *cultures* of Black people just as diverse, dynamic, variable, unpredictable, alterable, and changeable over time as all other cultures? How is it that Black youth seem to maintain cultural values and aspirations uninformed by the prevailing European, middle-class, male, heterosexual values, norms, and mores of schools and other institutions in which they participate?

---

4 Indeed, Canadians admire and support their athletes – Canadian-born athletes like National Basketball Association star Jamaal Magloire and teams such as the Toronto Raptors and Argonauts with their many Black players.

Ferber (2007) argues that there is a "naturalization of racial difference in sports discourse" that sustains the idea of natural athleticism in Black men, and a masculinity that is overly physical, driven by instinct, aggressive, threatening, prone to violence, and hypersexual (p. 20). The enduring historical "naturalized" images of Black males not only continue to instill fear of Black male bodies but also contribute to the obsession that they must be controlled and tamed. The message is that Black males are "essentially bad boys" but some can become "good guys" if tamed (Ferber, 2007, p. 20).

Sport serves as a mechanism through which coaches[5] and sports figures, operating as mentors and role models, provide Black male youth with the message that it is possible to succeed in this society regardless of their colour. Successful athletes are seen as representing the fact that if young Black males live by the discipline and moral codes of sport, they too can succeed – the opportunities are there for them to take. Athletes commonly bring this colour-blind "bootstrap message" (Ferber, 2007; Schick & St. Denis, 2003) to students in North American schools, and some young people, mesmerized by the perceived successes – the scholarships, money, clothing, women, and travels of these "role models and mentors" – fall for the message. They try to emulate their mentors and role models, even wearing sports attire that bears their names and numbers.

Ironically, many of these same role models and mentors, who today encourage young people to stay in school, did not apply themselves to their education – secondary and postsecondary – as they would have their young protégés believe. Their struggles to find meaning in an alienating, inequitable schooling experience is typically missing from their message. Missing also are the stories of individuals who did not make it in sports despite emulating their mentors and role models. Such talks usually do not address the downsides of focusing exclusively on sports (or on one sport) – for example, not being available to pursue other possibilities or develop abilities and skills in other areas in case of injuries or when one's sporting life ends.

Often, mentors are presented (or present themselves) as stand-in fathers[6] for the many father-absent young Black men about whom there

---

5 Ferber (2007) references Hill Collins (2004) as saying that "there is a traditional family script in place in sports that works to minimize the threat of Black masculinity. The coach is similar to the White male father figure, whereas Black male athletes are like the children, under the father's control and subject to his rule. It is only when they accept and play this role that they are fully embraced and accepted and seen as nonthreatening" (p. 20).
6 Coaches are regularly thought of as father figures.

is growing concern, particularly regarding gang membership and violence. Reporting on the question "Why do kids join gangs?" *Toronto Star* reporter Moira Welsh (2006) writes:

> These high-risk boys are poor, often from dysfunctional homes or ones where one parent has left, usually a father. Many fail in school, where teachers cannot cope with unfocused students. At home, there are no rules. Some of their mothers work 14-hour days, and when their sons say they are at Boys and Girls Club playing basketball, they believe them. The neighbourhoods they come from are populated by blacks and other minorities, as are the schools, in pockets of the inner city.

Concerns about young Black males have been well canvassed in various media reports and editorials. In 2005, referred to as Toronto's "Year of the Gun" because of shootings involving young Black men as both victims and perpetrators, the *Toronto Star* ran a series of articles focusing on what has been termed gang violence within the Black community. In many news stories, editorial comments, and letters to the editor, fatherlessness was put forward as being largely responsible for delinquency among Black males. The situation was seen as a "moral panic" that the Black community needed to address. To this end, CBC Radio held a series of interviews, town hall meetings, and online moderated discussions with members of the Black and non-Black communities on the topic "Growing Up without Men."[7] In addition to prominent Canadian scholars and community members invited to talk on the topic, as always happens with Canadian media, notable African Americans from the United States were also invited into the discussion. For the most part, guests on the various programs agreed that fatherlessness (or not having a father in the home) was responsible for the behaviour of young men in Black communities.

Professor Orlando Patterson, a prominent African-American scholar, proffered that much of the behaviour manifested by young Black men relates to a culture of "hypermasculinity" and sexual prowess, which involves "being a father – at least having children" (Barrie, 2006b). He

---

7 Townhalls on the topic, "What does it mean to grow up without a father?" were held in different areas of Metro Toronto during the fall of 2005. These were aired on CBC Radio One, Toronto, which also featured interviews with reporter Mary Wiens on the lives of four Torontonians. On 22 and 27 January 2006, the CBC Toronto program *Metro Morning* with host Andy Barrie aired a series of interviews with guests Eugene Rivers, David Popenoe, Anne Cools, Chris Spence, and Orlando Patterson on the topic "Growing Up without Men" (Barrie 2006a, 2006b).

agreed that the absence of fathers from the home reflects the community culture. Another American, Reverend Eugene Rivers of Boston, commented that "there is a high correlation between father absence, single-parent households, and criminal behaviour, particularly on the part of young males" (Barrie, 2006a). He contended that

> Canada's black community faces a crisis. A generation of poor, predominantly black youth is in violent rebellion against their fatherlessness and, by logical extension, against law and order and an established middle-class Black leadership that purports to speak for them. (Barrie, 2006a)

Rivers, like others who participated in the series, attributed the problems Toronto was experiencing with its Black youth to their families and the Black community, suggesting that these institutions needed to take responsibility for the problems. "Internally," Rivers said, "the black community has to make a decision that it will move beyond excuses, asking for funding to do programs which can be initiated without funding" (Barrie, 2006a).[8]

Ever since a record number of gun-related homicides among young Black men in Toronto, the media have continued to give voice to those who say that the source of problems for Black youth is their lack of "positive" role models, particularly for those living in "inner city" neighbourhoods. For example, the *National Post* carried an article by Wendell Adjetey (2009), stating:

> Young, Black males are falling by the wayside primarily because they lack positive male role-models. Census data reveals nearly 60% of all Black Canadian children live with a single parent mother. For this particular reason, it is imperative that social service providers focus more specifically on establishing mentorship networks that would provide inner-city males with positive role models who are also family oriented. (para. 3)

The call for institutionalizing mentorship and role model programs for Black youth by community members accords with this long-standing media message in which the skills and abilities of Black single mothers to raise their children are called into question and the children's problems diagnosed as stemming from fatherlessness and the moral

---

8 It seems that what Reverend Rivers had to say impressed the members of the Ontario Progressive Conservative Party sufficiently that they invited him to speak at their convention the following year.

ethos of Black masculinity. And since there are Black men who have demonstrated that it is possible to live honest, productive, successful, and respectable lives, many of whom are willing and able to become mentors and "positive role models," then the implicit message is that it is individual efforts, and not social structures, that account for one's successful outcomes.

On the premise that "corrective agents" provided by mentorship and role model programs enable individuals to live successful lives within the current structure, such programs are proliferating in schools and social service agencies. As mentioned earlier, one such program is Boys to Men, in which male teachers and other volunteer mentors work with at-risk Black male middle school and high school students in the Toronto area. Their job is to give the kids "positive images" of Black males that will change their "negative attitudes towards life and academic achievement," and revive their self-esteem, which, as Spence (2002, p. 71) writes, has been "battered by the pervasive negative images of people like themselves."

While Spence did not explicitly say it, his call in fall 2009 for a boys-only school builds on the Boys to Men model for at-risk Black males.[9] But it would appear that while institutionalizing a gendered approach to addressing the needs of boys – all boys – is acceptable, a school for *Black* boys would be summarily rejected – if we take the negative reactions to the establishment of an Africentric school as a precedent. While "a male-focused school" still accords with the discourse of multiculturalism, a "Black-focused school" entails segregation. Then-premier of Ontario Dalton McGuinty, who was vehemently opposed to the Africentric school, quickly endorsed the idea of a boys-only school, saying that "our boys are not doing as well as our girls when it comes to reading and behavioural challenges … You can put in place a curriculum that speaks to their special needs and opportunities and that focuses on some of their challenges, including reading and behavioural" (Talaga et al., 2009, paras. 16, 19). When asked about having a school that would to do the same for Black students as for boys, the premier responded by saying, "This is an all-boys school – not a some-boys school. All colours, all faiths, all cultures, all heritages and traditions. All boys" (para. 18).

Putting aside the fact that there is no way of knowing which boys will attend a "boys-only" school, it seems that the idea of a school that will centre the experiences of Black students and engage Black males in an

---

9 Spence was sure to say that attendance at such a school would be based on "choice" and it would not be "segregation" (Talaga et al., 2009).

education program and curriculum that speak to their experiences is unacceptable to many people, and white people in particular. The implicit message is that there is nothing wrong with the current schooling system – Black youth can succeed if only they behave in a disciplined manner and apply themselves to their schoolwork. The evidence to prove this is not applied in the same way to meet the needs of Black male students for whom mentorship and role modelling programs are expected to suffice.

Many male teachers enter the profession hoping in fact to become mentors and role models. In her study of male teachers working in elementary schools, Kimberley Tavares-Carter (2009) noted that mentoring was one of the key ways these teachers felt they could act in the interest of young Black males. Martin, a teacher in her study, "feels that mentorship is about working with and for students to provide the 'aggressive, proactive intervention' he and others felt is needed to support Black males as they navigate the school system. This is why they became teachers" (p. 51). Five of the eight respondents saw working in an elementary school as a "proactive measure" as opposed to "reactive" – or as Martin stated, "trying to get them [young students] on track when they're in Grades 8, 9, 10, it's a bit more difficult" (p. 51). Speaking to these teachers' desire to be mentors and role models to young black males at a stage in their lives when they are still "saveable," Tavares-Carter writes:

> Martin felt that he had to "cultivate a sense of self and cultivate this very confident progressive person in the student." Omar sought to "enrich the lives of the next generation by helping kids who are marginalized" ... For Kevin, being a teacher gave him the opportunity to "create a different experience for people who experience the world from the same place as me." Roy wanted to ensure that students "know that you are not coming just to talk about sports but trying to help them with life itself." (p. 50)

I find Tavares-Carter's (2009) starting point particularly interesting. She had set out to assert the need for having Black male teachers working with Black male high school students. She felt that as a Black female teacher, she was only able to partially connect with her Black male students and attributed this to gender differences; she assumed the students could more fully relate to male teachers. This assumption is consistent with the discourse about the need for father figures in the lives of young Black males.

But her respondents' experiences should signal that the lack of males – more precisely the absence of fathers – does not mean that Black boys do not live respectful and ambitious lives and attain important careers through strong support from their single mothers. Tavares-Carter (2009) noted that six of her eight respondents, all teachers, "grew up solely with their mothers, who nurtured, guided, and gave them a solid foundation" that helped to propel them through the difficult education and social systems (p. 54). One respondent talked of having "a strong mother and grandmother who pushed him," and others talked of doing things to make their mothers "proud" of them.[10]

Ainsworth Morgan, featured in the documentary mentioned earlier, *Invisible City* (Davis et al., 2009), now a successful parent, teacher, mentor, and role model, also talked of growing up with his single mother, from whom he was separated for about five years. He too talked of the significant role his mother played in his life in making him the person he is today – an experience upon which he drew to make the youth he mentored appreciate their own mothers' efforts.

Similarly, Conrad (pseudonym), who participated in a study I conducted with about twenty university students from a low-income, high-density, largely racialized minoritized community in Toronto, talked of his mother as someone who "understood you go to school, do your homework, you do well." This was an understanding that he internalized, and which has contributed to his success – an MBA and in the early stages of corporate law (James, 2010).[11] Indeed, as Lawson-Bush (2004) writes about the participation of Black mothers in their sons' lives, "no aspect or component of Black male life eluded these mothers in their ability to teach lessons that were necessary for manhood or the development of masculinity" (p. 384).

While male mentors and role models do have a role to play in the lives of Black boys, the evidence suggests that simple exposure to "corrective agents" will not necessarily result in young Black males pulling "themselves up to social respectability by their bootstrap" (Shannon, 1998). It is also simplistic to suggest, as one of Tavares-Carter's (2009) respondents said, that "no other than a Black man can teach a Black kid how to be a responsible Black adult" (p. 54). Such thinking negates the structural inequity that restricts life opportunities and possibilities for individuals on the basis of race – a reality despite the colour-blind message of Canadian multicultural discourse.

The idea that Black male mentors and role models are best positioned to provide Black youth with the specific moral education they

---

10 One respondent even went further to talk of his admiration for his older sister and how he did "things to make her proud" of him, like spending more time on his schoolwork (Tavares-Carter, 2009, p. 73).
11 Like Morgan, Conrad joined his mother from Jamaica at age twelve.

lack rests on an assumption that their racial or cultural identity alone will make them effective translators of the prevailing moral ethos; that they will be able to solve all the problems confronting disempowered Black youth; and that without systemic change they on their own can "eradicate racism or have special knowledge about how to effectively challenge it" (St. Denis, Bouvier, & Battiste, 1998, p. vii).

This idea of Black corrective agents having "special knowledge" is premised on the racializing discourse that treats minorities, in this case Black youth and adult mentors and role models, as homogeneous. In the end, white teachers, social service agents, and others are neither expected nor asked to do anything other than point Black male students in the direction of Black male role models and mentors (e.g., teachers), let alone address or evaluate how white teachers, social service agents, and others – and importantly, the system itself – are complicit in the marginalization and racialization of Black youth.

Conclusion

Let me be clear, having Black male mentors act as role models for Black youth carries value. But much more is needed in a society where inequity, marginalization, and racialization exist, and where racism, now couched in cultural terms, obscures the fact that neither individual disposition nor community cultural ethos is responsible for Black and other minoritized young people's life circumstances.

Liberal notions of colour-blindness and individualism, articulated by reporters, educators, human service agents, and government personnel, would have us believe that equity has been established and everyone has the same experience and quality of life in Canadian society. The evidence indicates otherwise. Hence, corrective agents should not simply collude with the existing social and educational system, producing uncritical young people; neither should they convince young people to conform to the status quo with regard to prevailing values, role expectations, and societal beliefs. Mentors and role models need to give attention to the complexity and contradictions of young people's existence in a society where they do not feel a sense of belonging.

Furthermore, as I have written elsewhere (James, 2009, p. 113), unless mentorship and role-model programs interrogate the "hegemonic structure of the normalized white male masculinity into which black males are being socialized and expected or forced to fit," they are unlikely to be effective. The starting point in re-educating or re-socializing young Black males need not be about their single mothers or their fatherlessness or absent fathers; rather, it should be about providing them with the critical skills and tools they need to understand how the cultural forces in schools and other socializing agencies have helped shape their lives and their construction and performance of Black heterosexual masculinity. Role models and mentors can best help the young Black males with whom they work by teaching them to recognize their own agency in the world as well as their social and cultural capital, and helping them to better understand their relationship to society's power structures.

REFERENCES

Adjetey, W. (2009, August 19). Inner-city youth need positive role models. *National Post.* https://www.pressreader.com/canada/national-post-latest-edition/20090819/281736970471927

Augoustinos, M., Tuffin, K., & Every, D. (2005). New racism, meritocracy and individualism: Constraining affirmative action in education. *Discourse and Society, 16*(3), 315–40. https://doi.org/10.1177/0957926505051168

Balibar, E. (2007). Is there a "neo-racism"? In T. Das Gupta, C.E. James, G-E. Galabuzi, & C. Andersen (Eds.), *Race and racialization: Essential readings* (pp. 83–8). Toronto, ON: Canadian Scholars' Press.

Barrie, A. (2006a, January 22). *Growing up without men* [radio broadcast]. CBC Radio Metro Morning.

Barrie, A. (2006b, January 27). *Growing up without men* [radio broadcast]. CBC Radio Metro Morning.

Bonilla-Silva, E. (2003). *Racism without racists: Color-blind racism and the persistence of racial inequality in America* (1st ed.). Oxford, UK: Rowman & Littlefield.

Brown, L., & Rushowy, K. (2009, October 21). Schools plan calls for boys-only classes. *Toronto Star.* https://www.thestar.com/life/parent/2009/10/21/schools_plan_calls_for_boysonly_classes.html

Davis, H. (Director), Lentin, M., & Flahive, G. (Producers). (2009). *Invisible city* [documentary film]. Ottawa, ON: National Film Board of Canada.

Diebel, L. (2007, August 19). Where are the men? *Toronto Star*, p. A1.

Ferber, A. (2007). The construction of Black masculinity: White supremacy now and then. *Journal of Sport & Social Issues, 31*(1), 11–24. https://doi.org/10.1177/0193723506296829

Gordon, P., & Klug, F. (1986). *New right, new racism.* London, UK: Searchlight.

Henry, F., & Tator, C. (2004) *The colour of democracy: Racism in Canadian society* (3rd ed.). Toronto, ON: Thomson Canada.

Hill Collins, P. (2004). *Black sexual politics: African Americans, gender and the new racism.* New York, NY: Routledge.

Hinchey, P.H. (2008). *Finding freedom in the classroom: A practical introduction to critical theory.* New York, NY: Peter Lang.

James, C.E. (2000). "You're doing it for the students": On the question of role models. In C.E. James (Ed.), *Experiencing difference* (pp. 89–93). Halifax, NS: Fernwood.

James, C.E. (2005). *Race in play: Understanding the socio-cultural worlds of student athletes.* Toronto, ON: Canadian Scholars' Press.

James, C.E. (2009). Masculinity, racialization, and schooling: The making of marginalized men. In W. Martino, M. Kehler, & M.B. Weaver-Hightower (Eds.), *The problem with boys' education: Beyond the backlash* (pp. 102–23). New York, NY: Routledge.

James, C.E. (2010). *Seeing ourselves: Exploring race, ethnicity and culture.* Toronto, ON: Thompson Educational Publishing.

James, C.E. (2012). Troubling role models: Seeing racialization in the discourse relating to "corrective agents" for Black males. In K. Moffat (Ed.), *Troubled masculinities: Re-imagining urban men* (pp. 77–92). Toronto, ON: University of Toronto Press.

Johnson, C. (2006). Shall we overcome? The Black American condition today. *Society, 43*(5), 13–14. https://doi.org/10.1007/BF02687566

Jorge, V. (2009). Expressions of "new" racism. *International Journal of Psychology, 44*, 1–3. https://doi.org/10.1080/00207590802057548

Lawson, E. (2012). Single mothers, absentee fathers and gun violence in Toronto: A contextual interpretation. *Women's Studies, 41*(7), 805–28. https://doi.org/10.1080/00497878.2012.707903

Lawson-Bush, V. (2004). How Black mothers participate in the development of manhood and masculinity: What do we know about Black mothers and their sons? *Journal of Negro Education, 73*(4), 381–91. https://doi.org/10.2307/4129623

Leach, C.W. (2005). Against the notion of a "new racism." *Journal of Community & Applied Social Psychology, 15*, 432–45. https://doi.org/10.1002/casp.841

Lee, S. (2005). *Up against whiteness: Race, school and immigrant youth.* New York, NY: Teachers College Press.

Macfarlane, J. (2006, February). We used to think of guns as an American problem. *Toronto Life, 40*(2), 17.

The many fatherless boys in Black families. (2005, November 26). *Globe and Mail.* https://www.theglobeandmail.com/opinion/the-many-fatherless-boys-in-black-families/article1331802/

Pon, G. (2000). Beamers, cells, malls and Cantopop: Thinking through the geographies of Chineseness. In C.E. James (Ed.), *Experiencing difference* (pp. 223–34). Halifax, NS: Fernwood.

Schick, C., & St. Denis, V. (2003). What makes anti-racist pedagogy in teacher education difficult? Three popular ideological assumptions. *Alberta Journal of Education Research, 49*(1), 55–69. https://journalhosting.ucalgary.ca/index.php/ajer/article/view/54959

Shannon, P. (1998). *Reading poverty*. Portsmouth, NH: Heinemann.

Spence, C.M. (2002). *On time! On task! On a mission! A year in the life of a middle school principal*. Halifax, NS: Fernwood.

St. Denis, V., Bouvier, R., & Battiste, M. (1998). *Okiskinahamakewak – Aboriginal teachers in Saskatchewan's publicly funded schools: Responding to the flux: Final report – October 31, 1998*. Regina, SK: Saskatchewan Education Research Networking Project.

Talaga, Y., Daubs, K., & Rushowy, K. (2009, October 21). Boys-only schools "issue of choice," not segregation, director says. *Toronto Star*. https://www.thestar.com/life/parent/2009/10/21/boysonly_schools_issue_of_choice_not_segregation_director_says.html

Tavares-Carter, K. (2009). *The dearth of Black male educators in the secondary panel* (unpublished master's thesis). Faculty of Education, York University, Toronto, ON.

van Dijk, T.A. (2000). New(s) racism: A discourse analytical approach. In Simon Cottle (Ed.), *Ethnic minorities and the media* (pp. 33–49). Milton Keynes, UK: Open University Press.

Walsh, E.T. (2009). Representations of race and gender in mainstream media coverage of the 2008 Democratic primary. *Journal of African American Studies, 13*(2), 121–30. https://doi.org/10.1007/s12111-008-9081-2

Welsh, M. (2006, April 29). Why kids join gangs. *Toronto Star*.

Response to Chapter 7

Black Role Models and Mentorship under Racial Capitalism

SAM TECLE
Assistant Professor, Community Engaged Learning, New College, University of Toronto, Ontario, Canada

On each reading of Carl James's chapter "Troubling Role Models: Seeing Racialization in the Discourse Relating to 'Corrective agents' for Black Males," I think of it in relation to my role as a core staff member in a community-based organization that works in partnership with a large school board in Canada. This organization holds role models and mentorship as a core tenet. I also think of the many times, particularly during Black History Month, that I am asked to speak to Black high school and undergraduate students as, presumably, a successful Black male – PhD candidate and community advocate. In reflecting on James's argument, I will use my experiences in my various roles to think through the implications of role modelling and mentorship in community-based projects on which I have worked. In addition, I will explore the *possibility still* for what Katherine McKittrick (2006), referencing Harriet Jacobs (1987), calls a "loophole of retreat," and ask if there exists a space of subversive possibility where role modelling and mentorship could operate differently for Black people, particularly Black youth.

I grew up at the intersection of Jane and Finch, which is a neighbourhood very much like Regent Park, the focus of the documentary *Invisible City* to which James refers. Coming of age in a deeply stigmatized, marginalized, racialized, poor, and working-class neighourhood was the subject of an essay I wrote (2012) in James's book *Life at the Intersection: Community, Class and Schooling*. I ended that essay by saying:

> I think of being praised by my professors now and by my teachers in the past for my aspirations and the heights to which I have ascended. I am appreciative and humbled by their praise and support. But I wonder if, within the deficit thinking about Jane and Finch, these admirers are seeing me as "an example" of what this "troubled community" can produce. (Tecle, 2012, p. 122)

In that passage, I was trying to articulate the ways in which it was possible to simultaneously heap praise on me for my individual aspirations and achievements, while also thinking of how far I have come – in relation to their notion of the "troubled" Jane and Finch community. I also think of how my story comes to be framed as the "successful Black male." And to rooms full of Black youth, my story framed in that way is designed to represent proof positive that the communities from which Black youth come, the conditions of poverty that make upward social mobility nearly impossible, and the family make-up that creates structural barriers are not insuperable obstacles. Despite these obstacles, yes, they too, with enough "grit," dedication, hustle, and grind, can "make it out." And in spite of all the deficits of their communities and neighbourhoods, they can also dream big and wide, and make it. Given my experiences and the messages I endeavour to put out, I wonder how being positioned as a "successful Black role model" entangles me in what James calls "corrective agent" logic. What is at stake when speaking to Black youth when this is the framing?

What makes the use of role models and mentorship programs so prevalent is that they are premised on the possibility of a pathway leading to escape from the barriers and limits that inherently come from growing up in a marginalized community. When community agencies and youth workers turn to Black role models and mentorship programs, they do so while also framing Black youth as at-risk (see chapter 4 in this volume). This has the effect of turning (and keeping) critical attention away from the historical and structural barriers that operate to reproduce and pathologize Black youth, without giving attention to the conditions under which Black communities are so often forced to live. As James points out, highlighting successful individual stories of Black men from a tough neighbourhood who have "made it" – in effect, "the rose that grew from concrete" trope[1] – affirms neoliberal values like individualism, hard work, and personal responsibility.

---

1 This is the title of Tupac Shakur's book of poetry (1999).

Stuart Hall's (2007) concept of managerial neoliberalism is particularly apt when considering the way James posits Black role models as corrective agents. For Hall, managerial neoliberalism focuses on the *process* of how neoliberalism comes to be mobilized as a prevailing ideology governing ethics, behaviour, and politics. Managerialism is neoliberalism's prime mover, and is also "how neoliberalism then gets into the system" (p. 111). In this regard, role models can be conceived not merely as "corrective agents," as James puts it, but also as people brought in to "manage" unruly "at-risk" Black youth from assumed "broken" Black families.

Of course, this is not just a contemporary phenomenon, because historically under capitalism, Black people have always required "management" for the sole purpose of maintaining society's economic and social arrangements in the accumulation of capital, which is a component of what Cedric Robinson (2000) calls "racial capitalism." According to Robinson, this arrangement mobilizes the ways race contributes to deep and severe inequity, displacement, dispossession, and uneven life chances that are a product of racialized historical exploitation. Robinson's framework encourages us to always remember that the mostly Black and racialized people who live in the types of communities that need role modelling and mentorship programs experience the realities they do because of a set of global and historical exploitations, rather than as a result of any biological, social, or cultural traits.

No one better represents the problematic logic of "role models as corrective agents" than former President Barack Obama. Both the policies and the mentorship programs he supports reflect his stance. Take for instance his landmark policy initiative, "My Brother's Keeper," which at its core is a nationwide mentorship program focused on uplifting young Black boys and men. On 27 February 2014, in front of an assembled group of national media reporters and concerned stakeholders in the East Room of the White House, President Obama signalled his thinking about what would help uplift young Black men in the United States. The audience of mostly young Black men – presumably the types of young Black men whom My Brother's Keeper was designed to help – heard him talk of helping "young men who show a lot of potential but may have gotten in some trouble to stay on the right path" (Obama, 2014, para. 2). Obama then turned to the personal to detail his own overcoming "at-risk" beginnings to instantiate the transformative possibilities of neoliberal values like self-reliance and hard work:

> When I was their age I was a lot like them. I didn't have a dad in the house. And I was angry about it, even though I didn't necessarily realize it at the

time. I made bad choices. I got high without always thinking about the harm that it could do. I didn't always take school as seriously as I should have. I made excuses. Sometimes I sold myself short. (para. 4)

As James notes, the discourse of absent fathers in the upbringing of Black male youth is an assumed attribute which marks them as lacking and "at-risk," hence even more in need of Black male mentorship. In drawing on this widely held assumption, Obama declares that it was through role models and mentorship programs that he received important direction, filling the void created by an absentee father. Obama shared this particular story so that Black boys and young men in attendance might envision the types of rewards they would receive from taking part and fully engaging in My Brother's Keeper. These rewards include developing the capacity to "make good choices, and to be resilient, and to overcome obstacles, and achieve their dreams," and that they would understand clearly My Brother's Keeper's central tenet, which is "the idea of opportunity for everybody; the notion that no matter who you are, or where you came from, or the circumstances into which you are born, if you work hard, if you take responsibility, then you can make it in this country. That's the core idea" (Obama, 2014, para. 8).

Loophole of Retreat

While I take James's argument seriously, I plan to continue supporting Black youth as I have been doing through mentorship programs, as a role model, and through speaking engagements, despite the problematic ways in which this might be framed. In that case, the critical question becomes: Is there a "loophole of retreat" to the critique James provides?

For the loophole, I turn to Fanon's *Black Skin, White Masks* (1952/2008) – in particular, a quote found towards the end of that important text, where Fanon makes the following charge to both himself and the reader, "O my body, make of me always a man who questions!" Rather than functioning as a "corrective agent," and a vehicle for the transmission of a set of neoliberal values, what if, despite how we are framed, we work to reproduce a Fanonian ethic in our mentoring and encourage critical questioning? What if role models presented a counternarrative to the mantra of individualized personal success that we are so often tasked with conveying? And rather than being corrective agents, what if role models were to operate on a collective and communal ethic? What if we were to actively reject the easy symbolism of individualized success of

Black role models, and instead focus on helping Black youth to develop and sustain critical structural analyses of our society and our communities so that they come to understand how economic, political, cultural, and educational structures make and keep Black life difficult?

After this most recent reading of the chapter, I am renewed in my determination to focus on these difficult questions which require answers that move us away from already prevalent ready-made "solutions." The challenge to think much more critically about "positive" Black role models and to question mentorship programs as solutions to historical and structural conditions is an open one. And if we are to break with neoliberalism's values and ethics, then the challenge must be taken up collectively.

REFERENCES

Fanon, F. (2008). *Black skin, white masks* (R. Philcox, Trans.). New York, NY: Grove Press. (Original work published 1952)

Hall, S. (2011). The neo-liberal revolution. *Cultural Studies, 25*(6), 705–28. https://doi.org/10.1080/09502386.2011.619886

Jacobs, H.A. (1987). *Incidents in the life of a slave girl: Written by herself.* Cambridge, MA: Harvard University Press.

McKittrick, K. (2006). *Demonic grounds: Black women and the cartographies of struggle.* Minneapolis, MN: University of Minnesota Press.

Obama, B. (2014, February 27). *Remarks by the President on "My Brother's Keeper" initiative.* https://obamawhitehouse.archives.gov/the-press-office/2014/02/27/remarks-president-my-brothers-keeper-initiative

Robinson, C.J. (2000). *Black Marxism: The making of the Black radical tradition.* Chapel Hill, NC: University of North Carolina Press.

Shakur, T. (1999). *The rose that grew from concrete.* New York, NY: Pocket Books.

Tecle, S. (2012). Growing up in a stigmatized community ... and making it. In C.E. James, *Life at the intersection: Community, class and schooling* (pp. 117–22). Halifax, NS: Fernwood.

8 "Up to No Good": Black on the Streets and Encountering Police[1]

> They [police] have their stereotypes: If you are Black and male, the cops think that you are up to no good, and if you are Black and female, it's not so bad, but we are still harassed. (Research participant)

One of the most controversial aspects of police discretion has been the right of police to stop, question, and search citizens in public places. Many allege that this aspect of discretion often leads to harassment, which has contributed to strained relationships between police and particular communities. Newspaper reports in many Canadian cities, including Toronto, Halifax, Ottawa, and Montreal, have recounted numerous incidents involving racial-minority youth and police.

In Toronto, for instance, one reported incident involved two brothers who were harassed and assaulted by the police while they waited at a bus stop on their way from a church meeting one Friday evening. Another concerned an alleged police assault on a young man who was eventually found dead from drowning in the Ottawa River. Meanwhile, tensions between Black youth and police in Cole Harbour, near Halifax, continue to undermine attempts to build trusting relationships. These incidents, along with police shootings of Black people,[2]

---

1 This chapter was originally published in 1998. See C.E. James (1998). Reprinted with the permission of the publisher. I wish to acknowledge the contributions of my colleagues Tony Xerri, Robynne Neugebauer, Joy Mannette, and Rinaldo Walcott who gave generously of their time and provided critical comments and suggestions.
2 Between 1978 and 1997, at least thirteen Black people in Ontario were shot and killed by police. Another six were injured – in some cases paralyzed – by police bullets. Of the nineteen Black people injured or killed by police, thirteen were youth: twelve males (eight were killed) and one female. See Commission on Systemic Racism in the Ontario Criminal Justice System (1995) which reports on shootings from 1978 to 1995 (p. 378).

have contributed to Black communities' concern about police-community relations and the tendency to criminalize their youth. This concern must be addressed if we are to change Toronto Caribbean youth's view of "the police as the 'ultimate oppressor'" (Henry, 1994, p. 202).

In this chapter, I explore the nature of Black people's encounters with police, focusing in particular on Black youth. I examine how both the youth and police understand and experience the street, a major arena in which their encounters initially play out. I argue that discretion by police and security personnel[3] to use such techniques as "stop and question" in their encounters with Black youth constitutes a cultural articulation of patriarchy and systemic racism that is deeply embedded in our consciousness – that we construct some members of Canadian society as more prone to crime and hence more in need of close observation and surveillance.

Racism, Policing, and Black Youth

Colonial discourse provides a framework within which we might understand the experiences of Black youth and their encounters with police. According to Weis and Fine (1996), whites use such discourse to engage in a process of Othering, wherein "'white' becomes the norm against which all other communities of colour are judged (usually to be deviant)" (p. 8). Colonialism and neocolonialism have both contributed to "the marginalization of people of colour and the resulting normality of whiteness." Under this system, the dominant white population members are able to engage in the process of establishing "boundedness."[4] Thus, much of white-identity formation, from colonial times to now, involves drawing boundaries, engaging in boundedness, and configuring rings around the substantively empty category *white*, while at the same time decisively constructing "others" (Weis & Fine, 1996, p. 8).

Part of the process of social construction and marginalization is reflected in, as Alan James (1981) contends, language. In his exploration of "the pejorative associations" with the English word *black* and their relationship to the social construction of Black people, A. James points out that "the offensive connotations of the word 'black' in English impose on the users of the language, black-skinned and white-skinned,

---

3 We recognize the difference in the functions of police and security personnel. However, for the purposes of this discussion, we explore how both have used discretion in the process of Othering and criminalizing Black youth.
4 The concept, referenced by Weis and Fine (1996), is borrowed from Trinh T. Minh-ha, who discusses it in *Woman, Native, Other* (1989).

an interpretation of reality that is hard to break" (p. 19). He notes that the associations of the word *black* with, among other things, "dirt and sin, evil and taboo" are so pervasive that people are tempted "to regard them as 'natural,' part of the common sense knowledge of the world and our own humanity" (p. 19).

Referring to the influence of Western Christendom, A. James (1981) demonstrates how Black people, as the "frightening and fascinating children of Cham," continue to be socially constructed by the "folk-racism" of medieval society. While the colour *white* is seen to represent "the unattainable ideal, virginal purity, bodily incorruption, social order, and peace," the colour *black* represents "the violent and disturbing urges of the human body and excretion ... [and] the repressed, dark elements of the mind, both fearful and fascinating" (p. 29).

Judith Butler's (1993) essay "Endangered/Endangering: Schematic Racism and White Paranoia" discusses the case of Rodney King, the African-American man who was badly beaten by the Los Angeles police in 1991. She points out that even in its indefensible state, the Black male body is seen as a physical threat (p. 16). She states that "this is not a simple seeing, an act of direct perception, but the racial production of the visible, the working of racial constraints on what it means to 'see.'" Butler writes further:

> In Fanon's citation of the racist interpellation, the black body is circumscribed as dangerous, prior to any gesture, and raising of the hand, and the infantilized white reader is positioned in the scene as one who is helpless in relation to that black body; as one definitionally in need of protection by his/her mother or, perhaps, the police. The fear is that some physical distance will be crossed, and the virgin sanctity of whiteness will be endangered by the proximity. The police are thus structurally placed to protect whiteness against violence, where violence is the imminent action of that black male body. And because within this imaginary schema, the police protect whiteness, their own violence cannot be read as violence; because the black male body ... is the site and source of danger, a threat, the police effort to subdue this body, even if in advance, is justified regardless of the circumstances. (p. 18)

These constructions of Black people as *other*, as *physical threats*, and as *violent* help justify the ways they are managed, contained, and policed by Western law enforcement and security personnel. In their research comparing African Americans' and white Americans' relations with police, Browning, Cullen, Cao, Kopache, and Stevenson (1994) conclude that police were more likely to hassle minoritized people without cause. In large urban settings – where racialized people constitute a higher percentage of the population – they are more likely to be targeted by police, and once targeted, they are likely to receive harsh treatment (Dannefer & Schutt, 1982; see also Anderson, 1990; Lieber, 1994; Staples, 1975).

In Britain, Norris, Fielding, Lemp, and Fielding (1992) found that Black people, particularly young Black men, were more than twice as likely to be stopped by the police (see also Landau & Nathan, 1983). As in Britain and the United States, Canadian studies show that racialized people, and Black youth in particular, experience differential treatment in their contacts with police (Commission on Systemic Racism in the Ontario Criminal Justice System, 1995; Gaskell & Smith, 1985; Head, 1975; Henry, 1994; C.E. James, 1990; Neugebauer, 1996; Waddington & Braddock, 1991). In her study comparing Black and white male youth experiences with the police in Toronto, Neugebauer (1996) found that Black youth were treated with "contempt" by police. While officers stopped young white men occasionally, they stopped young Black men as a matter of routine. Further, the youth's experiences with police often involved harassment, mistaken identity, and arbitrary arrest resulting in harsher penalties at all stages of the criminal justice system. Neugebauer argues that a "folk history" of frightening experiences with the police have become part of a collective consciousness shared by Blacks – even in the absence of direct personal experience with police.

The nature of policing in Canada, as in other stratified societies, "inevitably leads to policing the poor and minorities," who are identified as the social classes capable of creating problems if they are not "heavily policed" (Chambliss, 1995, p. 256). For young working-class Black men, whose lives are tormented by overpolicing, current police and security personnel practices elicit from them hostile responses (Chambliss, 1995; Gaskell & Smith, 1985; Henry, 1994) as they resist the "confinement and definition" imposed upon them by police. As Walcott (1995) argues: "By resisting imprisonment within the boundaries and borders, black cultures refuse to accept what Frantz Fanon called 'amputation'" (p. 49).

As part of this "amputation" or Othering, images of Black people as *working-class* and *immigrants*[5] persist even though Black people have resided in Canada since 1628, many who are immigrants today entered Canada with professional qualifications, and many hold responsible positions in society (Henry, 1994; Plaza, 1996). Although police

---

5 This perception of Black people as immigrants reinforces "their inside/outside position" in Canadian society (Walcott, 1995, p. 52).

are likely to have had contacts with many middle-class professional Black people, the entrenched historical construction of Black people as "criminals" remains (Gilroy, 1987; Henry, 1994; C.E. James, 1997) and is articulated in the complex constructions of police discretion. According to Franklin (1996), writing about the African-American situation in the 1990s, "Many whites are having status anxieties in a global context of rapid technological and social change. Fear of unemployment and downward mobility contributes to white scapegoating" of racial minorities, including Blacks and new immigrants (p. 142). This situation does not leave the Black middle-class unscathed. In fact, as Franklin also argues, "regardless of their occupational success, the black middle class does not escape from the various forms of race exclusion and insults" (p. 139).

This is why the *Toronto Star's A Minority Report* (Ward, 1985) noted that Black-Canadian community members expressed their belief that the police operate based on stereotypical images of Black people, particularly with respect to males, imagining that they make money primarily through hustling, dealing drugs, or pimping for prostitutes. Participants in the *Toronto Star's* study claimed that regardless of social-class status and education, Black people have to deal with police images and stereotypes of them as "criminals, layabouts, and disruptive elements." In the words of one participant, "You're always under suspicion" (Ward, 1985, p. 6). This finding is corroborated by Head (1975), Henry (1994), and Ginzberg (1985), whose studies have reported on the differential ways Black people are represented in the media and on their negative experiences with police in Toronto.

From her study of Caribbean people in Toronto, Henry (1994) concludes that police–Black community relations are "fraught with tensions" (p. 224). She explains that "the increased policing of the Black community, the stop-and-search procedures, and other forms of harassment have become so severe that tensions have been exacerbated"; these in turn have contributed to the criminalization of young working-class Black males.

The Commission on Systemic Racism in the Ontario Criminal Justice System (1995) reached the same conclusion. It reports that discriminatory police practices, particularly against Black men, manifested in how police exercised their discretion to stop and question citizens:

About 43% of black male residents, but only 25% of white and 19% of Chinese males report being stopped by the police in the previous two years. Significantly more black men (29%) than white (12%) or Chinese (7%) report two or more police stops in the previous two years. (p. ix)

In accounting for the particular encounters and negative experiences that racial minorities have with Canadian police, researchers such as Andrews (1992), Desroches (1992), Forcese (1992), Henry (1994), Henry, Tator, Mattis, and Rees (1995), and Vincent (1994) point to "police culture" as the basis for individual constables' attitudes and behaviours. In his audit of the Metropolitan Toronto Police force, Andrews (1992) writes,

> The culture of police forces in general tends to produce a "we and they" philosophy. Part of this is probably necessary, related to the need to maintain a detached view of the world being policed; part is brought about over time by virtue of the high level of contact with people who break the law; part is undoubtedly due to the image of policing as portrayed on television and other media. (p. 17)

Similarly, Desroches (1992) argues that the negative stereotypical images that police hold about "ethnic minorities" helps them to make the group's behaviour "more understandable and predictable, thus reducing the unexpected." This in turn predisposes law enforcement agents to enter encounters with members of "ethnic minority groups with a negative and closed-minded attitude" (p. 53). These police cultural attitudes, views, and behaviours stem from the patriarchal and gendered nature of law enforcement and the justice system (Brophy & Smart, 1985; Harris, 1993; St. Lewis, 1996). According to Forcese (1992),

> Most police in service have been recruited from working-class and lower-middle-class backgrounds, and there is little reason to expect them to have attitudes other than those associated with such class backgrounds. These attitudes include distrust of immigrants and minorities, and outright racism. (p. 76)

Socialized within a male, Anglo-Celtic, paramilitary culture, police are expected to control and maintain order in society – a society that is stratified by, among other things, race, class, and gender.[6] As Henry et al. (1995) point out, "The 'street' is exalted as a *raison d'être* of policing, and the 'street' experience is asserted to be the foundation of police

---

6 Black police officers and security personnel are socialized within this dominant culture and therefore are likely to act in similar ways to their white counterparts (see Desroches, 1992; Forcese, 1992; Henry, 1994; Henry et al., 1995) and have similar understandings of, and approaches to, the enforcement of law, regulations, and policies.

knowledge" (p. 120). Perceiving themselves as "pseudopolice," security personnel, many of whom have similar backgrounds to police (and in some cases are ex-police officers), tend to have similar understandings of, and approaches to, enforcing the law, regulations, and policies.

The Streets, Police, and Youth[7]

The streets serve many purposes. For car owners, the street may be the "public" asphalted path used to drive from one place to another and/or a place to park one's vehicle. For pedestrians, particularly those with no alternatives, the street, or more specifically, the sidewalk, plays a much larger role. It is a public path to move about, to get from one place to another, and also a social space – probably the most available, accessible, and relatively nonrestrictive social space in which to meet, "hang out," and converse. For some "street users," particularly young working-class apartment dwellers, because of their limited access and opportunities to alternative leisure and recreational spaces, the sidewalk, the street, the street corner, and the mall become an integral part of daily living and a part of cultural life. These social and recreational spaces are free from the adult-controlled rigid organizations that are often culturally indifferent and insensitive to youth's needs and interests, and into which they have little input.

In patriarchal societies, including Canada, the streets are typically the domain of males, where many have grown up participating in recreational and sport activities. For poor and working-class young men generally, and apartment dwellers in particular, the streets may be the only free and available spaces that afford them the opportunity for recreational and social activities on their terms.

Shopping malls can be seen as "roofed streets" and "street corners," where "outside" has been turned into "inside,"[8] and where public spaces have been turned into private spaces. Given Canadian weather conditions, especially in winter, these covered spaces offer much-needed shelter from the cold and rain. Busy shopping malls typically house video arcades, cinemas, and fast-food restaurants, all key entertainment outlets for many youth. Inevitably, therefore, one finds youth congregating in malls. But insofar as malls are indeed private spaces, business owners and mall authorities, through their "legal right" and private security agents, can enforce formal regulations on behaviour, dress,

---

7 My colleague Tony Xerri was particularly helpful in assisting me with the development of this section.
8 These descriptors were offered by Tony Xerri.

congregation, and attitudes of the "street users," who might be outside police jurisdiction. In other words, these security personnel have authority to enforce the very things that the police have been enforcing on the "public" streets. Here, "enforcement of the law" becomes problematic when one considers that the "right to evict from private property" has now come to include what had effectively been the street prior to "the roofing" – the only way to get from one shop to another, to attend the cinema or other places of business and entertainment, and at the same time to window-shop, meet, and talk with friends and engage in what the youth might have regarded as honest and legal activities.

This interpretation of the streets, street corners, and malls as meaningful spaces for a sector of the community contrasts significantly with the accepted, traditionally held view.[9] This view, perpetuated and maintained by those more privileged, stems from an assumption that leisure and recreational spaces and activities are accessible to all; therefore, there is no need for people to be on the streets or hanging out in malls. This population believes that there are enough community and recreational centres, parks, clubs, and other free or inexpensive places to congregate that cater to the needs and interests of those who currently use the street. Consequently, people who use the street in ways that don't conform to "acceptable" norms are considered unlawful, "up-to-no-good," suspicious characters who need to be controlled and contained.

Often, young people's perceived *lack* of activity (Brogden, Jefferson, & Walklate, 1988) creates the concern. As Brogden et al. (1988) write:

> Just walking round the streets "doing nothing," or "simply hanging around," felt innocent enough to the youths themselves. But, to a police force imbued with the virtues of useful toil, and its corollary – "the devil finds work for idle hands" – such unstructured, unsupervised and essentially "disorganized" inactivity is always vaguely suspect, and potentially threatening. "Doing nothing" is all too close, from a police viewpoint, to "loitering with intent" – especially if you belong to a group, male youth, with a "known" propensity for crime. (p. 106)

Informed by this view, and given the nature of policing, laws concerning property, and the normative behaviour they are charged to enforce,

---

9 In her article "Whiteness as Property," Harris (1993) makes the point that "when the law recognizes, either implicitly or explicitly, the settled expectations of whites built on privileges and benefits produced by white supremacy, it acknowledges and re-enforces a property interest in whiteness that reproduces Black subordination" (p. 1731).

police are likely to target particular groups of people, in this case Black youth, for special attention – believing that in taking preemptive action, they are preventing crimes from happening and/or escalating (Brogden et al., 1988). Such preemptive actions by police are often regarded as proactive policing; as Hagan (1994) points out, this policing of youth occurs in *offensible space*, where police believe that a disproportionate amount of crime occurs. Smith (1986) suggests that such scrutiny results in a process of *ecological contamination* in which all residents from designated areas are stereotyped as potential suspects. But as Brogden et al. (1988) argue, the overattention youth receive from police may well create the very culture that police are supposedly trying to prevent. Further, imposing a disreputable label contributes to an individual's stigmatization (Goffman, 1961, 1963) and the self-fulfilling prophecy wherein those individuals internalize the label and react to the police accordingly.

Social ideologies, along with cultural and generational differences, influence police perceptions, attitudes, and actions towards racial-minority youth. In other words, racism and stereotyping operate to "form at one and the same time both instigation for the initial contact by the police and the treatment received by the youth upon contact" (Brogden et al., 1988). Criminalization of Blacks, especially working-class youth, happens through these contacts as police, in the case of Toronto, carry out their "war on drugs" (Henry, 1994). While working-class communities might be the primary target, middle-class youth do not escape similar practices.

In my study of Black youth experiences with racism in Toronto, one research participant reported that he was stopped by police while walking in his middleclass neighbourhood because the police believed that he did not live there. The participant commented that the police suspected him of committing a crime; they did not suspect the white friends who accompanied him. These experiences with police proved fairly common; so too the police explanations for them. The reasons included claims that the youth "looked like" someone the police were seeking (C.E. James, 1990, p. 22). In their study of Black high-school dropouts in Toronto, Dei, Holmes, Mazzuca, McIsaac, and Campbell (1995) quote one young woman as saying,

> When you're a Black male ... you don't have to do anything ... You could be a good student, you could be a good father or whatever, [but] when you're out on the street, you're seen as a criminal ... a drug dealer. (pp. 51–2)

In naming this social construction of Blacks as a "problem," one high-school student commented that "there is no positive image of

Black people," and as a result police "assume all Black people are the same" (Frater, 1991, p. 68).

In our economically and racially stratified society – where stereotyping, classism, sexism, racism, and discrimination inform institutional policies and practices – it is quite easy to attribute negative police-youth encounters to those questioned, arrested, and otherwise singled out by law enforcement officers. While certain practices might be attributed to officers' "just doing their jobs," these practices do not always justify or legitimate police actions. As Forcese (1992) points out:

> The police officer is a very powerful person. He [sic] has the delegated right to arrest persons, even to use force against persons. An officer's interventions are usually discretionary, in that he or she must decide whether the conduct warrants police action ... [and] generally persons subject to police interventions are very vulnerable. The citizen carries the burden of reacting to police, who carry the full weight of social authority, and who have the benefit of a high degree of public and court confidence. (p. 49)

While we tend to believe that a person who has been stopped by the police must have done something wrong (Armour, 1984, p. 34), we must realize that policing can and sometimes does initiate a "self-fulfilling prophecy" (Brogden et al., 1988, p. 112). That is, once perceived to be potential lawbreakers and therefore targeted, once stopped by police, the youth's actions in their vulnerable state might then fit the stereotype as they react to police attitudes and behaviours towards them.

Black Youth Experiences with, and Perceptions of, Police

In this section, I present narratives from Black youth regarding their experiences with, and perceptions of, police. I focus on what the youth had to say about their encounters with police on the streets, the nature of these encounters, and their views about police perceptions of Blacks generally. The data were collected through focus groups and individual interviews in six Ontario cities (Toronto, Ottawa, London, Windsor, Hamilton, and Amherstburg) held in 1994.

About seventy racial-minority youth participated in the interviews, which were conducted in community centres, malls, and on "the streets." Here I focus on contributions from the approximately fifty Black youth (60 per cent male and 40 per cent female) who participated in the discussions. They represent a diversity of backgrounds in terms of social class and birthplace. While the majority were born in Canada, most of their parents come from the Caribbean (Jamaica, Trinidad and Tobago, Guyana, and other Caribbean countries) and Africa (e.g., Somalia). The discussion below attempts to show how the youth's encounters with police contribute to a criminalization process (Henry, 1994) and to cultural struggles for both parties.

"They Look at Colour First"

Many of the youth who participated in this study stated that they were frequently stopped and questioned by the police; this was a common occurrence for them. They shared the belief that skin colour operated as a primary determinant in attracting police attention and suspicion. One youth expressed this sentiment poignantly when he said, "You can't win. As long as you are Black, you are a target." Another argued that Black youth were stopped more often because of the negative stereotypes held by the police: "I think they think that once there is a group of Black youth, they think that there is going to be some sort of violence, some fight or something like that."

While most youth felt that their clothes increased their chances of being stopped, some insisted that colour, or race, and not merely clothes had been the prime determinant of police action towards them. On this point, and with reference to his own experiences with police, one youth commented that it was "not the clothes we wore. Standing waiting for a bus around nine in the evening, two police came up and asked us what we were doing; where we were going; and which bus we were taking. I wasn't wearing any hat, hood, or anything." The youth was asserting that they were not judged by their clothes but by their skin colour. The following comments support this point:

> They drive by. They don't glimpse your clothes; they glimpse your colour. That's the first thing they look at. If they judge the clothes so much, why don't they go and stop those white boys that are wearing those same things like us?

> I think that if you are black and wearing a suit, they would think that you did something illegal to get the suit. They don't think that Black people have money.

> If you're a Black youth with a white person, the white person is not approached usually. White youth can dress the same as Black youth and not be harassed, other than to be told by police that they should not be hanging out with Black youth.

> Clothes is nothing. It's your colour, your colour, and it's your colour.

"It Also Depends on What You Are Wearing and Your Hairstyle"

Suggesting that police used clothes, jewellery, and hairstyles to reinforce their stereotypical images of Black youth, many of those interviewed alleged that that they, as well as their relatives and/or friends, were stopped and harassed by the police on this basis. They felt that hairstyles, particularly "locksy hairstyle," dress, and jewellery were used by the police as indicators that they were suspicious persons engaging in suspicious activities. They were perceived as "candidates for crime." The following comments illustrate this point:

> If you dress in a suit every day, with a nice haircut, they won't harass you.

> With Black youth, you see them wearing baggy clothes, lots of rings and necklaces, they automatically think that they are drug dealers.

> There is the stereotype of Blacks – baggy pants, flashy jewellery, baseball caps, flashy colours, and so on. All Black people who dress like this are [seen] as pimps or drug dealers. White people dress like this too, [but are] not seen as pimps, et cetera.

> It's all how you present yourself. If you look like a rude girl, lots of gold chains et cetera, you'll get harassed. But if you are in your church clothes – pleated skirts – they won't trouble you.

> The chances of me catching a policeman's eyes increases with how I dress, and what I am wearing. If I am wearing a cap, et cetera, has a lot to do with how I am treated.

> I have been stopped on the street many times. I guess it's just the way I look – my hairstyle, the kind of people I hang out with. I go to a lot of parties, for example, and we are always being stopped for one thing or another. I guess my hairstyle attracts attention – the different colours.

> A bald head is a message. If you are white and you have a bald head, you are probably seen as a skin head. If you are Black and you have a bald head, you will probably be [seen as] a gang member.

> If you cut your hair low, cop ask you why you cut your hair like that. Are you trying to be like Ice Cube? Or say: "Nice haircut, who are you trying to imitate, Michael J.?" They will always find something to say to you – tie, suit, hair, no hair, big Afro, whatever.

"Not Just Colour but also Your Socio-economic Level"

Some of the study participants felt that other factors, such as socio-economic status, also contributed to the way they were perceived and treated by the police. They believed that police typically held the preconception that Black people were poor and therefore unable to buy and wear expensive clothing. The youth reasoned that all these factors go together to influence police perceptions of and actions towards Black people. One youth articulated this sentiment in the following way:

> I think that a lot of the times police look at someone and just because they are of another race or colour, and they are wearing expensive clothes, they are wondering, "How did they get these clothes?" Or if you are not wearing clothes that are expensive, they think that they must be up to trouble. A lot of times, it's not even your colour but your socio-economic level. If you are poor looking, they are going to think that you are up to no good.

"We Fit the Description"

Many of the study's participants claimed that the police were indiscriminate in stopping them, claiming either that "it was a routine check," or that they "matched the description of a crime suspect." They saw this as racism, believing police were operating on the notion that "all Blacks look alike." As one participant sarcastically remarked, "It is funny how white officers think that every Black male looks the same."

Noting that police perceptions were influenced by media images of Black people, one young man argued that when the media described, for example, a robbery suspect as "Black male, six foot something, hundred and something pounds," police often took this to mean that every Black man fitting this description would be a possible suspect, without consideration for other descriptors. He claimed that this was not the case for white youth. In their case, further descriptions would be taken into consideration.

Reflecting on the treatment they received from police, because police perceived Black people to be "bad people" who were likely "to steal and kill people," some of the youth said:

> There was a robbery in the area. The cop pulled me over, and all of a sudden a whole swarm of cops came. It was eight cops. I was with three guys. The cops said that we fit the description of the robbers, who were five in number, but we fit the description of three. They surrounded us and asked us to lie on the ground, and they had their guns out.

Once we were stopped by police because they said that we fit the description of robbery suspects. The description was that the robbers were Black. The cops asked us to open our bags, and they took everything out. There were also people with suitcases, and they searched them too.

"Black, Immigrant, and ..."

The youth believed that all Black people are perceived as *immigrants* by most Canadians and police in particular. But while this construction of Black people was often generalized to the entire population, they felt that certain constructions (or stereotypes) relating to particular Black immigrant groups affected how they were perceived and treated by the police. Jamaicans and Somalis were two of the groups named. According to the study participants, Jamaicans were perceived as "drug dealers and gangsters." On this basis, the participants claimed that police often made an association between criminal activities and national origin and/or immigrant status. The participants suggested that "even if you are not Jamaican, if you're Black, [you are] considered Jamaican," and the police would proceed to deal with them on this basis.

Most of the youth who participated in the study agreed that police perceptions of Somalis, while different, were not any better than those of Jamaicans. One Somali participant stated that although

> as Somalis we don't have that much criminals – we don't do drugs and all that, we stick to religion – it does not matter. We get the image – all the stereotypes – like the last set of Black people. We inherit the perceptions or the views that the police have of the last group of [Black immigrant] people.

Other Somali youth who participated in the study said that they were generally perceived as refugees who were "violent, crazy, bad-tempered, less educated, terrorists with guns" and people who were "living off the taxes" of Canadians. They felt that they had "double pain" in addition to being Black – that is, "the pain of being Somali and being immigrant." Some of the Somali youth felt that police treated them "worse" than other Black youth.

> No matter what the situation that you're in, what your dress is like ... they will find a negative way of thinking about you, because you're Black, and secondly because you're Somali, and thirdly because you're an immigrant, and you speak a different language.

I was stopped by the police ... for nothing ... He asked me when I came to Canada, how long I had been here, am I on welfare assistance? Questions I was not expecting from a police officer. Then I told him that "that doesn't concern you," and he just said have a nice day and left.

"White People Window Shop, Black People Loiter"

Based on the stereotypes that police and security personnel believe about Black people, and Black youth in particular, the participants believed that police made the assumption that any "standing around" of one person, or a number of Black youth, meant that "something is going down." For this reason, unlike their white peers, their presence on the street or in a mall was always suspect, particularly when they were believed to be "doing nothing." As one youth explained:

When I was in Grade 9 ... everybody used to go downtown after school, and it used to be a bunch of Black girls ... We weren't allowed to "linger" in one area. If we were in the food court, you had to eat your food and "done." You couldn't stay around for nothing. You couldn't stay in front of the mall. You know how you are waiting for a friend at the side and talking; you couldn't do that. You stay there for five minutes, and all of a sudden a security guard comes up and tells you: "What are you doing here? You are loitering. Get outside." And then if there are too many of you, all of a sudden you see cruisers circling J-Square. Next you know, there's police in the mall.

"If You Are Black and Female, It's Not So Bad, but Still We Are Harassed"

Participants noted that while females were viewed with the same suspicion as males, they were harassed less often and, when stopped, they were dealt with differently from the males. In the words of one participant, "Like if a bunch of girls is standing there, [the police] won't search the girls, but if a group of guys is standing next to them, they would go directly to the guys." The participants reasoned that this stemmed from the stereotypes that police had about Black males in particular.

They also speculated that fear of being accused of sexual harassment may have created a deterrent for police, particularly with respect to searching females. But as one young woman claimed, "Nowadays ... sometimes [girls] are treated the same way [as guys] because you could get a woman and a male cop working together, so the woman cop would do the searching." So today there is no escape for Black females from receiving somewhat similar treatment to Black males.

The study participants believed that location played a role in the young women's chances of being stopped, searched, and harassed. As one participant remarked,

> I think that girls get harassed now by the police, but I think in different settings. I think in schools and in malls, they get harassed just as much as the guys. This is because mall security guards think that the girls have the money and the boys don't.

Another participant said, "The security guards think that the girls are okay because they go to school." According to the youth, stereotyping underlies the perceptions that were held of Black males and females and thus the treatment they were likely to receive from police.

Conclusion: Criminalizing the Young Black Male or Protecting Him from Himself?

Within racist colonial discourse, as Gilroy (1987) argues, the streets and indeed "private roofed streets" (i.e., malls) are racialized spaces. They are white-defined locations, to be used in culturally prescribed manners. Insofar as Blacks, and young Black males in particular, violate the cultural norms of the streets and malls by their presence and actions, either alone or in groups, they will be targets. They will be targets of police officers and mall security personnel who operate within the dominant construction of Black young men as "up to no good," security risks, and potential lawbreakers (Commission on Systemic Racism in the Ontario Criminal Justice System, 1995; Dei et al., 1995; Four-Level Government/African Canadian Community Working Group, 1992; Head, 1975; Henry, 1994; C.E. James, 1990). As the youth have so eloquently argued, it is not a matter of clothes, jewellery, or hairstyle, but a matter of race and colour. And as they further argued, race, gender, social class, and "perception of being immigrants" are intricately linked and together form the basis of the assumptions and stereotypes by which the police and security personnel exercise discretion.

Why are Black males more likely to be stopped by the police? Franklin (1996), referring to Black youth in the United States, offers the following reason: "Whites fear young Black males" (p. 138). In Canadian society as well, Black young men have historically been represented as potential criminals who should be feared (C.E. James, 1997). This racist representation[10] of Black young men, coupled with what may appear to be their aimless strolls or congregation on the streets, contribute to their image as potential criminals. But as Brogden et al. (1988) point out,

> Once a group has been statistically identified as criminal and satisfies other criteria, such as low status and relative powerlessness, the resulting police "over-attention" begins to produce the sorts or results that justify the original over-attention. This then leads to continued over-attention. (p. 112)

What about Black females? In Dei et al.'s (1995) work, a young woman is quoted as saying that just being a young Black man on the street is enough for him to be regarded as a criminal or drug dealer (p. 52). Many of the youth who participated in this study concur, for they too pointed out that "it's not so bad for females." They suggested that while young Black women tended to be harassed less often than young men, this is changing. Police and mall security personnel are beginning to suspect females as potential lawbreakers. Females are also being searched, likely by female officers if only to avoid accusations of sexual harassment. But why this increased suspicion of Black females? Are they also to be found on the streets and in shopping malls in larger numbers than before? Is it that, with increased confidence in their citizenship rights, young Black females today, like Black males, are asserting their right to be on the streets and in malls? Are police increasingly constructing young Black women as criminals insofar as they are perceived as supporting males in their criminal activities?

Consistent with other studies (Henry, 1994; C.E. James, 1990), this study's findings demonstrate that middle-class young Black men are just as likely as working-class young Black men to be stopped, questioned, harassed, and searched by law enforcement personnel. This is understandable, since style of dress and/or jewellery today don't necessarily indicate socio-economic status. As Walcott (1995) suggests, clothing has become "one of the new markers for blackness" (p. 36).[11]

---

10 Butler (1993) also makes the point that the "white male's racist fear of the black male body" is also, to some degree, based on homophobia, which in turn contributes to his anxiety (p. 18).

11 Walcott (1996) argues that the wearing of jewellery can be read as the youth's assertion of their status in society, and a type of Black nationalism and Afrocentrism. He continues to say that "style and fashion carry for diasporic blacks important cultural practices and signifiers that tell us about their histories and desires. In particular, such practices can be read as signifying black histories of domination and subordination, suggesting some of the ways in which black cultural practices respond by revising dominant symbolic orders" (p. 131).

There is clearly more going on than just being perceived by police as poor immigrants who do not have the financial means to afford the same clothes and styles as their white counterparts. It seems that whatever the class background or attire, and regardless of the community in which young Black males and females stroll, they will be regarded as suspects. This helps explain why being Somali, Jamaican, Muslim, or Christian did not make a difference in the youth's experiences during encounters with police – they were simply all subjected to the existing social construction of Black youth.[12]

A curious irony of the police claim to being astute observers of people's appearances, behaviours, and movements manifests in the repeated mistakes they make with regard to Black youth fitting the descriptions of the suspects they seek. But are they really mistakes? Or is this phrase part of the racist discourse in which, having stopped the youth, the police must account for their actions and hence give their "best" line? Interestingly, every youth knows "the line," and police seemed not to be shy in saying it (Neugebauer, 2000). The rationalization that the youth "fit the description" forms part of the process of Othering, whereby the police engage in bounded actions that serve to marginalize Black youth. In some cases, the youth's responses to their marginalization are expressed through hostility, which sometimes results in them being charged – a further component of the marginalization process.

As in other studies (Head, 1975; Henry, 1994; C.E. James, 1990), the youth in this study who reported that they were often stopped, questioned, searched, and harassed by police were predominantly male, and they were often perceived to be working-class "immigrants" or "refugees." To suggest that these individuals defy laws and/or regulations, necessitating their being stopped and questioned, does not tell the entire story; neither does it justify the actions of many law enforcement personnel. The act of having been stopped further adds to the layered and constructed image of young Black males as a "troublesome" group of people. For as Snider (1983) argues, this is not "as arbitrary and irrational a focus as it would at first appear; indeed, it is a rational, though not humane, way of preserving the status quo" (p. 433) – to target a certain type of people who commit a certain type of crime, thus "leaving the majority of lawbreakers virtually unscathed."

---

12 In discussing the ways in which Blacks are criminalized, Henry et al. (1995) point out that "police and some members of the justice system commonly believe that Blacks are responsible for more crimes and that Blacks come from a crime-prone culture, notably Jamaica" (p. 113).

Despite Black people vociferously expressing their public outrage regarding police actions for years, indeed decades (Four-Level Government/African Canadian Community Working Group, 1992; Henry, 1994), clearly very little, or indeed nothing, has changed. Even after receiving cross-cultural, race relations, or antiracism training (Andrews, 1992; Fleras & Elliott, 1992; Forcese, 1992; Race Relations and Policing Task Force, 1989), police continue to construct Black youth as potential troublemakers who need to be constantly policed.

Much of the overattention given to youth on the streets or in shopping malls as a result of this social construction has little to do with any statistical evidence of their over-representation in criminal activities.[13] Rather, this overattention reflects structural and institutional assumptions about these youth rooted within the colonial discourse of policing, which legitimizes Othering of Black youth in their encounters. Within this discourse, any suggestions that police and security personnel's actions are based on racism and discrimination would be seen as an attempt to shift the issue from "the one stopped for questioning" to the police or security personnel. For it would be generally accepted that police base their actions upon social norms, which are not considered racist. In auditing police policies, procedures, programs, and practices, Andrews (1992) thus concludes:

> We found no evidence at all of organized, intentional prejudice or bias against racial minorities. Nor did we find evidence that the force attracts individuals who are overtly racist. We did find evidence that, over time, officers develop strong feelings and beliefs as to attributes of individuals based on factors such as appearance and racial background. These attitudes, when taken collectively, can and do produce a bias, which produces unequal treatment of individuals of different cultural or racial background.

Essentially, in policing Black youth – stopping, questioning, harassing them, and placing the onus on them to prove that they are not the "suspects" the police are seeking – law enforcement agents engage in a process of othering which, in turn, contributes to the criminalization of

---

13 The value of collecting and reporting data on criminal activities based on race has been debated strongly. While it would be useful to ascertain statistically the extent to which police overattention on youth is justified, Blacks are reluctant to support this practice. They understand that any analysis and reporting of such information must be contextualized by the colonial and racist discourse that informs police cultural practices, the construction of Black people, and their responses to their criminalization.

Black youth. This reflects the formal social control mechanisms under which law enforcement agents operate, which represent an extension of historical and colonial attitudes towards Black people – their use and abuse of power informed by racist ideologies (Harris, 1993).

The perception of Black youth on the street as "up to no good" – a theme that captures their perception of how police see them – becomes a self-perpetuating, cyclical phenomenon founded on four conditions: (a) a notion of the street as "white property" to be protected by police; (b) the concomitant issue of how and why spaces where youth congregate come to be recognized as "in need of policing"; (c) what gets defined as "criminal activities"; and (d) how the overattention or oversurveillance of youth and the areas they traverse increases the probability of contact, thus initiating and perpetuating this cyclical process.

Hidden within this cycle is how youth perceptions mirror police perceptions of them. Although it may sound superfluous to ask which comes first, one can easily see that the youth end up in a reactive position, due not only to their discriminatory treatment by law enforcement agents (and the a priori negative assumptions that both guide and lead to that treatment) but also to their treatment by society generally. All this acts as a backdrop to what many of the youth told us was simple, wholesome, normal travelling on their own, or social interaction with friends on the street. The youth's perception of their behaviour contrasts sharply with that of the police. As Corrigan (1979) argues:

> The boys see trouble as something connected purely with the police ... At no stage do they perceive it as doing wrong, or breaking rules ... What wrongs are they doing if they just walk around the streets, and the police harass them? The reasons for the harassment lie with the police, and NOT inside any rule that the boys arc breaking, since for the boys the streets are a "natural" meeting place. (p. 139)

The adversarial nature of their encounters with the police contributes to their hostility towards the police, a hostility that, as Smith (1991) argues with reference to African-Caribbean Blacks in Britain, is related to the assertion of their identity as Blacks and as citizens.

Given that most police officers and security agents operate with the dominant white, Anglo-Celtic, middle-class, patriarchal cultural values of Canadian society, we can see how a situation involving police patrolling the streets where youth are present can turn into "an incident with the law." For young members of communities judged to be different from the "norm," in particular, working-class Black youth, contact with police becomes even more dangerous. It is dangerous because the constructions of age, race, gender, and social class converge to form a suspicious image for the police, which in turn triggers their expectations and actions. There is nothing the youth can do (even if they wanted to) to escape the "up to no good" label and over-surveillance they receive. While they might be able to change their clothes, they can do nothing about their colour or their class position and what these signify.

Despite the potential for being stopped, questioned, detained, and harassed by police while on the streets and in shopping malls, the Black youth with whom we spoke did not give any indication that fear of law enforcement and security personnel would make them change their practices. They saw their dress, behaviours, and congregations as cultural practices and expressions of their identity. And insofar as they are denied the right to express their cultural identity, they are prepared to struggle. Much of this struggle will continue to occur in these public arenas – the streets and the malls. For Black youth, the struggle involves identity, representation, and the right to public space – a struggle in which they resist their "confinement and definition" in Canadian society (Walcott, 1995). For law enforcement personnel, the struggle involves exercising their power and control over the streets and the malls as "public"[14] spaces which must be used in particular ways. Their irritation with the youth is likely to produce periodic explosions, and their encounters continue.

To address these negative experiences that Black youth have with the police, educational and legal institutions must take steps to change what Black youth have identified as the limited knowledge and misinformation on which Canadian people in general, and police in particular, operate in their dealings with them. We can think of how frightening, but moreso vexing, it must be for these youth to live with the constant trepidation and knowledge that by simply walking down the street they might be perceived as lawbreakers, and the police will treat them accordingly.

It becomes a sad commentary on our institutions when we realize that the rationale used to justify policing certain streets and spaces and particular groups operates to disguise racism and discrimination that are consciously and unconsciously practised. Having identified, explored, and researched the issues relating to police–minoritized community relations, numerous commissions have made dozens of recommendations, including antiracism and cultural training and local community-based policing structures (see Commission on Systemic

---

14 It should be noted that "public" is inscribed in gender, race, class, and generational terms. In some cases malls are thought of as private spaces.

Racism in the Ontario Criminal Justice System, 1995). While these are useful, we must also change our paramilitary approach to policing and create a justice system that acknowledges how the social construction of race in Canadian society affects laws and their enforcement.

REFERENCES

Anderson, E. (1990). *Streetwise: Race, class and change in an urban community.* Chicago, IL: University of Chicago Press.

Andrews, A.G. (1992). *Review of race relations practices of the Metropolitan Toronto Police Force.* Toronto, ON: Municipality of Metropolitan Toronto, Metropolitan Audit Department.

Armour, M. (1984). Visible minorities: Invisible: A content analysis of submissions to the Special Committee on the Participation of Visible Minorities in Canadian Society. *Currents: Readings in Race Relations,* 2(1).

Brogden, M., Jefferson, T., & Walklate, S. (1988). *Introducing police work.* London, UK: Unwin.

Brophy, J., & Smart, C. (Eds). (1985). *Women in law: Explorations in law, family and sexuality.* London, UK: Routledge.

Browning, S.L., Cullen, F.T., Cao, L., Kopache, R., & Stevenson, T.J. (1994). Race and getting hassled by the police: A research note. *Police Studies,* 17(1), 1–11. https://www.ncjrs.gov/App/publications/abstract.aspx?ID=152672

Butler, J. (1993). Endangered/endangering: Schematic racism and white paranoia. In R. Gooding-Williams (Ed.), *Reading Rodney King/Reading urban uprising* (pp. 15–22). London, UK: Routledge.

Chambliss, W.J. (1995). Crime control and ethnic minorities: Legitimizing racist oppression by creating moral panics. In D.F. Hawkins (Ed.), *Ethnicity, race, and crime: Perspectives across time and place* (pp. 235–58). Albany, NY: State University of New York Press.

Commission on Systemic Racism in the Ontario Criminal Justice System. (1995). *Report.* Toronto: Queen's Printer for Ontario.

Corrigan, P. (1979). *Schooling the smash street kids.* London, UK: Macmillan.

Dannefer, D., & Schutt, R. (1982). Race and juvenile processing in court and police agencies. *American Journal of Sociology,* 87(5), 1113–32. https://doi.org/10.1086/227557

Dei, G.J.S., Holmes, L. Mazzuca, J., McIsaac, E., & Campbell, R. (1995, October). *Drop out or push out? The dynamics of Black students' disengagement from school.* Toronto, ON: Ontario Institute for Studies in Education, Department of Sociology in Education.

Desroches, F.J. (1992). The occupational subculture of the police. In B.K. Cryderman, C. O'Toole & A. Fleras (Eds.), *Police, race and ethnicity: A guide for police services* (pp. 45–54). Toronto, ON: Butterworths.

Fleras, A., & Elliott, J.L. (1992). *The challenge of diversity: Multiculturalism in Canada.* Toronto, ON: Nelson Canada.

Forcese, D.P. (1992). *Policing Canadian society.* Scarborough, ON: Prentice-Hall Canada.

Four-Level Government/African Canadian Community Working Group. (1992). *Towards a new beginning: The report and action plan.* Toronto, ON: City of Toronto.

Franklin, R.S. (1996). The response to Black youth crime by a new breed of bleeding heart conservatives. *Race Gender & Class: An Interdisciplinary & Multicultural Journal, 3*(3), 137–46.

Frater, T. (1991). Just my opinion. *Our Schools/Our Selves, 3*(3), 24–6.

Gaskell, G., & Smith, P. (1985, August). How young Blacks see the police. *New Society, 23,* 261–3.

Gilroy, P. (1987). *"There ain't no Black in the Union Jack": The cultural politics of race and nation.* Chicago, IL: University of Chicago Press.

Ginzberg, E. (1985). *Power without responsibility: The press we don't deserve.* Toronto, ON: Urban Alliance on Race Relations.

Goffman. E. (1961). *Asylums.* Chicago, IL: Aldine-Atherton.

Goffman, E. (1963). *Stigma: Notes on the management of spoiled identity.* Englewood Cliffs, NJ: Prentice-Hall.

Hagan, J. (1994). *Crime and disrepute.* Thousand Oaks, CA: Pine Forge Press/Sage.

Harris, C. (1993). Whiteness as property. *Harvard Law Review, 106,* 1709–91. https://doi.org/10.2307/1341787

Head, W. (1975). *The Black presence in the Canadian mosaic: A study of perception and the practice of discrimination against Blacks in Metropolitan Toronto.* Toronto, ON: Ontario Human Rights Commission.

Henry, F. (1994). *The Caribbean diaspora in Toronto: Learning to live with racism.* Toronto, ON: University of Toronto Press.

Henry, F., Tator, C. Mattis, W., & Rees, T. (1995). *The colour of democracy: Racism in Canadian society* (1st ed.). Toronto, ON: Harcourt Brace.

James, A. (1981). "Black": An inquiry into the pejorative associations of an English word. *New Community, 9*(1), 19–30. https://doi.org/10.1080/1369183X.1981.9975656

James, C.E. (1990). *Making it: Black youth, racism and career aspirations in a big city.* Oakville, ON: Mosaic Press.

James. C.E. (1997). The distorted images of African Canadians: Impact, implications and responses. In C. Green (Ed.), *Globalization and survival in the Black diaspora.* Albany, NY: State University of New York Press.

James. C.E. (1998). "Up to no good": Black on the streets and encountering police. In V. Satzewich (Ed.), *Racism and social inequality in Canada: Concepts, controversies and strategies of resistance* (pp. 157–76). Toronto, ON: Thompson Education Publishing.

Landau, S., & Nathan, G. (1983). Selecting delinquents for cautioning in the London Metropolitan Area. *British Journal of Criminology*, 23(2), 128–49. https://doi.org/10.1093/oxfordjournals.bjc.a047353

Lieber, M. (1994). A comparison of juvenile court outcomes for Native Americans, African Americans and whites. *Justice Quarterly*, 11(2), 257–78. https://doi.org/10.1080/07418829400092251

Minh-ha, Trinh T. (1989). *Woman, native, other: Writing postcoloniality and feminism*. Bloomington, IN: Indiana University Press.

Neugebauer, R. (1996). *Police-community relations: The impact of culture on the control of colour* (unpublished doctoral dissertation). Department of Sociology, York University, Toronto, ON.

Neugebauer, R. (2000). Kids, cops and colour: The social organization of police-minority youth relations. In R. Neugebauer (Ed.), *Criminal injustice: Racism in the criminal justice system* (Chapter 5). Toronto, ON: Canadian Scholars' Press.

Norris, C., Fielding, N., Lemp, C., & Fielding, J. (1992). Black and blue: An analysis of the influence of race on being stopped by the police. *British Journal of Sociology*, 43(2), 207–24. https://doi.org/10.2307/591465

Plaza, D. (1996). *The strategies and strategizing of university educated Black Caribbean-born men in Toronto: A study of occupation and income achievements* (unpublished doctoral dissertation). York University, North York, ON.

Race Relations and Policing Task Force. (1989). *Report*. Toronto, ON: Government of Ontario, Solicitor General.

Smith, D. (1986). The neighborhood context of police behaviour. In A.J. Reiss & M. Tonry (Eds.), *Communities and cities* (pp. 313–41). Chicago, IL: University of Chicago Press.

Smith, D. (1991). The origins of Black hostility to the police. *Policing and Society*, 2(1), 1–15. https://doi.org/10.1080/10439463.1991.9964628

Snider, L. (1983). The criminal justice system. In D. Forcese & S. Richer (Eds.), *Social issues: Sociological views of Canada* (pp. 395–439). Scarborough, ON: Prentice-Hall Canada.

St. Lewis, J. (1996). Race, racism, and the justice system. In C.E. James (Ed.), *Perspectives on racism and the human services sector: Case for change* (pp. 104–19). Toronto, ON: University of Toronto Press.

Staples, R. (1975). White racism, Black crime, and American justice: An application of the colonial model to explain crime and race. *Phylon*, 36(1), 14–23. https://doi.org/10.2307/274841

Vincent, C.L. (1994). *Police officer*. Ottawa, ON: Carleton University Press.

Waddington, P.A.J., & Braddock, Q. (1991). Guardians or bullies? Perceptions of the police amongst adolescent Black, white and Asian boys. *Policing and Society*, 2(1), 31–45. https://doi.org/10.1080/10439463.1991.9964630

Walcott, R. (1995). "Voyage through the multiverse": Contested Canadian identities. *Border/Lines, 36,* 49–52.

Walcott, R. (1996). *Performing the post-modern: Rap, hip-hop and the Black Atlantic.* (Unpublished doctoral dissertation). Toronto, ON: Ontario Institute for Studies in Education/ University of Toronto.

Ward, O. (1985). *A minority report.* Toronto, ON: Toronto Star.

Weis, L., & Fine, M. (1996). Notes on "white" as "race." *Race Gender & Class: An Interdisciplinary & Multicultural Journal, 3*(3), 5–9.

Response to Chapter 8

It Could Have Been Written Today: A Montrealer's Reflection

ADELLE BLACKETT
Canada Research Chair in Transnational Labour Law and Development, Labour Law & Development Research Laboratory, Faculty of Law, Université McGill University, Québec, Canada

It is near the end of 2018 and I am in Montreal. As I reread the chapter "'Up to No Good': Black on the Streets and Encountering Police," I find it hard to believe that it was published twenty years ago. It could have been written today, sadly, as yet another recently released report of the Ontario Human Rights Commission (2018) on racial profiling attests. What is more, it could have been written about Montreal.

On 4 November 2018, more than 100 people marched through the streets of one of Canada's most racially diverse neighbourhoods – Montreal's Notre-Dame-de-Grâce – to protest the fatal shooting by police of an unarmed Black man, twenty-three-year-old Nicholas Gibbs (Derfel, 2018). As in other cities, the release of a disturbing video, shot on a cell phone by a witness in an apartment building above, has led top experts and community activists, like former police officer Will Prosper, to conclude that police acted with excessive force on that fateful night, 21 August 2018 (Wilton, 2018a). Civil rights activists from the Montreal-based Coalition Against Repression and Abuse by Police Officers have recently released letters from Quebec's Bureau of Independent Inquiries. The documents suggest that Montreal police officers involved in the shooting of civilians are flouting the basic rules of writing reports independently and refraining from contact with other officers who were also involved in or witnesses to the same shootings (Wilton, 2018b). On 12 December, the Black Coalition of Quebec announces that it has launched a multimillion-dollar lawsuit against the police ("Black Coalition Files," 2018). The family of Nicholas Gibbs is also suing. Says his mother, Erma Gibbs, "I don't want another Black family to go through this" (Derfel, 2018).

Erma Gibbs's actions reflect her knowledge of the Black families that have continued to pay with their lives for anti-Black racism in Montreal. These include the family of the young unarmed Black man, Anthony Griffin, who was fatally shot on the streets by Constable Allan Gosset on Remembrance Day, 11 November 1987. The manslaughter and criminal negligence trial of Constable Gosset ended with his acquittal on appeal. While Griffin's mother received some financial compensation, her claims under the Quebec Charter of Human Rights and Freedoms (adopted in 1975) and the Canadian Charter of Rights and Freedoms (adopted in 1982) that the parent–child relationship had been violated were rejected (see Sheppard, 2004).

Griffin's shooting mobilized the Montreal Black community against systemic anti-Black racism (see Thornhill, 2008). And the case sparked the establishment of an official enquiry by the Quebec Human Rights Commission (which subsequently merged into the Quebec Human Rights and Youth Rights Commission, known by its French acronym, CDPDJ) on relations between the police and racialized communities. However, as I sat as a human rights commissioner in 2011 when the contemporary report on racial profiling (Commission des Droits de la Personne et des Droits de la Jeunesse, 2011) was adopted, it felt like déjà vu. The report reminded us of what James had already theorized: "The streets and indeed 'private roofed streets' (i.e., malls) are racialized spaces." What the CDPDJ's report added from years of experience is that profiling occurs beyond the police, and beyond the streets. The CDPDJ's work stressed that public security, education, and youth protection are sites where, in Robyn Maynard's (2017) terms, Black lives are policed. James's work was an early example of literature attuned to the devastating impact of perpetual policing of youth whose very identity socially constructs them as a problem, and whose defiant resistance yields further policing (this aspect of his work resonates with Coates, 2015).

James's article especially stands the test of time when it engages with Black women. One of his interviewees suggests that "if you are Black and female, it's not so bad. But still we are harassed." James's treatment of gender and race retains nuance, but fuller engagement with the emerging research on intersectionality would have yielded analyses that are less tentative and more grounded (see in particular Crenshaw, 1989). A very particular kind of violence is reserved for Black women (see Zellars, 2018, detailing the unprecedented, ongoing legal battles faced by the first Black and first female president of the CDPDJ, Me Tamara Thermitus, Ad. E.).

Some might protest that in Quebec, the fault line of race, and consequently any analysis of racism, must be the politics of language. Certainly language matters in Quebec, as it is deeply intertwined with the Quebec French majority's knowledge of its past and historic subordination to the English ruling class – "speak white" meant "speak English" (see Livingstone, Rutland, & Alix, 2018, focusing on the Saint-Michel district of Montreal). This knowledge coincides, however, with the need to acknowledge and engage with Quebec's history as a space of settler colonialism and its handmaiden, the enslavement of both Indigenous people and people of African descent (see Cooper, 2006). Blackness is not received in contemporary Quebec as a site of innocence. Because the history of slavery is a global history, in Quebec as elsewhere it is racialized as subordinate, and the object of violence. In the current political context of backlash to equality, it further remains necessary to contend with popular refusal to contemplate that there is "systemic" discrimination in Quebec (Shingler, 2015). This refusal seems impervious to the fact that courts and tribunals in Quebec and Canada have developed and deepened the notion of systemic discrimination consistently as they have interpreted the Quebec and Canadian charters. Some commentators also seem unable to come to terms with results like those from a situational test carried out by the CDPDJ in 2012, which revealed that two applicants with equivalent curricula vitae – including equivalent ability in French – were treated differently, with applicants with Quebec French-sounding names being at least 60 per cent more likely to be invited to an interview than applicants with names that sounded African, Arabic, or Latin American (Eid, 2012).

Each challenge needs to be addressed on its own terms. The challenges also need to be situated within the current context of populist, divisive politicking that is taking hold in Quebec, in Canada, and internationally. The moment we are in makes it all the more urgent to deliberately and decisively challenge arbitrary, unchecked exercises of police power against historically marginalized communities like the Black communities across Quebec and Canada. History continues to provide all-too-sobering reminders of where the empowerment of racialized hatred can lead if it is not vigorously resisted and ultimately transformed by a social justice anchored in love (King Jr., 1967).

REFERENCES

Black Coalition files $4M class-action lawsuit over racial profiling. (2018, December 12). *CTV News*. https://montreal.ctvnews.ca/black-coalition-files-4m-class-action-lawsuit-over-racial-profiling-1.4214642

Coates, T.-N. (2015). *Between the world and me.* New York, NY: Spiegel & Grau.
Commission des Droits de la Personne et des Droits de la Jeunesse. (2011). *Racial profiling and systemic discrimination of racialized youth: Report of the consultations on racial profiling and its consequences.* http://www.cdpdj.qc.ca/publications/Profiling_final_EN.pdf
Cooper, A. (2006). *The hanging of Angélique: The untold story of Canadian slavery and the burning of old Montréal.* Toronto, ON: HarperCollins.
Crenshaw, K.W. (1989). Demarginalizing the intersections of race and sex: A Black feminist critique of antidiscrimination doctrine, feminist theory and antiracist politics. *University of Chicago Legal Forum, 1989*(1), Article 8. http://chicagounbound.uchicago.edu/uclf/vol1989/iss1/8
Derfel, A. (2018, November 5). "The police didn't have the right to kill my son," Nicholas Gibbs's mother says during protest. *Montreal Gazette.* https://montrealgazette.com/news/local-news/vigil-planned-for-n-d-g-man-killed-by-police
Eid, P. (with Azzaria, M., & Quérat, M.). (2012, May). *Mesurer la discrimination à l'embauche subie par les minorités racisés: résultats d'un « testing » mené dans le Grand Montréal.* Cat. no. 2.120-1.31. Montreal, QC: Commission des Droits de la Personne et des Droits de la Jeunesse. http://www.cdpdj.qc.ca/Publications/etude_testing_discrimination_emploi.pdf
King, M.L., Jr. (1967). *Where do we go from here: Chaos or community?* Boston, MA: Beacon Press.
Livingstone, A.-M., Rutland, T., & Alix, S. (2018, December). *Le profilage racial dans les pratiques policières: Points de vue et expériences de jeunes racisés à Montréal.* Rapport de recherche. Montreal, QC: MTLSansProfilage.
Maynard, R. (2017). *Policing Black lives: State violence in Canada from slavery to the present.* Halifax, NS: Fernwood.
Ontario Human Rights Commission. (2018, November). *A collective impact: Interim report on the inquiry into racial profiling and racial discrimination of Black persons by the Toronto Police Service.* Toronto, ON: Author.
Sheppard, C. (2004). Intimacy, rights and the parent-child relationship: Rethinking freedom of association in Canada. *National Journal of Constitutional Law, 16*(1), 103. https://ssrn.com/abstract=2290994
Shingler, B. (2018, April 22). Quebec balked at investigating systemic racism, but some groups went ahead anyway. Here's what they found. *CBC News.* https://www.cbc.ca/news/canada/montreal/quebec-systemic-racism-community-groups-1.4630113
Thornhill, E.M.A. (2008). So seldom for us, so often against us: Blacks and law in Canada. *Journal of Black Studies, 38*(3), 321. https://doi.org/10.1177/0021934707308258
Wilton, K. (2018a, October 30). Family of Montreal man fatally shot by police files suit. *Montreal Gazette.* https://montrealgazette.com/news/local-news/family-of-n-d-g-man-fatally-shot-by-police-to-file-suit-against-montreal

Wilton, K. (2018b, November 5). Cops are ignoring Quebec's police watchdog rules, activists say. *Montreal Gazette*. https://montrealgazette.com/news/local-news/montreal-cops-are-ignoring-police-watchdog-rules-civil-rights-activists

Zellars, R. (2018, December 12). *The glass cliff: Tamara Thermitus and Quebec's Human Rights Commission*. Ricochet. https://ricochet.media/en/2460/the-glass-cliff-tamara-thermitus-and-quebecs-human-rights-commission

9 "Colour Matters": Suburban Life as Social Mobility and Its High Cost for Black Youth

Reporting in the *National Post* on Canada's 2011 census, Sarah Boesveld (2012) wrote,

> Nearly all of Canada's population growth over the past five years occurred in the suburbs ... While the downtown of Canada's six largest metropolitan areas made modest gains, urban cores have been "dwarfed by the scale of suburban population increases," which made up 93% of the nation's growth. (para. 1; see also Bula, 2011)

Between 2006 and 2011, 94 per cent of the population growth in Canada's Census Metropolitan Areas occurred in suburban and exurban areas.[1] Much of this suburban growth stems from migration by city residents – mostly first- and second-generation Canadians[2] – who have moved to these outer (many of them new) neighbourhoods or communities with the expectation of a having a "better" life.

Immigrants tend to settle first in affordable areas within metropolitan cities – in some cases, described as *inner-city areas* or an *in-between*

---

1 Specifically, 88 per cent of the Toronto metropolitan area's growth occurred in the suburbs, as did 98 per cent of Montreal's growth, 86 per cent of Vancouver's, 96 per cent of Ottawa-Gatineau's, 97 per cent of Calgary's, and 98 per cent of Edmonton's (Gordon & Shirokoff, 2014; see also "Canada Census 2011: Toronto's Suburbs Are Growing," 2012).

2 In this chapter, first-generation refers to those individuals who immigrated to Canada (in other words, first-generation immigrants) and second-generation refers to the children of these immigrants. Those individuals who were born elsewhere and immigrated before high school are referred to as "one-and-a-half generation." Indeed, these individuals would have very different experiences than their immigrant parents and others who were born in Canada for they have a level of understanding – albeit a childhood understanding and imagination – of the society they left.

city (Young, Wood, & Keil, 2011) – often populated by low-income, immigrant, and minoritized people. Many do so with the expectation that in time, once they "settle," become financially stable, or have children, they will move to "homes" – affordable houses – which in today's society typically means going to the suburbs.

In Toronto, for instance, many first- and second-generation families move from the *reception* areas of the city, which include the downtown core and the *inner suburbs*, to the *outer suburbs*, such as Mississauga, Brampton, Ajax, Markham, Richmond Hill, and other such areas outside the City of Toronto boundaries. In their bid to get out of poverty-stricken, racialized neighbourhoods, where schools often fail to meet their children's educational needs, interests, expectations, and aspirations, they migrate to new houses in newly established areas outside the city.

Relatedly, they seek to escape reception-area neighbourhoods, where the socio-economic conditions and racialized, immigrant population serve as sources of stigma. In the imagination of "mainstream" people, this stigmatization bolsters perceptions of downtown neighbourhoods as "dangerous" – beleaguered with drugs, delinquency, criminal activity, and thus under constant watch by surveillance agency personnel. Motivated by their need to create conditions for their children to succeed – educationally, socially, and economically – parents understandably seek to escape these conditions and move to suburban neighbourhoods, where they believe their children will be safer and will receive a higher quality of education. For some immigrant parents, such a move also represents upward social mobility – something for which as immigrants they consistently strive.

In this chapter, I examine what this migration to the suburbs means for Black youth, particularly those of Canadian-Caribbean background. My findings echo those of Maureen Brown (2003). Her study *Growing Up Black in Oakville: The Impact of Community on Black Youth Identity Formation and Civic Participation* reveals that despite the financial and social sacrifices parents make to move to more affluent outer suburban communities, their children – who now constitute a small minority of atypical residents – experience stereotyping and racial profiling. In the new environment, they experience the burden of expectations to be "good Blacks," heightened difficulties in parent–child relationships, financial obstacles, schools that are (still) unresponsive to their educational needs and interests, and a sense of being singled out in the community even as they try to fit in.

I revisit data from studies I conducted with youth who were living, or had lived, in the outer suburban areas of Toronto, noting the social, economic, cultural, and psychological effects – essentially the "cost" – for Black youth of growing up in the suburbs. In particular, I am interested in ascertaining what it means for these youth to grow up in suburban spaces which, for their parents, represent social mobility and related opportunities, possibilities, and safety.

Upward Social Mobility and the Chances of Economic and Social Success

We are socialized with the belief that our society is democratic, open, and meritocratic, so that with ambition, hard work, and perseverance, all members of society – including those at the lower end of the socio-economic hierarchy – will be able to fully participate and attain the things to which they aspire in life. According to this ideal, growing up in a poor family in Canada or coming to Canada from a small Caribbean island should not pose a barrier to achieving one's educational, career, and social ambitions. The notion here is that upward social mobility is possible, even for "small island" individuals; for with the necessary credentials, attitudes, and ambitions, they will be able to migrate to a country in the North and pursue their dreams. In reality, we live in a class-based society, in which income, education, and occupation help determine our position in the socio-economic hierarchy, and there is broad acceptance that our society is stratified and unequal and that social mobility is extremely difficult.

Social mobility – the movement of individuals from one social position to another within a socio-economic hierarchy – is thought to be a motivator. The movement that occurs in the course of a person's lifetime is referred to as *intragenerational mobility*; and mobility occurring between generations (i.e., children having a different class position from their parents') represents *intergenerational mobility* (Saunders, 2010, p. 1).

My interest here is *upward* social mobility – the advancement of individuals from a lower- to a higher-class position in Canadian society (Saunders, 2010, p. 1) – and the chances for first- (or immigrant) and second-generation Black-Canadian parents to achieve such mobility, or to create opportunities and possibilities for their children to so do. Numerous studies have identified people who migrate as having a drive – referred to as the "immigrant drive" (James, 2010) – to better themselves and/or their children (Anisef, Axelrod, Baichman-Anisef, James, & Turrittin, 2000; James, 2010; James & Chapman-Nyaho, 2018).

To that end, they try to do everything possible to achieve their goals. But in a society structured by inequality, are they able to access the necessary opportunities and conditions to do so?

Breen and Jonsson (2005) remind us to distinguish between *inequality of opportunity* and *inequality of condition*. The liberal notion of inequality of opportunity holds that "a person's chances to get ahead (attain an education, get a good job) should be unrelated to ascribed characteristics such as race, sex, or class (or socioeconomic origin)"; we can add to this list one's generation or citizenship status. Inequality of condition, on the other hand, relates to "the distribution of differential rewards and living conditions, either in the simple form of distribution of scarce goods or in relation to different inputs such as effort or rights (such as citizenship or employment)" (p. 223).

Essentially, upward social mobility requires access to the necessary opportunities. But in an inequitable society, individuals' access to opportunities and subsequent outcomes will be related to their social, economic, and other conditions. Our tendency to view participation in schooling and educational attainment as the means by which individuals can achieve upward social mobility places most of the responsibility or blame on students and their families or parents as opposed to the educational system (Smyth & Wrigley, 2013).

Unsurprisingly, parents will go to great lengths – such as relocating to particular neighbourhoods – to have their children attend a school that they believe will provide them with the education needed to achieve social and economic success (Holloway & Pimlott-Wilson, 2013; James & Chapman-Nyaho, 2018; McCreary, Basu, & Godlewska, 2013). But as Raffo (2015) writes in his review of Smyth and Wrigley's 2013 book, *Living on the Edge*, while working-class parents envision education as a means for their children to succeed in society, they "have not been provided with the appropriate 'road maps' to navigate an understanding of how to help young people in transition" (p. 296). This assertion applies in particular to first-generation (immigrant) parents – who have neither the networks nor the recognized social and cultural capital to give their children sufficient support for upward mobility. Regardless of a parent's background in their country of origin, in the new society they tend to occupy an "entrance status" (Porter, 1965) or marginalized position informed by ethnicity, race, accent, and language (or linguistic competence), often irrespective of their educational and occupational status. Within Canada's multicultural discourse, Black and other racialized bodies are marked as "foreign."

Given this, Black presence in the suburbs disrupts the taken-for-granted whiteness of the community; it is seen as "out of place."

Thus, Black suburban residents have to contend with questions about their social-class backgrounds and the legitimacy of their presence in the neighbourhood. Middle-class (having satisfied the measurement used to determine class) or not, Black parents and their children will be subjected to, and will have to navigate, the classist and racist discourses – and concomitantly the discrimination – that permeate these suburban spaces.

Rollock, Gillborn, Vincent, and Ball's (2011) study of middle-class Black families in Britain helps us understand the experiences and perceptions of suburban middle-class and "pretend" middle-class Black parents and their children in Canada. In their article "The Public Identities of the Black Middle Class: Managing Race in Public Spaces," Rollock and her colleagues examined how Black Britons "construct strategies and forms of being in light of the perceived normative constrictions of blackness" (p. 1080). They assert, with reference to Lacy (2007), that these Black parents "have at their disposal a range of resources – what Moore refers to as "a cultural toolkit" – such as language, mannerisms, clothing, and credentials that allow them to create … public identities to maximize or mediate against discriminatory treatment" (pp. 1080–1).

For Toronto residents, the decision to live in the suburbs might be considered (Lacy, 2007, as cited in Rollock et al., 2011, p. 1081), a "purposeful, instrumental" strategy employed by Black parents to "either reduce the probability of discrimination or curtail the extent of discrimination" that they and their children are likely to face "in their public interactions with white strangers." Living in the suburbs might not only represent their upward social mobility but provide a "public identity" they adopt to appear to others as – if not convince others that they are – rightful members of Canadian society and the middle class.[3]

But living in the suburbs does not mean eschewing Blackness (in terms of identities, cultural origin, and migration history), for Blackness has informed their choice of residence in the first place, and they must reference it to inoculate and equip their children against

---

3 Recall that many of these new suburbanites are first- and second-generation Canadians and for the most part have yet to attain the economic means to be able to purchase houses in the city. They migrate to suburbs because houses there tend to be new and more affordable. In fact, in a paper prepared for the Diversity in Education Parents' Forum, Schugurensky (2007) observes that many suburban families have low income, are "mortgage poor," and cannot afford some of the material resources ascribed to their neighbourhoods. As such, few of them are likely to have the necessary social networks and social and cultural capital that would confirm them as middle class.

racism, classism, and discrimination.[4] Rollock and her colleagues (2011) contend that

> the black middle classes are living through not a double consciousness (DuBois), but instead through a set of multiple consciousnesses as they move back and forth through the class and race divides within different social spheres populated by audiences and actors of varying races and class backgrounds. (p. 1088)

Gosine (2008) found a similar multi-consciousness among African-Canadian youth in his study. The Canadian-identified recent university graduates felt a sense of estrangement from their Black community – to which they were politically committed – because their "Anglo-Canadian accent, middle-class ideals of success, and in particular political viewpoints" were viewed as "antithetical to Blackness" (p. 322).

The Context: Toronto Outer Suburbs

As noted earlier, Toronto's growing suburban areas are increasingly populated with first- and second-generation Canadians, who are choosing to live in large single-family houses (with small yards) in new developments, located farther and farther away from the city. And while these newly established neighbourhoods have basic infrastructure, such as roads and schools, they tend to lack the community, recreational, and entertainment centres, libraries, and social services that many families in urban areas take for granted.

Furthermore, limited-to-nonexistent public transportation means that many suburbanites must depend on cars – especially to get to work, which is frequently some distance from their homes (thus often necessitating two cars for one family). While having a car might cut down on the time

---

4 In their article on the strategies that middle-class Black parents in Britain employ to equip and sustain their children to live in a white-dominated society and protect them from racism and inferior positioning, Vincent, Rollock, Ball, and Gillborn (2012b) reference US studies indicating that parents engage in "dual socialization," "strategic assimilation," and "selective distancing" (p. 432). The authors assert that these middle-class parents engaged their children in "concerted cultivation" through organized activities that serve to "minimize the perceived educational and social threats" to their children's full participation in the society and ultimately to attaining their aspirations – including those which their parents had for them. In providing their children with social advantages, the middle-class parents restrict them from mixing with poor and working-class Black children by educating them in distant, more affluent areas.

it takes to commute and to access distant social and recreational activities, it brings material costs, such as gas, maintenance, and insurance,[5] with which families must contend. If we consider that on average Black people tend to earn less than white Canadians, then we must recognize that the financial cost of living in the suburbs will be higher for them. For instance, in her study of Black families in Oakville, Ontario, Brown (2003) revealed that the average Black family income was about $20,000 less than that of the region. This difference in income might go unrecognized by teachers, social service providers, politicians, and others, given our society's prevailing ethos of colour-blindness, meritocracy, and democracy.

With much of their income going into mortgages and car payments, many new Black suburbanites are likely to be unable to afford their new life outside the city. Yet this scenario contradicts what one might expect of a middle-class family's financial capacities and carries implications for their children's schooling. Many teachers assume that their students are homogeneously middle class and hence can easily afford extra costs like class trips, music lessons, enrichment programs, and so on – ways to build children and youth's social and cultural capital consistent with school values. This adds obvious stress to Black children and their families and complicates relationships. Hence, if suburban teachers, along with their urban counterparts, do not learn to appreciate their students' cultural realities and work with them in ways that take into account their educational needs, interests, and aspirations, they will contribute to their students becoming alienated from both their school and community.

Apart from having to contend with their schooling situation, suburbanite Black youth must also work to come to terms with the incongruity of their parents' outward appearance of social mobility and their inability to pay for things that their white or other racialized peers have (Brown, 2003). Their parents often read their discontent at not having their needs and desires met as a lack of appreciation for the concerted efforts that the parents put into providing them with a better life – by moving to the suburbs.

Attitudes and Experiences of Black Suburban Parents and Youth

Parents' Motivation and Messages: "It's about Where You Live"

In discussing how parents feel about their move to the suburbs, their motivations, and the messages they pass on to their children, I will

---

5 Having teenagers or young adults with drivers' licences adds considerable costs to their car insurance.

use data from research I conducted in communities west of Toronto in 2002–3 and in 2014.

In the tradition of research triangulation (Patton, 2002), I interviewed Black youth and their parents. In the 2002–3 study, I conducted focus group interviews – three focus groups with twenty-one young people (six to eight in each group) between the ages of sixteen and twenty years old – and one focus group with twelve parents. The parents had been living in the community for three to ten years, with the majority having lived there about five years on average. I also interviewed youth workers and community workers. Finally, I gathered data through an online survey of twenty-three Black youths, focus group interviews with thirty Black residents, interviews with thirty service providers, and twenty key informant interviews.

While I draw mainly from the 2002–3 study, I will also use insights obtained from the 2014 study, which looked at another suburban community northwest of Toronto and helped to substantiate some of the earlier findings. In the 2014 study, I explored the experiences of youth with schooling, employment, social services, police, and recreational activities. All of the parents in these studies were first-generation Canadians of Caribbean background and had immigrated to Canada in the late 1960s and early 1970s – most of the children were second-generation (and a few were third-generation) Canadian.

Unlike other racialized groups, such as South Asians and East Asians, there is no outer suburban neighbourhood in the Greater Toronto Area (GTA) where Black families make up a majority of the population.[6] Hence, in moving to the suburbs, parents and their children will have lost close contact with and often support from members of their own ethnoracial communities. Parents believed this was a cost worth incurring, for eventually they will have secured for their children a safe, constructive environment in which to grow up. As one parent put it:

Parents live here because it's safe; it's a nice place to raise kids, and that's one of the reasons I moved here. It's quiet and away from the hectic life of Toronto and Scarborough, which was a hustle-bustle place – a keep going, going kind of thing. The more I looked at my kids, the more I saw that they were growing too fast and absorbing too many things that I didn't want

---

6 In fact, in a study my colleague and I conducted in a suburban community west of Toronto, about 70 per cent of the students were South Asians, which reflected the population of that community (James & Chapman-Nayho, 2018). In his study, Johal (2015) revealed that Sikh South Asian youth benefited from living in communities where they were a significant majority of the population.

them to absorb, so then I moved to [a southern Ontario town] and then to [this community]. The kids don't like it here, but I am here as a favour to the kids.

In addition to the safety and quiet of the community, parents feel the discipline their children are forced to cultivate is also important. Many assumed that in their bid to "fit in," their children would be inspired to develop the necessary behaviour, dress, values, and comportment consistent with the norms of the community. In the words of one father:

It's about where you live. I go to Toronto, and I go to a bank; and I go: "I'd like to deposit this cheque." The guy goes: "Where do you live?" And I go, "[Community]." All right, it's how I dress. I'm not going to dress in baggy pants because I don't want to ... It's about where you live. You can't be running around [Community] dressed in baggy pants, hoods, do-rags, acting like nobody cares. That won't fit well in [Community]. It's a rich retirement place.

For many of these parents, where one resides matters; it provides an address that can gain them respect insofar as it can signal one's social-class status and "ultimately minimize the effects of racial discrimination" (Rollock et al., 2011, p. 1089).

Along the same lines, it matters how one dresses. "I hate the way they dress," said one mother, lamenting her inability to persuade her teenage son to wear "nice" clothes rather than the "big, baggy" ones he favoured. Similarly, with regard to taste in music, another mother complained, "I love different types of music, and I want [my son] to learn about different types of music ... Reggae, soul, violin, you name it. It's good that they have a wide choice."

Underlying the parents' intent is that their children develop the necessary social and cultural capital that will enable them to fit into the "rich" or middle-class community where they have settled. While they might not be "middle-class," they expected that their children will experience the material conditions that will help structure "the way to do things." This is consistent with Vincent, Rollock, Ball, and Gillborn's (2012a) findings about Black middle-class Caribbean parents in Britain. Referencing Bourdieu's notion of *habitus*, Vincent and her colleagues' findings identify "parents' strictures to their children on speech and dress (particularly disapproval focused on low-hanging trousers on boys), and also more taken-for-granted aspects of lifestyle, such as regular eating-out at non-fast-food restaurants, enrollment in extra-curricular activities, or if and where a family goes on holidays" (p. 342).

Shaping many of these parents' messages to their children are the ones they received from their parents – such as "you have to be better, [and] you have to watch your step," as one mother said she received from her mother. She went on to say:

> When I am dealing with my children ... I say: "In your conduct you have to watch yourself, [and] you have to be the best." We set the standards for our children so high. I also tell them, no one owes you anything, but the colour of your skin is Black, and it doesn't make any difference in how well educated you are or what position you have in life. You always have to strive to prove to them that you are better. And so yes, I do set high standards for my children, and I hope that they live up to that standard ... In doing all of that, hopefully, we will not teach them the negativity around always assuming that when things don't work their way, [they can] use the excuse, [it's] because of the colour of their skin, because they are Black.

For these parents, the suburban community serves as a necessary, if not a fundamental, resource among others (dress, attitude, education, etc.) that will enable their children to become "the best." They believed that in such a community – away from the "hustle and bustle" and the dangers of the downtown area – they will be able to inculcate the "high standards" of values, behaviour and expectations they have for their children.

While it may appear that these parents are physically distancing themselves from areas with higher proportions of Black residents, the following comment illustrates the ambivalence some of the parents felt as they expressed how the choice to live in the suburb is a way of lessening – if not eliminating – the "stigma" that comes with being Black in Canadian society:

> On the one hand, you want to live near Black families, [yet] on the other hand, there is the stigma by society as to who and what they are. You think that by coming here you become less of that, and yet when you're here you wish for it. You wish for the good things about being in a community with many Blacks. My reality is based on what I'm given. How do I allow my children to grow and to be successful and to be part of a community? I like [the community]. I like ... the fact that there are fewer Black people here, yet I wish there were more.

Rather than thinking that they were subjecting their children to racialization, racism, and discrimination by moving to white-dominated communities, these parents believed they were inoculating their children from societal impediments to their advancement and success. To this end, as they reported, they told their children that colour – or being Black – should not be regarded as a negative, a deterrent to doing what it takes to achieve their educational or career ambitions, or something to be used as "an excuse." Besides, many of these parents believed that they were living well, taking actions, and pursuing their dreams, which should serve as exemplars to their children. As one father remarked:

> I told my children, "Stand up for your rights. Stand up for yourself. Don't back down from anyone. Don't let anything or anyone stand in your way. If you see something you want and know that you can get it because you've got the ability, reach for it. Don't stop until you reach it." On the other hand, you've got to be better than the white person. You've got to better than your friend; and then you've got to be Black. You've got to hold on to your culture. You've got to hold on to your being Black.

Similarly, another parent said:

> We are Black parents. To survive here, you have to beat the white man at his own game. I tell my children that they have to excel; that they shouldn't forget that they are Black; that for them to be comfortable they have to work extra hard.

The messages that parents pass on to their children are heavily weighted with an individual ethos – that as individuals their children should be able to "stand up" for themselves, and with skills and abilities, do "better" than their white peers while holding on to "being Black." At the same time, the parents concede that racism and discrimination are structures with which their children will have to contend. So, it is not that parents are oblivious to the ways in which structures of racism (stereotypes and discrimination) have operated and will continue to operate to thwart their own and their children's efforts to succeed in the society. They remain optimistic and confident – if not fully convinced – that through individual efforts, these structures can be sidestepped or surmounted. They see themselves as evidence of this happening – for after all, as one parent said, "It's an individual thing." He went on to say, reflecting on his early years in the community:

> Are we at any particular advantage or disadvantage living in [the community]? ... From time to time, we found ourselves to be the first of many things ... How do we fit in? All the problems that we have expressed here

tonight [in the focus group] seem to me to be the normal daily living for any minority ... It's how you approach a problem. Sometimes we do well. Sometimes it's ourselves that make or break things. It's in the way that we perceive ourselves.

For many of these parents, ultimately individuals have to and must take responsibility for their lives; whatever experiences and struggles they might have as minoritized members of society should be taken as merely a part of everyday life. However, they focused a critical part of their effort on education, which as one parent advised would help their children deal with whatever struggles or "pitfalls" they might experience because of race:

You're going to school, you're going to do well, and you will succeed. That should be your primary concern. Because of the colour of your skin, you should be aware that there are pitfalls ... [But] don't let [being Black be] the primary concern ... The moment they make it the central concern ... then it distracts from their focus to succeed ... The balance between white and Black and succeeding [is] being aware of colour. But go to school, and do well.

It is not that these parents had experienced a life free of racism in their community. One parent explained that her husband wanted to buy a luxury car, but she objected because their family was "already under the microscope." For this reason, even though they both had "decent jobs," worked hard, and came by their money "100 per cent honestly" by investing "just like the next guy," they sought to avoid the "unnecessary" attention. Her husband added,

Race is an issue ... Being Black means we have to resort to extraordinary means to keep quiet what others do openly – flaunt their wealth. The result, we'll keep driving our present understated car in the hopes that we won't attract attention to ourselves.

Another parent spoke of an incident in which a youth from the neighbourhood told his son that the youth's mom "did not want him playing with a Black boy." The father, who heard this from a third party, explained that this was a misunderstanding – for the mother explained that she was not referring to his son. Yet another parent recalled going into her child's class at school and observing that the teacher did not pay attention to the fact that "the Black kids are picked on more than the others." She said that the teacher's "teaching technique stinks" for she tended to favour students who were "sitting right in front." The result was disengaged students. With these kinds of experiences, it is understandable that the parents would be concerned about their children's well-being; indeed, as they admit, they worry about their children – something they observed their children do not seem to understand:

> They [my children] get angry come Friday nights when I say no, they can't go out if they can't get home by ten or eleven o'clock. I still worry about them. There's this maternal instinct. I say to them: "Don't bump anyone. Don't touch anyone." Every day you hear of someone getting shot ... I always worry about them when they go out. Parents try to protect the kids – do they appreciate what parents have done for them? They don't understand that you are trying to protect them.

Even in their suburban neighbourhood, parents still worry about their children's safety and the problems they might face. While these parents would like to think that they left the unsafe city behind, they are realistic in acknowledging that they cannot fully protect their children in this society. How young people experience the neighbourhood and what they make of their parents' messages are discussed in the following section.

The Struggles of Youth in Suburbia: "Too Black to Be White, and Too White to Be Black"

Rollock and her colleagues (2011) found that Black middle-class children in Britain developed "an understanding of an identity which is minoritized and which is wholly distinct from their parents, whose racialized identities were mainly formed under a geographical, temporal, and postcolonial context very different from theirs" (p. 1084). The same could be said of the children growing up with Black parents in Toronto's outer suburbs. Specifically, they seemed to believe and understand their parents' insistence about the need for them to recognize the significance of race in their lives and realize that, because they were Black, they had to "fight harder to accomplish their goals." The youth generally accepted this narrative, but many only really understood the significance of colour after moving to their new neighbourhood. For example, as one youth claimed:

> I didn't know I was Black until I came to [the area] ... In Toronto, I lived in a 95 per cent Italian neighbourhood and went to a multicultural school. Everyone would have a good time. We were kids. I don't understand the

shift between when you are twelve and fourteen. All of a sudden colour matters. People look at me. They do a double-take, like: "Is that a Black person?"

"You are treated differently," is how another youth termed it:

> I grew up in Jamaica, and race was never really an issue. I didn't even know white people existed till I was in high school. I moved to Canada, and we had to look at race a whole different way ... People treat you differently.

Many of the youth talked about the effort it took for them to understand and come to terms with reactions to their "colour" – specifically their Blackness – in the neighbourhood and their school. That people would "do a double-take" was to them sending a message that they were out of place – as a Black person, they did not belong in that community. Caught between their parents' insistence that they take pride in their Blackness and reactions they received from community members, it's certainly understandable that they would experience some confusion.

Some youth explained that it was not enough for them to be affirmed by their parents. They needed to see, hear, and experience the message in the broader society. According to one young woman:

> As much as my mom said, "Yes, I think you're cute, don't listen to them ..." It's your mom, you know. You feel that your mom is compelled to tell you these things. It helps for the moment. But to go back to the playground the next day knowing that my mom thought differently didn't help me. It didn't give me any way to combat the name-calling. I needed to hear it from other places. I needed to see it in magazines. I needed to have things where I could see people that looked like me ... big butts and thick thighs, not totally skinny with long, flowing hair.

Several parents downplayed the significance of Blackness, while simultaneously asserting that their children should be prepared to deal with whatever problems they might encounter. For instance, one young woman related:

> My parents were always telling me that even though being Black doesn't really matter, living in certain areas of society where Black people have that negative aspect, you have to fight harder for what you want. People will always be trying to hold you down ... If you're a Black person, your

outlook on life will be completely different from a Caucasian, or Indian, or Spanish ... They may not have gone through the same harsh, hostile [situation] we Black people have grown up in.

Is it possible that that this young woman's parents, and others like them, were trying to make her feel positive about being Black – or is it how she chose to interpret her parents' words in an attempt to deal with the dissonance or contradiction inherent in the message? Whatever the case, all of the youth in the studies seemed to accept that their parents were preparing them for life as Black people even as they expounded the benefits of their suburban life – a life that for some isolated them from other Black people, which had its consequences. Here is how one young woman described her experience:

> My mom tells me I should go out and mix with other races. But the problem is, I don't get a chance to be with Black people enough, so when I see Black "thugs" on the street, I get a little nervous; 'cause I don't know how to act around them. At school, I'm quiet around white people. I ask questions, but I don't really talk that much because I talk about Black music and stuff, and they don't understand. It's kinda bad 'cause I can talk to them about their music.

When some of the youth associated with other Black people, they developed feelings of dissonance – or as one termed it, having "real difficulty" – which left them in a quandary:

> It was nice to see people who looked like me and to know that I was not the only person out there who looks like this. But I found it really difficult to relate to them because we were from two completely separate environments. Basically, I was in a situation where I was too Black to be white and too white to be Black.

Many of the young people talked about grappling with questions, contradictions, ambivalences, and conflicts inspired by the messages they received from their parents combined with their own lived experiences. They admitted to grappling with such questions as, "What is it to be Black?" To this question, one participant stated,

> It really bothers me when people say I'm not Black enough. What is it to be Black? We don't say that that girl is acting out of her whiteness or Asianness. So why is there a double standard for Black girls? If we act in one way, we are being whitewashed. If we act Black, we are being ghetto.

This "double standard" and dualism (i.e., "whitewashed" or "ghetto") with which Black suburban youth (particularly females) had to contend meant that they tended to experience their identity as one-dimensional, consumed by race and related "performance" rather than recognized as complex, fluid, contextual, and contradiction-prone.[7] The question of which particular attitudes, behaviours, dress, skin colour, and peer relations constitute Blackness became an ongoing concern for many – particularly when they were judged on their peer associations, speech patterns, and social performance by both white and Black peers (obviously each rooted in varying racialized conceptions of Blackness).

This concern seemed especially difficult when their Black peers judged them as "different" because of their association with their white peers. One self-identified "biracial" participant complained that her friends would always remind her that she is "really half-Black" – something which for her negated the reality of her hurtful experiences with racism. "This makes me angry," she said, "because if I can feel the isolation of racism, then I'm enough Black to be called Black. I get the bad effects of it, so why can't I say I'm Black too?"[8]

For a number of research participants, schools appeared to have served as an incubator for some of the identity, social, and educational problems with which they struggled. They talked about their teachers being ambivalent or doubtful about their educational ability:

> It's almost like you have to prove to the teacher that you are smart. They don't believe you at first until you have the test in your hand.

> The first thing [the teacher] thinks is: "Oh my god, this guy is going to fail; his marks are not going to be as high as the others." But he's surprised when he sees that first test ... They don't think we are smart [because of] the way we dress or the way we act ... We just have to show we are smart.

> You always have to show that you are not the stereotypical Black. Wherever you go, people have this view [of us] because most of the whites at our school watch BET [Black Entertainment Television], and they get the

---

7 "When I'm around whites," said one young woman, "I am conservative, quiet. When I'm with other Blacks I'm different. I ask myself, why am I different? Why is my neck wobbling? Why am I falling into that stereotype? It's almost like a subconscious thing. It's almost disturbing."

8 These findings echo those of Gosine (2008), who observed that some high-achieving Black youth with middle-class aspirations grappled with the discursive constraints of a specific culturally constructed definition of Blackness.

wrong impression ... You put up your hand, and they [teachers] might ask you the hard question like they don't think you know the answer.

They [teachers] come up to you and pat you on the back and go like, "Good job!" Like, "She's got 95, wow!" But they are saying it so loud that everyone in the class can hear. So even though they are praising you, they are still making you feel like you struggled. They go, "Oh, did you find it hard?" I don't need you to come up and ask me that. I knew what I was doing. Obviously, I was listening ... But they are taking it like, "Oh my gosh, she got it. Wow!"

The low academic expectations these students encountered from their teachers are consistent with other studies of Black students in Toronto that have been conducted over the years (Dei, 2010; Dei & Kempf, 2013; James, 2012a). Ironically, these students' parents had been trying to protect them from precisely such teachers' perceptions to ensure their academic success. But as their experiences indicate, even as suburban students, the stereotype of the underachieving Black student prevailed.

This stereotype also influenced the educational and career advice students received at school. For example, one aspiring engineering student recalled that his guidance counsellor discouraged him from doing a full Ontario Academic Credit (OAC) course load in his final year of high school because the counsellor felt that this would be too demanding for him.[9] Living in such a climate of racism with its damaging stereotyping and discrimination, students would receive a teacher's compliments with some level of scepticism.

The differential treatment these students received from their teachers accounted for other problematic interactions and relationships between them. One student explained: "You can feel the tension" resulting from teachers' attempts to get the Black students "to turn down the hip-hop music they [were] playing," because, as teachers alleged, other students were afraid to pass through the area of the building where the Black students "chill." This young man saw this as unfair since white students were not similarly asked to turn down their music. The fear, which contributed to teachers' differential treatment, is rooted in the racial profiling of Black students as loud, impertinent, aggressive troublemakers and lawbreakers (see chapter 4).

But as some of these Black youth revealed, it was their white peers with their illegal activities who should have been subjected to the

---

9 Some students were "pressured" by teachers to participate in sports as opposed to their academic work.

teachers' supervisory attention and surveillance. One participant described the suburban area as "a big drug scene," saying,

> It's mostly the white people who are into it. We are not into it. They're into drugs like mad, and they are always asking if you want to buy some, or if you are selling. They tend to be like, "Well shouldn't you be into drugs?" Well, I have no interest in drugs.

These suburban Black youth reported experiencing racial profiling not only from their teachers, but also their white peers.[10] Many of them identified interactions with police as being based on the police's preconceived ideas of Blackness. They saw this as one of the disadvantages to living in the community. One young man talked of instances when he was unnecessarily stopped in a car when travelling with friends, "rudely" questioned, and threatened with being "beaten" by police (see also James, 2018). He said that he was asked to present his driver's licence even though he was not the driver, while his two white female friends with whom he was travelling were never questioned.

Another young man described an instance where he was walking home from work with his friend when two police cars stopped and the officers "interrogated" them, saying that they "fit the description of two Black youth who had robbed a convenience store earlier." Realizing that they were wearing their fast food restaurant uniforms when stopped, this youth reasoned to the officers, why, dressed as they were, would they have committed such an offence, "and why would I be walking towards the scene of the crime if I had robbed the store?" The officer, he said, responded saying, "That's a really good question" and let them go. But before reaching home, he was stopped again by police for the same reason. However, as he noted, except for race, the apprehended alleged robbers looked "nothing" like him and his friend and coworker.[11]

---

10 In recalling experiences with white peers, one young man disclosed: "It's a whole stereotyping thing. I don't know why, this guy came up to me. And was like: 'I got some fried chicken and watermelon in my car. Want some? Let's go to my house and watch some BET [Black Entertainment Television].'" Another added: "It was cold, and I was walking out of the store with my hood on. Someone came up to me and said: 'Watch out gangster.'" Yet another shared that she had gone to a friend's house a number of times and received "dirty looks" from her grandmother. In apologizing for her grandmother's behaviour, the friend said her "grandmother does not like Black people."

11 The youths in these studies also told stories of surveillance measures used by store owners and security officers to monitor them. For instance, one young man recounted that on one occasion he asked a corner store owner to leave him alone because he was "really a good kid." This was in response to the store owner asking him to buy something and leave the store while others were allowed to browse.

Most of the interviews and focus groups revealed the role that gender played in the lives of suburban Black youth (James, 2012b). For example, compared to females, males had greater opportunity to travel or roam around their community and as a result developed the social and cultural capital needed to effectively navigate the contours of the social, cultural, educational, and security structures of the community. Both race and gender informed the way these youth were profiled – while males reported that they were stereotyped as aggressive, troublemakers, and potential lawbreakers; females said they were largely seen as loud and brazen. "Ghetto" was ascribed to both males and females on the basis of their hip-hop clothing or dress.

These gendered ascriptions also played a role in the way boys and girls interacted with one another – particularly in their perceptions of one another as potential dating partners. The young women in the study claimed that young Black men in the community thought they had "too much attitude" and were intimidated by their academic, career, and personal ambitions. They encountered young men who, upon hearing that they planned to attend or were attending university, would counter with, "You're washed.[12] So, what, do you think you're better than me?" Besides, caught between young Black men's desire for white women because "they were prepared to put out more" (putting up with the young men's attitudes and giving them "compliments"),[13] and receiving little to no attention from their white male peers,[14] young Black women felt that they had little option but to accept the affections of young Black men whom they felt

---

12 That is, "whitewashed," suggesting behaviour in keeping with white values, ideas, and norms.
13 One female participant commented, "Black guys nowadays are the thing. The white girls are after them like white on rice."
14 According to one young woman, "The archetype of beauty at my school was a blonde, rich, driving around in a Mercedes, grew up in [the community] their entire life, generally didn't have too much of a religious background. I'm Black, I do not drive a Mercedes, religion is important to me ... School was so completely not me. It was so unimportant. If I tried to define myself according to the standards of my high school, I'd go insane." And in reflecting on her encounters with white males, one female talked of going out with her white girlfriends and being "looked over" by white guys. "The guys," she said, "are standing there looking at you, but you don't really feel that it's you they are looking at. You know that it's the tall, blond, blue-eyed that they are after. After being constantly, constantly looked over – it is so hard on a girl's self-esteem ... you begin to think, 'I guess I'm not really an attractive person.'"

did not measure up to their standards; otherwise, they would remain dateless.[15]

How do these young people navigate the structures of their community that mediate their opportunities? What do they tell themselves about these structures that enable them to make sense of their situation, their parents' viewpoints and expectations, and their perceived possibilities? How do they negotiate their positioned "difference" about which, as one parent said, "It was made very clear to my kids that they were different. It was not a situation that we created. It was created for them, and they responded." Findings indicate that some youth seemed resigned to the fact that the "odds were against them," and they had to struggle: "In certain situations the odds are against me. I can't be ignorant to these facts. But there's no point in me asking why any more. I just deal with the fact, that's just the way it is." In her rejoinder, another added:

> Deep down I knew I had to struggle, but just watching history, especially Black history, slavery, and the whole civil rights movement ... Just learning that, you realize that, yes, I am going to have to struggle harder because of my skin colour.

It appears that for some of these youth, the history of Black struggle not only provided evidence that change is possible, but also hope – a sense that, just like their ancestors, their "struggle" will eventually yield the opportunities and outcomes they seek. To this end, they seemed prepared to work harder knowing that it comes with being Black – a message they have long heard from their parents.

While their identity as a Black person was largely understood to be central to who they were (for as one youth said, "I don't go a day without hearing that I'm Black"), they wanted it known that Blackness does not constitute their entire being:

> I say to myself, don't just say you are a Black person – show them who you are. Let them know that you are a Black person and you are proud of it, but that's just one aspect of who you are.

---

15 One parent observed that "when the cops see them [young Black men] with white girls that becomes a problem ... When the [white] parents see them with their daughters that's a problem. These are problems that these [white] people have created ... and they [our sons] really don't want that. And they are not hiding it ... It's not like we are some place where people don't tell you their opinion."

Race was indeed "just one aspect" of their identity. To fully understand their experiences, one needs to take an intersectional approach (Gillborn, 2015) and better understand how social inequities – and the processes that create, structure and sustain them – spawn or account for the situations in which these youth find themselves. Hence, it is justifiable to insist, as did one young woman in an echo of Pat Parker (1978):

> Don't view me as just a Black person, but do understand that I am Black and that when you make racial comments, they do insult me. I am Black, and I don't forget that; but there is more to me than that.[16]

Not surprisingly, some of these young people had come to believe in a neoliberal rhetoric of individualism. That is, they assumed that the situations in which they found themselves were likely of their own making – perhaps they had not been open-minded enough to see or appreciate the perspectives of others, or perhaps the white people with whom they associated had only had negative experiences with Black people. In the words of one youth, "I don't just limit myself to being Black. I try to see things from other people's perspectives too." Along the same lines, another youth rationalized, "If we only hang out with people like ourselves ... that's where the prejudice starts. We need to take time to understand others." This kind of understanding led the youth who reported being told by a store owner not to browse in the store[17] to conclude that "that lady may have had experiences in the past that caused her to be like that." Similarly, one young man expressed a desire to give the police the benefit of the doubt:

> The thing I think about cops is that cops are people, just like us. If I saw them out of uniform, I wouldn't even know they are cops unless they told me. They are just like anybody else: they cuss, they smoke, whatever. The thing is, some of them think, some of them don't think. They just do their job, and they don't question anything. Some of them have the capacity to question things: those are the ones I like.

Clearly, these youths understood that their experiences had to do with race and the pernicious racism they faced daily. But they understood that racism as "prejudice" – they believed they could change

---

16 The first two lines of Parker's poem, "For the white person who wants to know how to be my friend" read: "The first thing you do is to forget that I'm black. Second, you must never forget that I'm black." She suggests that being Black does not mean that she should be held responsible for Black people's actions.
17 See note above on surveillance by store owners and security personnel.

individuals' attitudes through interactions with them. To this end, they saw themselves as taking responsibility to associate and socialize with their white peers and other community members, and present themselves as good, disciplined, worthy community members.

Others among the group felt that it was not worth putting so much energy into thinking about white people and their concerns, for they were not doing the same for Black people:

> We're focusing so much on our race. I'm sure that white people don't spend their whole lives thinking about the fact that they're white. They think about their career, their families ... But we tend to think about whether we will be treated fairly at a job interview, are people going to give me funny looks? ... You are automatically living your life in comparison to the lives of the majority.

DiAngelo (2011) points out the difficulty for Blacks in not doing so:

> White people in North America live in a social environment that protects and insulates them from race-based stress ... Whites are rarely without these "protective pillows [resources and privilege]," and when they are, it is usually temporary and by choice. (p. 55)

Therefore, while it might be plausible for these youth not to live their lives in comparison to whites, they would have to do so with an understanding of how race structures operate and have the tools to navigate these structures.

Conclusion: "We're Here as a Favour to the Kids" – A Costly Mobility Strategy for Black Youth

> We stand out, because we are Black. Society does not let them forget that. (Parent)

> How is it possible not to be living through your children as you try to work through your own sense of fear? As immigrants, we come to better ourselves and to live for our children, [but] in that process there's all this unpacking which many of us haven't done because we're too busy living life, trying to survive, trying to get where we want to go ... Our kids become caught. (Parent)

In deciding to move to the suburbs, many of the parents in these studies were motivated by seeking a better life for their children – doing them "a favour," as one parent put it. But as their children's experiences and struggles demonstrate, this "favour" carried a significant social, educational, cultural, and familial cost. While many of these suburban parents believe that "where you live matters," simply having a suburban address in a reputable community did not save their children from having to contend with racism. Parents said that they "did not even give a thought" to the implications of moving into a predominantly white community once they had found the house they liked. But their children's experiences with teachers, police, community members, and white friends and peers should alert Black parents that care must be given to choosing the neigbourhood where they want to raise their children.

That many of the young people in the research expressed a desire to leave the community "as soon as they were able to," because they found it "boring," was partly due to lack of recreational, cultural, and social facilities, as well as access to transportation and part-time work opportunities. As one youth put it, "There is nothing to do." It didn't help that the youth's experiences with racial profiling and discrimination represented a constant in his life (see US studies, notably Holland, 2012; Ispa-Landa, 2013; Ndiaye, 2013; Russell, 2013). There were also struggles with finding dating partners. Indeed, the individualistic middle-class ethos that characterizes suburban life had little to no appeal to youth who yearned for the sense of community they had experienced in Toronto's culturally diverse diaspora urban neighbourhoods.

The difficult role of gender and its influence on the high cost for Black youth who live in the suburbs also cannot be underestimated. Recent studies (Holland, 2012; Ispa-Landa, 2013; Ndiaye, 2013; Russell, 2013) involving Black youth living in suburban communities in the United States report that compared to Black girls, Black boys have an easier time with life in the suburbs, including with their schooling. While the masculine characteristic of being "cool and tough" serves to valorize and celebrate the boys, "the girls were sanctioned and stigmatized in part because they did not embody the same gender performances as their suburban classmates" (Ispa-Landa, 2013, p. 230).

In her examination of racialized students' schooling experiences, Holland (2012) found that males were "able to gain social status at the school through their participation in athletics and their physical embodiment of the urban 'Hip-Hop star,'" and also by engaging in strategies to play down negative stereotypes (p. 116). In contrast, females do not have access to similar avenues for social status and do not engage in such strategies. The way school is organized contributes to these gender differences by facilitating interracial contact for the males under ideal conditions, while providing the females with less opportunity for contact (p. 116).

But as the data for these studies indicate, boys tend to have a more difficult time being scrutinized and surveilled by neighbours, police, and security agents. This is consistent with Clampet-Lundquist, Edin, Kling, and Duncan's (2011) study of youth who moved to live in US suburban areas. Referencing the experiences of male respondents, the researchers surmise that "it was virtually impossible to have a social life in the suburbs" (p. 172).

Black parents, like all parents, seek the best for their children and see education and positive peer group membership as playing significant roles in helping their children to realize their aspirations. That should not come at the cost of self-efficacy – a cost created and sustained by social inequities and racism.

Life in the suburbs need not be one of isolation, alienation, and cultural distancing – as Johal (2015) showed for Sikh youth, living in an ethnic enclave can help to reinforce identity, parental values, and aspirations; supplement schooling (in terms of cultural reference); and offer peer support. Clearly, parents need to be more conscientious and sensitive in choosing the communities in which they wish to raise their children. In the absence of suburban neighbourhoods populated by large numbers of Black people, the high cost of growing up in the alienation of the suburbs remains. The fact is, upward social mobility is a reasonable ambition, but we must bear in mind the cost to our children.

REFERENCES

Anisef, P., Axelrod, P., Baichman-Anisef, E., James, C.E., & Turrittin, A. (2000). *Opportunity and uncertainty: Life course experiences of the class of '73*. Toronto, ON: University of Toronto Press.

Boesveld, S. (2012, February 16). City hall take note: You can't fight suburbia. *National Post*. https://nationalpost.com/news/canada/city-hall-take-note-you-cant-fight-suburbia

Breen, R., & Jonsson, J.O. (2005), Inequality of opportunity in comparative perspective: Recent research on educational attainment and social mobility. *Annual Review of Sociology, 31*, 223–43. https://doi.org/10.1146/annurev.soc.31.041304.122232

Brown, M. (2003). *Growing up Black in Oakville: The impact of community on Black youth identity formation and civic participation*. Oakville, ON: Canadian Caribbean Association of Halton.

Bula, F. (2011, April 8). Home in the suburbs, heart in the city. *Globe and Mail*. https://www.theglobeandmail.com/news/british-columbia/home-in-the-suburbs-heart-in-the-city/article585820/

Canada Census 2011: Toronto's suburbs are growing at an explosive rate. (2012, February 8). *National Post*. https://nationalpost.com/news/canada/canada-census-2011-torontos-suburbs-are-growing-at-an-explosive-rate

Clampet-Lundquist, S., Edin, K., Kling, J., & Duncan, G. (2011). Moving teenagers out of high-risk neighborhoods: How girls fare better than boys. *American Journal of Sociology 116*(4), 1154–89. https://doi.org/10.1086/657352

Dei, G.J.S. (2010). The possibilities of new/counter and alternative visions of schooling. *English Quarterly, 41*(3–4), 113–32.

Dei, G.J.S., & Kempf, A. (2013). *New perspectives on African-centred education in Canada*. Toronto, ON: Canadians Scholars' Press.

DiAngelo, R. (2011). White fragility. *International Journal of Critical Pedagogy, 3*(3), 54–70. https://libjournal.uncg.edu/ijcp/article/view/249

Gillborn, D. (2015). Intersectionality, critical race theory and the primacy of racism: Race, class, gender and disability in education. *Qualitative Inquiry, 21*(3), 277–87. https://doi.org/10.1177/1077800414557827

Gordon, D.L.A., & Shirokoff, I. (2014, July). *Suburban nation? Population growth in Canadian suburbs, 2006–2011*. Toronto, ON: Council for Canadian Urbanism. http://www.canadiansuburbs.ca/files/Gordon_Shirokoff_2011.pdf

Gosine, K. (2008). Living between stigma and status: A qualitative study of the social identities of highly educated Black Canadian adults. *Identity: An International Journal of Theory and Research, 8*(4), 307–33. https://doi.org/10.1080/15283480802365304

Holland, M.M. (2012). Only here for the day: The social integration of minority students at a majority white high school. *Sociology of Education. 85*(2), 101–20. https://doi.org/10.1177/0038040712440789

Holloway, S.L, & Pimlott-Wilson, H. (2013). Parental involvement in children's learning: Mothers' fourth shift, social class, and the growth of state intervention in family life. *Canadian Geographer, 57*(3), 327–36. https://doi.org/10.1111/cag.12014

Ispa-Landa, S. (2013). Gender, race, and justifications for group exclusion: Urban Black students bussed to affluent suburban schools. *Sociology of Education, 86*, 218–33. https://doi.org/10.1177/0038040712472912

James, C.E. (2010). Schooling and the university plans of immigrant Black students from an urban neighborhood. In H.R. Milner (Ed.), *Culture, curriculum, and identity in education* (pp. 117–39). New York, NY: Palgrave Macmillan.

James, C.E. (2012a). *Life at the intersection: Community, class and schooling*. Halifax, NS: Fernwood.

James, C.E. (2012b). Students "at risk": Stereotyping and the schooling of Black boys. *Urban Education, 47*(2), 464–94. https://doi.org/10.1177/0042085911429084

James, C.E. (2018). "Singled out": Being a Black youth in the suburbs. In L. Foster, L. Jacobs, B. Siu, & S. Azmi (Eds.), *Racial profiling and human rights in Canada: The new legal landscape* (pp. 133–51). Toronto, ON: Irwin Law.

James, C.E., & Chapman-Nyaho, S. (2018, November 11). Too busy for the PTA, but working-class parents care. *The Conversation*. https://theconversation.com/too-busy-for-the-pta-but-working-class-parents-care-104386

Johal, R. (2015). *Contradictions and challenges: Second generation Sikh males in Canada* (unpublished doctoral dissertation). Graduate Program in Education, York University, Toronto, ON.

Lacy, K. (2007). *Blue-chip Black: Race, class and status in the new Black middle class*. Berkeley, CA: University of California Press.

McCreary, T., Basu, R., & Godlewska, A. (2013). Critical geographies of education: Introduction to the special issue. *Canadian Geographer, 15*(3), 255–9. https://doi.org/10.1111/cag.12031

Ndiaye, A. (2013, October 21). Black boys have an easier time fitting in at suburban schools than Black girls. *The Atlantic*. https://www.theatlantic.com/education/archive/2013/10/black-boys-have-an-easier-time-fitting-in-at-suburban-schools-than-black-girls/280657/

Parker, P. (1978). For the white person who wants to know how to be my friend [poem]. In *Movement in Black* (p. 73). Ithaca, NY: Firebrand Books.

Patton, M.Q. (2002). *Qualitative research and evaluation methods*. London, UK: Sage.

Porter, J. (1965). *The vertical mosaic: An analysis of social class and power in Canada*. Toronto, ON: University of Toronto Press.

Raffo, C. (2015). Living on the edge – rethinking poverty, class and schooling [book review]. *Journal of Education Policy, 30*(2), 294–7. https://doi.org/10.1080/02680939.2014.969589

Rollock, N., Gillborn, D., Vincent, C., & Ball, S. (2011). The public identities of the Black middle classes: Managing race in public spaces. *Sociology 45*(6), 1078–93. https://doi.org/10.1177/0038038511416167

Russell, L.S. (2013). Negotiating identity: Black female identity construction in a predominantly-white suburban context. *Urban Education Research and Policy Annuals, 3*(1), 9. https://journals.uncc.edu/urbaned/article/view/349

Saunders, P. (2010). *Social mobility myths*. London, UK: Civitas: Institute for the Study of Civil Society.

Schugurensky, D. (2007, November 17). Does education equalize opportunities? The implications of the TDSB cohort analysis for democracy and meritocracy [Paper presentation]. Paper presented at the Diversity in Education Parents' Forum, Ethnocultural Community Network of the Toronto District School Board (ECN-TDSB), Toronto, ON.

Smyth, J., & Wrigley, T. (2013). *Living on the edge: Rethinking poverty, class and schooling*. New York, NY: Peter Lang.

Vincent, C., Rollock, N., Ball, S., & Gillborn, D. (2012a). Being strategic, being watchful, being determined: Black middle-class parents and schooling. *British Journal of Sociology of Education, 33*(3), 337–54. https://doi.org/10.1080/01425692.2012.668833

Vincent, C., Rollock, N., Ball, S., & Gillborn, D. (2012b). Raising middle-class Black children: Parenting priorities, actions and strategies. *Sociology, 47*(3), 427–42. https://doi.org/10.1177/0038038512454244

Young, D., Wood, P.B., & Keil, R. (Eds.). (2011). *In-between infrastructure: Urban connectivity in an age of vulnerability*: Kelowna, BC: Praxis (e)Press.

Response to Chapter 9

"What Floats in the Air Is Chance": Respectability Politics and the Search for Upward Mobility in Canada

ANDREA A. DAVIS
Humanities Department, Faculty of Applied Arts & Professional Studies, York University, Ontario, Canada

In the chapter "'Colour Matters': Suburban Life as Social Mobility and Its High Cost for Black Youth," James discusses the findings from interviews with first-generation parents of Caribbean descent and their second- and third-generation children living in suburban neighbourhoods outside Toronto. James argues that a desire to rearticulate family life and aspirations beyond the narrow perceptions of racialized poverty/crime, which circumscribe urban definitions of Blackness in Canada, encourage Caribbean immigrant families to move into the suburbs in search of better educational opportunities for their children and greater class insulation from the effects of racism.

James critiques this upward social impulse not only as misguided but also as harmful to Black youth, who experience the greatest impact from these demographic moves and who suffer from cultural isolation and increased vulnerability to anti-Black racism and stereotyping in overwhelmingly white suburban enclaves. James's critique suggests that Caribbean families, when faced with the limitations of race in Canadian society, draw on social strategies they learn on arrival to navigate the treacherously racialized terrain. The pursuit of middle-class respectability, thus, becomes a learned strategy in the pursuit of the promise of an illusory "Canadian dream" in societies framed, on the one hand, by competitive capitalism and, on the other, by widespread racial inequity.

Would it be possible, however, to pose another set of questions? To what extent might Caribbean immigrant families, rather than merely drawing on strategies of respectability politics they acquire upon migration, be activating deep-seated ideas about respectability they bring with them from the Caribbean? And what might their inability to actualize their dreams through previously proven strategies of social advancement mean?

The theory of respectability politics centres Black people's accountability in ensuring their self-preservation from acts of racialized violence and in maximizing opportunities for successful social integration in neoliberal capitalist and settler colonial states dependent on race, class, and gender inequities (Kerrison, Cobbina, & Bender, 2018; M. Smith, 2014). According to this way of thinking, if young Black men in the United States and Canada want to avoid discrimination in the workforce, they should take off their hoodies and pull up their pants. If they want to protect themselves from police violence, they should not stand on the corner looking as if they are "up to no good." If young Black women want to be treated with respect, they should check their clothes. Black men and women shouldn't talk so loudly; they shouldn't seem so angry all the time. As a distinct worldview – marking the diverse politics of a range of Black thinkers from Booker T. Washington to Marcus Garvey, W.E.B. Du Bois, Martin Luther King Jr., and Barack Obama – Black respectability politics suggests that "marginalized classes will receive their share of political influence and social standing not because democratic values and law require it" but because of their ability to demonstrate "compatibility with the 'mainstream' or non-marginalized class" (M. Smith, 2014, para. 1). The onus for the right of existence consequently falls on the marginalized group that is tasked with proving its civility and legitimizing its humanity.

While used predominantly to discuss the response of racialized groups to racism and racial violence in the United States and Canada, respectability politics also has deep roots in the former British colonies of the Caribbean. In the Caribbean, ideas about middle-class respectability are reinforced by educational and religious institutions and are played out in ongoing beliefs about marriage, morality, family life, self-restraint, work, and education (Boucher, 2003; Wilson, 1973/1995). The demands of respectability are particularly onerous for Black middle-class women, who are the ones most pressured to perform the idealized white British standards of femininity from which they have been historically barred. "Culture" (as signified by education) and "respectability" (as signified by deportment) are the two most singularly important markers of difference separating Black middle-class women from their working-class contemporaries in Caribbean societies where class differences are not always clearly visible in economic terms

(F. Smith, 1994). In this regard, Cooper (1995) identifies the "'high/low' cultural divide" endemic to Caribbean societies as one that is "(re)produced in the hierarchical relations of gender and sexuality" and expressed as a "Slackness/Culture dialectic" (p. 11).

These ideas about Caribbean respectability, framed as they are by colonial ideas of British moral behaviour, provide an important lens through which Caribbean immigrants to the UK and Canada (the two sites of migration James cites) perceive and understand their relationship to their new host societies. Indeed, by the middle of the twentieth century, the formal education system that had inculcated values of middle-class respectability had also convinced the new Caribbean educated classes (middle class by education but poor by North American and European standards) that immigration was the surest route to social mobility and "the dream of self-fulfillment" (Foster, 1996, p. 35). Since women have consistently represented a larger percentage of Caribbean immigrants to Canada from at least the 1970s (Mensah, 2002, p. 101), it is also likely that they brought with them these deeply entrenched attitudes of middle-class respectability. In her discussion of the recruitment of Jamaican domestic workers into Canada through the 1950s West Indian Domestic Scheme, Johnson (2012) identifies qualities of "honesty, respectability, industriousness and health" as primary assets among potential recruits (p. 38). These qualities, determined internally by local recruiters, were based on the same criteria used within the Jamaican domestic service sector to place working-class women in middle-class homes. Ideas about middle-class respectability, thus, originated in the Caribbean and found expression in neocolonial relationships outside the region.

While Caribbean immigrant families are often, therefore, working-class by birth, a commitment to education in their own nations provided access through a merit-based immigration system for their entry into Canada. Since they were often locked out of land ownership in the Caribbean, home ownership in Canada becomes essential to the valorization and creation of a new middle-class identity. This, along with education, is the new ancestral inheritance they bequeath to their own children.

In short, everything in the socialization of Caribbean children and parents has inculcated a carefully articulated respectability politics as a necessary protection from poverty and violence, and as the only sure means to upward social movement in their societies. When Caribbean immigrants arrive in Canada and face new versions of racialized poverty and crime, the traditions of middle-class respectability that have already guaranteed their partial movement across class lines provide critical strategies of resistance that can be redeployed in the new host society through a North American politics of Black respectability. While second- and third-generation Caribbean youth in Canada are justifiably more inclined to critique ideas about Black respectability and the primacy of education, as James points out, they are still forced to function within capitalist societies where success is measured in terms of the "sociopolitical and economic gains" one secures (Wright, 2015, p. 43).

Caribbean immigrant families will be unable to reject the desire of upward social mobility as long as Canadian society remains loyal to the impulses of neoliberal capitalism, patriarchy, and imperialism. While the problems of racial profiling by the police and low expectations from teachers may be exacerbated in Canadian suburbs, these problems are very much present in Canadian cities. Caribbean immigrant families have to deal with problems of social marginalization and racial stereotyping wherever they are situated: "What floats in the air ... is chance. People stand or sit with the thin magnetic film of their life wrapped around them" (Brand, 2005, p. 4). Every day, aspiring middle-class families leave the Caribbean dreaming of self-fulfilment and a chance to rewrite their stories in cities like Toronto, New York, and London, where reinvention seems possible. But when the dream falters, they redraw the thin magnetic film of their lives around them and shift their horizon elsewhere in search of yet another dream, another chance – this time, if not for themselves, then surely for their children. In this context, James's chapter may ultimately be the story of the shared failure of Caribbean migration to Canada.

REFERENCES

Boucher, L. (2003). Respectability and reputation: A balancing act. *Totem: The University of Western Ontario Journal of Anthropology, 11*(1), 85–7. https://ojs.lib.uwo.ca/index.php/uwoja/article/view/8820/7014

Brand, D. (2005). *What we all long for: A novel*. Toronto, ON: Vintage Canada.

Cooper, C. (1995). *Noises in the blood: Orality, gender, and the "vulgar" body of Jamaican popular culture*. Durham, NC: Duke University Press.

Foster, C. (1996). *A place called heaven: The meaning of being Black in Canada*. Toronto, ON: HarperCollins.

Johnson, M. (2012). "To ensure that only suitable persons are sent": Screening Jamaican women for the West Indian domestic scheme. In C.E. James & A. Davis (Eds.), *Jamaica in the Canadian experience: A multiculturalizing presence* (pp. 36–53). Halifax, NS: Fernwood.

Kerrison, E.M., Cobbina, J., & Bender, K. (2018). "Your pants won't save you": Why Black youth challenge race-based police surveillance and the demands of Black respectability politics." *Race and Justice, 8*(1), 7–26. https://doi.org/10.1177/2153368717734291

Mensah, J. (2002). *Black Canadians: History, experiences, social conditions.* Halifax, NS: Fernwood.

Smith, F. (1994). Coming home to the real thing: Gender and intellectual life in the Anglophone Caribbean. *South Atlantic Quarterly, 93*(4), 895–923. http://doi.org/10.33596/anth.234

Smith, M. (2014). Affect and respectability politics. *Theory & Event, 17*(3 Suppl.). https://muse.jhu.edu/article/559376

Wilson, P. (1995). *Crab antics: A Caribbean case study of the conflict between reputation and respectability.* Prospect Heights, IL: Waveland Press. (Original work published 1973)

Wright, M.M. (2015). *Physics of Blackness: Beyond the Middle Passage epistemology.* Minneapolis, MI: University of Minnesota Press.

10 Towards Equity in Education for Black Students in the Greater Toronto Area[1]

Black students are as capable, as competent, as creative, and as determined as all other students. The ways that Black students are constantly misjudged and mistreated by teachers and guidance counsellors is an injustice to our community. As educators who seek to enrich an increasingly diverse nation, it is your duty and responsibility to encourage, motivate, challenge, and strengthen us like all others. When you begin to see us as part of your community, only then will you effectively fulfil your job as an educator. (Student)

Having a caring adult to guide and mentor our youth in making decisions that affect their education and future is important. Having adults who believe in our young, Black youth, and making leadership opportunities available to them is important. We do not need teachers having low expectations for our children with a limited capacity to engage in real discussions with our youth. (Parent)

Some Black students struggle to relate and feel motivated due to the curriculum that is often being centred around European success. (Teacher)

As a lawyer, I have noticed that, for the most part, behavioural issues in schools transcend race and socio-economic status. However, the outcomes are very much dependent on these factors. Black students are far more likely to be perceived as threatening, defiant, and violent, and are disproportionately suspended and expelled from school. Perhaps more than any other group, Black students require present and involved parents and advocates to protect their right to an education. (Lawyer)

Given Black students' prevailing schooling, educational, and welfare situation – disengagement from school, poor academic performance,

---

1 This chapter is an edited version of a larger report (James & Turner, 2017).

encounters with racial stereotyping, excessive surveillance at school and in communities, and educational underachievement – colleagues Tana Turner, Rhonda George, Samuel Tecle, and I undertook a study aimed at hearing from parents, community members, students, and educators about their current (in 2016) schooling experiences (James & Turner, 2017). In this chapter, drawing on critical race theory (CRT) principles, I report on the study's findings based on the observations and comments from participants at sessions held at the four Boards of Education in the Greater Toronto Area (GTA).

Conducted in the fall of 2016, our study came seven years after the Ontario government introduced the *Equity and Inclusive Education Strategy* (2009) and about eight months after the Anti-Racism Directorate was established (February 2016). Both mechanisms were designed to bring awareness to and address systemic racism – particularly in government-regulated institutions – and promote policies and practices that would lead to racial equity (Government of Ontario, 2017). Given the lack of data about students' schooling and well-being, reporters, political leaders, and government officials would consistently reference the Toronto District School Board's (TDSB) Student Census data to support their assertions. No other school board at the time collected the demographic data needed – especially race data – to gain insights into students' educational performance and academic achievements.[2]

Nevertheless, there was a need to know about students' schooling situation – particularly Black students, whom the TDSB data repeatedly showed were over-represented in nonacademic programs, least likely to graduate, least likely to apply to postsecondary institutions, and suspended and expelled from schools at higher rates (see Toronto District School Board, 2017, chap. 1). The question for many parents, especially parents with children in the Toronto Catholic School Board and in the suburban public and Catholic school boards of Peel, York, and Durham regions was: What was their children's situation in these boards, and how did their situation compare with that of TDSB students?[3]

---

2 In 2006 with community support, the TDSB initiated a system-wide census of students in Grades 7 to 12. The survey was conducted again for the 2011–12 and 2016–17 school years. While data on race were collected, it was only in the 2016–17 census that data on religion were collected. Such student data allow for an analysis of disparities in opportunity and achievement by gender, race, religion, area of residence and other demographic factors. Other GTA public school boards begin to collect student data, including racial identification, in 2018 (see also Spencer, 2016a).

3 Missing also are data from French and French Catholic school boards, which are attended by Black students particularly from Haiti and French Africa. In 2016 the

An exploratory investigation of Black students in Peel and Durham regions showed that Black students in these areas were not doing any better than their Toronto counterparts. A 2015 investigation into the social well-being of Black youth in Peel Region used interview data from service providers, youth workers, and Black youth themselves. The study found that common to their experiences were the following: low expectations from teachers and administrators; stereotypes about their educational commitments and intellectual abilities; more harsh discipline compared to their white peers; feelings of exclusion from their school; and having school programs, curricular materials, and a teacher population that were not reflective of them (James & Turner, 2015).

Another study of Black students in the region explored the practices and strategies that account for their poor social, academic, and emotional experiences and schooling outcomes. Citing their experiences with racism, the poor perceptions teachers had of them, and the discriminatory treatment they regularly received from their peers, the students, especially the males, pointed to the Board's lack of attention to their schooling needs and interests (Gray, Bailey, Brady, & Tecle, 2016). And a more recent (2019) research report[4] concludes:

> Students across four schools in the Board expressed several challenges they encountered in their journey through school. From the students we learned that teachers' lack of attention to their needs, interests, concerns and aspirations, and racial stereotyping and differential treatment by many of their white teachers fostered a schooling environment that made learning tough and challenging – hence, their lowered educational achievement. (James, 2019, p. 32; see also James & Turner, 2015)

In Durham Region, local media revealed that parents were raising concerns that Black students were being "racially profiled" in both the public and Catholic schools (Szekely & Pessian, 2015a). Reporting on a case brought before the Ontario Human Rights Tribunal by parents

---

Catholic school board in Peel promised to introduce a student survey (Spencer, 2016b); and in 2015, York Region District School Board initiated the process, but stopped shortly after doing so. However, in 2018, York, Peel, and Durham regions' public school boards conducted student censuses.

4 The research was conducted in one elementary, one middle, and two secondary schools in the Peel District School Board (PDSB), in the spring of 2018. Forty-four students – thirty-two males and twelve females – participated in four focus groups of students.

from the region, one online newspaper presented data showing that Black students at a school in the Durham Catholic District School Board were about eight times more likely than white students to be disciplined for such things as fighting or bullying. In his ruling, the vice-chair of the Human Rights Tribunal is reported to have written, "In my view, the racial disparity is so glaring as to cry out for further investigation and review by the respondent school board" (Szekely & Pessian, 2015b, para. 7).

Even the United Nations' Working Group of Experts on People of African Descent, which made an official visit to Canada in October 2016 and consulted with Black community members on human rights issues, commented on the schooling and education of students. In its statement to the media following the visit, the Working Group noted that it was deeply concerned about the situation of African Canadians. Among its recommendations, the Working Group identified what needed to be done in educating Black students.

- Ensure that textbooks and other educational materials reflect historical facts accurately as they relate to past tragedies and atrocities, in particular enslavement, so as to avoid negative stereotypes.
- Implement a nationwide African-Canadian education strategy to address the inordinately low educational attainment, high dropout rates, suspensions and expulsions experienced by African-Canadian children and youth.
- Strengthen Afrocentric education and implement recommendations of the Black Learners Advisory Committee Report, Expanding from Equity Supports to Leadership and Results, Education Act and Education and Early Childhood Development. The provincial ministries should collect disaggregated data and ensure adequate remedies are available to African-Canadian students impacted by discriminatory effects of disciplinary policies, including racial profiling. (United Nations Human Rights Office of the High Commissioner, 2016, 84d, p. 16; 94d & e, p. 19)

Getting the Information

Within this context, my colleagues and I conducted five consultation sessions in October and November 2016 with members of Black communities in Toronto and the regions of Peel, York, and Durham, that is, the Greater Toronto Area (GTA). In total, 286 students, parents, educators, school administrators, trustees, and community members participated in the sessions, as follows:

- Toronto West (North York) – 32 participants
- York Region – 45 participants
- Durham Region – 43 participants
- Peel Region – 110 participants
- Toronto East (Scarborough) – 56 participants

Not to be left out, a group of university students contacted us asking to have their own sessions. We held three focus groups – two in January 2017 at the University of Toronto with fifteen students in each group, and one at York University with eight students. The thirty-eight participants included current and former university and college students. In total, 324 people participated in the sessions. A substantial majority (approximately 80 per cent) were Black parents, community members, educators, school staff, and board trustees representing the various Black ethnic communities. Participants also included white and other racialized educators, school staff, trustees, and parents of Black children. Following the sessions, we received written email communication from some attendees.

We feel strongly that our investigation marked an important and necessary step towards (a) documenting the schooling and educational experiences of today's Black students, and (b) beginning a necessary conversation among parents, students, community members, and educational leaders.[5] Data provide a significant mechanism for advocacy and a means to measure levels of equity and inclusivity in the school system. The TDSB data from its 2006–11 cohort of students by ethnoracial makeup, highlighting Black students, thus offered a useful reference.[6] We focused on students' programs of study, graduation rates, application to postsecondary institutions, enrolment in special education, and suspension and expulsion rates. We highlighted the

---

5 The consultations were also used as an opportunity to educate participants about their legal rights and responsibilities as parents and students. Lawyers from the African Canadian Legal Clinic gave presentations at the sessions on the law pertaining to school attendance, participation, behaviour, obligation, suspension, and expulsion.
6 We acknowledged that while the TDSB data have their limitations, in that the data only pertain to students in that board, they nevertheless provide one of the most comprehensive snapshots of the schooling and educational participation and outcomes of Black students in Canada's largest school board. Despite their limitations, and in absence of other data, these data offer useful insights into things we need to know about Black students beyond what any other data source – including the Canadian census – currently provides, and represent the only source of their kind in Ontario and in Canada.

intergenerational and intragenerational differences among Black students (see chapter 2 of this volume) and invited participants to discuss the following questions:

- What conditions at their schools and school boards might be contributing to Black students' schooling and educational participation, performance, and outcomes?
- What is occurring in Black students' homes and communities that might be contributing to their schooling and educational lives?

Fundamental to our inquiry was an understanding of the permanence of racism – which renders colour-blindness, cultural neutrality, objectivity, and meritocracy as myths – and the need to engage in counter-storytelling about the lived experiences of racialized people in the tradition of critical race theory (Gillborn, 2015; Ladson-Billings & Tate, 1995; Yosso, 2005). With that understanding, in what follows, I discuss two of the major themes that emerged from our investigation: (a) the process of streaming Black students into nonacademic educational paths, and (b) the racism of low expectations and educators' role in normalizing it. In my conclusion, I proffer that a "web of stereotypes" (Howard, 2008, p. 966) within "white racial frames" (Feagin, 2006) structures the racialization and marginalization of Black students as underachievers, athletes, and not academically inclined. Feagin (2006) defines "white racial frames" as "an organized set of racialized ideas, stereotypes, emotions, and inclinations to discriminate" (p. 25). These frames are so ubiquitous that it is "difficult to get people to think ... in terms other than those of the accepted frame. If facts do not fit a person's frame, that person typically ignores or rejects the facts, not the frame" (pp. 25–6). This frame, which Zuberi and Bonilla-Silva (2008) refer to as "white logic," is understood to be "'the epistemological arm of white supremacy.' Rather than leading to a science of objectivity, white logic has fostered an ethnocentric orientation" (p. 332).

Streaming Black Students and the Resulting Schooling and Educational Inequities

Referencing the TDSB data, parents, community members, students, and educators alike commented that streaming – the grouping of students based on perceived ability and/or potential – explained many Black students' problems with school participation and educational performance. Reflecting on the lower expectations educators and other school staff often have for Black students, participants observed that streaming commonly leads to these students being placed in courses below their ability level. Over-representation of Black students in Applied and Essential Programs of Study[7] reflects the assumption that they do not have the capacity to succeed, or do not belong, in Academic courses.

Participants shared stories of students who had a B average in Grade 8 and were told that they "could get As if they took Applied courses in high school."[8] Some students with an A average in Grade 8 were told that high school would be "much harder" if they took Academic courses, and on that basis, they were "encouraged to take Applied courses to maintain their A average." Still other students were told that there was no point in taking Academic courses because they "are not cut out for postsecondary education."

When meeting with guidance counsellors for their Grade 9 course selection, students reported that, without any prior knowledge of them and without even reviewing their academic record, the guidance counsellor assumed they would be enrolling in Applied courses. Students who planned to attend university were never told by their teachers or guidance counsellors that taking Applied courses, regardless of their achieved grades, would limit their chances of attaining their postsecondary ambitions. These students, enrolled in an Applied Program of Study, were later "surprised to find out" – especially in their final year of high school – that they did not have the academic requirements to apply to university. Some students reported that they had selected, and their parents had signed off on, Academic courses, but educators had nevertheless enrolled them in Applied courses.

A number of the students in our sessions claimed that while their white peers were encouraged to take Academic courses and were "supported to do well" even as they struggled with their courses, Black students did not receive the same support and encouragement. One social worker from suburban York Region concurred, noting:

> As a social worker, during student success meetings, I am infuriated at how often the guidance counsellor suggests changing pathways for Black and visible minority students whenever they are not receiving a passing

---

[7] Some participants pointed out that the existing data of the graduation rates of students do not show that students who took the Essential Program of Study may have graduated from high school, but are often unprepared to find suitable employment, and if and when they do, they are likely to be trapped in precarious, low-wage jobs.

[8] All quotations from participants in the following section appear in James and Turner (2015), the report we wrote following these sessions.

grade. This is not suggested as often for white students. Over and over again, I notice how a white student's poor grades are explained away based on mental health issues, family circumstances, and other concerns. The assumption is that their grades will improve, and there will be no need for them to move down to the Applied level. However, Black students who struggle must be "placed in the proper track for their academic potential."

A white educator who teaches Applied courses added: "I routinely see Black students in my classes who should be in Academic. I never see students from other races in applied who should not be there."

Participants contended that schools in low-income neighbourhoods with a significant population of racialized and predominantly Black residents tended not to receive funding that would enable their students to take Academic courses and go on to university. School resources were thus, in part, thought to account for the high rate at which Black students are streamed into Applied and Essential school programs. In the words of one student: "I went to a school that had a great kitchen and trades classrooms. They are decked out with all the newest equipment and tools. But in the Academic classes, like law, we had to share textbooks."

Students who wished to attend university were therefore required to attend a school outside their neighbourhood where they could take Academic courses and have more course options. Participants agreed that children in low-income neighbourhoods, where limited resources and poverty were part of the reality, start off with disadvantages, which are later exacerbated by a school system that does not provide the needed resources and infrastructure for their educational, employment, and social success.

Participants reasoned too that elementary and middle school teachers' low expectations of their Black students – premised on the notion that they were not academically inclined – contributed to their becoming emotionally and academically unprepared for an Academic program when they entered high school. As one teacher in a Toronto session stated, "These students are so damaged by the time they get to high school; they believe they can only take Applied courses." Another teacher from Peel Region echoed this sentiment: "The overrepresentation in Applied is a manifestation of their [students'] conditioning." And a parent added: "Black students are treated by the school like they are unwanted. Why would they stay?"

Groups also identified the focus on the athletic prowess and aptitude of Black students – especially males – as a means by which they were streamed away from Academic programs. As one student stated, "Black boys are encouraged to excel in athletics, at the expense of academics." As another participant suggested: "There are two ways Black students are treated. High-performing athletes get attention. The rest are ignored." And many participants mentioned that Black students were being recruited to ensure success for the school's sports teams. One participant observed, "Black students like sports because when they are in sports, they get positive reinforcement. They don't get this in the classroom."

But being recognized (sometimes recruited) primarily on the basis of their athletic contributions to the school ultimately proved to work to their detriment; it did not translate into genuine care and attention to their academic success. While Black students were lauded for their athletic skills, competencies, and achievements, their academic abilities and educational potential were not similarly supported. According to several participants, Black students were allowed to continue playing on their schools' athletic teams even while having poor grades and/or not attending classes. Reflecting on this profile of Black students, one participant noted, "Teachers need to know that Black students are not thugs or just people who are good at sports."

In sessions with young people, we heard about the important role their parents played through their advocacy in helping them to resist educators' suggestions that they take Applied courses. Those who successfully resisted and were in university also credited their own persistent advocacy against being steered into Applied courses. As one young person revealed, "I was forced to fight with the guidance counsellor to stay in the Academic program." Another added: "The guidance counsellor was pushing me into Applied classes. She asked me to drop all my STEM courses. I had to stop going to the guidance counsellor and went to the VP to choose courses." But other students who were stuck in the Applied programs into which they were placed contended that in many cases their parents did not always understand the different Programs of Study and the impact that course selection would have on their opportunities to pursue postsecondary education. As such, many felt that their parents were not equipped to advocate for them and to ensure they were enrolled in courses that reflected their abilities and supported their interest in pursuing postsecondary education.

That only 0.4 per cent of Black high school students in the TDSB were identified as gifted and placed in the gifted program reflects the fact that stereotypes of Black students limited the teachers' ability to see them as academically competent individuals whose abilities, talents, and strengths went beyond music and sport. One participant remarked that "nobody knows what to do with bright Black students." Another added, "No one expects Black students to be successful." While participants in Toronto expressed concern that Black students in the TDSB were "robbed" of the opportunity to get into this enriched program, those with children in the suburban region schools insisted that if data were available, we would see that Black students in these other regions were also under-represented in gifted programs. It was noted that Black parents tended to rely on schools and the efficacy or good intentions of teachers to have their children tested for giftedness as well as special education needs (such as learning disabilities).

Despite the cultural biases inherent in gifted tests[9] – recognized as an assessment problem for Black students – Black parents sought to have their children assessed for giftedness. Several parents reported having difficulty accessing a gifted assessment, an experience that one student related in one of the sessions. Now a university student, she described her experience of coming to Canada and being placed in a grade with children of the same age "despite," as she said, "having been in school since I was two years old." She indicated that she was academically "far ahead of my classmates, and rather than being given an enriched curriculum or being evaluated for giftedness, I was simply given more of the same work to complete." She explained that in class she was bored; consequently, she slacked off and acted out. She went on to say that even though her mother repeatedly asked that she be assessed for giftedness, teachers refused. She concluded: "If my mother hadn't pulled me out of public school and enrolled me in [a private Christian school with predominantly Black students], I would not have even graduated from high school."

Participants hypothesized that, by contrast, over-representation of white students in gifted programs likely reflected their parents being better "able to lobby the teachers and principal" to assess their children. Also, given their "higher and more disposable income," white parents were more likely thought to have the financial resources to pay for independent assessments of their children.

That the gifted programs in the respective school boards tended to be located mainly in white middle-class neighbourhoods was identified as yet another barrier to access these programs for Black students. Many Black students who were assessed and identified as gifted were required to travel out of their neighbourhoods for school; and in a

---

9 Parents and educators who were familiar with the testing instruments advised that the tests, and all standardized tests, should be assessed for cultural biases.

number of cases, parents decided to have their children (who would have agreed) remain at their neighbourhood schools. Further, because of the alienating culture of gifted classes, some Black students withdrew from these programs and returned to their home schools.

Submitting that the culture of gifted programs tends to be marginalizing for Black students, some educators in the sessions wondered about the "negative effects" that placement in such programs had on students' well-being, mental health, and behaviours. One educator observed that "Black kids don't last long in gifted programs. They don't fit in with the school culture, so they choose not to come back. Or they are identified as having a behavioural issue, and they are sent back." In such circumstances, parents and students must choose between prioritizing the students' academic performance and their psychological well-being, which can be more appropriately nurtured by a school setting that is culturally relevant and responsive to their needs and interests.

Rather than being assessed for giftedness, participants suggested that Black students were more likely to be given "diagnostic tests" by which they were identified as having learning disabilities, and as a consequence were often streamed into special education programs. Even though the reliability of these "diagnostic tests" was called into question, school authorities continued to administer the tests – even going as far as to test students for learning disabilities at very early ages and, in some cases, without parental knowledge or consent. There were also occasions when teachers would "diagnose" students as having a learning disability or attention-deficit/hyperactivity disorder (ADHD) and then go on to suggest that the child be given medication. Participants reported that in these cases, the teachers' "diagnosis" was often done without any form of testing and without getting to know the child so that the teachers might better explain specific learning patterns, educational performances, and behavioural tendencies.

A significant aspect of participants' concern regarding assessment was the lack of adequate resources and support given to students once they were identified as having special learning needs. A parent wrote to us following one of our sessions:

> As the mother of an energetic eight-year-old boy, I have felt the pressure from the school board to have my son identified as having a learning disability or ADHD. The school was willing to encourage me to have him tested but were not capable of providing me with any resources to have him assessed by a professional psychometrist. Instead, they advised me that the wait list for that service would be 1–2 years. Luckily, I was able

to access a private psychometrist who was able to assess my son, but the fee was substantial, and required a great deal of financial planning on my part. The reports were thorough and provided his teachers with the tools needed to support him. Without them, he would have most definitely fallen through the cracks and not received the appropriate supports needed for him to be successful. It has been my experience that the school is willing to identify children as having special education needs, but not provide them with any tools to be successful.

Schools' inadequate or inappropriate assessment of English-language needs also came up as a problem for many Black students and their families. Students for whom English was their first language were sometimes unnecessarily placed in classes for English-language learners. Some of the university students hypothesized that their misplacement in such classes was based on the assumption that because their parents spoke English with "an accent" and came from an African country, they lacked the necessary English-language skills. Others shared that their English-language needs were not assessed. One student, who reported that she did not speak English when she entered school, said that she was assessed in English and identified as "intellectually deficient" as opposed to merely having English-language learning needs. The placement – or more to the point, misplacement – of newcomer students means that they were unable to access the appropriate educational services and much needed social supports.

The labelling of Black students' behaviours arose as yet another concern relating to placement or streaming of students. Participants suggested that such labelling contributed to the placement of some students into "behavioural classes" – a practice many said begins as early as kindergarten – which involved removing students from regular classrooms or excluded from programs such as French immersion. Some parents reported that teachers or school authorities used "behavioural problems" as the reason for such removal; in a number of cases, school superintendents used threats of expulsion ("over minor behavioural issues") to get them to "voluntarily" move their children to another school or program. The message that some participants took from this practice was that teachers did not want active, engaged Black students. On this point, one participant in the York Region session surmised that "the goal is to have docile Black students, who are quiet and do things right."

A group of participants argued that special education and behavioural classes had become "warehouses" for Black students and the process by which they were removed from regular classrooms. This process, they claimed, led to racially stratified school environments and inequitable educational outcomes. Some participants even wondered whether the overidentification of Black students as "special-needs students" was part of a strategy to increase ministry funding for the schools – funding which is then diverted into general revenues.

Essentially, participants identified the labels given to some Black students following inappropriate testing as a problem in all of the regions. Some educators expressed concern that such labelling of Black students discouraged parents from getting their children tested when indications of learning issues or problems arose. They understood parents refusing to have their children tested over fears that their children would be stigmatized and their success in school undermined. Nevertheless, some of these educators advanced the idea that an Individual Education Plan (IEP) can, in fact, help students.

The Racism of Low Expectations and the Place of Teachers in Its Normalizing Process

Stereotypes of Black students as intellectually limited and having behavioural problems contributes to the low expectations teachers and school administrators often have of them. This in turn informs educators' recommendations regarding key aspects of these students' educational trajectory – schooling programs, course selections, and educational pursuits. Having identified how stereotypes shaped educators' perceptions of Black students, participants went on to discuss how these labels and stereotypes are rooted in anti-Black racism, noting that, in the words of a York Region participant, "racism is a barrier that blocks the ability of Black students to focus on academics" (see also Javed, 2016).

Parents, students, and educators alike reported having experiences in which low expectations were openly communicated to Black students, with teachers actively discouraging Black students from working hard. One parent shared the following:

> I was appalled the first day of my son's Grade 9 math class when the teacher expressed that not all students are capable of Academic-level work. Before teaching a single class, he planted in their minds the idea that they should move down to the Applied if they found the work too challenging.

High school students at the sessions revealed what they too heard from teachers:

One teacher said, "I'm not going to bother teaching you guys because all of you are going to be back next year."

A teacher told us, "Your work is good enough for college, don't worry."

Reflecting on their experiences, other students shared that, in some cases, teachers seemed to be annoyed by their abilities, since their doing well in school challenged the teachers' long-held assumptions about Black students:

> Teachers don't seem to like Black students – especially if they do well in school without even trying.

> Some teachers interpret student engagement, such as asking questions, as a threat to their authority.

It was noted that teachers of high-achieving Black students, whose school work and educational commitment contradicted the stereotypes, often attributed their good work on submitted assignments and tests to plagiarism or cheating. As a consequence, students would be accused, sometimes in front of their classmates, of copying from their peers or having someone do their work for them. One student who helped her brother with a class assignment told of his experience with his teacher:

> My brother submitted an essay on Nelson Mandela and was told in front of the whole class that he was incapable of writing the essay. The teacher refused to mark it, because he said that it was not his work. The issue went to the principal, and the principal sided with the teacher because he said that my brother is a class clown and called him a nuisance to the school and the community.

Participants also recalled that the low grades that they and others received from teachers did not reflect the quality of their work. In some cases, they suspected that teachers gave such grades without reading the assignments. In support of this assertion, one student recalled an occasion when his teacher gave him a grade of 50 per cent for an essay; seeing no comments or corrections for spelling or grammar, he challenged the grade. This student supported his action by saying that for the same assignment his white friend received a higher grade for the essay he submitted, which the student felt was not as well written as his. In the end, the teacher agreed to regrade the essay, and this time the teacher gave him a grade of 80 per cent. Similarly, a parent reported that when she questioned the poor grade her child received on an assignment, which she felt did not reflect the quality of the work, she was told by the teacher that her child "was not an A student." The parent asked other teachers to review the assignment. Those teachers agreed with the parent and felt that the student should have received a higher grade. With experiences like these, participants agreed that students become demotivated and, as a result, put less and less effort into their school work.

The racism that leads to teachers' low expectations of Black students contributes to normalizing the process through which those students are streamed into courses below their level of ability. Participants believed this normalized expectation is sustained by a racially stratified high school system in which "Black students are always at the bottom." Reflecting on their experiences in the high schools they attended, some students shared the following:

> I went to a majority Black school, yet the awards still went to Asians.

> My school was not full of Black kids, but Applied was full of Black kids. This tells me they were picking and choosing which kids were put into Applied.

> I never saw a white kid in Applied. They were in Academic, unless they had a special need.

Several students voiced their suspicion that some of their teachers resented Black students who had the ambition to attend university:

> I didn't have issues with teachers until I said I wanted to go to university. That's when the relationships went bad.

> They told me to go to college; that it is "more realistic, practical, and attainable."

> When I got into university, one teacher was telling everyone that it was because of the principal. She said I wasn't smart enough to get into university on my own.

These comments are consistent with the negative experiences of some students with their guidance counsellors, whom they would meet with to complete their university applications. They felt that the guidance counsellors actively tried to keep them from attending university; in doing so, they would suggest college instead, "without even looking up my marks," as one student recalled. And one community member added, "The guidance system is not set up to point Black students to long-term success." This is consistent with the "minimal assistance" students said they received in the process of applying for postsecondary education, gaining an understanding of the differences between the various universities or the programs offered, and in getting to know the difference between university and college. According to two university students:

> I can see why Black students don't apply to university. We are told that "it is not for you." I would have dropped it if my parents didn't push me to apply to university.

> My guidance counsellor didn't want me to apply to the University of Toronto. When I insisted, she said, "Don't be discouraged when you don't get in."

The university students with whom we spoke indicated that they planned their school participation, academic performance, and educational outcomes not only to ensure that they obtained the grades needed to attend university but also to counteract their teachers' construct of Black students as threats, thugs, low achievers, and uneducable. According to these students, even though they achieved high grades on their assignments and tests, their teachers still saw them as intellectually limited. They suggested that their teachers "refused" to recognize their academic abilities and to engage them in their classes the way they engaged other students. They in turn refused to be discouraged. The following excerpt from a university course paper, written by a participating student about her high school experiences and shared with us, captures the experiences of many of the students:

> Whenever I would raise my hand to speak, teachers would hesitate to call on me because they couldn't quite gauge what I was going to say. More often than not, I surprised them with my grasp of class content and my understandings of the English language. Some of the things they would say were "I'm glad to see you're keeping up" or (whenever I raised my hand during discussion) "Did you have a question," as if I was constantly confused with nothing to contribute ... I find these comments demeaning and hurtful on all accounts, but on the greater scale, there's something at work here. My experience as a "Hijabi" is one that denotes how exactly these attitudes towards Muslim students are understood as part of the hidden curriculum. (Moallim, 2015)

Participants agreed that the racism of low expectations was manifested throughout the schooling process – beginning in kindergarten. They emphasized that this form of racism has particular and significant implications for Black male students, whom teachers expect to be underachievers, troublemakers, and more interested in athletics than academic work. These students are thought to be, as one person put it, "throwaway kids," unworthy of their teacher's empathy and time. Hence, when Black male students engaged in relatively minor inappropriate behaviours, the behaviours were taken to be more serious and used to push these boys or young men out of regular classrooms or, by applying suspensions, out of school altogether.[10] One parent shared an example of teachers' and administrators' treatment of Black male students in their early schooling years:

> I have found that it has been very difficult for my son. Early on, he was identified as having a speech and language delay; and due to his young age, he would become frustrated with teachers and ECEs [Early Childhood Educators] that were not trained to address his needs. When the teachers grew frustrated, they would send him to the office; at which point I would receive a phone call from the principal. There was one incident that I will never forget. The principal advised me that if my son, four years old at the time and in JK, had been in Grade 6 or 7, he would have to call the police on him for his behaviour. As shocked as I was, he said it in a very cavalier manner.

A number of participants suggested that these problems were particularly evident in schools where the teachers were predominantly white and socialized to fear Black students. Commenting on this culture of fear in her high school, one student-participant observed, "The teachers disliked Black students or feared them." Another said, "We can sense that they fear us and view us as criminals in schools."

Because of this fear, and lacking the skills and/or willingness to engage with Black students and create a positive social and learning environment conducive to educational success, teacher–student

---

10 TDSB data show that by the time Black students graduate from high school, 42 per cent of them would have been suspended at least once compared to only 18 per cent of white students (also see Rankin, Rushowy, & Brown, 2013). While data for elementary students are not available, US data for the 2013–14 school year show that even Black preschoolers are suspended 3.6 times more than their white peers (Schott Foundation for Public Education, 2016).

relationships remain antagonistic and difficult. Participants therefore expressed concerns about Black students who attend schools with a substantial population of Black students but where the teachers are mostly white. They wondered: If white teachers were afraid of Black students, why would they be assigned to schools with a large population of Black students? And why would they choose to work in such schools?

Participants admitted that it might not always be possible for the teaching staff to mirror the diversity of the student population, but they felt it critical for educators and staff to have the skills, abilities, and desire to work in culturally diverse and marginalized communities. Therefore, they insisted that more needs to be done to create a diverse teaching workforce that reflects or at least approximates the increasingly diverse student population. Participating students decisively affirmed this contention, with some saying that they had had only one or two Black teachers, while others reported that they had not had a single Black teacher over their entire public-school career in GTA schools.

Relatedly, students reported that the few Black teachers in their schools were often assigned the responsibility of disciplining Black students. Consequently, many of these students' interactions with these Black disciplinarian teachers tended to be negative. Similarly, the only interactions that these Black teachers had with a number of Black students were also negative.

This was submitted as a concern for the students, because their interactions with Black teachers likely contributed to these teachers forming negative impressions of them. Additionally, the students asserted that since Black teachers are critical to creating safe and positive environments in schools with large numbers of Black students, more Black teachers needed to be hired. This was not merely to be role models or mentors, but to offset the one Black teacher or few Black teachers having to address the issues of Black students and to counter the negative construct of Black students and related expectations.

Throughout the consultations, many people spoke about the positive role that Black teachers have played and will likely continue to play in counteracting the commonly held stereotypes about Black students' educational abilities and skills.[11] It was suggested that while racial

---

11 A Johns Hopkins University study found that having a Black teacher reduces the chances of dropping out of high school by 39 per cent and increases interest in pursuing postsecondary education by 29 per cent (Gershenson, Lindsay, Hart, & Papageorge, 2017). In fact, it was shown that low-income Black students who have at least one Black teacher in elementary school are significantly more likely to graduate from high school. According to co-researcher Nicholas Papageorge, "We're

representation is important and that all students need to see capable and compassionate teachers and school administrators of all racial backgrounds, Black teachers' presence in schools goes far beyond the symbolic. Parents shared the excitement their children expressed for school when they had a Black teacher and recounted the impact Black teachers had on their children's learning. Further, they felt that the high academic and behavioural expectations that Black educators had for Black students[12] meant that these teachers would go out of their way to support Black students' successes (Turner, 2015); in turn, these students' academic performance was enhanced. The following comments of two students speak to this sentiment:

> Black teachers made an effort for us. They went above and beyond to help us succeed.
>
> I had one Black teacher, and it was the greatest game changer.

Nevertheless, a Black teacher shared that "Black teachers are afraid to advocate for students for fear of losing their jobs."

Understandably, the conversations among participants – particularly in the two Toronto sessions – turned to the value of a school focused on Black students. People spoke about the significant effect the Africentric Alternative School had in fostering high expectations of Black students. Participants talked about the benefits and value of Black students seeing themselves reflected in the curriculum and having school administrators and teachers who believe in them. In praising the school, one parent said:

---

seeing spending just one year with a teacher of the same race can move the dial on one of the most frustratingly persistent gaps in education attainment – that of low-income black boys. It not only moves the dial, it moves the dial in a powerful way" (Rosen, 2017).

12 A Yale University study found that Black teachers tend to have more positive perceptions of Black students. This contributes to their more positive relationship with and assessments of Black students, as well as their view of Black students' approaches to learning, self-control, and other behaviours. The study also shows that Black students are three times more likely to be identified as gifted by a Black teacher than a white teacher (Nicholson-Crotty, Grissom, Nicholson-Crotty, & Redding, 2016). Furthermore, when comparing Black and white teachers' assessment of the same student's abilities, Gershenson, Holt, and Papageorge (2016) found (also a US study) that white teachers were 40 per cent less likely to expect the Black students to graduate from high school and 30 per cent less likely to predict that they will complete university.

> The Africentric school is a place that fosters a sense of pride and not a sense of being a minority. Children benefit from being the centre of the conversation. Their mental wellness is supported by seeing themselves reflected within the curriculum and the school family. There should be an Africentric school in the east [area of Toronto].

At the Durham Region session, a parent whose daughter attended the Africentric school in Toronto commented on the impact the school has had on her child: "She raves about the experience. Her academic performance has improved, and her self-esteem has as well."

In signalling that what we were hearing from parents, students, and community members was generally true, a number of educators, school administrators, and board staff in each region commented that they did not need quantitative data to know that there are disparities in the treatment of Black students in their schools. They felt that the stark differences in the racial makeup of gifted, behavioural, and special education classes offer sufficient evidence of a problem – a systemic problem that has simmered for years and desperately needs to be addressed. Suggesting that the TDSB data represent the situation of Black students in school boards across the GTA, participants asked why a 69 per cent graduation rate for Black students was not enough to elicit alarm bells across all school boards and gain the Ministry of Education's attention. According to participants, allowing these outcomes to continue for decades has allowed them to become normalized and entrenched. They felt that educators used Black students' poor educational outcomes to justify their marginalization in the schools and to support prevailing stereotypes about them, rather than to highlight a problem with the education system.

Contrary to the stereotypes, participants argued that Black children begin kindergarten with ambition, confidence, excitement to learn, and high self-esteem, but are "gradually worn down" by teachers' attitudes towards them and by the education system in general. They noted that without a firm grounding in academics and study skills and confidence in their ability to learn during their elementary- and middle-school years, Black students are likely to fail in high school. Given the current schooling context, it was assumed that by the time Black students enter high school, many have internalized the negative messages the education system has been sending them, and therefore resigned themselves to those low expectations. Participants expressed concern that by high school, some Black students are so far behind their peers academically that they are unable to compete successfully.

Discussion and Conclusion

When asked to share a message they would like passed on to educators about what they should know and understand about Black students and parents, participating students responded with the following:

> Black students are not dumb, have behavioural issues, and come from broken homes. Black students are also bright and important.

> We are equally capable. We are equally able to succeed. We just need fair treatment and support.

> Black students are capable of performing at the highest level. If provided with adequate resources and support, we too can succeed.

> We don't bite. Invest some time, and you might find we're just like any other student.

> Your investment, passion, and love for learning matters to us.

> Black parents care about their children's academic success. They want them to excel in their studies without the fear of being marginalized in the school system due to their socio-economic status or ethnicity.

> Teachers should know that Black parents do care about their children's education and so should the teacher. End the stereotype that Black parents don't care about their children's education, causing you not to care too.

> You should know that Black parents trust you. They trust the system too much, and they are not thinking that anything could go wrong. When they seem like they don't care because they don't show up to meetings to talk about their child's success, it's because they think you know more than them. Parents need to know that you need them to help, so ask for their help.

These students' assertions and appeals point to their desire, and that of most participants in the seven consultation sessions, that their "difference" be recognized and respected – but not used to set them apart from other students. For like other students they, as their parents have advocated, have a desire to learn, are capable of learning, and have the ability to intellectually perform like any other students. While they contended that their parents often have too much trust and faith in the education system and too often believed teachers over their children when issues arose, they nevertheless understood that there is little beyond the existing education system. Given that, they want their caring parents not to "trust the system," which fosters the stereotypes to which they are subjected. They also suggest that Black parents need to become fully involved in their schooling, and in doing so come to better understand the school system and how to effectively engage with teachers – through questioning and advocating for their children's right to a high-quality education. The students offer these suggestions as ways to improve parent–teacher–school partnerships, thereby building and fostering positive relationships.

The students' experiences – like those of their parents, teachers, and community members – are mediated by the "web of stereotypes" (Howard, 2008) nestled within the "epistemological arm of white supremacy" (Zuberi & Bonilla-Silva, 2008) that serve to construct their "difference." Students and parents alike wish educators would recognize how the "white racial frame" (Feagin, 2006) produces the "white logic" that sustains educators' thinking about Black students – as dumb, as incapable of learning, as having behavioural issues, as coming from broken homes, and as individuals to be feared. All of this contributes to poor and unfair grades, leading to other negative school experiences and unfair treatments, such as unwarranted suspensions, which often go unquestioned, unchallenged, and hence unaddressed. They appeal to educators to invest in these students, treat them equitably in relation to other students, believe that they are just as capable as others of excelling academically, and know that with adequate resources and teachers' support they can successfully graduate from high school and move forward.

The stories students and parents shared not only helped to personalize the TDSB data, they also served to affirm how racial stereotyping of Black students contributes to the racial stratification we observe in classrooms – with Black students concentrated in Applied and Essential Programs of Study and in special education and behavioural classes. The resulting racial disparities account for, among other things, the high academic failures, the low number of Black TDSB students entering and graduating from university, and high dropout and stop-out rates (see chapter 2 of this volume).[13]

---

13 It is therefore understandable that the schooling and educational profile of Black students – especially Black males – would lead to their interactions with police inside school buildings and the community (see Na & Gottfredson, 2013).

The dominant logic of the white racial frame would have us seeing the problems as evidence of the failings of students and their parents rather than of our public social and educational institutions – in which educational workers and policymakers do not recognize or reflect on systemic issues. As one African-Canadian participant said to the Four-Level Government/African Canadian Community Working Group created in 1992 to develop an action plan following the uprising or so-called Yonge Street riot, "The school system seems to have a built-in deafness; it doesn't hear what it doesn't want to hear" (Four-Level Government/African Canadian Community Working Group, 1992, p. 75).

Dropout rates provide an indication of future life chances for Black students, given that failure to obtain a high school diploma significantly reduces one's chances of securing a good job and creating a promising future (Crenshaw, 2015, p. 8). The high social cost associated with failure to complete high school connects to the likelihood of low-wage jobs, precarious employment or high unemployment, and reliance on social assistance, public housing, and other public services, and also to involvement in the justice/correctional system. One US study quantified the cost of a student not completing high school and calculated the public cost – from lost tax revenue, increased health care costs, and increased criminal justice expenses – to be USD$755,000 over the life of each student (Rumberger & Losen, 2016). This highlights the importance of keeping students in school and supporting their educational success.

Finally, we must also focus our attention and efforts beyond the public-school system. While the postsecondary students who participated in the study forcefully recounted their high school challenges, they also expressed their concern that little attention is being paid to their experiences in Ontario colleges and universities. They shared feelings of isolation within their programs, lack of engagement with curricula that teach and reinforce anti-Black racism, and alienation from campuses on which they experienced anti-Black racism.

While these students were organizing conferences for Black high school students to encourage and support them to pursue postsecondary education, they wished for the same support and encouragement for themselves. In the meantime, Black student groups at both the University of Toronto and York University have issued demands for these universities to acknowledge and address the anti-Black racism that students experience. The following are among their demands: the collection of disaggregated race-based student and faculty data, addressing the under-representation of Black students and Black faculty, and providing culturally appropriate mental health services for Black students.

REFERENCES

Crenshaw, K.W. (with Ocen, P., & Nanda, J.). (2015). *Black girls matter: Pushed out, overpoliced, and underprotected*. New York, NY: African American Policy Forum & Columbia Law School, Center for Intersectionality and Social Policy Studies. http://www.law.columbia.edu/null/download?&exclusive =filemgr.download&file_id=613546

Feagin, J.R. (2006). *Systemic racism: A theory of oppression*. New York, NY: Routledge.

Four-Level Government/African Canadian Community Working Group. (1992). *Towards a new beginning: The report and action plan*. Toronto, ON: City of Toronto.

Gershenson, S., Holt, S.B., & Papageorge, N.W. (2016). Who believes in me? The effect of student-teacher demographic match on teacher expectations. *Economics of Education Review, 52*, 209–24. https://doi.org/10.1016 /j.econedurev.2016.03.002

Gershenson, S., Lindsay, C.A., Hart, C.M.D., & Papageorge, N.W. (2017, March). *The long-run impacts of same-race teachers*. Discussion paper 10630. Bonn, Germany: IZA Institute of Labor Economics. http://legacy.iza.org /en/webcontent/publications/papers/viewAbstract?dp_id=10630

Gillborn, D. (2015). Intersectionality, critical race theory and the primacy of racism: Race, class, gender and disability in education. *Qualitative Inquiry, 21*(3), 277–87. https://doi.org/10.1177/1077800414557827

Government of Ontario. (2017). *A better way forward: Ontario's 3-year anti-racism strategic plan*. Toronto, ON: Queen's Printer for Ontario. https://www.ontario .ca/page/better-way-forward-ontarios-3-year-anti-racism-strategic-plan

Gray, E., Bailey, R., Brady, J., & Tecle, S. (2016, September). *Perspectives of Black male students in secondary school: Understanding the successes and challenges*. Mississauga, ON: Peel District School Board.

Howard, T.C. (2008). Who really cares? The disenfranchisement of African American males in preK–12 schools: A critical race theory perspective. *Teachers College Record, 110*(5), 954–85.

James, C.E. (2019, March). *We rise together: A report to the Peel District School Board*. Toronto, ON: York University, Faculty of Education, Jean Augustine Chair in Education, Community & Diaspora.

James, C.E., & Turner, T. (2015). *Fighting an uphill battle: Report on the consultations into the well-being of Black youth in Peel Region*. Mississauga, ON: FACES of Peel Collaborative. http://www.bcanpeel.com/wp-content /uploads/2016/11/fighting-an-uphill-battle-sm.pdf

James, C.E., & Turner, T. (with George, R., & Tecle, S.). (2017, April). *Towards race equity in education: The schooling of Black students in the Greater Toronto Area*. Toronto, ON: York University, Faculty of Education, Jean Augustine

Chair in Education, Community & Diaspora. http://edu.yorku.ca/files/2017/04/Towards-Race-Equity-in-Education-April-2017.pdf

Javed, N. (2016, December 2). Parents file human rights complaint against York school board. *Toronto Star*. https://www.thestar.com/yourtoronto/education/2016/12/02/parents-file-human-rights-complaint-against-york-school-board.html

Ladson-Billings, G., & Tate, W.F. (1995). Toward a critical race theory of education. *Teachers College Record*, 9(1), 47–68.

Moallim, B.A. (2015). *Caught being Black, Muslim and a woman at school: Mapping my schooling experience* [Unpublished manuscript], University of Toronto, Toronto, ON.

Na, C., & Gottfredson, D.C. (2013). Police officers in schools: Effects on school crime and the processing of offending behaviors. *Justice Quarterly*, 30(4), 619–50. https://doi.org/10.1080/07418825.2011.615754

Nicholson-Crotty, S., Grissom, J.A., Nicholson-Crotty, J., & Redding, C. (2016). Disentangling the causal mechanisms of representative bureaucracy; Evidence from assignment of students to gifted programs. *Journal of Public Administration Research and Theory*, 26(4), 745–57. https://doi.org/10.1093/jopart/muw024

Rankin, J., Rushowy, K., & Brown, L. (2013, March 22). Toronto school suspension rates highest for Black and Aboriginal students. *Toronto Star*. https://www.thestar.com/news/gta/2013/03/22/toronto_school_suspension_rates_highest_for_black_and_aboriginal_students.html

Rosen, J. (2017, April 2). Black students who have at least one Black teacher are more likely to graduate. *Johns Hopkins Magazine*. http://hub.jhu.edu/2017/04/05/black-teachers-improve-student-graduation-college-access/

Rumberger, R.W., & Losen, D.J. (2016). *The high cost of harsh discipline and its disparate impact*. Los Angeles, CA: University of California, Los Angeles, Civil Rights Project, Center for Civil Rights Remedies. https://www.civilrightsproject.ucla.edu/resources/projects/center-for-civil-rights-remedies/school-to-prison-folder/federal-reports/the-high-cost-of-harsh-discipline-and-its-disparate-impact/UCLA_HighCost_6-2_948.pdf

Schott Foundation for Public Education. (2016, October 24). The school-to-prison pipeline starts in preschool [Blog post]. http://schottfoundation.org/blog/2016/10/24/school-prison-pipeline-starts-preschool

Spencer, J. (2016a, November 24). Student census coming to Peel board, data on race, sexual orientation could be collected. *Mississauga News*. http://www.mississauga.com/news-story/6983871-student-census-coming-to-peel-board-data-on-race-sexual-orientation-could-be-collected/

Spencer, J. (2016b, December 14). Student survey to drill down into equity issues in Catholic board. *Mississauga News*. http://www.mississauga.com/news-story/7020301-student-survey-to-drill-down-into-equity-issues-in-catholic-board/

Szekely, R., & Pessian P. (2015a, August 6). *Parents warn black youth are being racially profiled in Durham schools.* DurhamRegion.com. https://www.durhamregion.com/news-story/5787027-parents-warn-black-youth-are-being-racially-profiled-in-durham-schools/

Szekely, R., & Pessian P. (2015b, August 6). *Ontario Human Rights Tribunal finds there is a "racial disparity" in Durham.* DurhamRegion.com. https://www.durhamregion.com/community-story/5787114-ontario-human-rights-tribunal-finds-there-is-a-racial-disparity-in-durham/

Toronto District School Board. (2017, April). *Expulsion decision-making process and expelled students' transition experience in the Toronto District School Board's caring and safe school programs and their graduation outcomes.* Toronto, ON: Toronto District School Board, Research and Information Services.

Turner, T. (2015). *Voices of Ontario Black educators: An experiential report.* Toronto, ON: Ontario Alliance of Black School Educators. http://onabse.org/ONABSE_VOICES_OF_BLACK_EDUCATORS_Final_Report.pdf

United Nations Human Rights Office of the High Commissioner. (2016). *Statement to the media by the United Nations' Working Group of Experts on People of African Descent, on the conclusion of its official visit to Canada, 17–21 October 2016.* http://www.ohchr.org/EN/NewsEvents/Pages/DisplayNews.aspx?NewsID=20732&LangID=E#sthash.ipnZs5h7.dpuf

York Region District School Board. (2015, December 8). Collection of student demographic data. https://yrdsb.civicweb.net/document/55359

Yosso, T.J. (2005). Whose culture has capital? A critical race theory discussion of community cultural wealth. *Race Ethnicity and Education, 8*(1), 69–91. https://doi.org/10.1080/1361332052000341006

Zuberi, T., & Bonilla-Silva, E. (2008). Telling the real tale of the hunt: Toward a race conscious sociology of racial stratification. In T. Zuberi & E. Bonilla-Silva (Eds.), *White logic, white methods: Racism and methodology* (pp. 329–41). Lanham, MD: Rowman & Littlefield.

Response to Chapter 10

"I Will Treat All My Students with Respect": The Limits of Good Intentions

LEANNE TAYLOR
Faculty of Education, Brock University, Ontario, Canada

Not long ago, my goddaughter Jade (pseudonym), currently a Grade 12 student in an Ontario school, told me she did not think she was cut out for college or university. "I'm not sure it's for me," she explained. To some, such a comment may not seem especially problematic. I am sure that at some point or another many students, unsure of what to expect, ask this question about postsecondary education. But I read Jade's comments differently. Jade is a young Black woman whose entire schooling experience has been informed by a racist system that has bombarded her, subtly and overtly, with a host of negative messages. Perhaps being her godmother has heightened my concern. But from my perspective as a university professor who teaches student teachers about issues of equity and about racism and other forms of oppression, her remark and experiences highlight deeper structural barriers. Jade's story bears striking resemblance to the stories articulated in chapter 10, and I reflect on it in relation to teacher candidates' responses to the report *Towards Race Equity in Education: The Schooling of Black Students in the Greater Toronto Area* (James & Turner, 2017), from which James constructed the chapter.

When Low Expectations Negate Good Intentions

I recall Jade's first overtly racist experience at school. She was eight years old when she was called "Black trash" by a white student. When Jade showed a reluctance to return to school, teachers did not address the issue, and her mother intervened and arranged a meeting with the principal. The principal did not investigate the issue further, but instead expressed concern that Jade was an overly sensitive child. The principal explained that "kids say all sorts of things," suggested the incident may have been misinterpreted, and admonished Jade and her mom for "crying racism" because of hurt feelings. Shortly after this incident I accompanied Jade's mom to a parent–teacher interview night. After a general discussion with the teacher about Jade's academic performance in class (she was an A student), I asked the teacher how she had supported Jade through her recent experience of racism and her subsequent reservations about attending school. She stiffened at my question and adjusted her posture in her chair, explaining, "We take diversity seriously here and do not tolerate negative behaviour." With a sweeping hand gesture she drew my attention to the brightly decorated walls and bulletin boards, multicultural books, and posters of Black and Brown faces: "As you can see, we do everything we can to ensure all students feel safe and welcome." I got the message that I was meant to have faith in the curriculum, and in her good intentions.

I would argue that this was Jade's first lesson that teachers will not always advocate for her in times of crisis; that bringing up race and racism will create discomfort and may position her as a troublemaker; and that questioning teachers' practices, and by extension their curriculum, pedagogy, and otherwise good intentions might be to her detriment. But as Jade moved through elementary school, her faith in school and in her teachers continued to waver. By Grade 8, despite her good grades, her guidance counsellor told her to take mostly Applied stream courses (including English and math). The teacher explained that high school would be difficult, and, if Jade wanted to succeed and avoid unwanted stress and anxiety, she should not take too many Academic stream classes. Jade obliged. By Grade 11, she realized that she might want to become a teacher but was lacking the requisite course requirements for university. She spent the next two years, begrudgingly, retaking her Applied courses at the Academic level to "catch up." By Grade 12, her frustration turned to anger as teachers increasingly told her to tone down her views, politics, and personality; respect teacher authority; adhere more closely to dress code policies; and rein in her "Angela Davis" attitude. Now in her final year of high school, after years of negotiating the racism of low expectations and challenges to her identity, Jade is questioning whether a postsecondary education is "for her."

Student Teachers' Reactions to Inequity: "It Comes Down to Individual Teachers Who Care"

I find it useful to consider Jade's story and the stories articulated in chapter 10 alongside my experiences teaching a compulsory course in "Diversity Issues in Schooling" at Brock University to second-year education students. The course is designed to teach students about systems of inequity and power in schooling, inclusive practices, and strategies for change. Last year (2018), I assigned *Towards Race Equity in Education: The Schooling of Black Students in the Greater Toronto Area* as required reading, in part because students are often quick to dismiss articles and readings that are not Canadian, using them to bolster their claims that racism is less pervasive here. I used the report as a way to highlight student, parent, teacher, and community voices, to shed light on the concerns of Black youth and their experiences in school, and to expose the impact of structural racism in Canada's education system – noting the discriminatory policies that systematically marginalize racialized youth.

The student teachers' immediate reactions to the report included expressions of surprise and anger that there has been so little progress made to address racism in schools. One student remarked, "I thought we were supposed to be past this?" Another asserted, "I honestly never thought that this was happening here – not really. I honestly had no idea." The student teachers also turned their attention to what they saw as the failures of individual teachers and educators whom they suggested were morally responsible for guiding and supporting students. They condemned the actions of teachers who were reported, for example, to have assigned Black students lower grades than their white peers and perpetuated stereotypes that limited their opportunities. One student explained that she never thought teachers "could be so biased" in that they would encourage Black students to take Applied courses. She said, "Streaming is not supposed to happen anymore – so why would teachers do that? It's so maddening." Appalled that such overt bias existed, the student teachers claimed that they would make sure they did not do the same thing in their practice. However, in suggesting that teachers need to "do better" by being more tolerant and fair, they were failing to acknowledge and understand how hierarchical structures of education sustain the race privileges that teachers exercise (Schick & St. Denis, 2003).

The data and counterstories presented in the report forced students, at the very least, to confront their lack of knowledge about how racism operates in schools. It seemed they were grappling with how students' and parents' counterstories challenged their liberal multicultural and meritocratic beliefs that uphold schooling as fundamentally good, curriculum as positive, and the majority of teachers as well-intentioned. Although they did not see schooling as perfect, these student teachers were surprised to learn that, in a context where we are "all supposed to be learning the same thing" and "have the same opportunities," there could be such inequitable access to resources, racialized differences in success, and blatant racism in schools. And they vowed that they would "not let racism play a role in my teaching" and that "racism won't be an issue in my classroom because I will treat all my students with respect." They indicated that they would do this by bringing in more diverse curriculum, celebrating differences, and treating their students "the same."

During the class discussion, I thought about my goddaughter Jade's experience with her teachers and decided to ask the class how they think teachers can use the data in the report to inform the way they engage with students and plan their classes. Students had a lot to say. Some questioned whether they, as mostly white students, have the knowledge to really be doing this work at all. They worried about saying the wrong thing and felt paralyzed by guilty feelings connected to their growing awareness of their privilege. Some expressed frustration: "How can we change anything if the institutions are so racist – where do I even start?"

After class, Nabil (pseudonym), one of only two Black students in the class of forty, came to me and disclosed that this was the most relevant class he had taken during his time in university. "This report really got me thinking," he said. "It basically explained my entire experience in school." Looking around to see if other students were in earshot, he continued: "I barely made it here. I had no idea whether I should or could come to university or not." Nabil then went on to offer a profound critique of teachers: "The students in this teaching program need to understand what they will be facing in the classroom as teachers." And he added, "I worry sometimes. Most of them have no idea; they have no idea the kind of damage they can do if they don't take this stuff seriously." I asked him what he felt teachers should take more seriously. He replied,

> I was lucky. I had a Black teacher who cared. He knew what I was going through. He took time to know my family, where I lived, and what mattered to me. Teachers – Black or white – need to know what kids' lives are about. It can't just be about curriculum ... At the end of the day they need to actually get their hands dirty and be there for their students every day.

I understand Nabil's concern, for we know that the majority of teachers entering the profession are white, middle-class women (Ryan, Pollock, & Antonelli, 2009) who often struggle with making the shift from being unaware of their whiteness and privilege to a critical appreciation of the role power, culture, and oppression play in their lives and in schools (Picower, 2009). Although many teacher educators, like myself, try to help student teachers develop critical consciousness about racialization, we must at the same time fight against an imposing "neoliberal multiculturalism" (Darder, 2012) that centres individuals, preserves colour blindness, secures the myth of meritocracy, and encourages palatable and easily digestible approaches that cater to "fragile" white consumers (DiAngelo, 2011). As in many teacher education classes, the majority of my students are over-representative of the dominant group. They often hold good intentions and want to do right by their students, but they routinely express discomfort when addressing race and racism, confronting their privileges, and engaging racialized students in ways that might, as Nabil said, "get their hands dirty."

Not all felt "stuck," however. Some were optimistic. For example, although the report "opened their eyes" and tended to be "surprising," various students admitted it helped them to better understand institutional racism and how policies and administrative processes can be racist. They started to think about how documents and policies might need to be adjusted to reflect the stories they were reading about. Many seemed to understand from the report that school approaches need to reflect students' lives and experiences. They recognized the importance of the data for thinking about family and community differently and discussed with passion the need for schools, teachers, and principals to use this information in their practice and "just listen to the kids." On some level, they understood the report as a "call to action" and noted the value in hearing students' voices, feeling that the stories "make it more real."

Final Thoughts

I do not believe that one twelve-week course on diversity is enough. There is only so much anyone can do in one course. Students need to understand the context, history, and importance of anti-Black racism and the principles of critical theories of race and racism, so they can at least recognize racism and consider how to address it. They need this training throughout their programs. In the end, if teachers – like Jade's teacher – cannot name racism, continue to believe in and prioritize celebratory approaches in their teaching, and do not stand up for their students or address the systemic inequities that permeate schooling, change will remain elusive. In my class, I try to connect theory and research to stories like Jade's and those of others to remind student teachers (especially young white students) of the everyday lives and experiences of those they will one day teach. I help them to develop language so that they are able to dialogue more effectively with colleagues and students about racism and student achievement. I try to illustrate how and why their words, actions, and knowledge matter as much as or more than just the content of the courses, and I try to demonstrate that fairness is about more than advocating a multicultural classroom or celebrating diversity.

If we do not address the complex ways in which racism is embedded within every social system and structure, we will be not only unable to address inequities in schools but also be at risk of reinforcing them. If we are to truly understand and address Black students' success, we need to understand how community, home, and educators contribute to their experiences and identities. For me, the collection of stories presented in chapter 10 – much like Nabil's and Jade's – serve as important reminders of the urgent need for action. Their stories motivate me to do the work I do in the classroom and beyond.

REFERENCES

DiAngelo, R. (2011). White fragility. *International Journal of Critical Pedagogy*, 3(3), 54–70. https://libjournal.uncg.edu/ijcp/article/view/249

Darder, A. (2012). Neoliberalism in the academic borderlands: An on-going struggle for equality and human rights. *Educational Studies*, 48(5), 412–26. https://doi.org/10.1080/00131946.2012.714334

James, C.E., & Turner, T. (with George, R., & Tecle, S.). (2017, April). *Towards race equity in education: The schooling of Black students in the Greater Toronto Area*. Toronto, ON: York University, Faculty of Education, Jean Augustine Chair in Education, Community & Diaspora. http://edu.yorku.ca/files/2017/04/Towards-Race-Equity-in-Education-April-2017.pdf

Picower, B. (2009). The unexamined whiteness of teaching: How white teachers maintain and enact dominant racial ideologies. *Race Ethnicity and Education*, 12(2), 197–215. https://doi.org/10.1080/13613320902995475

Ryan, J., Pollock, K., & Antonelli, F. (2009). Teacher diversity in Canada: Leaky pipelines, bottlenecks, and glass ceilings. *Canadian Journal of Education*, 32(3), 591–617. https://journals.sfu.ca/cje/index.php/cje-rce/article/view/3053

Schick, C., & St. Denis, V. (2003). What makes anti-racist pedagogy in teacher education difficult? Three popular ideological assumptions. *Alberta Journal of Education Research*, 49(1), 55–69. https://journalhosting.ucalgary.ca/index.php/ajer/issue/view/4442

Epilogue

MICHELE A. JOHNSON
Department of History, York University, Ontario, Canada

In this examination of the "experiences, issues, and concerns of Black youth" based on research conducted over a period of more than two decades, Carl James opens a series of windows on the "gendered, complicated, shifting and challenging paths" along which the youth and their families must tread and analyses the disheartening resilience of the anti-Black racism which they encounter in a variety of contexts. Focusing on multiple and overlapping manifestations and articulations of race-based discrimination and prejudice, especially within the parameters of "the hegemonic schooling structures [which] have mediated the educational experiences and outcomes of Black students," James's interrogations of the experiences of Black students begin in the 1970s, run through the last portion of the twentieth century, and end in 2016–19. This comprehensive evaluation – which offers a closer scrutiny of the experiences of Black male students – probes the "social construction of African-Canadian males as 'at-risk' students," as athletes, and as individuals supposedly in need of direction, correction, and control. James is able to further his definitive arguments through his use of a series of longitudinal studies that allow access into the development of individuals' life expectations and experiences as well as assessments of the impacts of socio-historical contexts.

The publication is further enriched by the scrutiny offered to James's arguments, methodologies, and conclusions by scholars who have been invited to offer reflections on the chapters. In addition to commenting on the book's chapters, this epilogue seizes the opportunity to comment on James's comprehensive treatment of wide-ranging data that cover a significant period of time, as well as the scholarly conversations that introduce additional layers, perspectives, comparisons, suggestions, and nuances to an important series of considerations.

In chapter 1, James begins with a historical treatment of education among Blacks in Canada by examining the experiences of Black

Caribbean migrants to Canada in the 1970s and 1980s who, despite their high aspirations for success in educational pursuits and careers, tended to be disappointed with their achievements. He contends that while arguments were offered about the migrants' poor adjustment and psychological problems, lack of ability, and poor social conditions (especially parenting), which supposedly led to their congregation in lower-school levels, vocational training, and special education, the (almost) identical experiences of the extant African-Canadian population challenged the trope of the maladjusted Black migrant. As he makes clear, with few attempts to address their concerns, Black students became increasingly discouraged, resistant to school authorities, and disengaged from the academic process, which resulted in levels of educational achievement that were far less than ideal. As the charges of racism in the school systems grew ever louder, as community organizations advocated on behalf of the youth and families, and as recommendations of various reports sought policies and programs from school boards (including an end to streaming and the deleterious effects of a "multicultural" education which left racist structures and sentiments intact), an aura of neglect, despair, and failure settled on large portions of the community as schools continued to fail Black students.

In her response to chapter 1, Funké Aladejebi supports James's conclusions, but also urges an expansion of his analysis to include African Canadian communities in southwestern Ontario – in order to include a discussion of the occurrence of separate (segregated) schools – as well as the experiences of Black youth in Montreal and those of continental African students, who are often neglected by researchers. Further, Aladejebi argues that while James envisions possibilities in an Afrocentric approach to education and focuses on the activities of students, families, and the wider community, the chapter included limited data on Black girls and Black female educators, many of whom offered support to Black youth and created resistive pedagogies, even in the face of institutional and personal hostilities.

There is little doubt that James's discussion would have benefited from a more robust and consistent inclusion of the experiences of Black females (both as students and teachers), and that a geographical expansion would have tested his conclusions from a wider frame. It might also have been helpful to extend the "historical" foundations of the chapter into the eighteenth and nineteenth centuries to capture the long histories of absented, segregated, under-resourced, neglected, and restricted educational options available to Black children and youth, which contributed to the limitations on their career and life possibilities. In addition, laying deeper historical foundations would have interrupted the portrayal of the Black presence in Canada as defined by the difficulties of relatively recent migrations of inherently "problematic" foreigners.

Some of the concerns Aladejebi outlines are answered in the following chapter where James mines data from the Student Census (2011), compiled by the Toronto District School Board (TDSB), regarding Black students' experiences (including Programs of Study, graduation status, and postsecondary education) through the lens of gender, students' families' country of origin, and the length of their residence (by generation) in Canada. After a comprehensive analysis, James concludes that while second-generation Black students were performing better than the first, third-generation students were performing worst. In addition, he argues that Black students are less likely than others to be identified as gifted, to be encouraged to pursue advanced programs, and to graduate; generally, they have poorer educational outcomes than white or other racialized groups. None of this is helped, James argues, by a consistent lack of relevant curriculum and culturally skilled teachers.

In her engagement with the data and James's arguments in chapter 2, Shirley Anne Tate's reponse endorses his conclusions and explanations for the poor performances of Black students: double consciousness, complex interrelationships of generational status, gender, and social, economic, and political context; and the impact of school and classroom, including a lack of relevant curriculum, culturally skilled teachers, and inclusive pedagogy. Tate's comparison with the similar experiences of Black British Caribbean students, especially boys (in a country that considers itself "post-race") offers an international context for James's discussion. For her, institutional racism in UK schooling is widely accepted; indeed, "its persistence has led to it being also taken as a given within the educational system so that if against all odds Black boys achieve then they are exceptions and performing above the expectation of their group." She argues that there is a lack of political will to rectify the situation, and similar to their Black Canadian counterparts, British Black youth experience an achievement gap, are more likely to be temporarily and permanently excluded from school, and have a low presence in university. In Tate's assessment, poor leadership from head teachers, institutional racism, stereotyping, teachers' low expectations, curriculum irrelevance and barriers, lack of workplace diversity, and a lack of targeted support combine to ensure poor educational results for Black children and youth and their continued placement in the basement of most occupational pyramids. Since the groups with whom Tate is concerned (descendants of Black Caribbean migrants) mirror those who are the focus of James's analyses, the similarities of their arguments and conclusions serve to bolster both. As with James, Tate's reflections indicate that researchers tend to focus on Black boys; there is a great need to redress the balance in the scholarship and, as importantly, to pay attention to the experiences of youth whose experiences do not conform to the expectations, ideologies, and performances of normative gender categories.

Using the ideas that emerge from the assessment of the TDSB's data, in chapter 3 James presents a longitudinal study with a young man, "Mark," in the "1.5 generation" through a series of interviews (in 2001, 2002, 2007, and 2013). Using this method, James is able to trace an individual's experiences of migration and settlement; educational and occupational expectations and outcomes; and the roles of parents, teachers, coaches and peers; as well as a sense of belonging, processes of acculturation, and the (re)construction of identity. To this innovative analytical frame, James adds another layer by including a response to the chapter from "Mark." This not only gives him a chance for reflection and clarification, but – as is seldom the case – an opportunity to complete the cycle of research. This study serves to confirm, in the life of a "real" person, the larger conclusions explored by James's sociological methodologies; it offers insight into the significant gains in unravelling complexities that might be made by long-term studies. However, it also confirms James's focus on the experiences of Black males. A similar, parallel study of a Black female or other gender categories would have allowed for other means to give voice to the complexity of Black experiences.

If James's focus is on "Mark," in her response to chapter 3, Amoaba Gooden shifts the emphasis to the motivations, sacrifices, contributions, and framing experiences of Mark's mother, Brenda, and his othermothers, including his grandmother (who looked after him for five years) and his Grade 8 teacher (who was also a female Caribbean migrant). She points out that Brenda was one of the many Black Caribbean women engaged in a gendered model of migration and argues that "Mark's narrative ... must be understood within the context of his mother's love, her temporary transnational mothering, and her strategy of using migration to seek a better life for herself and her sons." It was Brenda's mothering that created the context for Mark's life that James follows so closely; as Gooden contends, if Mark knew that life in Canada would be challenging because of his "skin colour," it was Brenda who "taught her sons to be race-conscious."

Opening more widely the intersected prisms of race, gender, and class to reflect on the experiences of migration, settlement, and growing up Black in Canada, Gooden considers her "own experiences as a 1.5 generation immigrant young woman athlete with working-class parents," and gestures towards how studies about similar experiences might address "the knowledge gaps and silence in the academic scholarship relating to the experiences of Black female students." This is absolutely critical because, as Gooden points out, while they might share important experiences that are "grounded in historical complexities, we also know that racialized girls and boys experience migration and settlement differently." In her discussions of the differential experiences of individual mentoring and institutional support, Gooden points to "intersectional inequities that occur along gender, race, class, and citizenship lines, and that contribute to devaluing people of African descent." As she argues, when experiences such as hers are placed "alongside Mark's narrative" and the scholarship that lies at the heart of James's contribution, "we can see that gender – along with the settlement, schooling, and aspirational experiences of Caribbean Canadians – all factor into the experiences of the 1.5 generation."

In an assessment of the categorization of and solutions offered for "at-risk" students in chapter 4, James examines the role of stereotypes, the education of Black boys, and concepts and policies to "instill discipline" as mechanisms of social control. He makes the point that not enough attention is paid to the correlation between students being "at risk" and their close ties to the "vulnerability index" (experiencing poverty, incomplete formal education, poor parenting practices, low teacher expectations). He examines the roles played by overlapping stereotypes (that the students are immigrants, fatherless, athletes, troublemakers, underachievers), which together "serve to categorize, essentialize, and disenfranchise young, Black male students" operating within schools with Eurocentric curricula, homogeneity in approach to teaching/learning, and culturally inappropriate assessments. In the face of these circumstances, James argues, some Black youth express resistive attitudes and behaviours that seem to confirm preexisting stereotypical designations.

Joyce E. King's response to chapter 4 begins with lists of Black boys and men killed by the police in the United States and Canada as part of her discussion of the role of anti-Black stereotypes in both contexts. She emphasizes the findings of James's chapter and points to the effects of the combined neglect of Black culture and history as well as the reinforcement of ideas of European ideological superiority. King advocates "using action verbs" to shift the discourse of culpability (absented fathers and histories, impeded achievers and resource-starved schools, among other concerns) as one means of "becoming unapologetically Black" to avoid the "spirit-murdering" that so many Black youth face. She argues for moving away from an overreliance on testing, and for reframing what it means to do well in school "from a Black epistemological and ideological position." While King's focus on Black boys once again points to the relative paucity in the scholarship on Black girls in schools, her call for discursive, epistemological, and ideological shifts expands the discussion significantly, as does her focus on the protection of generations of Black youth from the forces of anti-Black racism.

In another deep analysis of the impact of social forces on individual lives, in chapter 5 James presents another longitudinal study that follows the aspirations and career trajectories of two young Black men. Analysing interviews conducted in 2001–2, 2006, and 2011, he unpacks the prevalent narrative about individual achievement (including the roles of hard work, intellectual ability, luck, and assistance), which often ignores the fact that this path is "contingent on many social, institutional, and structural factors that are beyond an individual's control." James argues that the two young men's paths towards their career goals "have been shaped by how effectively they were able to ... navigate the layered, multifaceted structures of inequity [that] sustained the hegemonic ideology and commonsense rhetoric of neoliberalism which presents confounding obstacles."

Annette Henry engages with the arguments that James offers in chapter 5 by pointing out that he moves beyond the factors of individual ability and hard work to discuss the "roles that colonialism, race, and racism play in the historical and contemporary lives of Black people," and analyses instead "the pervasive negative societal stereotypes of Black people as lazy, helpless, ignorant, and residing in single-parent families." From Henry's perspectives, given the structural barriers that they face, many Black youth are situated where they will be cast as statistics or anomalies. While Henry supports James's conclusions that young Black men are essentialized and expected (and sometimes helped) by teachers, coaches, and others to perform as athletes as opposed to scholars, her work on Black girls takes the conversation in interesting directions. Living at the intersections of gender ideologies and racialized expectations, according to Henry, Black girls are expected to perform gendered roles; are supposed to be invisible while also being assessed by their looks; and are often stereotyped as "loud, brash, unfeminine, less innocent, more mature for their age, needing less attention, and hypersexual." Speaking to long-extant tropes of Black (non) femininity, Henry's discussion offers layers and complexities to James's longitudinal study of young Black men. Her contribution suggests that similar long-term studies by James, taking the gendered, raced, and classed experiences of young Black female and other/nongendered persons, were likely to have added important layers to his analyses.

While the conjoined considerations of class, race, and athletics among Black male students were alluded to in previous chapters, in chapter 6 James now centres those concerns (in an essay originally published in 2012) and argues that for many Black student-athletes "sports is seen as a creative, viable, and socially acceptable way to navigate and negotiate the alienating and inequitable schooling environment" and as also a potential way out of poverty. For James, many Black student-athletes are involved in a "performance" of Black male athleticism – including an interest in sports, playing "Black" (fast, slick, flashy), and participation in Black athletic culture (clothes, hairstyles, music, language) – and, often supported by an influential coach, foster a desire to go to the United States on athletic scholarships.

In his response to chapter 6, Mark Campbell agrees with James that young Black students gravitate towards sports to navigate the hostility they face in schools and that teachers use Black males' athletic participation "as a way to set expectations that are aligned with the dominant society's fabricated rendition of blackness as unintelligent and ineducable." Campbell develops ideas about the creativity inherent in "various aesthetically pleasing athletic stylings," especially when young Black males play basketball, and argues that this creative labour should be understood as "acts of survival ... [which] mitigate the harm of colonialism and white supremacy" and also indicate "a critical desire to live beyond being 'units of labour' under Western capitalism."

Still, as Campbell makes clear, this creative labour often comes to naught since the educational system has done little to address the concerns of Black students and they continue to be positioned as intellectually inferior and their academic performance continues to be less than optimal. These poor academic results mean that, no matter how talented they might be, their prospects of going on to postsecondary education (in the United States) are, in reality, almost nonexistent. Campbell also invokes a class analysis to disaggregate the experiences of Black student-athletes and argues that, for youth whose parents can afford elite training, there are expensive clubs and the US prep school route, which increase the possibility of being noticed by the professional leagues. For others who enjoy a short-lived celebrity in secondary school through sports – and for whom school rules are bent to allow them to play despite poor academics – the path to success through professional sports is largely illusory. Campbell's engagement with James's arguments, including an examination of the creative labour in which Black youth invest and the classed differences in experiences, helps to complicate the notions of a culture of Black male athleticism. Conversations such as these, offering different perspectives, enhance the overall publication.

In his examination of role models as corrective agents for Black male in chapter 7 (also first published in 2012), James uses the framework of "new racism" (which obscures systemic and structural racism) to examine the roles of mentors. Often presented as "evidence" that success is possible despite the barriers and that setbacks build character, Black mentors (coaches, athletes, teachers) are expected to stand in the breach to guide Black youth and to address the tropes of fatherless families and their links to violence. According to James, Black male mentors might have value to individuals, but they are not all that is needed in a society "where inequity, marginalization, and racialization exist, and where racism, now couched in cultural terms, obscures the fact that neither individual disposition nor community cultural ethos is responsible for Black and other minority young people's life circumstances." James concludes that mentors run the risk of colluding with the existing social and educational systems in claiming that effort and discipline are all that are needed and advocates that rather than focusing on fatherlessness, youth should be provided with the critical skills and tools they need to negotiate their circumstances.

In his chapter 7 response to James's arguments about the potentially negative impact of mentorship on Black youth, Sam Tecle reflects on his role as a staff member in a community-based organization that works in partnership with a large school board and offers role models and mentorship as core tenets. Echoing Henry's caution about being labelled as an anomaly who serves to symbolize what effort and focus can accomplish, Tecle agrees that mentorship programs can have the effect of turning attention away from the "historical and structural barriers that operate to reproduce and pathologize Black youth, without giving attention to the conditions under which Black communities are so often forced to live." Not only can mentors operate as "corrective agents," but, as he argues, they can also be "brought in to 'manage' unruly 'at-risk' Black youth from assumed 'broken' Black families."

However, Tecle's intervention also speaks to the possibility of using a self-reflective and self-conscious praxis that would allow him to continue working with Black youth through "mentorship programs, as a role model, and through speaking engagements despite the problematic ways in which this might be framed." Where the act and impact of mentoring are concerned, Tecle uses the opportunity to ask whether a practice of "critical questioning" might help to construct "a space of subversive possibility where role modelling and mentoring could operate differently for Black people and Black youth." Cognizant of the potential for negative applications and outcomes in mentoring and role modelling programs, Tecle's determination to retrieve the possibilities for positive impact is worthy of consideration. It might be true that many who plan, launch, and conduct these programs remain unaware of, or remain unwilling to engage with, the pitfalls to which James points. However, as Tecle might maintain, it could be detrimental to suspend all such interventions, especially since – as James has argued repeatedly – educational institutions are continuing to fail Black youth. Perhaps a greater awareness of the potential hazards of these programs and a constant praxis of critical engagement with, between, and among mentors and mentees – Tecle's "critical questioning" – might offer some of the means to unpack these concerns.

As he has done for Black youth's experiences in educational systems, James examines the movement of Black youth into and through public spaces in chapter 8, previously published in 1998. Whether on the streets of the city (Toronto) or in spaces like shopping malls, the chapter captures some of the most problematic encounters of Black youth – with the policing arm of the state. While the original research is more than twenty years old, the contexts within which police officers stop, question, search, and generally harass Black youth have a tragic and current familiarity, as do James's arguments that police actions represent "a cultural articulation of patriarchy and systemic racism." James uses colonial discourse, linked to the pejorative tropes associated with Blackness (violence, fear, threat, other, criminal), to understand the experiences of Black youth who report that while young Black males are often the target of police actions, Black females are also harassed. And as James points out, in the equal-opportunity anti-Black racism that pervades the city, middle-class Blacks are not exempt.

For Adelle Blackett, in her response to chapter 8, that James's arguments hold up after twenty years is telling; that they could apply to contemporary Montreal is significant and indicative of the negative conditions facing Blacks in Canada. Police actions against Black youth in Montreal often point to systemic discrimination. In recounting these cases, Blackett assesses James's work as an early intervention and exercise in theorizing about the racism that Black youth face in public spaces. While James includes Black females in his analysis, Blackett maintains that there is need for a fuller engagement with the research on intersectionality since "[a] very particular kind of violence is reserved for Black women." In her extension of James's analysis into Quebec, Blackett makes the point that language is part of the discussion; further, she says, there is a need to examine Quebec as a place of settler colonialism and enslavement, where Blackness is "racialized as subordinate, and the object of violence." While Blackett is quite right to argue that James's essential arguments remain largely intact, there are aspects – such as some of the details of legal and/or acceptable police practices and references to youth in video arcades in shopping malls – that tie the chapter to its time and place. Still, as Blackett might argue, that so little had changed in twenty years is disheartening and frustrating – although, given the deep roots of anti-Black racism in Canada, not entirely surprising.

While the majority of James's work focusing on Black youth tends to centre on their experiences in Canada's largest urban city, as increasing numbers of Black families venture into the suburbs beyond Toronto, his analyses have widened to include the concerns of families in these areas. In chapter 9, James looks closely at surbuban experiences. According to him, the desire for improved social circumstances (amenities, educational institutions, safety) that often drives the move into suburban communities is accompanied by high costs for Black youth. These include expectations that they will be "good Blacks," increased tension between youth and their parents (who worry about and try to protect their children), financial stresses, unresponsive schools (teachers with low expectations), racialization, and hostility (such as name-calling). James reports that, similar to their counterparts in the city, young Black males in the suburbs are labelled as "aggressive, troublemakers, and potential lawbreakers," while Black female youth are "largely seen as loud and brazen." According to James, then, youth in the suburbs also seem resigned to the odds being against them.

Andrea Davis's reflection on James's portrayal of Black families' move into the suburbs as "not only misguided, but as harmful to Black youth" urges a vision beyond actions spurred by an illusory Canadian Dream. Instead, in her response to chapter 9, Davis expands the frame of reference to the places of origin of the Caribbean families and asks whether they might be "activating deep-seated ideas about respectability they bring with them from the Caribbean." Her discussion takes up the roots and manifestations of "respectability politics" in the English-speaking Caribbean, linked to a deep-seated belief that – given the conjoined legacies of colonialism and enslavement – migration is the "surest route to social mobility." From this perspective, Davis offers a number of rationales behind the movements into the suburbs outlined by James. While James's study focuses on the price paid by Black youth and their families for these decisions, Davis seeks to understand their source and so adds another layer to the discussion. While, as Davis says, James's work "may ultimately be the story of the shared failure of Caribbean migration to Canada," her contribution points to the multi-faceted approaches that might help to complicate the narrative.

Where James begins his examination of the experiences of Black youth in Canada in the 1970s, this work ends in chaper 10 with a close analysis of the *Towards Race Equity in Education* report (2017), which presents details about the schooling of Black youth in the Greater Toronto Area (GTA). According to James, the available data in the wider GTA confirm the concerns raised regarding Black youth in the TDSB with "low expectations from teachers and administrators; stereotypes about their educational commitments and intellectual abilities; more harsh discipline compared to their white peers; feelings of exclusion from their school; and having school programs, curricular materials, and a teacher population that were not reflective of them" were "common to their experiences." As James points out, while there continues to be a need for disaggregated data, there have been few moves to implement the recommendations that have been made. And since the outlined concerns seem to follow those Black youth who manage to traverse the many barriers in the educational systems into college and university, the possibilities of less than stellar results for Black youth are quite high.

In her response to James's analyses in chapter 10, Leanne Taylor reflects on the experiences of her Black goddaughter in navigating the educational system and her role as an education professor who teaches about inequity and power in schools. In one class, she had her students read the *Towards Race Equity in Education* report; she points to what she calls "the limits of good intentions." While the teacher-candidates who read the report expressed surprise and unease with the data about the barriers facing Black youth and indicated a determination to "do better," Taylor argues that "they were failing to acknowledge and understand how hierarchical structures of education sustain the race privileges that teachers exercise." If, as Taylor says, the educators on whom the system depends so heavily for its existence and functioning continue to be unaware of and/or unresponsive to the deeply ingrained anti-Black racism that pervades Canadian society and that is manifested in the systems of education with which Black youth have to contend, then the amount and range of corrective measures that remain to be implemented are quite daunting.

This publication brings together wide-ranging sets of data, scholarship, analyses, and arguments and lays out – in no uncertain terms – the dire circumstances of large numbers of Black youth in Canada. Whether in Toronto and the wider GTA or in the comparable communities in Montreal, the United Kingdom, and elsewhere, this work argues that Black children and youth often face the brunt of anti-Blackness in their communities, and especially within the educational institutions that they are expected to navigate, often without support or assistance. The anti-Black sentiment that informed the race-based systems of enslavement and hierarchies in the places that would coalesce into the geopolitical entity called Canada have neither disappeared nor dissipated.

326 Epilogue ~ Michele A. Johnson

Black youth – whether they are the descendants of long-extant African-Canadian communities, second- and third-generation descendants of migrants in the later twentieth century, or recent migrants – continue to face hurdles built on foundations that neither they nor their families helped to construct. Yet, as they go about their lives – observing the upward mobility of their non-Black peers while they remain circumscribed on every side by anti-Black racism – they can only echo the conclusion of one youth who told Carl James that, after all, "colour matters."

Acknowledgments

This book of essays, as is generally the case with any project, has been made possible through my good fortune of being surrounded by a supportive community of family, friends, colleagues, students, and activists. Here, I am especially grateful to one colleague, Professor Michele Johnson, who, as Principal Investigator of a SSHRC Collaborative Research Initiative (MCRI), "Slavery, Memory, Citizenship," encouraged my interest in pursuing this project as part of the larger initiative. I also benefited from the support of the Jean Augustine Chair and the Faculty of Education of York University.

Chronicling the lives of Black youth is important to comprehending the complex and diverse ways in which they grapple with, understand, assert, and perform identities as Canadians, maintain hope (avoiding what Harry Pettit [2019] calls "cruel optimism"), and resist the power and pervasive structure of racism normalized through social, educational, health, and recreational institutions. And every so often young people express words or phrases that succinctly capture the full meaning of what needs to be said – like the research participant who stated that "colour matters" and from whom I cribbed the title of this book. I am indebted to her for providing me the phrase on which I am engaging in this conversation about – as colleagues and friends Rinaldo Walcott and Idil Abdillahi (2019) put it – "Blacklife." They make the point that Blackness and life are inextricably linked in particular ways.

A common interest of mine is to periodically return to participants of earlier studies I conducted to "check up on them" years later to hear about their experiences and to know about their accomplishments. I do this believing that to fully understand individuals' experiences requires that we go beyond the one interview experience. This book project provided opportunities for me to return to some of these research participants for updates. I owe these participants my sincerest gratitude for putting up with my periodic impositions.

I am privileged to have remarkable university and community colleagues and friends whose presence, scholarship, advice, and guidance inspire me, provide encouragement, nurture intellectual growth, and sustain my work. It is this knowledge that guides my profound indebtedness to those on whom I called to make contributions to *Colour Matters*. My gratitude goes to Alissa Trotz and Michele Johnson for their deeply insightful and interrogative bookends that serve to scaffold the various perspectives and ideas in which we engage here. I extend the same gratitude to an outstanding group of colleagues: Funké Aladejebi, Shirley Anne Tate, Amoaba Gooden, Joyce King, Annette Henry, Mark Campbell, Sam Tecle, Adele Blackett, Andrea Davis, and Leanne Taylor for their generous and significant contributions to this project. I was encouraged and honoured that they agreed to respond to the essays, providing insightful comments and furthering the conversation I started.

My appreciation also goes to colleagues Robert Brown and David Cameron, for their help in accessing and preparing the Toronto District School Board data for chapter 2, to which Firissaa Abdulkarim and Gillian Parekh also contributed with data analysis. Thanks also to Tana Turner for her invaluable contributions to the work with the community, particularly with the consultations in which Rhonda Grege and San Tecle also participated that produced the *Race Equity* report from which chapter 10 was prepared.

I am also indebted to colleagues and friends at my academic residence, York University. I especially thank Tka Pinnock, whose help with the manuscript was invaluable to the writing process; and thanks to Firissaa Abdulkarim, Sam Tecle, Rhonda George, Julia Samaroo, Selom Nyaho Chapman, Tapo Chimbganda, Nemoy Lewis – all of whom, as part of the Jean Augustine Chair team, provided helpful research and/or organizational assistance and support that facilitated the completion of this book. I am also indebted to Andrea Torre for making possible some of the requirements for the completion of this project. As well, my thanks to colleagues Annette Boodram and Enakshi Dua for their support.

I am appreciative for the reviewers' commentaries and critiques, from which I have benefited and which, in turn, improved the manuscript. So too the manuscript has benefited from the editorial assistance and suggestions of Bob Chodos and Susan Joanis. I also acknowledge with gratefulness the encouragement, advice, and assistance I received from Douglas Hildebrand, the initial University of Toronto Press Acquisitions Editor, and Meg Farrell Patterson, who took over from Doug. Their belief in the project was important to the process of completion. Also, I acknowledge the work of the Publishing Team of the University of Toronto Press, in particular Janice Evans, and of freelance copyeditor Beth McAuley of The Editing Company in Toronto.

Finally, to Kai, who, over the years in many ways, has been a constant source of inspiration – your intuitions and our conversations, debates, and political arguments provided helpful insights; and to my mother and other family members, Dorne, Sammy, Nia, and Kito I offer utmost thanks – knowing the this simple word can never be enough for your nurturance, validation, and support that only you as family provide.

Copyright Credits

The following articles are being reprinted with the permission of the respective publishers.

Chapter 1 was published as Carl E. James with Keren S. Brathwaite (1996) under the title "Assessing the Educational Experiences of African Canadians." In K.S. Brathwaite & C.E. James (Eds.), *Educating African Canadians* (pp. 13–31). Toronto, ON: Our Schools/Our Selves & James Lorimer Ltd.

Chapter 3 was published as Carl E. James (2005), "'I Feel Like a Trini': Narrative of a Generation-and-a-Half Canadian." In Vijay Agnew (Ed.), *Diaspora, Memory and Identity: A Search for Home* (pp. 230–53). Toronto, ON: University of Toronto Press.

Chapter 4 was published as Carl E. James (2012), "Students 'At Risk': Stereotyping and the Schooling of Black Boys." *Urban Education*, 47(2), 464–94.

Chapter 5 was published as Carl E. James (2015), "Beyond Education, Brains and Hard Work: The Aspirations and Career Trajectory of Two Black Young Men." *Alternate Routes: A Journal of Critical Social Research*, 26, 332–53.

Chapter 6 was published as Carl E. James (2012), "Class, Race and Schooling in the Performance of Black Male Athleticism." In Christopher J. Greig & Wayne J. Martino (Eds.), *Canadian Men and Masculinities: Historical and Contemporary Perspectives* (pp. 176–90). Toronto, ON: Canadians Scholars' Press.

Chapter 7 was published as Carl E. James (2012), "Troubling Role Models: Seeing Racialization in the Discourse Relating to 'Corrective Agents' for Black Males." In Ken Moffat (Ed.), *Troubled*

Masculinities: Re-Imagining Urban Men (pp. 77–92). Toronto, ON: University of Toronto Press.

Chapter 8 was published as Carl E. James (1998), "'Up to No Good': Black on the Streets and Encountering Police." In Vic Satzewich (Ed.), *Racism and Social Inequality in Canada: Concepts, Controversies and Strategies of Resistance* (pp. 156–76). Toronto, ON: Thompson Education Publishing.

* * *

Funding for this publication came from the SSHRC Major Collaborative Research Initiative (MCRI) Program, "Slavery, Memory, Citizenship." Principal Investigator, Professor Michele Johnson.

Contributors

Carl E. James, PhD, FRSC, holds the Jean Augustine Chair in Education, Community & Diaspora in the Faculty of Education, York University, Toronto, where he is also the Senior Advisor on Equity and Representation in the Office of the Vice President of Equity, People and Culture. He holds cross-appointments in the Graduate Programs in Sociology and Social Work, and for over fifteen years was the visiting lecturer in the Teacher Training Department at Uppsala University, Sweden. In his studies of the experiences of Black youth, James seeks to move us beyond the racializing essentialist discourses that account for their situation and would have us engage in action for systemic changes in educational institutions, social agencies, workplaces, and society.

* * *

Funké Aladejebi, PhD, is Assistant Professor of History at the University of Toronto. She is currently working on a manuscript titled "Girl You Better Apply to Teachers' College: The History of Black Women Educators in Ontario, 1940s–1980s," which explores the importance of Black Canadian women in sustaining their communities and preserving a distinct Black identity within restrictive gender and racial barriers. She has published articles in *Ontario History* and *Education Matters*. Her research interests are in oral history, the history of education in Canada, Black feminist thought, and transnationalism.

Adelle Blackett, AdE, is Professor of Law and Canada Research Chair in Transnational Labour Law and Development at the Faculty of Law, McGill University, where she directs the Labour Law and Development Research Laboratory. Her most recent book is *Everyday Transgressions:*

Domestic Workers' Transnational Challenge to International Labour Law (Cornell University Press, 2019).

Mark V. Campbell, PhD, is Assistant Professor in the Department of Arts, Culture and Media at the University of Toronto Scarborough. Dr. Campbell is a former Banting Postdoctoral Fellow in the Department of Fine Arts, University of Regina, and is currently Principal Investigator on the SSHRC-funded research project on hip-hop archives. A DJ, scholar, and curator, his research explores the relationships between Afrosonic innovations and notions of the human. He has published widely, with scholarly essays appearing in cultural studies journals and popular writing in local and national Canadian newspapers and hip-hop magazines such as *Urbanology*.

Andrea A. Davis, PhD, is Associate Professor in Black Cultures of the Americas, Coordinator of the Black Canadian Studies Certificate, and former chair of the Department of Humanities at York University, Toronto. She also holds cross-appointments in the graduate programs in English; Interdisciplinary Studies; and Gender, Feminist and Women's Studies. She is the author of the forthcoming book *Horizon, Sea, Sound: A Cultural Critique of the Nation* (Northwestern University Press, 2021).

Amoaba Gooden, PhD, is an Associate Professor and Chair in the Department of Pan-African Studies at Kent State University. Her ongoing research includes the study of African Canadian organizing, leadership, and community building. She is the editor of a special edition of the *Southern Journal of Canadian Studies: Constructing Black Canada: Becoming Canadian*. Her publications can be found in *African Canadian Leadership: Perspectives on Continuity, Transition, and Transformation* (University of Toronto Press, 2019); *S'TENISTOLW – Moving Indigenous Education Forward* (edited by T. Ormiston, J. Green, & K. Aguirre, J. Charlton Publishing); and in the *Journal of Black Studies*; *Journal of Pan-African Studies*; *Wagadu: Journal of Transnational Women's and Gender Studies*; and *Canadian Woman Studies Journal*.

Annette M. Henry, PhD, holds the David Lam Chair in Multicultural Education in the Faculty of Education, University of British Columbia. She was a professor at the University of Illinois Chicago and University of Washington, Tacoma for eighteen years before coming to the University of British Columbia. Now professor and former head of the Department of Language and Literacy Education, she is cross-appointed to the Institute for Gender, Race, Sexuality and Social Justice.

Her research interests include Black life histories; Black feminisms; and race, class, language, gender, and culture in socio-cultural contexts of teaching and learning.

Michele A. Johnson, PhD, is a Professor in the Department of History at York University where she has served as the coordinator of the Latin American and Caribbean Studies Programme, as York's Affirmative Action Officer, and as Director of the Harriet Tubman Institute for Research on Africa and Its Diasporas. Her research interests include cultural history, gender relations, race/racialization, labour, domestic slavery, and domestic service in Jamaica and Canada.

Joyce E. King, PhD, holds the Benjamin E. Mays Endowed Chair for Urban Teaching, Learning and Leadership in the College of Education and Human Development at Georgia State University, Atlanta. She is a past-president of the American Educational Research Association and a member of the National African American Reparations Commission (USA). A recent publication (with E. Swartz) is *Heritage Knowledge in the Curriculum: Retrieving an African Episteme* (Routledge, 2018).

Shirley Anne Tate, PhD, is Professor in the Sociology Department at the University of Alberta, where she is Canada Research Chair Tier 1 designate in Feminism and Intersectionality; until 2018, she was Professor of Race and Education and Director of the Centre for Race, Education, and Decoloniality at Leeds Beckett University, Leeds, Britain. She is Honorary Professor, Chair in Critical Studies in Higher Education Transformation (*Cri*SHET) at Nelson Mandela University, South Africa, and Visiting Professor at CEREN, University of Helsinki, and at CRED, Leeds Beckett University. Her area of research is Black diaspora studies.

Leanne Taylor, PhD, is an Associate Professor in the Faculty of Education at Brock University. Her research explores racialized identities, particularly mixed-race identities, immigrant student aspirations, "at-risk" youth, and marginalized students' access to and experiences in postsecondary education. She teaches graduate and undergraduate courses addressing social justice, diversity, and activism in education; critical anti-racist practice; and the interrelationship between pedagogy, culture, and identity.

Sam Tecle, PhD, is Assistant Professor of Community Engaged Learning at New College, University of Toronto. His research is in the areas of Black and Diaspora Studies, Urban Studies, and Sociology of

Education. His doctoral work *Black Grammars: On Difference and Belonging* explored the experiences and perspectives relating to Blackness and Black identification of East African Diasporas across the UK, Canada, and the US. He has held graduate student fellowships in the African & African American Studies Departments of Harvard University (2016) and Northwestern University (2014). A former middle and high school teacher, Professor Tecle is a community advocate who has worked on a number of community projects concerned with the well-being, social lives, schooling experiences, and educational outcomes of Black students.

D. Alissa Trotz, PhD, is Professor of Caribbean Studies at New College and Women and Gender Studies at the University of Toronto. She is also affiliate faculty at the Dame Nita Barrow Institute of Gender and Development Studies at the University of the West Indies, Cave Hill, Barbados. She is co-editor, with Arif Bulkan, of *Unmasking the State: Politics, Society and the Economy in Guyana, 1992–2015* (Ian Randle Publishers, 2019), and editor of the anthology *The Point Is to Change the World: Selected Writings by Andaiye* (Pluto Press Black Critique Series, 2020). She is editor of "In the Diaspora," a weekly newspaper column in the Guyanese daily *Stabroek News*, http://www.stabroeknews.com/category/features/in-the-diaspora.

Index

1.5-generation. *See* generation-and-a-half
1.5-generation Caribbean Canadian. *See* generation-and-a-half Caribbean Canadian

Abdillahi, I., xvii–xviii
absent fathers. *See* fatherlessness
Academic POS. *See* Program of Study (POS) – academic courses
acculturation, 78–9
achievement: and generations, 47; and middle-class norms, 177; as problem for African Canadians, 5–6, 8, 10, 16–17, 19–20, 316; and racism, 295–7, 298; solutions for African Canadians, 11–14, 43, 316. *See also* underachievement
"achievement gap," Black students *vs.* others, 131
Adjetey, Wendell, 208
adolescence to adulthood life trajectories: example, xxv–xxvi; "hurdles" of racism and discrimination, xxv–xxvii; optimism of participants, xxvi–xxviii, xxxi
adolescents, and optimism *vs.* "hurdles," xxvi–xxvii

adults, and optimism *vs.* "hurdles," xxvii–xxviii
African-born Blacks, experiences in education, ix, 44, 48
African Canadian Legal Clinic, 287n4
African Canadians: at-risk students, 114–15; historical foundations, 316–17; and hope, 4; population and profile in Canada, 117
African Canadians and education: in 1970s and 1980s, 4–15; in 1990s, 15–21; in 2000s and 2010s, 21–34; achievement and performance problems, 5–6, 8, 10, 16–17, 19–20, 316; achievement solutions, 11–14, 43, 316; African heritage classes, 11; *vs.* Canadian-born Black youth, 6, 44; change(s) needed, 3, 4, 34–5; community education projects, 4–5; and discrimination, 5, 46; disengagement from education, 10; education as concern, 3–4; and language policies, 11; level of study in Ontario, 6; national picture, 44; race-relations policies and programs, 12–13; racism in school system, 8–9

African descent: educational outcomes, 68, 72–3; in TDSB cohort data, 49, 50
African heritage classes, 11
"African History Month," 4n4
Africentric Alternative School, 14, 24–5, 31, 33, 301
Africentric schools and schooling, 24–6, 31–4, 35, 209, 301–2
Afro-Caribbean Alternative Secondary School (ACASS), 13–14
aggregation, ix
Akande, Zanana, 13
Aladejebi, Funké, 43–6, 316–17
alternative schools in Ontario, 24–5
"amputation," 224
ancestry probing, 84, 117
Andrews, A.G., 226, 239
anti-Black racism. *See* racism, anti-Black
Anti-Racism and Ethnocultural Equity policy (Ontario), 15–16
Anti-Racism Directorate, 28, 284
antiracism in Ontario: education for, 32, 32n20; and institutional change, 16–19; legislation, 28; policies and programs, 15–16, 28
Applied POS. *See* Program of Study (POS) – applied courses
arts, role for enslaved populations, 192
Ashcraft, C., 124
Aston, C., 26–7
athlete, as stereotypes for at-risk Black male youth, 115, 124–7, 177
athletics and athleticism: assumptions and framework for Black student-athlete culture, 175, 178–88; and belief in overcoming racism, 9–10; and Black female youth, xxiii–xxiv; and Black male youth, xxiii; and disenfranchisement, 188; and education, xxiii–xxiv, 205; and gender, xxiii–xxiv, 110; inequities and schooling, 176; and natural ability, 205–6; participation in Black athletic culture, 181–3, 191, 192–3, 321; participation in school, 183; and Program of Study (POS), 290–1; race, class and gender in, 175–8, 187–8, 194; and race, 206. *See also* scholarships [athletic]; sports
The Atlantic, on Black male youth killed, 142
at risk: as construct and term, 113, 116–17; as social capital, 164
at-risk students and youth: Black male youth as, 114–15; cultural analysis and critical race theory approach, 115, 116–17; definition, 112; identification and intervention measures, 113–14; as label for Black male youth, 112, 117; as language, 112–13, 144; and masculinity standards, 116; and role models, 209, 217, 218–19; and stereotypes (*See* stereotypes for at-risk Black male youth); vulnerability factors, 113
attention-deficit/hyperactivity disorder (ADHD), 293

Bailey, B., 183
Bailey, Ian, 14
Bailey-Harris, Haille, 123–4
Baldwin, James, xi
Balibar, E., xviii–xix, 201, 202
Barrett, P., 144
Bashi, V., 117–18
basketball: and creative labour, 192, 195; and digital media, 193; dress and style in, 180, 181–2, 191,

192–3, 321; elite programs, 194; infrastructure in Toronto, 193–5; over-representation of Blacks, 187; and participation in Black athletic culture, 181–3, 191; and "play Black," 179–81, 191, 192; recruitment due to race, 125–6
behaviour of students, and placement, 294–5
Berns-McGown, R., 81
A Better Way Forward action plan (2017), 28
Bills, D.B., xvii
biology, and skills, 202, 203, 205
black, as word, 222–3
Black Africans, experiences in education, 44
"black" as social construction, 222–3
Black communities, and "othermothers," 108–9
Black educators/teachers: Black women as, 45–6; and discipline, 300; impact and contribution, 45–6, 109, 300–1, 300–301nn10–11, 312; need in Toronto schools, 300; as role models for Black male youth, 210–11; working in own community, 160
Blackett, Adelle, 246–8, 323–4
Black female youth: athletics and sports, xxiii–xxiv, 109, 110; career choices, 45; educational experiences, xxiv–xxv, 45, 171–2, 316, 320; experience as 1.5 generation, 109–10, 111, 318–19; graduation and academic performance, xxiii; "hurdles" of racism and gender, xxvi–xxvii; and police, 235–6, 237, 247; research on, xxiii, xxiv, 45, 316; responses to schooling environment, 22–3; stereotypes, xxv, 172, 320; and suburbs, 269–70, 273; and teachers, 171–2
Black-focused schools: for boys only, 209–10; in Britain, 26–7; change(s) in, 31–4; as option or solution, 23–6, 32, 35
Black History Month, 4n4, 13, 20–1
Black Learners Advisory Committee (BLAC), 19–20
Black male youth: optimism towards learning, 124; research on, xxiii; as troublemakers, 22. *See also* Black youth; specific topics
Blackness: diversity in, 44–5, 118–19; role, 146; in suburbs, 255–6, 263–6, 270–1
Black police officers, cultural attitudes and views, 226n6
Blacks, population and profile in Canada, 117. *See also* specific topics
Black Skin, White Masks (Fanon), 219
Black Student Achievement Advisory Committee (BSAAC), mandate, 29
Black student-athlete culture (Black athletic culture): assumptions and framework, 175, 178–88; inequities and schooling, 176; participation in, 181–3, 191, 192–3, 321
Black students: deficit thinking about, 130–1; differences and nuances in, 47; educational aspirations, 6, 130; educational trajectory, 302; experiences in education since 1970s, 315; future of, 305; lower expectations for, 288–9, 290, 295–6, 297, 299, 302. *See also* specific topics
Black women: as educators/ teachers, 45–6; immigration from Caribbean, 107–8;

Black women (*continued*)
and respectability, 279, 280; as school board directors, 30n19. *See also* Black female youth
Black youth: costs and "extra work," xxi; life trajectories, xxviii; and power relations, xviii; social and educational experiences in Toronto, xv–xvi. *See also* Black female youth; Black male youth; specific topics
"A Blinkered Report on Race" (*Globe and Mail*), 17–18
boards. *See* school boards
Boesveld, Sarah, 251
Bonilla-Silva, E., 202, 203, 288
boys-only school, 209–10
Boys to Men program, 200, 209
Brathwaite, Keren, 8–9
Breen, R., 254
Britain: African-Caribbean education in 1970s and 1980s, 14–15; Black-focused schools, 26–7; career choices of Black female youth, 45; educational outcomes for Black students, 73–4, 317; middle-class Blacks in suburbs, 255, 256n4, 263; organizing of 1970s–1980s by Blacks, xiii; police harassment of Black male youth, 224; school system as model, xiii; social class and perceptions by teachers, 176; systemic racism, 73–4, 317
Brogden, M., et al., 228, 229, 237
Brown, D.K., xvii
Brown, Jaylen, 195
Brown, Maureen, 252, 257
Brown, R.S., et al., 62
Browning, S.L., et al., 223–4
Butler, Judith, 223

Calliste, A., 6
Campbell, Mark V., 191–5, 321

Canadian-born Black youth, educational experiences, 6, 44
capitalism, 151–2, 218
Caribbean: education and gender in Britain, 14–15; immigration to Canada, xv, 5, 107–8; and respectability, 279–81, 325
Caribbean Canadian generation-and-a-half (Mark). *See* generation-and-a-half Caribbean Canadian
Caribbean students, in TDSB cohort data, 49, 50
Caribbean (descent) students, educational outcomes, 67–8, 72–3, 74
Caribbean women, immigration to Canada, 107–8
Case, Patrick, 30, 31
case studies, as approach, 153
case studies of two Black male youth: academics *vs.* sports, 171; aspirations and outcomes, 151, 170–1, 320; education and schooling, 169–71; research method and interviews, 152–4. *See also* Kobe; Trevor
CBC Radio (Canadian Broadcasting Corporation), on fatherlessness, 121, 207, 207n7
CDPDJ (Commission des Droits de la Personne et des Droits de la Jeunesse), 247
Census Metropolitan Areas (CMAs), population, 251
Centre of Excellence for the Education of Black Students, 29
Chadha, Ena, 30
Chung, R.C.-Y., 175–6
Clampet-Lundquist, S., et al., 274
class (social class): aspirations of Blacks, 6; and language, 183; and perceptions by teachers,

176; and police, 224–5, 237; and race and gender in athletics, 175–8, 187–8, 194; and sports, 175, 187–8; teachers and educational performance, 176–7; upward mobility, 253. *See also* middle-class; working-class

clothes. *See* dress and style

coachability, and academic performance, 126

coaches: and educational concerns, 186; as role models in sports, 101–2, 185–7, 205

Coard, Bernard, xiii, 73

Codjoe, H., 130–1

cohort data. *See* TDSB 2008–11 cohort data

college in Ontario: and gender, 62; and race, 59, 60

colonial discourse and colonialism, 222, 236, 239, 248

colour, influence and impact, 32

"colour-blind" discourse or approach, 32, 114, 133

"colour-blindness": belief in Canada, 94, 114n3; and Mark, 94–5; and new racism, 202–3; and sports, 94, 206

Commission on Systemic Racism in the Ontario Criminal Justice System (1995), 225

"common curriculum," 15–16, 15n11

common-sense approach, 201, 204

common-sense ideas/notions, 201, 203, 204

community: Black educators working in own community, 160; and fatherlessness, 208; resources for Black male youth, 152; role in lives, 153, 154, 170. *See also* neighbourhoods

community-based projects, and role models, 216–17, 219–20

"community cultural wealth" access, 152

community education projects for African Canadians, 4–5

Compendium of Action for Black Student Success (2018), 30

competition, in neoliberalism, xvi, 151

Connell, R., xvii

"The Construction of Black Masculinity" (Ferber), 205

Consultative Committee on the Education of Black Students in Toronto Schools (CCEBSTS), 7

Cooper, Afua, 13

Cooper, C., 280

"corrective agents": Blacks as, 212; description and role, 197; in role modelling programs, 209; and role models, 217, 218, 219

Corrigan, P., 240

COVID-19 pandemic impact, xxxii

"cradle to jail," 27, 74, 130

Crawford, C., 109–10

creative labour: definition and role, 191–2, 321; examples, 192–3, 195; as problem, 192, 195

criminalization of Blacks by police, 225, 229, 236–7, 238–41

critical hope, 4, 43

critical race theory: approach in case studies, 153; and at-risk students, 115, 117; and Black youth, xix–xx; and education, xix–xx; in graduation and postsecondary attainment, 48; and neoliberalism, 152; as theoretical framework, xviii–xix, xx–xxi, 116

cultural analysis: and at-risk students, 115, 116–17; as theoretical framework, xviii, xx–xxi, 115, 116

cultural capital, access to, 152
cultural groups, and neoliberalism, xvii–xviii
culture(s): function of, 175–6; individuals and cultural contexts, xx; and multiculturalism, 93–4, 118; and natural ability, 205; and schooling, 176
Curling, Alvin, 27
curriculum: as barrier to success, 12, 20; culturally informed education, 145–6; knowledge about Blacks, 20; problems with, 143, 144; reforms needed, 28
cyclical condition of perceptions, 240

data. *See* TDSB 2008–11 cohort data
data collection on race, 23, 28–9, 48n2, 239n13
dating, 269–70
Davis, Andrea A., 278–81, 324
Davis, J.E., 124
deficit thinking about Black students, 130–1
Dei, George, 23
Dei, G.J.S., et al., 229, 237
Demie, Feyisa, 74
democratic racism, 202
Dennis (pseudonym), 179–80, 181–2, 184, 185
Desroches, F.J., 226
destreaming in Ontario, 11, 16
"diagnostic tests" for Black students, 293
DiAngelo, R., 272
Diebel, Lisa, 199–200
digital media, and black athletic culture, 193
disaggregated data, 23, 28, 29, 47, 49, 61, 286, 305, 321, 325
disaggregation, ix
discipline, and Black educators, 300

discrimination: for African Canadians in education, 5, 46; *Equity and Inclusive Education Strategy*, 28; as "hurdle," xxvi; in Quebec, 248; and race, xviii
Discussion Group on "Focused Schools," 19
diversity course for student teachers, 311, 313–14
"Diversity Issues in Schooling" course, 311
Donnor, J.K., xix–xx
double-consciousness, 73, 80, 96–7
Dowd, N., 121
dress and style: in basketball, 180, 181–2, 191, 192–3, 321; and police, 231–2, 233, 237–8, 237n11
dropout rates, viii, 7–8, 14, 18, 21, 21n13, 113, 118, 155, 229, 286, 304, 305
duality, 80–2, 95–7
Du Bois, W.E.B., 96, 145
Dunne, M., 176
Durham District School Board (DDSB), equity initiatives, 31
Durham region, Black students situation and racial profiling, 285–6
Dwaine (pseudonym), 178–9, 181, 184, 186

economic class, and sports, 175
education: and aspirations, x–xi, 6, 130; and belief in overcoming racism, xxvii–xxviii, 9; change(s) needed in system, 3, 4, 34–5; and critical race theory, xix–xx; as process, 114; representation of experiences, 44–5; value, 6, 7–8. *See also* schooling; school system
education students. *See* student teachers

Edwards, Harry, 124
elementary school, teachers as role models, 210–11
employment: and "hurdles," xxvii; and neoliberalism, xvii, 163–4; and racism, xxvi
English-language learning and needs, and placement, 294
equality of opportunity, 150
equity: and data collection on race, 28–9; and limited opportunities for Blacks, 46; policies and initiatives by school boards, 28–31, 43–4. See also *Towards Race Equity in Education* report
Equity and Diversity Strategic Framework (2017), 31
Equity and Diversity Strategic Plan (DDSB), 31
Equity and Inclusive Education Strategy (2009), 28, 284
Equity Strategic Plan (YRDSB), 30
Erving, Julius, 192
essays and responses in book, xxviii, xxxi
Essential POS, 49–53, 289
Evans-Winter, V.E., xxiv–xxv
exclusion from schools, impact, 27
expelled students. *See* suspended students
external integration, 81

"Fab Five," 192
"The Fact of Blackness" (Fanon), 195
family structure and "breakdown," 120–1
Fanon, Frantz, 195, 219, 223, 224
Farmer, S., 129
fatherlessness: articles in media and on radio, 121, 123–4, 199–200, 207; link to violence, 199–200, 207, 208; and mothers, 120–1, 123, 210–11;

and role modelling programs, 208–9, 219; and role models, 122, 124, 199, 200, 206–7; seen as problem for Black male youth, 124, 200–1, 207–8; as stereotype for at-risk Black male youth, 115, 121–4; and successful lives, 210–11. *See also* single parenthood
fathers, need for Black male youth, 123, 200
father-son relationship in sports, 185–7
Feagin, J.R., 288
fear of Black youth, 236–7, 299–300
female youth. *See* Black female youth
Ferber, Abby, 201, 205, 206
Fine, M., 113, 222
first-generation (born outside the country): educational outcomes for Black students, 66–7, 68; groups by parental birthplace, 50; in TDSB cohort data, 48–9
"fitting the description," and police, 233–4, 238, 268
"Focused Schools" project, 18, 19
Forbes magazine article, 150, 169
Forcese, D.P., 226, 230
Four-Level Government/African-Canadian Community Working Group, 16
Franklin, R.S., 225, 236
Freire, P., 4
Friesen, Joe, 21
Fuligni, A.J., 78–9
Fuller, M., 14–15
funding of schools and education, 22

Gaymes, Alison, 22–3
Gazeley, L., 176
gender: and athletics, xxiii–xxiv, 110; and college in Ontario, 62;

gender (*continued*)
  and education in Britain, 14–15; gifted students and special education, 55–6; and graduation, 57, 59, 64, 65; as "hurdle," xxvi–xxvii; and immigration, 108; male privilege, xxii; perspective of 1.5 generation, 108–11, 318–19; and postsecondary institutions, 62; and Program of Study (POS), 52–3; and race, xxii–xxiii, 201; and race and class in athletics, 175–8, 187–8, 194; and racialization for Black male youth, xxii–xxiii; in suburbs, 269–70, 273–4
generational status, 47, 48–9, 50
generation-and-a-half (1.5 generation): concept, 77–8, 80, 251n2; experience of A. Gooden, 109–10, 111, 318–19; gendered perspective on, 108–11, 318–19; and identity, 80–2; and integration, 81
generation-and-a-half (1.5 generation) Caribbean Canadian (Mark): aspirations and parental influence, 88–90, 99–100, 101, 108; and colour-blindness, 94–5; comments from Mark on final essay, 97–9, 101–2, 318; duality as 1.5 generation, 95–7; gendered perspective on, 108–9, 318–19; high school experiences, 85–8; as interpretive account of life story, 79–80; interviews with author, 78, 82; as longitudinal study, 78, 79, 318; mother of, 82–3, 89, 90, 96, 99–100, 107, 108, 110–11, 318; move to Canada, 82–5; on multiculturalism, 92–4; national identity and self-identification, 76–7, 78, 84–5, 92, 95–7, 98–9, 102; and "othermothers," 108–9;

racialization avoidance, 97, 108; on racism, 92–4, 95, 97, 101; scholarship, 88–90, 96, 99; social network and cultural difference, 87; sport career as option, 91–4, 96; sports in high school, 86, 87, 88; and sports' role in life, 79, 100–1, 102; and stereotypes, 85, 88, 96
generations: and achievement, 47; breakdowns for Black students, 48–9; definitions, 251n2; differences in TDSB cohort data, 48–9, 69; educational outcomes for Black students, 56–7, 58, 65–8, 72–3, 317–18; and graduation after high school, 56–7, 58; and postsecondary institutions, 59–62, 64–5; and Program of Study (POS), 51–2; and social mobility terminology, 253; and special education, 53–5; and sports' role in life, 79; and suburbs, 251–2. *See also* first-generation; generation-and-a-half; second-generation; third-generation-plus
George, Rhonda, 109, 110, 284
Gershenson, S., et al., 301n11
"get-tough" approach to troublemakers, 130
Gibbs, Nicholas, and family, 246–7
gifted students: assessment of Black students, 292, 293; and gender, 55–6; race and generations in, 53, 54–5; under-representation of Black students, 291–3
Gilmore, Ruth Wilson, xi
Gilroy, P., 236
Girls for Gender Equity research, xxiv–xxv
Globe and Mail: on Africentric schools, 25, 26; denial of racism, 17, 26; on fatherless Black male

youth, 123–4, 199; and *Report on Race Relations in Ontario*, 17–18
Gooden, Amoaba, 107–11, 318–19; experience as migrant, 109–10, 318–19
Gordon, P., 204
Gosine, K., 154, 256
Gosset, Allan, 247
grades for Black students, 296–7
graduation rates for Black students, xi, xxiii, 302
graduation status after high school, 56–7, 58, 59
Gray, E., et al., 29
Grenada, xiii
Griffin, Anthony, 247
Griffith, A., 123
Growing Up Black in Oakville (Brown), 252
"Growing Up without Men" radio series, 121, 207
guidance counsellors, negative experiences with, 289, 297–8

Haberman, M., 112
habitus, 259
Hagan, J., 229
hairstyle, and police, 232
Halifax (NS), 5, 26
Hall, Stuart, 218
Harriet Tubman Centre, 13
Harris government (1995–2001), and "zero tolerance" policy, 27
Harrison, L., et al., 127
Hayles, Tanya, xxv
Head, W., 8, 9
Henry, Annette, xxii, 20, 169–72, 320
Henry, F., 128, 202, 225
Henry, F., et al., 226–7
Herbert, Suzanne, 30, 31
heredity, and skills, 202, 203, 205
Hernandez, K.C., 124

hidden curriculum, 44
high-needs schools and students, funding, 22
high schools: and basketball, 193–4; graduation status in TDSB cohort data, 56–7, 58, 59; non-completion impact, 305
Hill Collins, P., 203
history, and critical race theory, xix–xx
hockey, 126
"Holding It Down? The Silencing of Black Female Students in the Educational Discourse of the Greater Toronto Area" (George), 109
Holland, M.M., 273
hooks, bell, 4
hope, role and value, 4
"How the West Indian Child Is Made Educationally Sub-Normal in the British School System" (Coard), xiii
Howard, T.C., xviii, xix
Hunter, Mitzie, 30
Hutton, Clinton, 191–2

identity: and 1.5 generation, 80–2; and culturally informed education, 145–6; formation by whites, 222; national identity in Canada, 98; and sports for Black male youth, 178–9
"If I Were a Poor Black Kid" (Marks), 150, 169
immigrant, as stereotype for at-risk Black male youth, 115, 118–20
immigrants: ancestry probing, 84, 117; duality, 80–2; integration types, 81; and multiculturalism, 68, 93, 118; and police view of Black youth, 234–5, 238;

immigrants (*continued*)
  settlement pattern in Canada, 251–2; and social mobility, 253–4, 280; and suburbs, 251–2, 255n3, 256; support of education, 254; and systemic racism, 84
immigration in Canada: for a better life, 82–3; Black population increase in 1970s, xv, 4, 5; from Caribbean, xv, 5, 107–8; changes of 1967, xv; and gender, 108; and next generations, xv–xvi; nonwhite restrictions, 117–18
"Improving the Success of Black Students" program, 24
in-between neighbourhood, 155
inclusion policies, 28
Individual Education Plan (IEP), race and generations in, 53, 54, 55
individualism, xvi–xvii, 201, 271
individuals: and cultural contexts, xx; responsibility for successes and failures, 200–4
inequality of condition, 254
inequality of opportunity, 254
inequities: for Blacks, xxxi; intersectional inequities, 109–10, 172, 320; and race, 218; and role models for systemic change, 200–1, 211–12, 217, 220, 322; and schooling, 176
Integrated Equity Framework and Action Plan 2016–19, 29
integration, types and definitions, 81
internal integration, 81
Invisible City documentary, 198–9
"'I Really Do Feel I'm 1.5!': The Construction of Self and Community by Young Korean Americans" (Park), 80–1

Jacobs, Harriet, 216
Jamaicans, and stereotypes, 119, 234
James, Alan, 222–3
Jane and Finch community, 216–17
jobs. *See* employment
Johal, R., 274
Johnson, C., 200
Johnson, M., 280
Jonsson, J.O., 254
Jordan, Michael, 192
Jorge, V., 202

Kagawa-Singer, M., 175–6
Kani, and "play Black," 180
Keil, R., 155
Kelly, P., 113
Kendell, in *Invisible City*, 198–9
Kimmel, M., 116
King, Joyce E., 141–6, 319–20
King, Rodney, 223
Klug, F., 204
Kobe (pseudonym): aspirations and outcomes, 151, 160, 161, 164–5; and community, 153; description, 153; early life, 155; education and schooling, 158, 160–1, 164; employment and career, 160–1, 163–4; family and mother, 155, 156, 160; friends, 163n7; interviews and case-study approach, 153; and neighbourhood, 153, 154–5, 156; and neoliberal rationalities, 151; similarities and differences with Trevor, 154; sports at school, 158; teachers, 158–9. *See also* Trevor
Kumsa, Martha, 44

Lacy, K., 255
language: and at-risk students, 112–13, 144; and "black" as social construction, 222–3; in multiculturalism policies, 11; race and social class, 183; and sports, 183

language of dominance, reframing of, xi–xii, 144–5
Larter, S., et al., 7
Lawson, E., 200–1
Lawson-Bush, V., 122, 211
learning disabilities testing for Black students, 293
Lee, Enid, 12
Levin, B., 112, 113
Levine-Rasky, C., 26, 32
Lewis, Stephen, and report, 16–18
LGBTQ school, 25n17
life trajectories. *See* adolescence to adulthood life trajectories
Lincoln, Y.S., 80
lone-parent family. *See* single parenthood
longitudinal studies: as approach, 78–9; description and participants, xxvi–xxvii; example on racism, xxv–xxvi; optimism *vs.* "hurdles," xxvi–xxviii
"loophole of retreat" to role models, 216, 219–20
López, N., xxii
Los Angeles riots (1992), and language used, xi
Louie, V., 80
Love, B., 145
Luxton, M., xvi
Lynn, M., et al., 131–2

"Making Real Change for African Canadians" report, 143
"Making the Grade: Are We Failing Black Youth?" community forums, 23
Malcolm, Mike, 22
male-focused school, 209–10
male youth. *See* Black male youth
malls. *See* shopping malls
managerial neoliberalism, 218

Mark (pseudonym). *See* generation-and-a-half Caribbean Canadian
Marks, Gene, 150, 169
Martí, José, xiii
masculinity, 116, 152, 178, 179, 188
Maynard, Robyn, 144, 247
McDermott, R., xx, 134
McGhee Hassrick, E., 176–7
McGuinty, Dalton, on Africentric schools, 24, 209
McKittrick, Katherine, 216
McLean, Christabel, 74
McLeod, Donald, 31
McMurty, Roy, 27
media: digital media and basketball in Toronto, 193–5; on fatherlessness, 121, 123–4, 199–200, 207; and new racism, 204–5; and stereotypes, 128
men. *See* Black male youth
mentors. *See* role models
mentorship programs. *See* role modelling programs
middle-class Blacks: and police, 225, 237; and respectability, 279, 280; in suburbs, 255–6, 256n4, 263
middle-class norms to schooling system, 177
middle-class parents, 176–7, 188
Mikey, in *Invisible City*, 198–9
Milner, H.R., 116, 131, 144
Ministry of Education (Ontario), 11, 15–16
minoritized groups, and neoliberalism, xvii–xviii
minoritized people, harassment by police, 223–4, 226
Mirza, Heidi S., 15, 45
mobility. *See* social mobility
"model minorities," 203
Montreal, police and Black youth, 246–8, 323

"moral panic" response, 129–30
Morgan, Ainsworth, 198–9, 211
Morrison, Toni, 144
mothers: ability to educate their children, 122, 123, 124; and fatherlessness, 120–1, 123, 210–11
Mullings, D., et al., 109
multiculturalism: and antiracism education, 32n20; in Canada, xvii–xviii, xx–xxi; criticisms, xvii–xviii; and culture, 93–4, 118; for immigrants, 68, 93, 118; language as focus, 11; and neoliberalism, xvii–xviii, xxi; policies in education, 11, 12–13; and problems in African Canadians, 11; and race, xx–xxi, 143–4, 151; and racism, 12, 43, 92–4, 144; and "segregated" schooling, 25–6, 32
My Brother's Keeper initiative, 218, 219

National Post, 25, 208, 251
natural ability, and athletics, 205–6
negative stereotyping, 132
Negro History Week, 4n4
Negrophobia, definition and role, xx
neighbourhoods: and Academic courses, 289; "in-between" description, 155; reception-area neighbourhoods, 252; and stereotypes, 128–9. *See also* suburbs
neoliberalism: and anti-Black racism, ix; and critical race theory, 152; and employment, xvii, 163–4; and equality of opportunity, 150–1; as framework, xvi–xvii; and individualism, xvi–xvii, 271; and multiculturalism, xvii–xviii, xxi; for racialized people, 151–2; and role models, 218–19, 220; and success for Blacks, 150–1, 161, 165, 169–70; teachers working in own community, 160; youth in, xvii
Neugebauer, R., 224
New Democratic Party government (Ontario), antiracism policies and programs, 15–16, 19
new racism: and "colour-blindness," 202–3; definition, xviii–xix; as framework, 201, 202, 203, 204; and media, 204–5; and minoritized-group members, 204–5; and natural ability, 205–6
"The New School" lecture (Coard), xiii
N'ghana school, 19
Noguera, P.A., 134
Norris, C., et al., 224
Nova Scotia, 19–20, 26

Oakville (ON), income of Blacks, 257
Obama, Barack, 150, 218–19
Oliver, Jules, 7, 10
1.5-generation. *See* generation-and-a-half
1.5-generation Caribbean Canadian. *See* generation-and-a-half Caribbean Canadian
Ontario: antiracism (*See* antiracism in Ontario); Black male youth killed or injured by police, 221n2; Black students situation, 284–5; censuses on students, 284–5n2; *Equity and Inclusive Education Strategy*, 28; harassment of Black male youth by police, 221–2; level of study of African Canadians, 6; and multiculturalism policies, 11, 12–13; racially segregated schools, 23–4, 25; streaming dismantling, 11, 16; and systemic racism, 17–18,

26, 284; university (*See* university in Ontario)
Ontario Human Rights Tribunal, on racial disparity, 285–6
optimism towards learning, 124
optimism *vs.* "hurdles," xxvi–xxviii
"othermothers," 108–9

Palmer, H., 84, 117
Papageorge, N.W., 300–1n10
parents: birthplace and status, 49, 50, 57, 58; and coaches in sports, 186–7; engagement with school, 303; and meaning of schools, vii–viii; and Program of Study (POS), 51–2, 291; and social class, 176–7, 188; and suburbs, 258–62, 272–3, 274; and underachievement in Black students, 131–2; and upward social mobility, 254. *See also* single parenthood
Park, Kyeyoung, 80–1
Parker, Pat, 271
Patterson, Orlando, 207–8
Payne, Stephanie, 24
Peacock, K., 113
Peel District School Board: Black students situation, 285, 285n3; equity initiatives, 29–30
Peel region, Black students situation, 285
Phillips, Trevor, 27
Plaza, Dwaine, 77n2
police: and Black female youth, 235–6, 237, 247; and Blacks "as criminals," 225, 229, 236–7, 238–41; and Black youth on streets, 229–30, 233–4, 323–4; change of approach to Black youth, 241–2; cultural attitudes and behaviours, 226–7, 229; and dress of Black youth, 231–3, 237–8, 237n11; and

"fitting the description," 233–4, 238, 268; harassment of Black male youth, 221–2, 224, 225; harassment of minoritized people, 223–4, 226; in Montreal, 246–8, 323; perceptions by, and of, Black youth, 230–6, 237–8, 239, 240; and reactions to encounters, 240–1; relations with Blacks, 225–6; shootings of Black male youth in Canada and US, 141–2, 221n2, 246, 247; and social class, 224–5, 237; and stereotypes, 225, 226, 229–30, 231–6; in suburbs, 268; view of Black youth as immigrants, 234–5, 238; and young whites, 224; and youth, 228–30
police officers (Black), cultural attitudes and views, 226n6
Popenoe, David, 121–2
positive stereotyping, 127
postsecondary educational institutions: and gender, 62; and generations, 59–62, 64–5; and parental birthplace, 61; and race, 57–61; in TDSB cohort data, 57–62. *See also* university
poverty, 113, 175
prep-school route, and basketball, 194
Prince, Althea, 13, 20
Product of Canada study, 77, 77n2
Program of Study (POS): and Black students, 50–3; courses description, 49–50; and gender, 52–3; and generations, 51–2; and parents, 51–2, 291; and TDSB cohort data, 49–53; in *Towards ...* report, 289–91
Program of Study (POS) – academic courses: advocacy by Black students and parents, 291;

Program of Study (*continued*)
and athletics, 290–1; and resources for school, 289; and TDSB cohort data, 49–53; unsuitability for and streaming of Black students, 289–90, 310

Program of Study (POS) – applied courses: consequences, 289; over-representation and streaming of Black students, 289–90, 310; and TDSB cohort data, 49–53

Program of Study (POS) – essential courses, 49–53, 289

"progressive discipline" policy, 114n2

"The Public Identities of the Black Middle Class: Managing Race in Public Spaces" (Rollock et al.), 255

Quebec, anti-Black racism and discrimination, 247, 248, 323

Raby, R., 112
race: and athletics, 206; and discrimination, xviii; and gender, xxii–xxiii, 201; and gender and class in athletics, 175–8, 187–8, 194; generational status in TDSB cohort data, 48–9; and graduation, 56–7, 63–4, 65; and inequity, 218; influence and impact, 32; and language, 183; and multiculturalism, xx–xxi, 143–4, 151; and postsecondary institutions, 57–61; and special education, 53–4; and suburbs, 261–4, 266, 269, 271–2; TDSB students at university, 62–3; theoretical frameworks, xviii
race-based data collection, 23, 28–9, 48n2, 239n13
race-relations policies and programs, 12–13

racial capitalism, 218
racialization, xix, xxii–xxiii, 97, 108
racialized people, and neoliberalism, 151–2
racialized spaces, and streets, 236–7
racialized students, in TDSB cohort data, 48–9
racially segregated schools in Ontario, 23–4, 25
racial profiling, 128–9, 268, 285–6
racism: belief in overcoming, xxvii–xxviii, 9–10; and Black youth, xxi; coping strategy, 131; and data collection on race, 28–9; definition by Gilmore, xi; dismissal as issue, 309–10; in employment, xxvi; and fear of Black youth, 236–7, 299–300; as "hurdle," xxvi–xxvii; impact on Black youth and society, xxxi–xxxii, 313–14, 325–6; longitudinal studies example, xxv–xxvi; for Mark, 92–4, 95, 97, 101; and multiculturalism, 12, 43, 92–4, 144; post-civil rights era shift, 202; race-relations policies and programs, 12; and racialization, xix; and *Report on Race Relations in Ontario*, 16–18; resistance by Blacks, xviii; and sports, 9–10, 94, 205; and stereotypes, 142–3, 204, 295; strategies for overcoming, 10; and suburbs, 261, 262–3, 266, 271–2, 273, 278; and teachers, 295–9, 311, 312, 313–14; in *Towards ... report*, 288, 295–300, 302, 304. *See also* antiracism in Ontario; new racism; racism, anti-Black; systemic racism
racism, anti-Black: acknowledgement and structures needed, xxxi–xxxii; continuity

in schools, 43; documentation in Canada, 143; and education, 143; experiences since 1970s, 315; factors and forces, xv–xvi; materialization in schools, viii–ix; in Montreal and Quebec, 247, 248, 323; and neoliberalism, ix; promises without resources, ix; at university, 305. *See also* racism

Rae, Bob, and *Report on Race Relations in Ontario*, 16–17

Raffo, C., 254

reception-area neighbourhoods, 252

Report on Race Relations in Ontario (Lewis, 1992), 16–18

resources and references (educational), and Black stereotypes, 119

respectability politics, 279–81, 325

Richard, Shawn, 30

risk, vulnerability to, 113. *See also* at risk; at-risk students and youth

Rivers, Eugene, 208

Robinson, Cedric, 218

role modelling programs: author's experiences, 197–8; barriers and challenges, 197; *vs.* Black-focused schools, 210; and "corrective agents," 209; description, 197; effectiveness, 212–13; example from *Invisible City*, 198–9; and fatherlessness, 208–9, 219; and individualism, 201; and positive role models, 209; use and role of, 197, 217, 219, 322–3

role models: and at-risk Black youth, 209, 217, 218–19; Blacks as, 211–12, 216–17, 219–20; Black students as role model to others, 160; in community-based projects, 216–17, 219–20; and fatherlessness, 122, 124, 199, 200, 206–7; lack of positive role models, 208; and "loophole of retreat," 216, 219–20; males *vs.* females, 210–12; need for, 200, 201; and neoliberalism, 218–19, 220; and new racism, 205; problems with, 206–7; purpose, 213; sport as success for Black male youth, 206; sport coaches as, 101–2, 185–7, 205; "successful" Blacks as examples, 202–4, 216–17; and systemic change, 200–1, 211–12, 217, 220, 322; teachers as, 210–11

Rollock, N., et al., 255, 256, 263

The Roots of Youth Violence report (2008), 27–8

Royal Commission on Learning (Ontario), 16, 18–19

Russell-Rawlings, Collen, 30

Safe Schools Act (Bill 81, 2000), 21

Schissel, B., 112

Schneider, B.L., 176–7

scholarships (athletic): *vs.* academic for Mark, 88–90, 96, 99; aspiration to, 184–5; non-US options, 184n4, 185; at US universities and colleges, 79, 88–90, 158, 184–5

school boards: Black women as directors, 30n19; data collection on race, 23, 29; equity and inclusion policies and initiatives, 28–31, 43–4. *See also* specific boards

School Community Safety Advisory Panel, 28

schooling: and critical race theory, xix; cultural context, 132–3, 176; as process, 114. *See also* education

schools: meaning to parents, vii–viii; specialized programs, 25. *See also* specific topics; specific types of schools

school system: and African Canadians problems in 1970s, 5–6, 8; Britain as model, xiii; middle-class norms, 177; problems in, 305; and racism in (*See* systemic racism)
"school-to-prison pipeline," 27, 74, 130
Schugurensky, D., 255n3
second-generation (born in Canada to immigrant parents): educational outcomes for Black students, 68; groups by parental birthplace, 49, 50; in TDSB cohort data, 48–9
security personnel, 227, 228, 235
"segregated" schooling, and multiculturalism, 25–6, 32
segregation in schools, 23–4, 25, 33
Seif (pseudonym), stereotypes and race, 183
Semere (pseudonym), 174–5, 182–3, 184, 186
Sevier, B., 124
Shannon, Patrick, 197
shootings of Black male youth by police, 141–2, 221n2, 246, 247
shopping malls, as "streets" and social spaces, 227–8, 237, 239, 241, 323, 324
Shujaa, M.J., 114
Shuttleworth, Dale, 13
Simmel, G., 119
single mothers, and fatherlessness, 120–1, 123, 210–11
single parenthood: experiences of, 199–200; proportion in Blacks, 83, 121, 199; seen as problem for Black male youth, 120–2, 123
skin colour, and police, 231
slam dunks, and creative labour, 192
Smith, D., 229, 240
Smyth, J., 254

Snider, L., 238
social class. *See* class
social mobility: definition and terminology, 253; as drive for immigrants, 253–4, 280; move to suburbs, 252, 278; as possibility for all, 150. *See also* upward social mobility
society: and achievement problems of 1970s, 5–6, 8; ideal of *vs.* stratification, 253; impact of racism on Black youth, xxxi–xxxii, 313–14, 325–6; and masculinity, 116
Solomon, R.P., 10
Somalis, and police, 234
Sparkes, A.C., 98
special education, 53–6, 194
special learning needs, and placement, 293–4
speech pattern, and sports, 183
Spence, Chris, 122, 200, 209
"spirit-murdering," 145
sports: Black female youth experience, 109, 110; career as option for Mark, 91–4, 96; coaches as role models, 101–2, 185–7, 205; and "colour-blindness," 94, 206; as coping and resistance to racism, 9–10; and cultural significance, 126; engagement and meaning for Black male youth, 10, 174–5, 178, 179, 187; and exclusion of other pursuits, 127; "father-son" relationship, 185–7; and identity for Black male youth, 178–9; as intervention and preemptive strategy, 157; and masculinity, 178, 179, 188; and "play Black," 179–81, 191, 192–3; and racism, 9–10, 94, 205; recruitment due to race, 125–6; resistance to stereotype,

178; role for Black male youth, 179, 191; role in life for Mark, 79, 100–1, 102; and social class, 175, 187–8; and stereotypes, 177, 178, 179, 180, 183, 193–4; and success, 206, 291; support in Canada, 91, 92; use for attainment, 79. *See also* athletics and athleticism
stereotypes: Black female youth, xxv, 172, 320; Black youth, xxi–xxiii, 183; as circular process, 177; conform *vs.* resist response, 120, 132, 133, 178; consequences, 304–5; contribution to problems, 128–9, 133–4; and Mark, 85, 88, 96; negative stereotyping, 132; and neighbourhoods, 128–9; and police, 225, 226, 229–30, 231–6; positive stereotyping, 127; as problem, 133–4; and racial profiling, 128–9; and racism, 204, 295; and reframing of language, 144–5; and sports, 177, 178, 179, 180, 183, 193–4; and underachievement, 193–4, 267, 321; and "white racial frames," 288, 304
stereotypes for at-risk Black male youth: as athlete, 115, 124–7, 177; as fatherless, 115, 121–4; as immigrant, 115, 118–20; overview, 115, 117, 132–3, 177, 319; process of, 115, 133–4, 177; and racism, 142–3; as troublemaker, 115, 127–30, 144; as underachiever, 115, 130–2
Stevenson, H.C., 116
"stop and question" (stop, question, and search), 222
"the stranger" concept, 119
streaming: Black students placement, 6–7, 8; description, 288; dismantling in Ontario, 11, 16; impact, 7; nonacademic paths for Black students, 288–95, 310; as problem, 288–9
streets: and "doing nothing," 228–9; and police perceptions of Black youth, 230–6, 237–8, 239, 240; as racialized spaces, 236–7; as social space, 227–8; traditional view, 228. *See also* shopping malls
students. *See* Black students
student teachers (education students): diversity course, 311, 313–14; reactions to *Towards...* report, 311–13, 325; understanding of issues for Black students, 312–13, 325
style. *See* dress and style
suburbs: and aspirations for youth, xi; and Black female youth, 269–70, 273; and Blackness, 255–6, 263–6, 270–1; and cost of living, 257, 258; differential treatment for Black youth, 265–6, 267–8; experiences and attitudes of Blacks, 257–72; and gender, 269–70, 273–4; immigrants' settlement pattern, 251–2, 255n3, 256; infrastructure and transportation issues, 256–7; interviews and studies by author, 258; legitimacy of Blacks in, 254–5; and middle-class Blacks, 255–6, 256n4, 263; migration to by Black youth, 252–3, 257, 274; negative cost, 261–72, 273–4, 278, 324; and parents, 258–62, 272–3, 274; and police, 268; population in Canada, 251; positive cost, 258–62, 272–3, 274; and race, 261–4, 266, 269, 271–2; and racism, 261, 262–3, 266, 271–2, 273, 278;

suburbs (*continued*)
  and respectability, 279, 325; and social mobility, 252, 278; and teachers, 257, 266–8. *See also* upward social mobility
success: barriers to, 12, 20; and fatherlessness, 210–11; formula for Blacks, 150, 169; and initiatives of school boards, 31; and neoliberalism, 150–1, 161, 165, 169–70; and sports, 206, 291
"successful" Black individuals as examples, 202–4, 216–17
Sukarieh, M., xvii
Sullivan, Veronica, 13
suspended or expelled students, 21, 27, 299n9
systemic racism: and Africentric schools, 26; in Britain, 73–4, 317; change(s) needed in education, 34–5; definition, 10n7; denial, 17–18, 26; and immigrants, 84; impact in 1970s, 8–9; in Ontario, 17–18, 26, 284; policies and programs in 2010s, 28; as problem, 10

Tannock, S., xvii
Tate, Shirley Anne, 72–4, 317–18
Tator, C., 128, 202
Tavares-Carter, Kimberley, 210–11
Taylor, Leanne, 309–14, 325
TDSB (Toronto District School Board): Africentric Alternative School, 14, 24–5, 31, 33, 301; alternative schools, 24–5; Black-focused schools, 23–5; censuses, 284n1; creation, 6n6; data collection and use, 284; data collection on race, 23, 29; data from 2006–11 cohort, 287, 287n5; equity and inclusion policies and initiatives, 29; "Focused Schools" project, 18, 19; graduation rates for Black students, xi, xxiii, 302; N'ghana school, 19; School Community Safety Advisory Panel, 28; 2011 Student Census, xxiii
TDSB 2008–11 cohort data: description and numbers of Black students, 47–9, 48n2; educational outcomes for Black students, 65–9; and generational differences, 48–9, 69; graduation after high school, 56–7, 58, 59; for graduation and postsecondary attainment, 48; and parental birthplace, 49, 50; postsecondary institutions, 57–62; and Program of Study (POS), 49–53; and special education, 53–6; university entry patterns and graduation, 62–5
TDSB 2011 Student Census, xxiii, 47, 284
teachers: academics *vs.* sports for Blacks, 171; achievement problems of Black students in 1970s, 8; "bad schools get bad teachers" idea, 159; and Black female youth, 171–2; and Black male youth, 299; and coaches in sports, 186–7; diversity in, 28, 300; fear of Black students, 299–300; lower expectations for Black students, 288–9, 290, 295–6, 297, 299, 302; and racism, 295–9, 311, 312, 313–14; as role models for Black male youth, 210–11; social class and parents' role in education, 176–7; and suburbs, 257, 266–8; and underachievement in Black students, 131–2, 176, 267; understanding of issues for Black students, 312–13, 325; views of Black students, 304. *See also* Black educators/teachers; student teachers
Tecle, Sam, 216–20, 284, 322–3
test scores, as measure, 131

third-generation-plus (born in Canada to Canadian-born parents): educational outcomes for Black students, 65–6, 68; in TDSB cohort data, 48–9, 48n3

Thurston, Baratunde, 169

Toronto: Black educators need, 300; Blacks in suburbs, 255, 258; Black students situation, 284–5; community education projects, 4–5; digital media and basketball infrastructure, 193–5; move to suburbs 252, 256–7; recruitment of Black male youth in sports, 125–6; stereotypes for Black male youth, xxii–xxiii; violence and Black youth, 27

Toronto Board of Education, 6, 7, 23

Toronto District School Board (TDSB). *See* TDSB

Toronto Star: on Africentric Alternative School, 25; dropout rates, 21n13; on fatherless Black male youth, 199–200, 207; on inequities for Blacks, xxxi; on police and stereotypes, 225; programs for Black students in 1990s, 13–14

Tory, John, 24

Towards Race Equity in Education report (James & Turner, 2017): and achievement, 295–7, 298; Africentric schools and schooling, 301–2; assertions and suggestions of students, 302–3; conclusions, 304–5; consultations and participants, 286–8; data in, 288, 325; gifted students, 291–3; impact on student teachers, 311–13, 325; and initiatives of school boards, 31; overview, xxx–xxxi, 284–6, 325; and Programs of Study, 289–91; and racism, 288, 295–300, 302, 304; special learning needs and behaviour of Black students, 293–5; and streaming into nonacademic paths, 288–95; and teaching staff, 299–301; and university applications or guidance, 289, 297–8

Trevor (pseudonym): academic outcomes, 157; aspirations and outcomes, 151, 161, 164, 165; and community, 154; early life, 156; education and schooling, 161, 164; employment and career, 161–4; family and mother, 156; friends, 163n7; interviews and case-study approach, 153–4; and neighbourhood, 154–5, 156–7, 164; and neoliberal rationalities, 151; similarities and differences with Kobe, 154; sports at school, 157–8; teachers, 159. *See also* Kobe

Triangle school, 25n17

Trinidad, 87, 91–2

troublemaker, as stereotype for at-risk Black male youth, 115, 127–30, 144

Turcotte, M., 83

Turner, Tana, 284

underachievement: and middle-class norms, 177; reasons, 74; social class and perceptions by teachers, 176; as stereotype, 193–4, 267, 321; and teachers, 131–2, 176, 267. *See also* achievement

underachiever, as stereotype for at-risk Black male youth, 115, 130–2

United Nations' Working Group of Experts on People of African Descent, 286

units of labour *vs.* creative labour, 191, 192

university: entry patterns and graduation in TDSB cohort data, 62–5; guidance away from for Black students, 289, 297–8;

university (*continued*)
  support for Black students, 305; turning away from, 309, 310. *See also* postsecondary educational institutions
university in Ontario: and gender, 62; and generations, 59, 60, 61, 64–5; and race, 59, 60, 61
university in US and athletic scholarship: aspiration to, 184–5; for Mark, 88–90, 96, 99; use by Black male youth, 79, 88, 89, 158
University of Toronto, TDSB students by race, 62
upward social mobility: and appearances, 255, 257; cost of, 274; definition, 253; as ideal, 253, 281; support by parents, 254
US universities and colleges. *See* university in US

value on education, 6, 7–8
Varenne, H., xx, 134
Vincent, C., et al., 256n4, 259
violence, roots, 27
vocational classes, Black students placement in, 6–7

Walcott, R., xvii–xviii, 152, 224, 237
Wallace, A., 14
Webber, Chris, 192, 193
Weis, L., 222
Welsh, Moira, 207
We Rise Together action plan (2016), 29–30
"Where are you from?" question, 84, 117
white as word, 223
"white racial frames" (or "white logic"), 288, 304, 305
whites: and identity formation, 222; and police, 224

white students, in TDSB cohort data, 48–9
white supremacy, 202
white teachers, understanding of issues for Black students, 312–13
Williams, Castor, 19–20
Williams, P.J., 145
Wilson, Jackie, 13
women. *See* Black female youth; Black women
Woodson, C.G., 145
working-class Black male student-athletes, 175, 176, 187–8
working-class parents, and educational performance, 177
working-class youth, and streets, 227
Wotherspoon, T., 112
Wright, Ouida, 16
Wrigley, T., 254
Wynne, Kathleen, on Africentric schools, 24; government of (2013–2018), 28–9
Wynter, Sylvia, xi, 145

York Region District School Board, 30–1
York University, and TDSB cohort data, 48, 62–5
Yosso, T.J., 152
Young, D., 155
young Black men. *See* Black male youth
young Black women. *See* Black female youth
youth: educational aspirations, x–xi; and neoliberalism, xvii; and police, 228–30; and streets, 227–9. *See also* Black youth

Zamudio, M.M., et al., xviii
"zero tolerance" policy, 21, 27, 114n2
Zuberi, T., 288